Advanced Praise for
Truth Matters, Life Matters More

"Hank Hanegraaff's *Truth Matters, Life Matters More* is a remarkable tapestry of vast historical and scriptural knowledge, woven from personal experience, chronicles of faith journeys, and marvelous spiritual insights that mesh to create more than a compendium of theology. Indeed, he pulls the strands together with deftness and devotion, such that they form a map, a sacred topography of the life in Christ. And as a good cartographer would do, Hanegraaff makes sure that the reader has all the keys and legends to read his map. He knows how to point the reader in all the right directions, but he also knows that it is grace that 'will lead us home.'"

—Fr. Alex Karloutsos, Vicar General of the
Greek Orthodox Archdiocese of America

"Quoting from a wide range of sources, Hank Hanegraaff makes an impassioned case for calling the church back to her earliest roots in this book that is sure to stir and provoke any reader. *Participation*, *union*, and even the controversial word *deification* have been making a quiet comeback in the wake of more and more calls to broaden our collective understanding of what salvation entails. In this book, Hanegraaff wages a battle on two fronts. On the one hand, he wants to maintain that biblical truth matters. On the other hand, he insists that this truth is neither abstract nor impersonal, but a living truth because it is anchored in the living Christ. As someone passionately interested in recovering the reality of our union with Christ, I hope readers will thoughtfully engage with Hanegraaff's challenging conclusions."

—Rankin Wilbourne, Pastor of Pacific Crossroads Church Los
Angeles and author of *Union with Christ* and *The Cross Before Me*

"As Hank has masterfully pointed out, 'there can be no life without truth, but above all, no truth without life, deification is God's greatest gift. It is the high peak truth of redemptive revelation.' Hank elucidates this life-changing lesson revealing that 'while truth is necessary, it is hardly sufficient. That the map is not the territory. That the menu is not the meal. That we must never mistake the cradle for its occupant. And that we are destined even *now* to experience life that is life to the full.' This book will further allow us to take His life as source of our living, in our church life, for His satisfaction, to bring to light the Kingdom of God on earth."

—Samuel Nee, a fellow lover and partaker of
Christ, nephew of Watchman Nee

"In this moving and compelling book, Hank Hanegraaff recapitulates the apologetic themes that he has spent decades honing and defending—from human origins, to the reality of the resurrection, to the reliability of Scripture. But, more than that, he shows how this vital defense of truth must be part of the larger cause of uniting our life with the life of God. This is a theme that for too long has been missed by millions of believing Christians. Hank shows, with characteristic precision, how the traditional Christian idea of 'deification' is not some doubtful sidelight, but represents the culmination of the Christian life, and the source of Christian unity. Whether you've read all of Hank's books, or none of them, I urge you to read this one."

—JAY RICHARDS, PH.D., O.P., ASSISTANT RESEARCH PROFESSOR AT THE CATHOLIC UNIVERSITY OF AMERICA, SENIOR FELLOW AT THE DISCOVERY INSTITUTE, EXECUTIVE EDITOR OF *THE STREAM*, AND A *NEW YORK TIMES* BESTSELLING AUTHOR—HIS MANY BOOKS INCLUDE THE FORTHCOMING *EAT, FAST, FEAST*

"Truth Matters, Life Matters More is a cornucopia of good, nourishing things, the fruit of Hank's many decades of reading, reflection, and prayer. His gift for taking in complex ideas, digesting them, and then presenting them to readers clearly and briefly make his latest book a wise companion and enjoyable friend."

—FREDERICA MATHEWES-GREEN, AUTHOR OF *WELCOME TO THE ORTHODOX CHURCH: AN INTRODUCTION TO EASTERN CHRISTIANITY*

"This book portrays what the flower of a beautiful life looks like when it blossoms from the rich soil of Christian truth. The author is widely read and theologically astute in his articulation of selected doctrines of classical Christian faith. The book instructs, inspires, and bears witness to a godly life that blooms from our union with the Incarnate God."

—BRADLEY NASSIF, PH.D., PROFESSOR OF BIBLICAL AND THEOLOGICAL STUDIES, NORTH PARK UNIVERSITY, AND CO-EDITOR OF *THE PHILOKALIA: A CLASSICAL TEXT OF ORTHODOX SPIRITUALITY*

"Truth Matters, Life Matters More is an extraordinarily wise and thoughtful book, magnificent in its scope and inspiring in its presentation. From the way to detect counterfeit religions (and the importance of doing so) to the true meaning of the all-important but poorly understood Orthodox Christian concept of deification, Hank Hanegraaff brilliantly elucidates the pure joy of living a life in fidelity to truth, and to Truth Himself, the Author of all life. I thank God for my fellow Orthodox believer and for his unparalleled guide to the wonderful happiness of living as a Christian."

—ROBERT SPENCER, BESTSELLING AUTHOR OF *THE POLITICALLY INCORRECT GUIDE TO ISLAM (AND THE CRUSADES)* AND *THE HISTORY OF JIHAD*

"Hank Hanegraaff's *Truth Matters, Life Matters More* is a wonderfully written reminder that we are made for more than merely knowing the truth about God—we are made to be Christ's brothers and sisters, and the Father's sons and daughters, through deification. This is a forgotten, deeply biblical truth that the early Christians well understood, and one that all Christians must recover."

—BENJAMIN WIKER, PH.D., AUTHOR OF MANY BOOKS INCLUDING *A MEANINGFUL WORLD* AND PROFESSOR OF POLITICAL SCIENCE AND DIRECTOR OF HUMAN LIFE STUDIES AT FRANCISCAN UNIVERSITY

"Hanegraaff's masterpiece guides us toward ultimate Truth in the context of Christ's promise that He has come to give us life—deified life that is life to the full."

—NORRIS J. CHUMLEY, PH.D., AUTHOR AND EMMY AWARD-WINNING EXECUTIVE PRODUCER AND DIRECTOR, *MYSTERIES OF THE JESUS PRAYER*

"*Truth Matters, Life Matters More* details Hank Hanegraaff's life journey from his childhood to the present day, a voyage guided by Providence. Hanegraaff rightly recognizes salvation as a step towards a higher state—deification—which is not a reality to be expressed conceptually but lived out through the transformation of our life in Christ, through the Holy Spirit, by means of the grace communicated in the Church by the sacraments and the personal practice of spiritual disciplines.

"What makes Hanegraaff's approach interesting is that it is not a theoretical presentation but a testimony of his personal journey. Though Hank's reflections are rooted in personal experience, there is a clear desire for others to experience similar spiritual growth, exhibiting a youthful enthusiasm for evangelism. In traversing the stages of the long way that led him to True Life, he does not forget to pay homage to those who, often without knowing it, illumined his path."

—JEAN-CLAUDE LARCHET, PH.D., PH.D., PROFESSOR OF PHILOSOPHY IN A FRENCH LYCÉE IN STRASBOURG AND AUTHOR OF MANY BOOKS INCLUDING *THE THEOLOGY OF ILLNESS*

"My wife, Marsha, and I have known Hank and his family for over twenty-five years. We have traveled together, played golf, and experienced much time sharing our lives and the love of Christ. Years ago, Hank shared with me the revelation he received from Elijah Widjaja that 'truth matters, but life matters more' and the impact that statement has had on his life. *Truth Matters, Life Matters More* is a testament to the transformation of Hank's life since that revelation. I learned from this book that my relationship with Jesus Christ means everything to me and the more I allow Him to fill my life with His presence, the more I become complete in Him. May you be blessed by the reading of this profound book."

—JACK COUNTRYMAN, VICE PRESIDENT AND PUBLISHER EMERITUS, THOMAS NELSON, HARPERCOLLINS CHRISTIAN PUBLISHING

"The truth here is that salvation is so much greater than most people allow themselves to believe. We have been saved not only FROM sin, but FOR divine life. God has shared his inner life with us and made us partakers of his divine nature. This book tells how the Bible Answer Man arrived at the Bible's most important answer."

—Scott Hahn, Ph.D., Chair of Biblical Theology and the New Evangelization at Franciscan University of Steubenville

"Having appreciated Hank Hanegraaff's writings for decades, I find *Truth Matters, Life Matters More* to be his most personal and engaging work to date. It features the disciplined attention to detail we expect from Hank, but also gives us reflections from a man who's assessing the state of the modern church with a prophetic voice and a scholarly eye. Well worth reading."

—Joe Dallas, author of *Speaking of Homosexuality*

"Long convinced that we are truly human becomings more than human beings, I welcome the arrival of *Truth Matters, Life Matters More*. Having known Hank for nearly forty years and having worked closely with him for a good number of those years, I can testify to the journey of deep personal transformation that this book chronicles—a journey that beckons all those who wish to truly follow Christ. Unwilling to surrender to the pscyhosclerosis ('hardening of the categories') that characterizes far too many Christians, Hank's openness to the Spirit and his unquenchable thirst for truth have thankfully made him 'paradigm pliable.' Perhaps suggesting that truth is more a vital verb than a noetic noun, more a rushing river than a placid pond, this book provides fascinating insights into the enlarged and consequently enriched theological and existential perspectives possible when West meets East. This book will thrill many. It is also guaranteed to annoy and disturb others too settled and accustomed to seeing truth through the narrow chinks of their culturally conditioned intellectual and perspectival caverns. As with much of life, our reactions will reveal more about us, the readers, than the author. For those who have applauded and supported the work of this relentless defender and champion of biblical truth for decades, *Truth Matters, Life Matters More* is more than a spiritual milestone. It's a cairn marking the path toward higher ground."

—Larry F. Johnston, Ph.D., President, McConkey/Johnston International

Truth Matters, Life Matters More

Other Books by Hank Hanegraaff

Has God Spoken?
Memorable Proofs of the Bible's Divine Inspiration

Resurrection

The FACE That Demonstrates the Farce of Evolution

The Creation Answer Book

Christianity in Crisis: 21st Century

Counterfeit Revival

The Prayer of Jesus: Secrets to Real Intimacy with God

The Covering: God's Plan to Protect You from Evil

The Heart of Christmas

The Complete Bible Answer Book, Collector's Edition

The Apocalypse Code: Find Out What the Bible Really Says
About the End Times . . . and Why It Matters Today

MUSLIM: What You Need to Know About the
World's Fastest-Growing Religion

Truth Matters, Life Matters More

The Unexpected Beauty of an
Authentic Christian Life

Hank Hanegraaff

W Publishing Group

An Imprint of Thomas Nelson

Published in Nashville, Tennessee, by W Publishing, an imprint of Thomas Nelson.

Thomas Nelson titles may be purchased in bulk for educational, business, fund-raising, or sales promotional use. For information, please e-mail SpecialMarkets@ThomasNelson.com.

Unless otherwise noted, Scripture quotations are taken from the Holy Bible, New International Version®, NIV®. Copyright © 1973, 1978, 1984, 2011 by Biblica, Inc.® Used by permission of Zondervan. All rights reserved worldwide. www.Zondervan.com. The "NIV" and "New International Version" are trademarks registered in the United States Patent and Trademark Office by Biblica, Inc.®

Scripture quotations marked NIV 1984 are taken from the Holy Bible, New International Version, copyright © 1973, 1978, 1984, International Bible Society. Used by permission of Zondervan Bible Publishers. All rights reserved worldwide.

Scripture quotations marked NKJV are from the New King James Version®. © 1982 by Thomas Nelson. Used by permission. All rights reserved.

Scripture quotations marked ESV are from the ESV® Bible (The Holy Bible, English Standard Version®), copyright © 2001 by Crossway, a publishing ministry of Good News Publishers. Used by permission. All rights reserved.

Scripture quotations marked NASB are from New American Standard Bible®, copyright © 1960, 1962, 1963, 1968, 1971, 1972, 1973, 1975, 1977, 1995 by The Lockman Foundation. Used by permission. (www.Lockman.org)

Scripture quotations marked NRSV are from the New Revised Standard Version Bible. Copyright © 1989 National Council of the Churches of Christ in the United States of America. Used by permission. All rights reserved.

Scripture quotations marked KJV are from the King James Version.

Italics in Bible quotations indicate the author's emphasis.

Unless otherwise indicated, all cited URLs were last accessed in January 2019.

Any Internet addresses, phone numbers, or company or product information printed in this book are offered as a resource and are not intended in any way to be or to imply an endorsement by Thomas Nelson, nor does Thomas Nelson vouch for the existence, content, or services of these sites, phone numbers, companies, or products beyond the life of this book.

ISBN 978-0-7852-1611-7 (eBook)

Library of Congress Control Number: 2019946305

ISBN 978-0-7852-1606-3

Printed in the United States of America

19 20 21 22 23   LSC   10 9 8 7 6 5 4 3 2 1

It is with great affection that I dedicate this book to my dear friend Elijah Widjaja, without whom it would not—could not— have been written. "Gold there is, and rubies in abundance, but lips that speak knowledge are a rare jewel."

CONTENTS

FOREWORD BY LAUREN GREEN,
    CHIEF RELIGION CORRESPONDENT, FOX NEWS   XIII

BEFORE YOU BEGIN: STANDING FOR TRUTH—MY PORTAL INTO LIFE   XIX

PART 1: TRUTH MATTERS   1

    1: ANSWERS: APOLOGETICS IN THE MODERN AGE
        OF SKEPTICISM   7
    2: BIBLICAL INTERPRETATION: REMOVING THE VEIL   50
    3: COUNTERING COUNTERFEIT RELIGIONS: CONTRAST
        IS THE CONDUIT TO CLARITY   59

PART 2: LIFE MATTERS MORE   83

    4: DEIFICATION: BECOMING GODS BY GRACE   87
    5: ECCLESIA: THE CHURCH AS THE SOURCE OF LIFE   121
    6: FUSION: THE SECRET TO GLOBAL TRANSFORMATION   190

EPILOGUE: DISCOVERING THE AUTHENTIC CHRISTIAN LIFE   207

ACKNOWLEDGMENTS   217

NOTES   219

ABOUT THE AUTHOR   283

FOREWORD

by Lauren Green

Chief Religion Correspondent, Fox News

I had known of Hank Hanegraaff for many years. One cannot be the chief religion correspondent for a major news organization and not have heard of the Bible Answer Man. However, I only first met Hank face-to-face in 2017. It was a happenstance meeting, even though we'd planned to find time to talk at the Religious Freedom Conference in Washington, DC, sponsored by the Archons of the Greek Orthodox Church. Hank had just recently joined St. Nektarios Greek Orthodox Church in Charlotte, North Carolina, and that fascinated me because my husband is Greek Orthodox, and I am not.

So that's why it never occurred to me that becoming a member of an Orthodox church would be controversial for someone like Hank, but apparently it was. The controversy gained the attention of the Greeks, who welcomed him with open arms. His presence at the conference was part of that welcome wagon.

I arrived at the hotel eager to get to my room, change, and get on the shuttle bus to the next conference event, when this pleasant-enough gentleman passing in the hallway said, "Hello, Lauren."

I said hello back in that nice sort of greeting given to fans. Then I heard the words that turned the whole weekend around: "I'm Hank Hanegraaff."

My surprise—or even shock—was apparent. Although I had interviewed

Hank via satellite a few times, I'd never seen him in person. From that point on, he and I, and his wife, Kathy, and daughter, Christina, were buds for the whole of the conference.

A few months later Hank was the featured speaker for the Lenten retreat at a famed Greek Orthodox church in Southampton, New York. My husband and I rented a house for the week and invited the Hanegraaffs to be our guests. A closeness developed between his family and mine. My husband had an Orthodox scholar to talk with, and Hank had a Protestant Christian firmly in his corner.

I give this preamble to explain why I, of all people, would be asked to write the foreword to this book. I consider it an incredible honor. Of all the great religious minds Hank could have asked, it humbles me to be trusted with such an important task.

Truth matters, it matters a lot. Each of us is obligated to seek truth without compromise. But as I read the pages of the book, I learned how much more life matters.

There's an axiom in logic called the law of non-contradiction, which says if a statement is true, its negation cannot also be true. Or, colloquially: whatever is true, its opposite must be false. To say four plus four equals eight is true; to say that it is not eight is false. Even nine is false. And it's not a little bit false; it's 100 percent false. No matter if it is one number shy of the eight, it is still completely false.

It's easy to see the verity of the axiom in numbers because the heart is not involved. It's much harder to face it when it comes to something as personal as religion. I know, because it's my job to cover subjects concerning faith and belief systems, and there's hardly anything that's more divisive than our faith foundations.

But facing the Truth of faith is an ordeal encountered for centuries. Let me give you a most epic example. When Roman prefect Pilate interrogated Jesus after his arrest, Jesus told him, "Everyone on the side of truth listens to me" (John 18:37). Then in verse 38 Pilate made that infamous retort, "What is truth?" Pilate was asking a rhetorical question, not one for which he believed a clear answer exists. He was brushing off the answer with the implication that no one can know the truth. Of course, an astute apologist would quip back, "Is that true?"

Pilate was not asking for information. He was speaking from a typical secular, pagan mindset that "truth is what I say it is." Truth is what Caesar says it is. Truth is relative. Regardless of Pilate's brush with philosophy, he showed his hand. He didn't want to know the truth because that complicated his life. Pilate may have thought his purpose in life was climbing the Roman Empire's corporate ladder. Being prefect of the Roman province of Judea was a mere stepping-stone to earthly glory. But God had other plans, using Pilate's pagan mindset for an encounter with Christ, setting the stage for an existential showdown concerning the nature of truth.

After a brief moment with Jesus in which he sentenced Jesus to death for treason, Pilate seems to have disappeared from history's stage. His later years and death remain shrouded in mystery.[1] There are reports he committed suicide or was forced to. There are even reports that he became a follower of Jesus.

Regardless of what we don't know about Pilate, what we do know is what happened to Jesus. He was crucified on a cross. He died and was buried in a tomb. Three days later, the New Testament documents tell us, he rose from the dead. His followers grew from a handful to millions and billions. And more followers are coming into the fold every day, believing that Jesus is the Truth and the Life. That is either true or it is not. But if it is true—if Jesus is who he said he is—it changes everything.

Jesus makes us all uncomfortable. Like Pilate, many ask that same question in much the same manner: "What is truth?" For more than two thousand years Jesus has given the same answer, "I am the way and the truth and the life. No one comes to the Father except through me" (John 14:6).

As many theologians have pointed out, no other founder of a religion ever dared say what Jesus claimed. Buddha didn't. Muhammad didn't. All of them said, "Do this or that and you will achieve enlightenment; you will win God's favor." They gave instructions, "This is the way to find truth."[2]

Only Jesus said, "I am the way . . ."

It's an uncomfortable statement in a world where we just want to get along. Inclusiveness is the order of the day. A live and let live mentality rules the day, bringing a pseudo-peace perspective that equates to abject ambivalence concerning objective truth, creating a syncretistic, civil religion. It's where all the different faiths are coalesced into one big hodgepodge of relative truths.

Is Christianity true? If so, then Islam is false, then Mormonism is false. Then Judaism is woefully incomplete. It's an uncomfortable reality that most modern people have been taught to shun. We prefer living in the gray areas, contented to be "immersed in fog"; not because there's not enough information, but because truth in its pure form forces us to make changes, forces us perhaps even to sacrifice the idols that we have long believed will really save us: position, power, money, friends, relatives. Like Pilate, we shun the fires of truth, fearing its searing crucible. Yes, we will be changed, no doubt. But changed for the better. Changed for all eternity.

This book is Hank's magnum opus, a culmination of a life of research and theological course corrections. It is not just other faiths that Hank challenges, but many branches of Christianity as well. Jesus' Church suffers for what divides us. Because along the way, through two thousand years, his adherents have tacitly echoed Pilate's rhetorical query, "What is truth?" Incremental departures from the truth of Christ's Church have created wide fissures, first dividing West from East, then Protestants from Roman Catholics. Then a plethora of Protestant denominations, where today the fissures are still splintering off more microdenominations based on things that have nothing to do with the truth of the gospel but have more to do with human desires; where feelings have replaced facts.

The individualism and secularism rampant in culture today have infiltrated the Church. Many factions are a long way from, "I am the way and the truth and the life." And this lack of fusion in the Church is a direct result of truth ignored. It is a major stumbling block. Per Hank's own words: "Far easier to fissure than fuse. Yet there can be no doubt that you and I have been called for fusion."

So truth is step one. Now comes life. For "there can be no life without truth and no truth without life."

And I defer to Hank's magnum opus to explain the interplay of truth and life. Why should life matter more than truth? Because life is the arena in which truth is experienced. Truth is the third rail, the one with the electrical power that moves the train along. But it's there to serve the train. It is the train that matters. Without it, the third rail is unnecessary. It's much the same as the reason we need maps. You can stare at one all day long, but it's not a substitute for the green hills or blue waters you long to see. "You won't get anywhere by just looking at a map. But you will likely not get to where you're going without one. Thus, again, while it is true that life matters more than truth, the life that matters more is ultimately dependent on truth."[3]

This quote gets at the heart of the marriage needed between truth and life. It's the application, the journey, the standing up for what the Truth says is right and good, not what the culture says or the latest polls say.

We understand Pilate's predicament. When he looked into the eyes of Truth, his own incoherent pack of lies he'd lived by no longer supported him. The walls of his worldview came crumbling down as he experienced a self-quake, a disturbance in the force. To paraphrase that famous movie, "He couldn't handle the truth!"

We're not made just to know the truth—we are made to live it out and be in relationship with that Truth.

We have split the idea of truth and life, compartmentalized their application. But Hank has so importantly fused them back together as they were intended. Because, again, "There is no truth without life, and no life without truth."

—Lauren Green

Lauren Green serves as Fox News Channel's chief religion correspondent based in the New York bureau, host of *A Spirited Debate* for FoxNews.com, and author of *Lighthouse Faith* (Thomas Nelson, 2017).

Before You Begin

Standing for Truth—My Portal into Life

I am the way and the truth and the life.

—JESUS[1]

August 4, 2003, will forever remain etched in my mind. I was fifteen years into my tenure as president of the Christian Research Institute (CRI) when I met with a group of cultic Christians. Or so I thought.

The group I met with were the progeny of Nee Shu-tsu—better known around the world as Watchman Nee. Nee was a tall, handsome, well-spoken Chinese believer committed to feeding the spiritual hunger of Christians. I first heard of him from my father, who had been deeply moved by the simplicity and profundity of Nee's stories. Stories that made the complex simple and relatable.

One such story found Nee wandering into an orchard farm in Fukien, a southwestern province of China.[2] The orchard was thick with longan trees—the fruit of which is believed to be medicinal. The orchard trees were quite pathetic. The fruit they bore were the size of raspberries consisting of little more than skin and seeds. Upon being introduced to the orchard farmer, a miraculous illustration began to unfold.

The orchard contained a "father tree." In distinction to the other trees, it bore luscious fruit the size and consistency of plums. And it was this tree that changed all the other trees. The farmer had mastered the art of taking the nature of the father tree and grafting it into the trees bearing their useless fruit. He made cleavages in the bad trees and engrafted into them the nature of the good tree. Below the graft the fruit continued to be as useless as ever. But above it, the fruit the trees produced were radiantly rich and full of life.

Nee's application was intoxicating. If an orchard farmer can graft the life of a father tree into a bunch of fruitless longan trees, cannot the omnipotent Father engraft the life of his Son into us so that we may become partakers of the divine nature?

Nee did not mince words. Salvation was far more than justification. It was nothing short of deification: "To bring God into man, making God one with man as a God-man."[3] While Nee's views were consistent with Apostolic Tradition, within traditional denominationalism they sounded foreign—even frightening. Cultic. Particularly off-putting was his use of the word *mingling*—the notion that the life of God might be mingled with redeemed humanity such that the redeemed could legitimately be called god.[4]

Despite much controversy, Nee succeeded in multiplying his derisively branded "Little Flock" in "neighboring cities such as Hangzhou and Nanjing; north to Beijing and Shandong Province; south throughout Fujian; and west to the ports of Wuhan and Chongqing. Worshippers wrote down his talks and sermons and gathered them into books that were not only distributed among Christians in China but also translated for believers around the world."[5]

In 1934 Witness Lee (Lǐ Chángshòu) joined Nee in mission and vision. They proved a formidable team. By the time the Communist Party came to power (1949), the Little Flock had swelled to more than seventy thousand devotees in eight hundred locations across China.

Foreseeing ominous clouds on the horizon, Nee compelled Lee to leave the mainland. "Brother, you must realize that although in this desperate situation we trust in the Lord, it is possible that the enemy will one day wipe us out. If this happens, you will be out of China, and we will still have something left. So you must go."[6] Nee himself stayed in Shanghai and in time paid the ultimate price.

In the years following the Communist takeover, Nee's following became ever more expansive. "Many Christian congregations that had been dependent on foreign missions joined the Little Flock, which offered them financial help if they needed it. Some American and British missionaries were so grateful that they handed over their church property to the Little Flock before China kicked them out of the country."[7]

Zhou Enlai, the first premier of the People's Republic of China, cautioned Chinese Christians to rid their ranks of "imperialistic and feudalistic influences."[8] Being forewarned, Protestant leaders throughout China proactively "drew up a 'Christian Manifesto' and urged others to publicly sign on, pledging to terminate ties with overseas missions and support the new regime."[9]

The Manifesto, christened the "Three–Self Reform Movement," envisioned Christian churches as "'self-governing, self-supporting and self-propagating'—in real terms, free of foreign involvement of any kind in the fate, finances, or future growth of Christianity in China."[10]

In theory, the "Three–Self Movement" was not particularly onerous with respect to Little Flock distinctives. "They were 'three–self' even before there was a Three–Self Movement. The Little Flock members were 'self-supporting,' not relying on overseas funds to run their assembly halls. They were 'self-governing,' with no hierarchy like that of the Anglican House of Bishops. And they handled their own grassroots expansion, thus being 'self-propagating.'"[11]

Nevertheless, because of Nee's great influence on the burgeoning Christian population, the Communist Party viewed him as a threat. Predictably, they arrested Nee in 1952 as a "counterrevolutionary—*fan geming*. He faced accusations of spying; hostility to the government; fleecing fellow churchgoers; resisting land reform; and plotting against the People's Liberation Army. On top of all of that, he was tarred as morally corrupt, a philanderer who made a mockery of his marriage and paid regular visits to prostitutes."[12]

Nee's arrest culminated in a trial before the People's High Court in June 1956 where he was found guilty of counterrevolutionary crimes and sentenced to a fifteen-year imprisonment at the notorious Tilanqiao Prison in Shanghai. Adding to the pain, Nee's own church family turned on him. Their communiqué to Little Flock fellowships throughout China was nothing short of devastating. "We represent all brothers and sisters of the Shanghai Christian Assembly to support the sentence of the government heartily!"[13]

In 1972, twenty years after he had been arrested, Watchman Nee died in the midst of an onerous Cultural Revolution. "When relatives came to get his ashes at the labor camp, a guard gave them a piece of paper that had been tucked beneath his pillow. With a weak hand, [Nee] had written in Chinese characters: 'I shall die for believing in Christ.'"[14] Nee's ministry, however, did not die with him. Instead, a branch grew over the prison wall. A branch that in time stretched from East to West.[15]

Nee was not only faithful to the end but wisely arranged for his legacy to continue. As evidence, he had the foresight of sending Witness Lee to Taiwan. Within a handful of years some fifty thousand believers were meeting in local churches throughout the island. From Taiwan the "Local Churches" that had originated on China's mainland began to spread far and wide—to Singapore, Malaysia, Indonesia, Japan, Korea, and beyond.

In 1962, enthused by the growing interest in Watchman Nee's life and legacy in Western regions, Witness Lee moved to Los Angeles and began the mission of establishing Local Churches throughout the West.[16] As happened in Eastern regions, Local Churches spread rapidly from Lee's base in Southern California to far-flung places throughout the Western hemisphere.

But then came the pushback. Concurrent with the burgeoning growth of Lee's outreaches in the mid-seventies, the countercult efforts of the Christian Research Institute, founded by Dr. Walter Martin, were hitting their stride. Cults were rapidly proliferating across the continent, and CRI was strongly suspicious that Witness Lee might be the leader of one of them.

In October 1977 at a special meeting at Melodyland Christian Center in Anaheim, California, Walter Martin warned Christians that the teachings of Witness Lee and the Local Churches, also known as the Lord's Recovery, were "heretical and dangerous." In the considered opinion of Martin— popularly known as the father of the countercult movement—"A number of the basic teachings of Witness Lee and the Local Church are false, and it is man's carnal nature as well as Satan that breeds falsity. Such teachings are darkness, and the Christian must not walk in darkness."[17]

Martin and CRI called on devotees of the Lord's Recovery to cease walking in darkness and to walk instead in the light.[18] As Martin concluded in his bestseller *The New Cults*, "The fact that many immature Christians have been deceived into joining this group does not mean that the Local Church is close to orthodoxy, but only that it has become a clever counterfeit of the truth."[19]

With that the war between CRI and the Lord's Recovery began in earnest. Local Churches responded to Martin's conclusions by taking out full-page ads in the *Orange County Register* contending for the orthodoxy of their beliefs and denouncing "The Bible Answer Man." In turn CRI and Martin (then host of the *Bible Answer Man* broadcast) "published a booklet on the teachings of the Local Church and followed that up with a longer written treatment in 1978."[20]

CRI's published materials, along with Martin's book *The New Cults*,[21] created havoc for the Lord's Recovery. As did *The God-Men*[22] and *The Mindbenders*,[23] the latter of which featured "the Local Church" on its cover copy alongside such capricious cults as the Moonies and Hare Krishna. As noted by defenders of the Lord's Recovery, such "accusations were repeated in at least three hundred other books, articles and broadcasts." As a result, "the growth of the churches was stopped and the acceptance of Brother Lee's ministry was severely damaged. Families suffered estrangement, divorces were caused, jobs were lost, some members were physically assaulted, our children were confronted with the 'cult' charge, and many members were exposed to embarrassment and humiliation."[24]

Harassment and embarrassment in the West "[paled] in comparison to what the local churches and individuals suffered because of the 'cult' accusation in countries where freedom of religion was not protected. In those places, members suffered arrest, imprisonment and worse."[25] From the perspective of the Lord's Recovery, the fallout was an unmitigated tragedy. For CRI, the cost was more than justified by the ultimacy of truth.

CRI's perspective remained resolute until August 4, 2003. That evening, I met with leading ones in the Lord's Recovery who passionately affirmed the very things our Institute claimed they denied. I was particularly struck by the plain-spoken testimony of a tall lanky Texan by the name of Benson Philips. "I testify, brother Hank," began Philips, "we are not modalists[26] but thoroughly trinitarian. I testify, brother, that we do not believe we can become as

God is in the Godhead—we do not share his sovereignty or his persons and cannot be worshipped as God. I testify, brother, that we do not believe we are *the only church*—we are *only the church*."

A lively discussion ensued. Leading ones within the Lord's Recovery provided eye-opening clarifications to one alleged misunderstanding after another. We cited statements from the writings of Witness Lee, and they provided context not adequately accounted for in our evaluations. As the meeting drew to a conclusion, I purposed to remove CRI's statements from the web and withhold all commentary pending further investigation.

Thereafter, I commissioned Elliot Miller, editor-in-chief of our flagship magazine the *Christian Research Journal*, to initiate a primary research project. I subsequently invited Gretchen Passantino, a titan in the domain of theology and cult apologetics, to join him in the process. Both significantly contributed to Dr. Martin's writing and research, and I knew both to be ferociously committed to standing for truth no matter the cost.

Primary research commenced in 2003 and was not complete until 2009. It was conducted in the West and in Eastern regions such as China, Taiwan, South Korea, and Indonesia. It involved careful evaluation of literally hundreds of books, papers, church documents, and audio and video recordings. The result was encapsulated in three words. "We Were Wrong."[27]

Gretchen uttered those words to Li Li-hong in Shanghai. Years before in July 1983, when his daughter was but four months old, Li-hong was arrested, imprisoned, and sentenced to death. The intermediate court in the Jinhua region had him shackled with leg irons and handcuffs. Walking through the prison dragging his chains, he boldly preached the gospel to fellow prisoners and to prison guards alike. After five months, Li-hong received a second judgment. The Zhejiang high court changed his sentence to life imprisonment and exiled him to the frontier of Qinghai in the northwest of China. "Serving a life sentence with no hope of sentence reduction," wrote Li-hong, "meant that I had no hope in this life, but my heart was still joyful, because Christ was my hope of glory."[28]

Unlike Watchman Nee, Li-hong did not die in prison. In the end his life sentence was reduced five times. When he was finally released in 1998, his daughter was seventeen. Yet with a grateful heart, he wrote, "I thank the Lord for His grace in allowing me to be reunited with my family, and for the opportunity for us to serve Him together as a household."[29]

When Gretchen came to the realization that her writings had contributed to Li-hong's torturous seventeen-year imprisonment, she was undone. Amidst tears, she asked his forgiveness and experienced the sweetness of complete reconciliation.

Like Gretchen, Elliot experienced reconciliation with many brothers and sisters in the Lord's Recovery, with one of them being Lin Zilong, who had suffered imprisonment for a total of twenty-four years.[30]

Our research into the teachings and practices of Witness Lee and the Local Churches are memorialized in a special edition of the *Christian Research Journal*. Prominently displayed on the cover copy of the magazine are the words "We Were Wrong—A Reassessment of the 'Local Church' Movement of Watchman Nee and Witness Lee."[31] As Elliot wrote in our flagship magazine, we were "profoundly mistaken" and have come to the realization that the Lord's Recovery "represents a crucial work of God."[32]

The cost of our acknowledgment is significant. Integrity has been questioned, motives challenged, and slander has ensued. And CRI's financial support took a major hit. Leaders who once supported CRI were effusive in their denunciations. Dr. Norman Geisler is but one example. As dean of Southern Evangelical Seminary, he once awarded me an honorary doctorate and my bestseller *Christianity in Crisis* bore his endorsement—"Hank Hanegraaff has carefully documented one of the most popular and dangerous cultic groups to ever penetrate the contemporary evangelical church. The church owes a deep debt of gratitude to the leader of the world's largest countercult organization for unmasking the deceptive and poisonous false doctrines of the Faith Movement"[33]—yet after publication of our research, Dr. Geisler, in conjunction with Dr. Ron Rhodes (a former CRI staffer), called CRI's credibility into question.

"Not only does CRI no longer believe the LC ['The Local Church'] is a cult, as they once did, but they do not even believe they are an 'aberrant Christian group.' They now call the LC 'a *solidly orthodox* group of believers.'

Moreover, they say, members of the LC are in many ways 'an exemplary group of Christians.' All this has come as a great surprise to the majority of countercult ministries and apologists who have studied the matter and have come to the opposite conclusion."[34]

Geisler and Rhodes appeal to the study of sixty-plus evangelical scholars from seven nations who, in an open letter proliferated on the Internet, call on "the leadership of the 'local churches' and Living Stream Ministry to withdraw unorthodox statements by their founder, Witness Lee." Statements that "compromise essential Christian beliefs such as the doctrine of the Trinity."[35] They conclude by expressing their great disappointment "that one of the foremost countercult groups in the country could sacrifice its once high credibility in their nearly unqualified justification of this aberrant and cultic group."[36]

And therein lies the conundrum. On one side are sixty-plus evangelical scholars from seven nations who carefully examined this matter before taking the consequential step of affixing their names to an open letter deeming the Lord's Recovery cultic. On the other side is CRI, which is alleged to have sacrificed "its once high credibility." In the middle are multitudes who face enormous consequences. To label tens of thousands of Christians cultic or worse may lead to public humiliation and disgrace in the West—in the East, it may well lead to prison or death.

Considering the enormity of the consequences—and in the interest of truth—I purposed to personally contact the men who had affixed their names to the open letter. To my utter astonishment the first two scholars I contacted were not even aware of the open letter, said they did not endorse its conclusions, and never knowingly lent their names to it. A third signatory confessed he had *not* studied the matter—yet was unwilling to remove his name.

Most troubling for this scholar, and for the rest of the signatories, is context. Even the most cursory examination demonstrates conclusively that the open letter takes Witness Lee out of context—not only the broader context but the immediate context.

For example, respecting the matter of deification, the sixty-plus scholars from seven nations demand that the Lord's Recovery "disavow and cease to publish" the following declaration: "We the believers are begotten of God.

What is begotten of man is man, and what is begotten of God must be God. We are born of God; hence, in this sense, we are God."[37] What the scholars fail to disclose is the very next word—*nevertheless*: "*Nevertheless*, we must know that we do not share God's Person and cannot be worshiped by others. Only God Himself has the Person of God and can be worshiped by man."[38] Lee goes so far as to add, "It is a great heresy to say that we are made like God in His Godhead."[39] Even giving this cadre of scholars every benefit of the doubt, it is supremely difficult to imagine that every last one of them would have missed this obvious and crucial qualification.

Let me be clear. I do not pretend to judge the motivations involved. Perhaps it can be explained by what Dario Fernández-Morera (writing on the myth of the Andalusian Paradise) described as "'stakeholder interests and incentives,' which affect the research of academics in the humanities no less and perhaps even more than those in the sciences. Perhaps it has to do with what psychologists call 'motivated blindness,' which inhibits an individual's ability to perceive inconvenient data. Perhaps it has to do with the 'innocence of intellectuals.' Perhaps it is simply the result of shoddy research by a number of university professors repeated by many journalists."[40]

Whatever the motivation, one thing is certain. Rather than take Lee out of context, the open letter signatories should—in the interest of truth—consider the biblical and historical precedent for what he (in context) is communicating. As Athanasius of Alexandria, widely regarded as the greatest theologian of his time, has well said, God "was made man that we might be made God."[41]

This, of course, is not to say that we, though redeemed, possess God's incommunicable attributes. Who among us can claim self-existence, immutability, ineffability, eternality, omnipotence, omniscience, omnipresence, and absolute sovereignty? God is *eternal*;[42] humanity was created at a point in time[43] and has but a brief mortal existence on the earth.[44] God has *life in himself*,[45] but man is dependent on God to sustain him.[46] God is *all-powerful*,[47] but man is weak.[48] God is *all-knowing*,[49] but man is limited in knowledge.[50] God is *everywhere present*,[51] but humans are confined to a single space at a time.[52]

The great and glorious biblical truth communicated by both Nee and

Lee was well articulated in Paul's second letter to the Corinthians. "If anyone is *in Christ*, the *new creation* has come: The old has gone, the new is here!"[53] The Father's greatest gift to those saved through the death of his Son is the impartation of a new order of life. An order of life that is of the same quality as the life of Christ. For that is precisely what it is—the engrafting of the life of Christ. Thus, to be in Christ is more than a changed life; it is an exchanged life—an impartation of life by which the incarnation continues.[54]

Union with the divine is God's greatest gift to humanity. The apex of human existence. It is the high peak truth of redemptive revelation—the Everest of experiential epistemology. To recapitulate the words of the Apostle to the Gentiles, "If anyone is *in* Christ, the new creation has come: The old has gone, the new is here!" Such newness is not relegated to the felicity of forgiveness and purification—though it is most certainly that. It encompasses the great and glorious grace by which the forgiven now live in intimate union with the triadic One.[55] This is not merely an objective truth to be cognitively apprehended. "Life in the Trinity" is a living reality to be comprehended experientially.[56]

No one expressed this glorious grace more eloquently than did Martin Luther in his famed Christmas sermon of 1514. "For the word becomes flesh precisely so that the flesh may become word. In other words: *God becomes man so that man may become God*."[57] As such, the descent of the ineffable in incarnation provides the ladder of divine ascent by which fallen humanity may rise up to union with God—*and as such become new creations in Christ*. What that means, said Luther, is nothing less than the inviolate truth "that a man helped by grace is more than a man; indeed, the grace of God gives him the form of God and deifies him, so that even the Scriptures call him 'God' and 'God's son.'"[58]

This, of course, is not so much as to hint at heresy. Luther, should he have imagined that his aphorism, "word becomes flesh precisely so that the flesh may become word," would be taken as a confusion of essences, would no doubt turn over in his grave. Likewise the other greats of church history. Of one thing they were certain. While redeemed humanity may participate in the *energies* of God, the *essence* of God remains inviolate. As Gregory Palamas rightly observed, "the Logos became flesh and the flesh became Logos, even though neither abandoned its own proper nature."[59]

Thus, when the apostle Peter proclaimed that those in Christ "may participate in the divine nature,"[60] he was not suggesting that redeemed humanity may become what God is in his essence. That is not only impossible but heretical. Those in Christ become by grace what the Son of God is by nature[61]—"Children of God."[62] Gods by grace. Gods by participation in the divine nature.

Historically, the Christian church has illustrated this scintillating truth through the thrusting of a sword into the red-hot flames of a furnace. While the steel of the sword takes on the properties of fire, such that gray steel turns fiery red, the sword never becomes the fire nor the fire the sword. Likewise water and sponge. Though the sponge absorbs the ineffable waters of God's inexhaustible energy, it yet remains a sponge. The sponge does not become the water, nor the water the sponge. Again, to be in Christ—to experience his divine life—is to experience his *energies*, not to partake of his *essence*.[63]

The "tin man," to use a C. S. Lewis illustration, is being turned into a real man. Those who are in Christ have been transformed into new creations. The image and likeness of God, once ruinously marred, is being miraculously restored. Said Lewis: "The real Son of God is at your side. He is beginning to turn you into the same kind of thing as Himself. He is beginning, so to speak, to 'inject' His kind of life and thought, His *Zoe*, into you; beginning to turn the tin soldier into a live man."[64]

It is not a famous counselor or teacher who is changing the sensibilities of the redeemed from one thing to another. No! It is Jesus himself turning the tin man into a true man. Yes, he is God. The One who spoke and the limitless galaxies leapt into existence. But he is also very much a man. Not one who is dead, but one who is alive forevermore. Not only alive, but actively transforming you and me into a likeness of himself.

While I will expand on the matter of deification in part two, the matter at hand is truth. Truth matters. Regardless of one's disposition toward Watchman Nee, Witness Lee, and the Lord's Recovery, there is simply no justification for the deliberate distortion of truth. Moreover, if Lee and the Local Churches are to be branded heretics, why not Luther and Lewis?

As eminent social scientist Dr. Rodney Stark rightly noted long before the advent of the open letter, quoting Lee's theological statements so as to be diametrically opposed to what he was saying is not only libelous, but patently unfair.[65] And when J. Gordon Melton, founder of the Institute for the Study of American Religions, looked into this matter when *The God-Men* was published, he deemed it among the most painful experiences in his Christian life. Not because he found the Lord's Recovery to be a cult, but because as he began to check quotes used against Lee and the Local Churches, he discovered time and time again that they were placed "in a foreign context" and made "to say the opposite" of what was intended. As Melton made manifest, "This was done while ignoring the great truths of the Christian faith found throughout Lee's writings."

Moreover, numbers, whether sixty or sixty thousand, do not determine a matter to be true or false. When forty men bound themselves with an oath to kill the apostle Paul, they did so on false pretenses.[66] When *all* Israel grumbled against Moses and Aaron, they likewise did so falsely.[67] And as I have noted in a book titled *The Covering*, this is not an isolated instance.[68] In the past Christians have communicated the legend of Darwin's deathbed conversion; boycotted Procter & Gamble because its president allegedly confessed his company's ties to satanism; argued for the inspiration of Scripture on the basis of imbedded Bible codes; and told the tale of James Bartley, who was allegedly swallowed by a whale, to substantiate the biblical account of Jonah—all under the guise of truth.

As Os Guinness chronicled in *Time for Truth*, such creative storytelling is pandemic in the broader culture as well. It runs the gamut from "NBC television's staged report on the exploding General Motors trucks, later acknowledged to be planted detonations" to "Norma McCorvey's (AKA Jane Roe) fabricated story of rape, encouraged by proabortion leaders, that was so instrumental in the U.S. Supreme Court's 1973 decision, *Roe v. Wade*,"[69] to *Empire* actor and LGBTQ activist Jussie Smollett's shameful 2019 staging of a hate-crime hoax, presumptively depicted by Senator Kamala Harris as a "modern day lynching" as she exited "a Harlem, N.Y. restaurant with Al Sharpton," who himself "famously publicized the fraudulent hate-crime claim made by Tawana Brawley in the late 1980s."[70]

Such truth-twisting tactics are inevitably justified by the "Larger Truth that filmmaker Oliver Stone used in defending the facts in one of his films: 'Even if I'm totally wrong . . . I am still right . . . I am essentially right because I am depicting the Evil with a capital E.'"[71]

In 1999 I wrote *The Millennium Bug Debugged*.[72] Why? Because formidable intellects across the Christian landscape were busily propagating reckless rumors, spurious statistics, and anecdotal arguments respecting a technological bug that portended the demise of Western civilization. Although painful, the January issue of *Esquire* that year gave us a glimpse of the world's perspective on the lack of truthfulness within the Christian camp. Leaders were castigated for "mining the subjunctive, cultivating the seed of the threat buried inside each unrealized instance."[73] Not knowing how to discern between truth and error, tens of thousands of Christians were resigned to stocking up on freeze-dried food and generators, when what was really in short supply was truth.

In an age of fake news and sensationalistic distortions, the apostle Paul's words ring down through the ages with prophetic urgency: "Stand firm then, with the belt of truth buckled around your waist."[74] As your waist is the center of your body, so truth is central to the full armor of God. Without it, the covering that protects us from the Devil's schemes simply crumples to the ground, leaving us naked and vulnerable.

Truth, like all the other pieces of the armor, is in actuality an aspect of the nature of God himself. Thus, to put on the belt of truth is to put on Christ. For Christ is "truth."[75] And Christians are called to be bearers of truth.

And as Guinness has well said, Christianity is not true because it works (pragmatism); it is not true because it feels right (subjectivism); it is not true because it is "my truth" (relativism). It is true because it is anchored in the person of Christ. "The Christian faith is not true because it works; it works because it is true. It is not true because we experience it; we experience it—deeply and gloriously—because it is true. It is not simply 'true for us'; it is true for any who seek in order to find, because truth is true even if nobody believes it, and falsehood is false even if everybody believes it. That is why truth does not yield to opinion, fashion, numbers, office, or sincerity—it is simply true and that is the end of it."[76]

When I felt led to write large the words "We Were Wrong" on the cover of a special edition of the *Christian Research Journal*, it was not a matter of opinion—and it was most certainly not fashionable. Yet, while the toll this stand took on me personally and professionally was beyond anything I could ever have imagined, the reward has been equally astonishing. As a result of our research on the Lord's Recovery, I traveled to China on several occasions between 2003 and 2009. And those occasions not only changed me but forever altered our ministry.

In the West, theology, like politics, has become a veritable blood sport. In the East, things are somewhat different. More than a conceptual framework of faith, theology means something closer to the literal meaning of the word (*theos* meaning God and *logos* connoting knowledge). As such, far from signifying arguments about God, theology signified intimacy and communion with God. The creature encountering the Creator. The theoretical (though important) overshadowed by a living intimacy with the One who knit us together in our mothers' wombs.

This is precisely what I experienced during our primary research on the Lord's Recovery. The very people we were critiquing exemplified something beyond truth. They personified life. They proved to be humble Christians, so united with Christ that they naturally did the works of Christ. It was not that they considered truth to be unnecessary; they simply recognized it to be insufficient.

Flying back from East to West, toward the end of our research on the Recovery, I found myself staring into the clouds, pondering my own Christian experience. I had spent the better part of my career defining truth, debating truth, defending truth. I knew what I believed and why I believed it. Yet it had become clear to me that the Christians I had encountered in the underground church of China were experiencing something beyond truth. They were experiencing life—life that is life to the full.

As I stared into the vast expanse of the heavens from the vantage of my window seat, Thomas Aquinas flashed through my mind. Thomas had committed the whole of his mortal existence to the examination and explication of truth—his *Summa Theologica* is roundly regarded as one of the greatest intellectual accomplishments in all of Western civilization. His life's work was to codify all of truth into one coherent whole—truth from "the findings of anthropology, science, ethics, psychology, political theory, and theology all under God."[77]

But on the morning of December 6, 1273, Thomas had a eucharistic encounter with the real presence of God that radically rearranged his priorities. On that morning he had an experience that so viscerally impacted his being that the *Summa* was left unfinished. "While celebrating Holy Communion in the Chapel, he caught a glimpse of eternity. He was given a revelation from God that let him know that all his efforts to describe God fell so far short that he decided never to write again. When his secretary and friend, Reginald, tried to encourage him to do more writing, he responded, 'Reginald, I can do no more. The end of my labors has come. Such things have been revealed to me that all I have written seems as so much straw.'"[78]

My experience was not as immediate. Nor as dramatic. At least not at first. Yet standing for truth on August 4, 2003, has become my portal into life. The lifeblood of another has been engrafted within me, and even now I am experiencing the progression of union with God. Watchman Nee was right to say that salvation is far more than justification. That it is nothing short of deification. "To bring God into man, making God one with man as a God-man."[79] Nee's language might have been unnerving to detractors, but it was hardly novel. Orthodox theologian Vladimir Lossky, born the same year as Nee (1903), said much the same thing: "After the Fall, human history is a long shipwreck awaiting rescue: but the port of salvation is not the goal; it is the possibility for the shipwrecked to resume his journey whose sole goal is union with God."[80]

This, then, is my story—beginning with my personal search for truth as chronicled in the introduction to part one, *Truth Matters*, and continuing on with the unlikely discovery that *Life Matters More* as recounted in part two.

In essence *Truth Matters, Life Matters More* is two books in one. Part one emphasizes the absolute necessity and criticality of truth. You and I have no hope of standing against the deadly rip current of our insidious post-truth culture unless and until we grasp that the faith once for all delivered to the saints is grounded in history and evidence. That it corresponds to reality.

Part two makes plain that while truth is necessary, it is hardly sufficient. That the map is not the territory. That the menu is not the meal. That we must never mistake the cradle for its occupant. And that we are destined even *now* to experience life that is life to the full.

If you have suspected that there is more to the Christian life than what you are currently experiencing, read on—and discover *the unexpected beauty of an authentic Christian life.*

PART 1

TRUTH MATTERS

Truth is so obscure in these times,
and falsehood so established,
that unless we love the truth, we cannot know it.

—BLAISE PASCAL[1]

I was born in the Netherlands (Holland) in 1950, five years after the end of the Second World War. When I was but three, the Great Storm of 1953 blazed a trail of devastation along the North Sea coast of my homeland. The shambles of the post-war economy along with the worst peacetime disaster of the twentieth century impelled my parents to make a momentous decision. They became the first in a lineage stretching all the way back to the twelfth century to leave the motherland.

On March 19, 1953, we boarded *de Groote Beer* (the Great Bear) headed for Halifax, Nova Scotia, Canada. Ten years later, after my father nearly died of a mysterious disease, he purposed to abandon a comfortable suburban lifestyle, move our family to Grand Rapids, Michigan, and begin studies at Calvin College and Seminary to become a minister in the Christian Reformed denomination. And so, in September 1963, our family emigrated once again.

The details of our move to the United States are still vivid in my memory.

Scarcely two months into our move, President John F. Kennedy was assassinated as his motorcade snaked through Dealey Plaza in downtown Dallas, Texas. I can still remember precisely where I was when the news hit my thirteen-year-old ears.

Kennedy's murder proved a point of demarcation. As documented by PBS in *1964*, the assassination of JFK was "the moment that fundamentally altered the kind of nation America would become."[2] It spawned the war on poverty—what Lyndon Johnson dubbed *The Great Society*—and the war in Vietnam following the Gulf of Tonkin Resolution. It was the year of Berkeley and the Beatles. The year Cassius Clay took the Muslim moniker Mohammad Ali. The year of the Civil Rights Bill, *Bikini Beach*, and Joan Baez.

These were momentous times—especially for a fourteen-year-old immigrant to the United States from Holland via Canada. Nothing seemed to fit. I wore black socks; my peers wore white. I played hockey; they played basketball. I now inhabited the inner city, they suburbia. I felt disoriented, and Bob Dylan didn't help. "The Times They Are A-Changin'" pounded my ears.[3]

Betty Friedan was exploring abortion as the pathway to liberation from the perceived cancer of housewifery. Mohammad Ali was entertaining Allah as an alternative to the oppressive God of Christianity. The fab four were seeking solace in the transcendentalism of Maharishi Mahesh Yogi. And Lennon wanted listeners to "imagine" a world with "no religion."[4]

They, along with millions of others, were desperate for answers. And so was I. Was Mohammad Ali onto something? Were John Lennon, Paul McCartney, Ringo Starr, George Harrison? Perhaps Dylan was prescient. Maybe the old road was "agin'." The Beatles questioned their Christian background. Should I? The more I thought about it, the more I pined for answers.

For me, the biggest questions were directly related to God. Did God arrange the fall of Adam and Eve? Were multiplied millions fatalistically predestined to hell? My parents, my Christian school, my church, all seemed to answer in the affirmative. That the God of the Bible had created millions of people "doomed from the womb" to certain destruction.[5] That they could no more respond to God in faith than a cow could fly. Even in my untrained teenage mind, implications perpetually bubbled to the surface. If God arranged for the fall of humanity, God must be the author of evil. And if the God I had been taught to believe in from childhood onward was the author of evil, how did I separate this God from evil itself?

I can still remember sitting in our family pew listening to the pastor preach a sermon on predestination. I no longer recall the exact words, however I do remember the essence. It was the dictum of John Calvin. That "by predestination we mean the eternal decree of God, by which he determined with himself whatever he wished to happen with regard to every man. All are not created on equal terms, but some are preordained to eternal life, others to eternal damnation; and, accordingly, as each has been created for one or other of these ends, we say that he has been predestinated to life or to death."[6]

The reason that message is still vivid after all these years is that in the midst of listening, I purposed to blaspheme God. Though I doubted the premise of the message, I lived in mortal terror of having committed that unforgivable sin. During the Cuban Missile Crisis, when I feared the world might be vaporized in a nuclear holocaust, my father found me doubled up on the living room sofa. I quite literally trembled at the thought that I might soon be burning in hell. I told my dad about that day in church in which I had done something that could never be undone. To my amazement, my father simply smiled and told me that if I had committed an unpardonable sin, I would not now in the least be concerned about it.

As the cold-war tensions between the Soviet Union and the United States thawed, questions returned with a vengeance. If God created the universe, who created God? Was Eve tempted by a talking snake? If we can't see God, how do we know he exists? How can God be one and three? And what about the Bible? Is it truly a reliable authority? What about resurrection? Do dead people really come back to life? Did Christ? Will I?

As the questions churned through my teenage mind, I tormented my parents, my pastor, and my teachers for answers. Where answers were unsatisfying, or I was urged to just have faith, my doubts intensified. And all this in conjunction with wanting to experience life without borders. The sexual revolution was in full swing, and God seemed to me a cosmic kill-joy. In time I began to live life as a functional atheist. From time to time I would feel myself drawn back to Christianity. But there were always too many unanswered questions.

For the better part of fifteen years I slipped in and out of spirituality. I could never fully separate myself from the religion of my youth, nor could I fully embrace it. On balance Darwin's evolutionary hypothesis seemed a more appealing alternative. Not only was it the pervasive narrative of the culture, but it allowed me to escape the oppressive dictates of the Christian ethic.

All of that changed January 1979 when three Christians from a nearby church told me about a weekend workshop on origins. The workshop proved to be a game changer. It not only exposed cracks in the evolutionary veneer, it also impelled me to dig deeper. And so, I began to examine the issue of origins in earnest, and thereafter the trustworthiness of the Bible and the plausibility of resurrection.

After immersing myself in the quest for answers for what I believe are the three great apologetic issues, I embarked on a transformational "journey whose sole goal [was] union with God."[7] The church family I embraced engaged me in an evangelism ministry in which I learned to share my newfound faith. As I did, I encountered one question after another. My involvement in evangelism quite naturally drove me into education—into finding answers to questions I was encountering. To, as the apostle Peter put it, "always be prepared to give an answer to everyone who asks you to give the reason for the hope that you have."[8]

If there is one thing I have discovered in forty years of answering questions—over thirty as host of CRI's *Bible Answer Man* broadcast—it is that the Christian worldview corresponds to reality. And that in the swirling waves of doubt and despair that can threaten to submerge our faith, it is ever more critical to be familiar with the pillars or posts on which the Christian faith is founded—namely, God created the universe, Jesus Christ demonstrated that he is God through the immutable fact of resurrection, and the Bible is divine rather than merely human in origin.[9]

Like *answers* to the great apologetics issues, commitment to the maxim "truth matters" has inculcated within me a deep commitment to the art and science of *biblical interpretation*. Wrongly interpreted, one might well suppose along with the late Christopher Hitchens of *Vanity Fair* that "the Bible contains a warrant for trafficking in humans, for ethnic cleansing, for slavery, for bride-price and for indiscriminate massacre."[10] And if this is so, it is a game changer.

Take slavery, for example. If the Scriptures upheld the virtues of slavery, I could not uphold the virtues of the Scriptures. Nor should anyone else. While Scripture as a whole recognizes the reality of slavery, it never promotes the practice of slavery. In fact, it was the application of proper interpretive principles that ultimately led to the overthrow of slavery, both in ancient Israel and in the United States of America. Far from extolling the virtues of slavery, the Bible denounces slavery as sin. The New Testament goes so far as to put slave traders in the same category as murderers, adulterers, perverts, and liars.[11]

The same can be said for trafficking, ethnic cleansing, bride-price, or for indiscriminate massacre.[12] When the Bible is interpreted properly, all such accusations fall by the wayside. In an age in which Internet lies travel halfway around the world before truth has had a chance to put its boots on, it is axiomatic that you and I devote our lives to knowing how to read the Bible for all its worth.[13]

Finally, in the interest of truth, it is likewise crucial to counter the advocates of counterfeit religious systems ranging from Mormons to Muslims. When Mormons, in concert with their founder Joseph Smith, claim that their revelation, the Book of Mormon, is "*the* most correct of any book on earth"[14] and that conversely the Bible is fraught with error, there must be a counter.[15] Likewise, when Muslims claim that the Qur'an is uncreated and unalterable, without error, having ethics beyond question, and eloquent above anything the world has ever experienced, it is incumbent upon Christians to demonstrate that the emperor has no clothes. That the Qur'an in reality is fraught with faulty ethics and riddled with factual errors.[16]

Because truth matters, CRI is committed to equipping Christians to be so familiar with essential Christian doctrine that when counterfeit religions loom on the horizon, they will recognize their unbiblical revelations, linguistic subversions, theological perversions, and sociological deviances, instantaneously.

This, then, is the focus of part one. *Truth Matters*. While I argue in part two that *Life Matters More*, we must remain mindful that without a proper menu, our meal may well be toxic.

ANSWERS

Apologetics in the Modern Age of Skepticism

> Always be prepared to give an answer to everyone who asks
> you to give the reason for the hope that you have. But do this
> with gentleness and respect.
>
> —THE APOSTLE PETER[1]

I often refer to origins as not *an* apologetic issue but *the* apologetic issue. It is because how you view your origins will ultimately determine how you live your life. If you suppose you are a function of random processes, you will live your life by a different standard than if you know you are created in the image of God and accountable to him. In the final analysis, more consequences for society hinge on the issue of origins than on any other.

Friedrich Nietzsche, who provided the philosophical framework for Hitler's Germany, understood this better than most. He predicted that the death of God in the nineteenth century would ensure that the twentieth century would be the bloodiest in human history. And he was right. Not only about the twentieth century but about the twenty-first.

The supposed death of God ushered in an era in which humans proclaimed themselves sovereigns of the universe. Nowhere was this more evident than at the Darwinian Centennial Convention, celebrating the one hundredth anniversary of Darwin's *On the Origin of Species by Means of Natural Selection*. Sir Julian Huxley, the great-grandson of Thomas Huxley (who coined the term *agnostic*), declared, "there is no longer either need or room for the supernatural. The earth was not created: it evolved. So did all the animals and plants that inhabit it, including our human selves, mind and soul as well as brain and body. So did religion." Thus, said Huxley, "evolutionary man can no longer take refuge from his loneliness by creeping for shelter into the arms of a divinized father-figure whom he has himself created."[2]

Sir Julian hyperbolically dubbed the Darwinian revolution "the most powerful and the most comprehensive idea that has ever arisen on earth."[3] A revolution that shaped the worldview of hundreds of millions, beginning with Darwin himself. When he left Devonport, England, aboard Her Majesty's ship *The Beagle*, on December 27, 1831, Darwin was a self-proclaimed Genesis devotee.[4] "*The Beagle*," however, "proved the turning point of his life, a liberating journey through time and space which freed him from the constraining influence of Genesis."[5]

If Darwin's departure from a "strict and literal" interpretation of Genesis was anything at all, it was extraordinary. In *Origin*, he speculated that bears might well have evolved into whales. "I can see no difficulty in a race of bears being rendered, by natural selection, more and more aquatic in their structure and habits, with larger and larger mouths, till a creature was produced as monstrous as a whale."[6]

Humans, too, were in the midst of evolutionary flux. "At some future period, not very distant as measured by centuries, the civilised races of man will almost certainly exterminate, and replace, the savage races throughout the world. At the same time, the anthropomorphous apes," averred Darwin, "will no doubt be exterminated. The break between man and his nearest allies will then be wider, for it will intervene between man in a more civilised state, as we may hope, even than the Caucasian, and some ape as low as a baboon, instead of as now between the negro or Australian and the gorilla."[7] Dr. Benjamin Wiker rightly deduced that Darwin's ranking of races places "the Caucasian at top, and down at the bottom, dangling at the edge of humanity, 'the negro or Australian' who is just an evolutionary hair's-breadth away from the anthropomorphous gorilla."[8]

The racist implications of the evolutionary hypothesis are so horrendous that Darwin apologist Richard Dawkins attempted to absolve his exemplar from the disturbing realities of overt bigotry. "The misunderstanding of the Darwinian struggle for existence as a struggle between groups of individuals—the so-called 'group selection' fallacy—is unfortunately not confined to Hitlerian racism. It constantly resurfaces in amateur misinterpretations of Darwinism, and even among some professional biologists who should know better."[9]

This Dawkinsian slight of mind would be humorous if it were not so heartbreaking. The dichotomy between races and groups of individuals who share common characteristics is a distinction without a difference. Characteristics that groups of individuals share in common are a function of genetics. Darwin was largely ignorant of genetics, but the same cannot be said for Dawkins. Indeed, genetics is precisely what grounds his concept of race. The "professional biologists" should be better commended. It takes courage in today's politically correct climate to call things as they are. Moreover, to excuse the overt racism (and sexism) in Darwin's writings is itself inexcusable— particularly from the pen of a man who has the temerity to castigate those who do not believe in his evolutionary enterprise as "ignorant," "stupid," "insane," "wicked," "tormented," "bullied," or "brainwashed."[10]

For neo-Darwinians like Dawkins, God is little more than a troublesome myth. As such, a human being has no more intrinsic value than a hornet. In time a more sophisticated life form will supplant humankind, courtesy of the evolutionary paradigm. As hippos transitioned into whales, humans will inevitably transition into whatever. The fact that there is scant fossil evidence for this fundamentalist fervor seems of little consequence. Nor is molecular evidence to the contrary a stumbling block.[11] Woven tightly into the psycho-epistemological cocoons of their own making, evolutionary titans such as Richard Dawkins go on blindly spinning evolutionary tales. In their implausible paradigms, skin becomes impermeable to water, eye protection mechanisms appear like magic, as do myriad changes in the brain; diving and other mechanisms emerge, including a respiratory system that prevents the bends, lactation system, sonar, and so forth.

Anyone who has spent even a modicum of time looking at the progression of such scientific speculations knows full well that academics are not impervious to group-think—particularly when tenure, social dynamics, grants, and such are in play. One would be hard-pressed to come up with a better example of herd mentality than the collective embrace of eugenics. The moniker "eugenics" (the science of being well born) was coined in 1865 by Sir Francis Galton—a prestigious polymath, sociologist, psychologist, anthropologist, and cousin to Charles Darwin.[12]

In the celebrated British *Macmillan's Magazine*, Galton contended that eugenics must of necessity be applied to humans as well as horses.[13] Darwin famously followed suit in *The Descent of Man*, where he made explicit that his notorious subtitle, "The Preservation of Favored Races in the Struggle for Life," quite rightly applied to human races. Apart from eugenics, he opined, there is nothing to "prevent the reckless, the vicious and otherwise *inferior members of society from increasing at a quicker rate than the better class of men*." And when that happens, "the nation will retrograde, as has occurred too often in the history of the world."[14]

Group-think followed on the heels of Galton and Darwin. With the dawn of the twentieth century, eugenics was standard fare in high school biology classes. George William Hunter's textbook *A Civic Biology* is of particular note. I, like most other Americans, remember it as the infamous biology text at the center of the 1925 "Scopes Monkey Trial." As a professed progenitor of progress, John Scopes used this very text to convince impressionable students that humanity has an evolutionary hierarchy. That "if we follow the early history of man upon the earth, we find that at first he must have been little better than one of the lower animals." That "at the present time there exist upon the earth five races or varieties of man." That there are the "negro type, originating in Africa; the Malay or brown race, from the islands of the Pacific; the American Indian; the Mongolian or yellow race, including the natives of China, Japan, and the Eskimos; and finally, the highest type of all, the Caucasians, represented by the civilized white inhabitants of Europe and America."[15]

The text makes a stirring case for the pseudo-science of eugenics, going so far as to say that the remedy for those not "well born" should be *extermination*— "If such people were lower animals, we would probably kill them off to prevent them from spreading."[16]

The ramifications of eugenic reasoning are as rampant as they are racist. Dr. John Langdon Down famously labeled Down syndrome "Mongoloid Idiocy." Why? Because from his biased perspective, it exemplified "a 'throwback' to the 'Mongolian stage' in human evolution."[17] This is amplified by the late Stephen Jay Gould, who observed that the moniker "'Mongoloid' was first applied to mentally defective people because it was then commonly believed that the Mongoloid race had not yet evolved to the status of the Caucasian race."[18] Tragically, it wasn't until 1965 that the World Health Organization (WHO) finally resolved to abandon the expression at the behest of the People's Republic of Mongolia.[19] The bias against Down syndrome babies, however, remains intact to this very moment.

In a CBS News story subtitled "Inside the country where Down syndrome is disappearing," Julian Quinones pointed out that "since prenatal screening tests were introduced in Iceland in the early 2000s, the vast majority of women—close to 100 percent—who received a positive test for Down syndrome terminated their pregnancy." Geneticist Kári Stefánsson, founder of deCODE Genetics, observed that as a result of "heavy-handed genetic counseling" strategies, "we have basically eradicated, almost, Down syndrome from our society . . . that there is hardly ever a child with Down syndrome in Iceland anymore."[20]

While all this is being breathlessly touted by evolutionary establishment as evolvement, in reality it represents historical recapitulation—a throwback to nineteenth-century scientists who hypothesized that the gene pool was being corrupted by the less fit genes of inferior people. For evolution to succeed, they reckoned it as crucial that the unfit die as that the fittest survive. "If the unfit survived indefinitely, they would continue to 'infect' the fit with their less fit genes." The result is that fit genes are corrupted, and evolution compromised.[21]

As the late Michael Crichton appropriately pointed out, the theory of eugenics postulated that "the best human beings were not breeding as rapidly as the inferior ones—the foreigners, immigrants, Jews, degenerates, the unfit, and the 'feeble minded.'" Thus, in accord with eugenic theory, "the plan was to identify individuals who were feeble minded—Jews were agreed to be largely feeble-minded, but so were many foreigners, as well as blacks—and stop them from breeding by isolation in institutions or by sterilization."[22]

The logical progression from evolution to eugenics is hardly surprising. What is breathtaking, however, is the vast rapidity with which this baseless theory was embraced by the cultural elite. Crichton noted that its supporters ranged from President Theodore Roosevelt to Planned Parenthood founder Margaret Sanger. Eugenics research was funded through philanthropies such as the Carnegie and Rockefeller foundations and carried out at prestigious universities such as Stanford, Harvard, Yale, and Princeton.

As the herd marched onward, legislation to address the concern posed by eugenics was passed in blue states ranging from New York to California. Eugenics was even backed by the National Academy of Sciences and the American Medical Association. Those who resisted eugenics were considered backward and ignorant. Conversely, those like Margaret Sanger, the birth mother of Planned Parenthood, who embraced eugenics, were considered enlightened. German scientists who gassed the "feeble-minded," too, were considered forward-thinking and progressive and were rewarded with grants from such institutions as the Rockefeller Foundation right up to the onset of World War II.

It wasn't until the ghastly reality of eugenics reached full bloom in the genocidal mania of German death camps that it vanished quietly into the night. Indeed, after World War II few institutions or individuals would even own up to their insidious belief in eugenics. Nor did the cultural elite ever acknowledge the obvious connection between eugenics and evolution.

Apart from ongoing reparations, eugenics has faded into the shadowy recesses of history. The tragic consequences of the evolutionary dogma that birthed it, however, are yet with us today.

ANSWERS ON ORIGINS

As the vaunted R. Taylor Cole Professor of Philosophy at Duke University and codirector of the Duke Center for Philosophy of Biology, Dr. Alex Rosenberg is determined that no one—not his students, nor anyone else in today's generation—fails to understand the full implications of Darwin's evolutionary paradigm. "Scientism needs to show that blind variation together with environmental filtration is the sole route through which life can emerge in any universe. We have to understand why, in a universe made only by physics, the process that Darwin discovered is the only game in town."[23] In *The Atheist's Guide to Reality*, Rosenberg noted that "95 percent of the most distinguished scientists in America (along with their foreign associate members) don't believe in God."[24] The other 5 percent simply swallowed "the biggest conspiracy theory of them all: the story of how God put us here."[25]

But "science beats stories," said Rosenberg.[26] Stories about such things as meaning, purpose, free will, morality. Stories he believes we desperately need liberation from. "The answer to the persistent question, *What is the purpose of the universe?* is quite simply: There is none."[27] And, intones the famed philosopher and biologist, "in a world where physics fixes all the facts, it's hard to see how there could be room for moral facts." Why? "If Darwinism is true, then anything goes." "We need to face the fact that nihilism is true."[28] That there are no intrinsic moral values. "Our core morality isn't true, right, correct, and neither is any other. Nature just seduced us into thinking it's right."[29] Because "nihilism denies that there is anything at all that is good in itself or, for that matter, bad in itself."[30]

For people troubled by immortality, immorality, or who want "to know the nature of right and wrong, good and evil, why we should be moral, and whether abortion, euthanasia, cloning, or having fun is forbidden, permissible, or sometimes obligatory," Rosenberg has provided pithy answers:

Is there a God? No. What is the nature of reality? What physics says it is. What is the purpose of the universe? There is none. What is the meaning of life? Ditto. Why am I here? Just dumb luck. Does prayer work? Of course not. Is there a soul?

Is it immortal? Are you kidding? *Is there free will?* Not a chance! *What happens when we die?* Everything pretty much goes on as before, except us. *What is the difference between right and wrong, good and bad?* There is no moral difference between them. *Why should I be moral?* Because it makes you feel better than being immoral. *Is abortion, euthanasia, suicide, paying taxes, foreign aid, or anything else you don't like forbidden, permissible, or sometimes obligatory?* Anything goes. *What is love and how can I find it?* Love is the solution to a strategic interaction problem. Don't look for it; it will find you when you need it. *Does history have any meaning or purpose?* It's full of sound and fury but signifies nothing. *Does the human past have any lessons for our future?* Fewer and fewer, if it ever had any to begin with.[31]

If this summary sounds depressing, says Rosenberg, "scientism has good news. There is an ever-increasing pharmacopoeia of drugs, medicines, treatments, prosthetic devices, and regimes that will avoid, minimize, or reduce these unwanted conditions. Take them. And if you feel guilty for seeking surcease from the thousand natural shocks that flesh and especially gray matter are subject to, well there's probably a drug that reduces such guilt feelings, too."[32] Because there is no meaning. No purpose. No immortality. No moral compass. No free will. Rosenberg counsels the scientistic to "cultivate an Epicurean detachment. This is a disposition recommended by Epicurus, a Greek philosopher of the fourth century BC" who "believed that everything was basically atoms moving on determined paths forever. The physical facts, he rightly held, fix all the facts, and that made him an atheist. Epicurus held that there was nothing more to the mind than physical matter and that immortality was out of the question. He equated the morally good with pleasure and evil with pain."[33]

That's the sum of it! If it gives you pleasure—whatever it is—it's morally good. Pain? Pain is unredeemable.[34] As for punishment, "no one does wrong freely [there is no free will], so no one should really be punished."[35] And if all of this keeps you from sleeping at night, proffers Rosenberg, "you probably just need one more little thing besides Epicurean detachment. Take a Prozac or your favorite serotonin reuptake inhibitor, and keep taking them till they kick in."[36]

14

One thing Dr. Rosenberg may be lauded for is his candor. The myriad students he impacts as a professor of philosophy at the prestigious Duke Center for Philosophy of Biology are never left wondering about the implications of the naturalistic worldview he champions. Nor are the multitudes unimpacted by his writings. Rosenberg not only espouses what he believes to be consensus science (*95 percent of elite scientists don't believe in God*) but forthrightly underscores the draconian implications of his firmly held conviction that "what we know about physical and biological science makes the existence of God less probable than the existence of Santa Claus."[37] Adds Rosenberg, "the parts of science that rule out theism are firmly fixed."[38]

Really? We do well to remember that "when the barbarians destroyed the Roman Empire in the West, it was the Christian Church that put together the new order called Europe."[39] The foundational principle undergirding the new world was codified in a singular word—*revelation*. No matter how keen a person's eyesight, they can see nothing if confined to the pitch-black darkness of consensus thinking. As light is axiomatic to seeing, so revelation is needed for knowing. While truth may be comprehended by reason, the fountainhead of truth is revelation. Without divine disclosure we are but blind men grasping at the trunk of the proverbial elephant.

My personal experience illustrates the point. Shortly after we immigrated to Michigan, my parents purchased an encyclopedia set called the *Book of Knowledge*. In it I discovered an evolutionary paradigm that dispensed with the need for a rational Creator who ordered the cosmos in accordance with his nature. In place of a Creator, the *Book of Knowledge* posited chance. In the words of biologist Jacques Monod, winner of the prestigious Nobel Prize, "Chance *alone* is at the source of every innovation, of all creation in the biosphere. Pure chance, absolutely free but blind, at the very root of the stupendous edifice of evolution."[40]

It wasn't until I was twenty-nine that I realized such reasoning to be a departure from knowledge into a dangerous world of antiknowledge. What makes an Australian aborigine the equal of Dr. Rosenberg? Why suppose a woman to be the equal, much less the superior, of a man? Why not pontificate, as did Rosenberg (acclaimed by the *New York Times* as a "well-informed and imaginative philosopher"[41]) that "racism and xenophobia are optimally adapted to maximize the representation of your genes in the next generation, instead of some stranger's genes. Consider the almost universal patriarchal norms of female subordination. They are the result of Darwinian processes."[42] Or why not suppose, as Darwin did, that man can attain "to a higher eminence, in whatever he takes up, than can woman—whether requiring deep thought, reason, or imagination, or merely the use of the senses and hands."[43]

The answer again is revelation. As Genesis reveals, we are created in the *imago Dei* (image of God). And that makes all the difference in the world. The *imago Dei* ensures a Down syndrome child is afforded the same dignity given a distinguished scientist. The *imago Darwinii*, as Dr. Rosenberg makes plain, leads in quite an opposite direction.

It was the realization that revelation is axiomatic to knowledge that led medieval thinkers to crown theology queen of the sciences. Peter Paul Rubens personified this elegantly in his seventeenth-century painting *The Triumph of the Eucharist*. Seated in a chariot propelled by angelic beings is theology—queen of the sciences. Walking alongside are philosophy, the wise and grizzled veteran, and science, a newcomer in the cosmic conversation. The point is that theology is never absent philosophy and science.[44] However, philosophy and science absent revelation leads inexorably to the blind ditch of ignorance. Ignorance on the level of that personified by Rosenberg alongside peers and predecessors.

This is precisely why Greek philosophers like Epicurus were hardly a match for Christian theologians. While they were conversant with the laws of logic, they were woefully ignorant respecting divine revelation. Aristotle, ignoring the revelation "In the beginning God" (Genesis 1:1), embraced the implausibility of an eternal universe. Not so, said early Christian theologians. Their God was an omniscient, omnipotent deity, who has the will and power to reveal himself.[45]

The new world order that arose from the impotence of Greco-Roman thought was grounded in the premise that God has revealed himself as Creator and sustainer of the universe in the realm of nature. No one made this point more eloquently than did the apostle most responsible for spreading the

Christian ethic throughout the Roman Empire. "For since the creation of the world God's invisible qualities—his eternal power and divine nature—have been clearly seen, being understood from what has been made, so that men are without excuse."[46] The Apostle to the Gentiles went on to note that those who denied what could be clearly seen "became fools."[47] Not in the sense of lacking mental acumen. Epicurus, Darwin, Huxley, Dawkins, Rosenberg, and others have significant accomplishments to their credit. No, the fool Paul has in mind is one whose mind is darkened by the narrow confines of his naturalistic preconceptions.

It isn't that Christian apologists dwarf the intellects of pagan philosophers. The laws of reason are as accessible to one as to the other. It is the failure to apply the explanatory power of revelation to the mysteries of life that trapped pagan thinkers in the intellectual cul-de-sac of their own making. Pagan philosophers and their devotees idealize the world in terms of how they think it ought to be. Christian thinkers turned pages in the book of nature and discovered how it really was. The organization and complexity of the physical universe bear eloquent testimony to the existence of an uncaused First Cause—an Intelligent Designer.

Ocean tides caused by the gravitational pull of the moon are a classic case in point. If the moon were significantly larger, devastating tidal waves would submerge large areas of land. If the moon were smaller, tidal motion would cease and the oceans would stagnate and die. From its tides to its temperatures to the tilt of its axis ("23.5 degrees from perpendicular to the plane of its orbit"[48]), the earth is an unparalleled planetary masterpiece of precision and design.

As was readily apparent as I emerged from my own psycho-epistemological cocoon, the universe is not an illusion, it did not spring out of nothing (*nothing comes from nothing; nothing ever could*), and it has not eternally existed (the laws of thermodynamics and big bang cosmology tell us that the universe came into existence a finite time ago). Thus, the only philosophically plausible possibility remaining is that the universe was made by an unmade Cause greater than itself.

This is precisely why science did not—indeed, could not—have emerged from Greek philosophy any more than it could have evolved within the dreary environs of philosophical naturalism. Men of science were of necessity also men of God, as committed to revelation as they were to reason. Leonardo da Vinci, widely considered to be the real founder of modern science, could not so much as countenance the notion that nothing created everything. Instead he was deeply committed to the evidential notion that "God created the heavens and the earth."[49] Robert Boyle, the father of modern chemistry as well as the greatest physical scientist of his generation, was immovably committed to the reality of an uncaused First Cause. Sir Isaac Newton, a prodigious intellect who developed calculus, discovered the law of gravity, and designed the first reflecting telescope, would not abide the Epicurean predilection that there is "nothing more to the mind than physical matter and that immortality was out of the question."[50] Louis Pasteur, well known for the process of pasteurization and for utterly demolishing the concept of spontaneous generation, underscored the power of revelation and undermined the evident absurdities of an atheistic paradigm.[51]

Other intellects gracing the doorway of science include Johannes Kepler (scientific astronomy), Francis Bacon (the scientific method), Blaise Pascal (mathematician and philosopher), Carl Linnaeus (biological taxonomy), Gregor Mendel (genetics), Michael Faraday (electromagnetics), Joseph Lister (antiseptic surgery), Henrietta Swan Leavitt (astronomy), Clara Swain (medicine), and countless others. These men and women were highly allergic to the atheistic archetype.[52]

Perhaps Dr. Rosenberg is right. Perhaps the vast majority of elite twenty-first-century scientists are Darwinian atheists. But that hardly proves that evolution is the answer. Dr. Jonathan Wells, author of *Zombie Science*, aptly noted that "throughout history, the scientific consensus has often proven to be unreliable. In 1500, the scientific consensus held that the sun revolves around the Earth, a view that was overturned by Nicolaus Copernicus and Galileo Galilei. In 1750, the consensus held that some living things (such as maggots) originate by spontaneous generation, a view that was overturned by Francesco Redi and Louis Pasteur."[53] Numerous false scientific paradigms have enjoyed scientific consensus.

Answers, however, are not a function of consensus but of correspondence to reality.

Fossil Follies

To answer the question of origins one need look no further than to the fossil record. Darwin predicted that the fossil record would bear him out. However, as I discovered in my personal journey toward truth more than forty years ago, the fossil record is one of the greatest embarrassments of the Darwinian legacy. In place of the Genesis Tree of Life, Darwin planted an imposter.

According to the Darwinian version, humans and fruit flies share a common ancestor. As do boys and bananas. The Tree of Life appears in *The Origin of Species* to persuade the faithful that all species (kinds) are "lineal descendants of some few beings which lived long before the first bed of the Silurian [Cambrian] system was deposited."[54] At the root of the Tree are a handful of organic building blocks; at the tips of its budding branches are all modern species.

Darwin's Tree of Life is an icon. And not just *any* icon—it is *the* principal symbol of evolution. For multitudes the icon has become the argument. The mere mention of it invokes devotees to bow deeply before the twin altars of common descent and natural selection. "I should infer," the chief priest intoned, "that probably all the organic beings which have ever lived on this earth have descended from *some one* primordial form."[55]

Yet as I began my own liberating journey from Darwinian fundamentalism to a biblical worldview, I found Darwin's Tree of Life to be purely mythological. What seemed patently obvious upon closer examination is that in the geological period designated Cambrian, the highest orders in the biological hierarchy appear suddenly and fully formed. Which is precisely the case. Darwin's Tree of Life is not only uprooted by the Cambrian Explosion, the fossil record in general shows no evidence of the origin of species by means of common descent and natural selection. Instead, as Richard Dawkins candidly confessed, "It is as though they [the Cambrian fossils] were just planted there, without any evolutionary history."[56]

But then the plot thickened. Whenever I brought up the lack of fossil transitions from one species to another, my evolutionary friends would habitually point to Archaeopteryx as a transitional fossil between birds and dinosaurs. Wondering if this was so, I took a closer look. What I discovered was that, despite all the hype, Archaeopteryx was an unlikely candidate for the missing link, since birds and alleged ancestral dinosaurs happened to thrive during the same period (Jurassic).[57] In sober fact, Archaeopteryx appears suddenly in the fossil record, with masterfully engineered wings and feathers common in birds observable today.

Moreover, to believe that Archaeopteryx is a missing link between reptiles and birds, I would have had to convince myself against all evidence that scales evolved into feathers. That air friction acting on genetic mutation could have frayed the outer edges of reptilian scales. That over the course of millions of years, scales became increasingly like feathers until one fine day the perfect feather emerged. And that the fearsome flight of the falcon and the delicate darting flitter of the hummingbird are a miraculous function of unguided, purposeless processes.

Today, as forty years ago, whether in conferences or common conversation, if I say that the fossil record is an embarrassment to Darwin's evolutionary hypothesis, someone invariably brings up Archaeopteryx. This happens with such regularity that I coined the word *pseudosaur. Pseudo* meaning false and *saur*—reptile (literally, lizard). Thus, *pseudosaur* connotes a false link between reptiles (such as dinosaurs) and birds. As noted by evolutionist Pierre Lecomte du Noüy, an expert in the science of statistical probability, "We are not even authorized to consider the exceptional case of the Archaeopteryx as a true link. By link, we mean a necessary stage of transition between classes such as reptiles and birds, or between smaller groups. An animal displaying characters belonging to two different groups cannot be treated as a true link as long as the intermediary stages have not been found, and as long as the mechanisms of transition remain unknown."[58]

Likewise, Stephen Jay Gould of Harvard University and Niles Eldredge of the American Museum of Natural History (both militant evolutionists) have concluded that Archaeopteryx cannot be considered a legitimate fossil transition from one species to another. "At the higher level of evolutionary transition between basic morphological designs, gradualism has always been in trouble, though it remains the 'official' position of most Western evolutionists. Smooth intermediates between *Baupläne* [different types of creatures] are almost impossible to construct, even in thought experiments; there is certainly no evidence for them in the fossil record."[59] I remain grateful today, as in my early investigation, for such laudable candor.

Ape-Men—Another Evolutionary Icon

I will never forget the day I first saw the face of *Pithecanthropus erectus*. It virtually leapt off the page of my text. It had a sharply receding forehead that cascaded abruptly into a heavy brow ridge. Its mouth jutted open, revealing apelike teeth. His eyes—his eyes were deep set and pensive. The eyes of a philosopher (with a slightly worried look as though he'd just seen his tax accountant).[60] If ever a picture was worth a thousand words, this was it. Even at a tender age, I understood exactly what it meant. *This monkey was man in the making!* My earliest ancestor was not Adam but an ape. Twenty years would come and go before I discovered that *Pithecanthropus erectus*—the ape-man that walked erect—was fiction.[61]

Pithecanthropus Erectus. *Pithecanthropus erectus* is far and away the most famous "ape-man" fiction still being circulated as fact. While over time he has evolved into the new classification, *Homo erectus*, millions regard him an ancestor, and refer to him by the famed nickname "Java man."

It is generally known that Java man was initially discovered by a fellow Dutchman named Eugene Dubois on the Dutch East Indian island of Java back in 1891. What is not as well known is that Java man consists of nothing more than a skullcap, a femur (thigh bone), three teeth, and a great deal of imagination. Even more disturbing is the fact that the femur was found fifty feet from the skullcap and a full year later! Most unsettling of all is that for almost thirty years, Dubois downplayed the discovery of two human skulls that were found in close proximity to his original "finds."[62] This alone should have been sufficient to disqualify Java man as the ancestor of humankind.

The most thorough fact-finding expedition ever conducted on Java man utterly undressed Dubois's claims. This trek, commonly referred to as the

Selenka Expedition, included nineteen evolutionists bent on demonstrating that Dubois's conjectures about Java man were true. Nonetheless, their 342-page scientific report demonstrated conclusively that Java man played no part in human evolution.[63]

Despite evidence to the contrary, *Time* magazine proffered "How Man Began,"[64] an article that shamelessly treated Java man as though it were a true evolutionary ancestor. Even more incredible is the fact that Donald Johanson, best known for his discovery of Lucy (the famed fossil named after the Beatles' tune "Lucy in the Sky with Diamonds"), still regards Java man as a valid transitional form; and Harvard's Richard Lewontin thinks this information about Java man should be taught as one of the five "facts of evolution."[65]

Piltdown Man. While *Pithecanthropus erectus* (Java man) might be appropriately placed in the category of fiction, Piltdown man (*Eoanthropus dawsoni*) may be accurately described a fraud—a fraud cleverly conceived but crudely carried out, the jaw of an ape stained to match a human skull. Making matters worse was the unrefined reshaping of the Piltdown fossils.[66] As Marvin Lubenow explained, "The file marks on the orangutan teeth of the lower jaw were clearly visible. The molars were misaligned and filed at two different angles. The canine tooth had been filed at two different angles. The canine tooth had been filed down so far that the pulp cavity had been exposed and then plugged."[67]

Despite "doctoring," highly esteemed scientists affirmed the veracity of the Piltdown fossils. In *The Bone Peddlers*, William Fix reported that the two most eminent paleoanthropologists in England at the time (Sir Arthur Keith and A. S. Woodward) declared that Piltdown man "represents more closely than any human form yet discovered the common ancestor from which both the Neanderthal and modern types have been derived."[68]

It wasn't until 1953, after the Nature Conservancy had spent a considerable amount of taxpayer money to designate the Piltdown site a national monument, that Dawson's Dawn man (Piltdown) was formally declared a fake.[69] Although there is still a great deal of uncertainty as to who perpetrated the fraud, A. S. Woodward (keeper of geology at the British Museum), Pierre Teilhard de Chardin (a Jesuit priest), and Charles Dawson (the lawyer who unearthed Piltdown man in 1912) are front-runners in the long list of possible suspects.[70]

While Piltdown man may well be ranked as one of the most notorious scientific frauds in history, it was used for forty years to dupe students into thinking that evolution was a fact.

Peking Man. While Java man is fictitious and Piltdown man is a fraud, Peking man is pure fantasy—wish giving birth to reality. Peking man, fabricated on the basis of a dusty old tooth, was discovered by Canadian physician Davidson Black, just as he was about to run out of funds for his evolutionary explorations in 1927.[71]

The Rockefeller Foundation rewarded Dr. Black's discovery with a generous grant so he could keep on digging. Two years later, Black discovered what he fervently believed was Peking man's braincase and estimated Peking man to be a half million years of age. Unfortunately, Black's fame was fleeting. At age forty-nine, he died of a heart attack.[72] Black's death, however, did not end the charade. By the time World War II broke out, the evolutionary community had "discovered" fourteen skulls and an interesting collection of tools and teeth. All fourteen skulls were "missing in action" by war's end. Yet the pretense persisted.[73]

The photographs and plaster casts that remained had some interesting similarities. Apart from the fact that the lower skeletons were missing, the skulls had all been bashed at the base. Ian Taylor noted that Teilhard de Chardin (of Piltdown fame) made his former professor, Marcellin Boule, angry "at having traveled halfway around the world to see a battered monkey skull. He pointed out that all the evidence indicated that true man was in charge of some sort of 'industry' and that the skulls found were merely those of monkeys."[74]

Boule was not far from the truth. As has been duly noted, it appears likely that the tools found with Peking man were used on him, not by him.[75] While monkey meat is difficult to digest, monkey brains are delicious. To this day, natives of Southeast Asia lop off the heads of monkeys, bash them in at the back, scoop out the brains, and eat them as a delicacy.[76] If you watched *Indiana Jones and the Temple of Doom*, that's exactly what Jones and his cohorts were having for dinner—"Peking man on the half shell."[77] It should be clear to anyone looking at the evidence with an open mind that Peking man was not a distant relative but rather dinner.

Despite deceptions, Ape-man icons continued to appear with predictable regularity. Nebraska man was a beauty. In 1922, a tooth was discovered in Nebraska. With a little imagination the tooth was connected to a jawbone, the jawbone was connected to a skull, the skull was connected to a skeleton, the skeleton was given a face, features, fur, and by the time the story hit the London press, "Nebraska man" was pictured alongside "Nebraska mom."[78] All of that from an old tooth.

Sometime after the initial discovery, an identical tooth was found by geologist Harold Cook. This time the tooth was attached to an actual skull, the skull was attached to the skeleton, but alas the skeleton was that of a wild pig.[79] Thus, Nebraska man (known by the "scientific" designation *Hesperopithecus haroldcookii*) is unmasked as myth rather than a man in the making.

One might suppose that mental digestion would improve over time. But no! The illustration of a knuckle-dragging ape evolving into modern man through a series of imaginary transitional forms has appeared so many times in so many places that the picture evolved into proof. In light of the fanfare attending recent candidates, we would do well to remember that while past contestants have bestowed fame on their finders, they have done little to distinguish themselves as prime exemplars in the process of human evolution.

The 2009 discovery of *Dariwinius masillae*, affectionately nicknamed "Ida," is yet another in the long list of pretenders. Ida was dubbed the most important fossil discovery in forty-seven million years.[80] The "mother of all monkeys."[81] The "eighth wonder of the world."[82] The scientific equivalent of discovering the Holy Grail. Like finding the lost ark of the covenant.[83] In actuality, Ida proved little more than an in-house debate among evolutionists as to whether *Dariwinius masillae* was the ancestor of lemurs or monkeys.[84]

What I discovered during my journey from evolution to evidence is that the distance between an ape that cannot read or write, and a descendant of Adam, who can compose a musical masterpiece or send a man to the moon, is the distance of infinity.[85]

Recapitulation

One would think that ape-men fiction, fantasy, and fraud would suffi-ciently temper mental digestion. It hasn't. Evolutionary titan Ernst Haeckel's recapitulation icon is proof positive.

Recapitulation, better known by the popular evolutionary phrase "*Ontogeny recapitulates phylogeny*," is an iconic deception used to dupe the unsuspecting into believing that in the course of its development (ontogeny), an embryo repeats (recapitulates) the evolutionary history of its species (phy-logeny). The recapitulation icon illustrates the embryonic human looking somewhat fishy, then rather froggy, and finally fetus-like. This evolution-ary icon, first championed by the aforementioned German biologist Ernst Haeckel, is not only based on revisionism but has been used as justification for *Roe v. Wade* and as justification for racism.[86]

Revisionism. In *Ontogeny and Phylogeny* Harvard professor Stephen Jay Gould pointed out that German scientist Wilhelm His exposed such "shock-ing dishonesty" on the part of Haeckel that it rendered him unworthy "to be counted as a peer in the company of earnest researchers."[87] Despite the fact that the recapitulation theory has been roundly discredited, Dr. Gould wrote an entire book to demonstrate that it is still "one of the great themes of evolutionary biology."[88] "I do so," wrote Gould, "because it has fascinated me ever since the New York City public schools taught me Haeckel's doctrine, that ontogeny recapitulates phylogeny, fifty years after it had been abandoned by science."[89]

Sir Gavin de Beer of the British Natural History Museum was more circumspect. "Seldom has an assertion like that of Haeckel's 'theory of recapitulation,' facile, tidy, and plausible, widely accepted without critical examination, done so much harm to science."[90] Why? Because Haeckel not only used deceptive data but utilized doctored drawings to delude devotees.[91] His dishonesty was so blatant that he was charged with fraud by five professors and convicted by a university court at Jena.[92] His forgeries were subsequently made public with the publication of *Haeckel's Frauds and Forgeries*.[93] In truth human embryos never develop gill slits nor at any stage have fins or fishlike configurations.[94] Indeed, modern studies in molecular genetics demonstrate that the DNA for a fish, a frog, and a fetus is uniquely programmed for reproduction after its own kind.[95]

Such well-documented realities have not stopped evolutionary giants like Carl Sagan from affirming recapitulation. "Haeckel held that in its embryological development, an animal tends to repeat or recapitulate the sequence that its ancestors followed during their evolution." In full face of evidence to the contrary, Sagan went on to pontificate that during "human intrauterine development we run through stages very much like fish, reptiles, and non-primate mammals before we become recognizably human. The fish stage even has gill slits, which are absolutely useless for the embryo who is nourished via the umbilical cord, but a necessity for human embryology." Why? Because "gills were vital to our ancestors."[96]

What Sagan must surely have known is that what he cavalierly referred to as "gill slits" are essential parts of human anatomy. That far from being useless evolutionary vestiges, they are axiomatic to the development of human embryos.[97] And that under the guise of factual science he was blatantly dispensing science fiction.

Roe. In *The Dragons of Eden*, Dr. Sagan wrote that determining when a fetus becomes human "could play a major role in achieving an acceptable compromise in the abortion debate." According to his calculation, the transition to human "would fall toward the end of the first trimester or near the beginning of the second trimester of pregnancy."[98]

Shortly before he died, I watched him reiterate this odd predilection. Using recapitulation as the pretext, he shamefully defended the painful killing of innocent human beings. Without so much as blushing, he communicated the mythology that a first-trimester abortion does not constitute the termination of a human life but merely the termination of a fish or frog. As such, in Sagan's world, *Roe v. Wade* provided the legal framework for the slaughter of multiplied millions of creatures rather than the slaughter of multiplied millions of children.

It should go without saying that Sagan is wrong. The notion that a human being does not emerge during a pregnancy until after the end of the first trimester is merely the figment of a fertile imagination. While an emerging embryo may not have a fully developed personality, it does have full person-hood from the moment of conception. French geneticist Jerome L. LeJeune bore eloquent testimony to this truth while testifying to a United States Senate subcommittee: "To accept the fact that, after fertilization has taken place, a new human has come into being, is no longer a matter of taste or of opinion. The human nature of the human being from conception to old age is not a metaphysical contention. It is plain, experimental evidence."[99]

Dr. Hymie Gordon, professor of medical genetics and physician at the prestigious Mayo Clinic, offered a similar sentiment. "I think we can now also say that the question of the beginning of life—when life begins—is no longer a question for theological or philosophical dispute. It is an established scientific fact. Theologians and philosophers may go on to debate the meaning of life or the purpose of life, but it is an established fact that all life, including human life, begins at the moment of conception."[100]

Racism. *Roe* is not the only ghastly consequence of the recapitulation theory; racism is another. As previously noted, Dr. Gould rightly observed that recapitulation served as a basis for labeling Down syndrome "Mongolian idiocy"[101] because "it was thought to represent a 'throwback' to the 'Mongolian stage' in human evolution."[102] In an article titled "Dr. Down's Syndrome," Gould rightly referenced recapitulation's responsibility for the repugnancy of racism. "Recapitulation provided a convenient focus for the pervasive racism of white scientists: they looked to the activities of their own children for comparison with normal, adult behavior in lower races."[103]

Although Gould expressed doubts about recapitulation, he did not so much as consider abandoning the evolution paradigm. Instead, he pitifully attempted to prop up the crumbling edifice of evolution with other novel notions including punctuated equilibrium. According to Gould's account of the punctuated equilibrium paradigm, "In any local area, a species does not arise gradually by the steady transformation of its ancestors; it appears all at once and 'fully formed.'"[104]

It is more than sad to see the lengths to which credentialed scientists such as Gould have stretched to prop up the decaying corpse of evolution. Dr. David Berlinski likely said it best: "Darwin's theory of evolution is the last of the great nineteenth-century mystery religions. And as we speak it is now following Freudianism and Marxism into the nether regions, and I'm quite sure that Freud, Marx, and Darwin are commiserating one with the other in the dark dungeon where discarded gods gather."[105]

Chance

"Chance *alone*," wrote the esteemed French Nobel laureate Jacques Monod, "is at the source of every innovation, of all creation in the biosphere. Pure chance, absolutely free but blind, [is] at the very root of the stupendous edifice of evolution."[106]

Dr. Monod, a great admirer of Charles Darwin, went on to assert "man knows at last that he is alone in the universe's unfeeling immensity, out of which he emerged only by chance. His destiny is nowhere spelled out, nor is his duty."[107] No transcendent designer. No transcendent destiny. No transcendent duty.

Chance is the hell of the evolutionary paradigm. It posits a world without free will. It supposes that human beings, like the rest of creation, are fatalistically determined by their brain chemistry and their genetics. Consider the absurdity of it all. Your eyes. An egg. The earth. Each in its vast complexity, thought to be a function of pure chance—"Absolutely free but blind." Darwin himself, the perceived father of it all, found it hard to accede that a human eye could be the product of blind evolutionary chance. The very notion gave him "cold shudders."[108]

Eye. In *The Origin of Species by Means of Natural Selection*, Darwin conceded, "to suppose that the eye, with all its inimitable contrivances for adjusting the focus to different distances, for admitting different amounts of light, and for the correction of spherical and chromatic aberration, could have been formed by natural selection, seems, I freely confess, absurd in the highest degree possible."[109] In this Darwin was prescient.

In *Darwin's Black Box*, biochemist Michael Behe explicated that what happens when a photon of light hits a human eye was beyond nineteenth-century science. Thus, to Darwin vision was an unopened black box. The black box, now open, has revealed that "each of the anatomical steps and structures that Darwin thought were so simple actually involves staggeringly complicated biochemical processes" that demand explanation.[110] One cannot explain the origin of vision without first accounting for the origin of the enormously complex system of molecular mechanisms that make it work.

As science continues to advance, the "black box" of vision has revealed complexities that render the chance hypothesis pure farcicality. Think reflectively about your eyes for a moment. Extraordinary muscles surround them for motility and shape the lens for focus. They consist of balls with a lens on one side and a light-sensitive retina made up of rods and cones on the other. Your lenses have a sturdy protective covering called a cornea and sit over an iris designed to protect your eyes from excessive light. They contain a fantastic watery substance that is replaced every four hours; tear glands that continuously flush the outside clean; eyelids that sweep secretions over the cornea keeping it moist; and eyelashes that protect them from excess dust.[111]

While it is a stretch to suggest that the organized complexities of the eye evolved by chance; it stretches credulity beyond the breaking point to surmise that your eyes evolved in concert with myriad coordinated functions. For example, as you now read what I am presently writing, a vast number of impulses are traveling from your eyes through millions of nerve fibers that transmit information to a complex computing center in the brain called the visual cortex. Linking visual information from your eyes to motor centers in your brain is crucial in coordinating a vast number of bodily functions that are axiomatic to the very process of daily living. Without the coordinated development of the eye and the brain in synergistic fashion, isolated developments themselves are not only meaningless—they are counterproductive.[112]

Egg. As with the eye, evolution cannot account for the complex synchronization process needed to produce life from a single fertilized human egg. Through a process of incredible precision, a microscopic egg in one human being is fertilized by a sperm cell from another. This process not only marks the beginning of a new life but marks the genetic future that life will have.[113]

A single fertilized egg (zygote), the size of a pinhead, contains chemical instructions that would fill more than five hundred thousand printed pages.[114] The genetic information in this "encyclopedia" determines the physical aspect of the developing human from height to hair color. In time, the fertilized egg divides into thirty trillion cells that make up the body, including twelve billion brain cells, which form more than 120 trillion connections.[115]

In Darwin's day, a human egg was thought to be quite simple—for all practical purposes, little more than a microscopic blob of gelatin.[116] Today, we know that a fertilized egg is among the most organized, complex structures in the universe. In an age of scientific enlightenment, it is incredible to believe that people are willing to maintain that something so organized and vastly complex arose by chance. A child playing with tiles from the party game Scrabble can easily spell the phrase "the theory of evolution," while chance requires five million times the assumed age of the earth to accomplish the same feat.[117]

Earth. Like an egg or an eye, the earth is a masterpiece of precision and design that could not have come into existence by blind chance. The organization, complexity, and vastness of the physical universe (trillions of galaxies each with a hundred billion stars) bear eloquent testimony to the existence of an uncaused First Cause.

Consider plain old tap water. The solid state of most substances is denser than their liquid state. The opposite is true for water—which explains why ice floats rather than sinks. If water were like virtually any other liquid, it would freeze from the bottom up rather than from the top down, killing aquatic life, destroying the oxygen supply, and making the earth uninhabitable.[118]

And as previously mentioned, ocean tides play a crucial role in our survival. If the moon were significantly larger, thereby having a stronger gravitational pull, devastating tidal waves would submerge large areas of land. If the moon were smaller, tidal motion would cease, and the oceans would stagnate and die.[119]

Temperatures—not duplicated on any other known planet in the universe—are a significant consideration as well. If we were closer to the sun, we would fry. If farther away, we would freeze.[120] Even the tilt of earth's axis—"23.5 degrees from perpendicular to the plane of its orbit"—renders the chance hypothesis nothing more than special pleading. "This tilting, combined with earth's revolution around the sun, causes our seasons," which are essential to our food supply.[121]

The science of statistical probability demonstrates conclusively that forming an eye, egg, or the earth by undirected chance processes is not only improbable; it is impossible. As King David poignantly put it three thousand years ago, "The fool says in his heart, 'There is no God.'"[122]

Empirical Science

Leonardo da Vinci, Sir Isaac Newton, and Louis Pasteur are just a few of the great icons of science and technology who staunchly defended the reality of a cosmic Creator. Even Albert Einstein—though not a Christian—was driven to the inexorable conclusion that there must of necessity be an uncaused First Cause that did not create by chance but rather by mathematical, purposeful, and rational processes. "The harmony of natural law," said Einstein, "reveals an intelligence of such superiority that, compared with it, all the systematic thinking and acting of human beings is an utterly insignificant reflection."[123]

Effects and Causes. It doesn't take an Einstein to understand the empirically validated scientific reality that every effect must have a cause equal to or greater than itself. As science journalist Fred Heeren aptly put it, "This is common sense, and no one has ever observed an exception. Even the famed Julie Andrews sang about it: 'Nothing comes from nothing; nothing ever could.' That every effect must have a cause is a self-evident truth, not only for those who have been trained in logic, but for thinking people everywhere."[124]

Cause and effect, "which is universally accepted and followed in every field of science, relates every phenomenon as an effect to a cause. No effect is ever quantitatively 'greater' nor qualitatively 'superior' to its cause. An effect can be lower than its cause but never higher."[125] In sharp contrast to empirical reality, the evolutionary rigidity sabotages common sense by attempting to make effects such as organized complexity, life, and personality greater than their causes—disorder, nonlife, and impersonal forces.

The simple truth is that design always, always, always requires a designer.[126] An effect, like the sun, must of necessity have a cause. Likewise, the cosmos. It did not spring from nothing. To imagine it did is not just irresponsible, it is plainly irrational. An effect must have a cause, which is exactly what is left wanting in the untenable evolutionary philosophical theory.

One more point needs to be made before moving on. In saying that the universe is an effect that requires a cause equal to or greater than itself, one may well presume that this principle would apply equally to God. This, however, is clearly not the case. Unlike the universe, which according to modern science had a beginning, God is eternal. And as an eternal being, God can logically be demonstrated to be the previously mentioned uncaused First Cause.[127]

Energy Conservation. Today's physical sciences are built on three laws of thermodynamics that describe energy relationships of matter in the universe. These laws were established as a scientific discipline by Lord William Kelvin (1824–1907), a committed Christian, who, like Einstein, was a brilliant intellect. *The New Encyclopædia Britannica* states that he published hundreds of papers, was granted multiple patents, and that it was said of Lord Kelvin that he was "entitled to more letters after his name than any other man in Britain." One of his greatest contributions to science was his role in the development of the law of energy conservation.[128]

Like the law of cause and effect, the law of energy conservation is an empirical law of science. Also known as the first law of thermodynamics, the law of energy conservation states that while energy can be converted from one form to another, it can neither be created nor annihilated. Isaac Asimov considered it "the most powerful and most fundamental generalization about the universe that scientists have ever been able to make."[129]

From a purely logical point of view, it should be self-evident that nothing comes from nothing. Yet, this is precisely what philosophical naturalism—the worldview undergirding evolutionism—presupposes. This is analogous to the nineteenth-century concept of spontaneous generation, the false belief that simple living organisms could arise spontaneously from liquids such as milk or beer that were allowed to sit for several days.[130]

In an age of scientific enlightenment, we should know better than to believe in an evolutionary dictum that of necessity presupposes *something* comes from *nothing*. To hold to the law of energy conservation is to jettison impossible constructs for the infallible canon, which clearly communicates that since God finished the work of creating (Genesis 2:1–3), he has been sustaining (conserving) all things by his power (Hebrews 1:3).[131]

Entropy. While the law of energy conservation is a blow to the theory of evolution, the law of entropy is a bullet to its head. Not only is the universe dying of heat loss, but as entropy—also known as the second law of thermodynamics—necessitates, everything runs inexorably from order to disorder and from complexity to decay. The theory of biological evolution directly contradicts the law of entropy in that it describes a universe in which things run from chaos to complexity. In evolution, atoms allegedly self-produce amino acids, amino acids auto-organize amoebas, amoebas turn into apes, and apes evolve into astronauts.

Mathematician and physicist Sir Arthur Eddington demonstrated that exactly the opposite is true: the energy of the universe irreversibly flows from hot to cold bodies.[132] The sun burns up billions of tons of hydrogen each second, stars burn out, and species eventually become extinct. While I would fight for a person's right to have faith in science fiction, we must resist evolutionists who attempt to brainwash people into thinking that evolution is science.[133] In the words of Sir Arthur, "If your theory is found to be against the second law of thermodynamics I can give you no hope; there is nothing for it but to collapse in deepest humiliation."[134]

Rather than humbling themselves in light of the law of entropy, some in the evolutionary community dogmatically attempt to discredit or dismiss it. In doing so they contend that the law cannot be invoked because it merely deals with energy relationships of matter, while evolution deals with complex life forms arising from simpler ones. It should go without saying that this is false. In an energy conversion system entropy dictates that energy will decay; in an informational system entropy dictates that information will become distorted. *Scientific American* rightly acknowledged that "the conceptual connection between information and the second law of thermodynamics is now firmly established."[135]

Despite evidence to the contrary, evolutionists frequently contend that entropy does not prevent evolution on earth since earth is an open system that receives energy from the sun. This, of course, is nonsense. The sun's rays never produce an upswing in organized complexity without teleonomy (the ordering principle of life). In other words, energy from the sun does not produce an orderly structure of growth and development without information and an engine. If the sun beats down on a dead plant, it does not produce growth but rather speeds up decay. If, on the other hand, the sun beats down on a living plant, it produces a temporary increase in complexity and growth.[136]

In sum, evolutionists can provide only three explanations for the existence of the universe in which we live: (1) The universe is merely an illusion. This notion carries little weight in an age of scientific enlightenment. As has been well said, "Even the full-blown solipsist looks both ways before crossing the street." (2) The universe sprang from nothing. This proposition flies in the face of both the laws of cause and effect and energy conservation. There simply are no free lunches. The conditions that hold true in this universe prevent any possibility of matter springing out of nothing.[137] (3) The universe eternally existed. This hypothesis is devastated by the law of entropy, which predicts that a universe that has existed eternally would have died an "eternity ago" of heat loss.[138] Thankfully, there is another reality. It is found in the first chapter of the first book of the Bible: "In the beginning God created the heavens and the earth."[139] In an age of empirical science, nothing could be more certain, clear, or correct.

In case you did not notice, I intentionally used *F-A-R-C-E* as an acronym to make memorable salient arguments against evolutionary bias. I did so, in that, as previously noted, origins is not just *an* apologetic issue; it is *the* apologetic issue. As such I want you to remember, as I do, that: **F**ossil follies are an evolutionary embarrassment; **A**pe-men icons involve fiction, fraud, and fantasy; **R**ecapitulation is revisionist, racist, and ridiculous; **C**hance renders the evolutionary dictum improbable; and **E**mpirical science militates against evolutionary bias.

Darwinism is in the same condition Marxism was before its collapse. As the Soviet Union collapsed before our very eyes, so too the propped-up corpse of evolution is ready for a final fall. While insiders in the evolutionary community are aware of their theory's desperate condition, the general public is as yet in the dark. That's precisely where you and I come in. We have the inestimable privilege to share the news that nothing could be more compelling in an age of scientific enlightenment than "In the beginning God created the heavens and the earth."[140]

ANSWERS ON RESURRECTION

Apart from origins, no question begs an answer more insistently than does the question of resurrection. Christians are commissioned to confirm that God is "Creator of heaven and earth, and of all things visible and invisible" and to certify that "for us and for our salvation" he "came down from heaven and was incarnate of the Holy Spirit and the Virgin Mary and became man."[141]

According to Scripture (which I will establish shortly to be divine rather than merely human in origin), Christ "is the image of the invisible God, the firstborn over all creation. For by him all things were created: things in heaven and on earth, visible and invisible, whether thrones or powers or rulers or authorities; all things were created by him and for him. He is before all things, and in him all things hold together." And "he is the beginning and *the firstborn from among the dead.*"[142]

Resurrection is the ultimate game changer. If I face hardships in life "for merely human reasons," wrote Paul in his first letter to the Corinthian Christians, "what have I gained? If the dead are not raised, 'Let us eat and drink, for tomorrow we die.'"[143] As Paul expounded in the same letter, "If Christ has not been raised, your faith is futile; you are still in your sins. Then those also who have fallen asleep in Christ are lost. If only for this life we have hope in Christ, we are to be pitied more than all men."[144]

I heard all this and more before I ever graduated grammar school. But there were always lingering doubts. Doubts exacerbated by arguments to the contrary. When I was fifteen, for example, Hugh Schonfield published a 287-page volume titled *The Passover Plot*. To me, as to many others, the "plot" seemed perfectly plausible. Rather than suffering fatal torment, Jesus merely swooned. Magazines and ministers embraced the swoon theory in mass. *Time* magazine heartily endorsed Schonfield's contention that Jesus was resuscitated rather than resurrected, and television minister William

Barclay dubbed *The Passover Plot* "a book of enormous learning and erudition, meticulously documented."[145]

Schonfield was not the first, nor the last, to cast doubt upon the resurrection of Jesus. Seven years after *The Passover Plot* was released, journalist Donovan Joyce published *The Jesus Scroll*. Joyce contended that Jesus was revived by a doctor planted in the tomb.[146] Twenty years later (and to rave reviews) Professor Barbara Thiering surmised that Jesus imbibed snake poison to fake his death. Upon recovering, he married Mary Magdalene and later fell in love with Lydia of Philippi.[147]

The Islamic Allah is likewise certain that Christ was neither crucified nor resurrected. With great bluster the Muslim god averred, "They killed him not, nor crucified him, but so it was made to appear to them."[148] In forwarding the narrative that Christ's crucifixion was merely an illusion—that God made someone look like Jesus and the look-alike was crucified in place of Jesus—Muslims advance candidates ranging from Simon of Cyrene to Judas Iscariot. Yusuf Ali in his Qur'anic commentary seeks to bolster the denial of the crucifixion and subsequent resurrection of Christ through an appeal to the Gospel of Barnabas,[149] a late-medieval fabrication, not even concocted until the fourteenth century![150]

As with Professor Thiering, Muslims advance various theories to account for the whereabouts of Jesus subsequent to the crucifixion of his purported look-alike. A majority suppose he was taken into heaven and will one day return to earth where he will kill the antichrist and all pigs, destroy all churches and crosses, and accelerate the worldwide spread of Islam, before being buried in Medina next to the prophet Muhammad.[151]

Other theories concerning the resurrection of Jesus Christ can be found in pseudo-Christian cults such as the Jehovah's Witnesses who assert that a *physical* resurrection would not have been a tremendous triumph; it would have been a hopeless humiliation.[152] To explain away the empty tomb, Watchtower adherents argue that the body of Jesus was discarded and destroyed.[153] To account for Christ's post-resurrection appearances, they suggest that Jesus merely appeared and disappeared in different bodies—in essence fooling his disciples into thinking he had physically risen from the grave.[154]

If liberal scholars, adherents of Islam, or devotees of pseudo-Christian cults are correct, the biblical account of resurrection is fiction, fantasy, or fraudulent. No middle ground exists. The resurrection is history or hoax, miracle or myth, fact or fantasy. *Without resurrection, Christianity crumbles.* Because this is so, I invested a sizable amount of time in 1979 seeking to determine its veracity—ultimately concluding that the resurrection of Christ constitutes the greatest feat in the annals of recorded history.[155]

Fatal Torment

Did Jesus merely swoon? Was he revived by a doctor planted in the tomb of Joseph of Arimathea? Did he fake his death and live out the remainder of his pathetic life in obscurity? Was a look-alike crucified in place of Christ? Or did Jesus suffer fatal torment as narrated by the New Testament authors? The only reasonable conclusion is the latter—that "Christ died for our sins according to the Scriptures."[156]

The fatal suffering of the historical Jesus is one of the most well-established facts of antiquity. It is attested by Flavius Josephus,[157] an eyewitness to many of the details and descriptions found in the New Testament,[158] as well as by such historical luminaries as Cornelius Tacitus, widely deemed to be the greatest first-century historian of the ancient Roman Empire. In *Annals*, Tacitus forthrightly chronicled the death of the "Christus," who "suffered the extreme penalty during the reign of Tiberius at the hands of one of our procurators, Pontius Pilatus."[159] Tacitus not only provided corroborating testimony to the biblical account of Christ's fatal torment at the hands of Pilate during the reign of Tiberius Caesar but drew attention to the whole of the Christian movement, which had spread from Judea to Rome.[160]

Even in the modern age of scientific enlightenment, there is virtual consensus among New Testament scholars—both conservative and liberal—that Christ died on the cross, that he was buried in the tomb of Joseph of Arimathea, and that his death drove his disciples to despair.[161] While scholars in concert with the Allah of Islam have suggested a variety of alternatives, as noted, evidence clearly validates the historical account of Christ's crucifixion.

The fatal torment of Jesus Christ began in the Garden of Gethsemane after the emotional Last Supper. There Christ experienced a medical condition known as hematidrosis—tiny capillaries in his sweat glands ruptured, mixing sweat with blood.[162] After being arrested by the temple guard, he was mocked, beaten, and spat upon. The next morning, battered, bruised, and bleeding, he was stripped and subjected to the brutality of Roman flogging—a whip replete with razor-sharp bones and lead balls that reduced his body to quivering ribbons of bleeding flesh.

As Christ slumped into the pool of his own blood, soldiers threw a scarlet robe across his shoulders, thrust a scepter into his hands, and pressed sharp thorns into his scalp. After mocking him, the soldiers took the scepter and repeatedly struck Jesus on the head. A heavy wooden beam was thrust upon his bleeding body, and he was led away to "the place of the skull."[163] There he experienced excruciating torment in the form of the cross. The Roman system of crucifixion had been fine-tuned to produce maximum pain. Indeed, the word *excruciating*—literally "out of the cross"—was coined to fully codify its horror.[164]

At "the place of the skull," Roman soldiers drove thick, seven-inch iron spikes through Christ's hands[165] and feet. Waves of pain pulsated through Christ's body as the nails lacerated his nerves. Breathing became an agonizing endeavor as Christ pushed his tortured body upward to grasp small gulps of air. In the ensuing hours he experienced cycles of joint-wrenching cramps, intermittent asphyxiation, and excruciating pain as his lacerated back moved up and down against the rough timber of the cross.

And then, with his passion complete, Jesus gave up his spirit. Shortly thereafter, a Roman legionnaire drove his spear through the fifth interspace between the ribs, upward through the pericardium, and into Christ's heart. Immediately, there rushed forth blood and water, demonstrating conclusively that Jesus had suffered fatal torment.[166]

Empty Tomb

As it is incontrovertible that Christ suffered fatal torment, so, too, it is certain beyond reasonable doubt that Christ "was buried" in the tomb of Joseph of Arimathea and that he "was raised on the third day according to the Scriptures."[167]

As the reliability of the resurrection was undermined in magazines, manuscripts, and movies, it became increasingly crucial to look at the rationale for believing that Jesus was buried in the tomb of Joseph of Arimathea, and that on Easter morning some two thousand years ago, the tomb was indeed empty.

To begin with, it was heartening to discover that the late liberal Cambridge scholar John A. T. Robinson conceded the burial of Christ to be "one of the earliest and best-attested facts about Jesus."[168] Robinson's affirmation turns out to be more than a dogmatic assertion. It is a defensible argument. Liberal New Testament scholars such as Robinson, in concert with conservative scholarship, agree that the body of Jesus was buried in the private tomb of Joseph of Arimathea.[169] And that as a Sanhedrist in the court that condemned Christ to death, he is unlikely to be the figment of a fertile imagination.[170] It is also striking that no alternative burial account occurs in the historical record.[171] They also agree that the tomb quickly lost significance because the remains of Christ were not there to be venerated (which is noteworthy in that the graves of sages were profoundly reverenced).[172] And that the account of Jesus' burial in the tomb of Joseph of Arimathea as put forth in Mark's Gospel is far too early to have been the stuff of legends.[173]

Added to this is the reality that the Gospel writers highlight women as the heroes of their empty tomb accounts. Considering females were routinely considered little more than chattel, the empty tomb accounts are powerful evidence that the Gospel writers valued truth over cultural correctness.[174] Prior to the coming of Christ, females were so denigrated by society that first-century Jewish males routinely mouthed the mantra, "I thank Thee I am not a woman."[175] Had the Gospel accounts been legendary, males would most certainly have been heroes of the narrative.[176]

It is also heartening to realize that Jewish antagonists take the empty tomb for granted. Instead of repudiating the empty tomb, they accused Christ's disciples of stealing his body.[177] And had the tomb not been empty, enemies of the resurrection could have easily put an end to the pretense by displaying the remains of Christ.[178] In the centuries following the resurrection of Christ, the fact of the empty tomb was forwarded by friends and foes alike.

Simply stated, the tomb was empty. Were it not, Christianity would not have survived the tomb containing the remains of Messiah.[179]

Appearances of Christ

One thing can be known with iron-clad certainty: the apostles did not merely propagate Christ's teachings; they were absolutely positive that he had appeared to them alive in the flesh after his crucifixion and burial. Although two thousand years removed from the actual event, you and I can be absolutely confident in Christ's post-resurrection appearances as well.

To begin with, in 1 Corinthians 15:3–7, Paul reiterated a Christian creed that can be traced all the way back to the formative stages of the early Christian church.[180] "Christ died for our sins according to the Scriptures, that he was buried, that he was raised on the third day according to the Scriptures, and that he appeared to Peter, and then to the Twelve. After that, he appeared to more than five hundred of the brothers at the same time, most of whom are still living, though some have fallen asleep. Then he appeared to James, then to all the apostles."[181]

Scholars of all stripes have concluded that this very creed can be dated to within mere months of Messiah's murder.[182] The short time span between Christ's crucifixion and the composition of this early Christian creed precludes the possibility of corruption in the form of legend.[183] As has been roundly reported, the creed is early, free from the contamination, unambiguous, specific, and ultimately rooted in eyewitness testimony.[184] As eyewitnesses, Peter, Paul, and the rest of the apostles claimed that Christ appeared to hundreds of people who were still alive and available for cross-examination.[185] It would be one thing for the apostles to attribute such supernatural appearances to people who had already died. It is quite another to attribute them to multitudes who were still alive.[186]

And nothing other than the appearances of Christ can account for the utter transformation of Paul,[187] who abdicated his position as an esteemed Jewish leader, a Rabbi and a Pharisee—one who had studied under Rabban Gamaliel 1, the leading authority of the Sanhedrin.[188] Paul gave up his avowed mission to stamp out every vestige of what he considered the insidious heresy of Christianity[189] and in the end, paid the ultimate price for his faith—martyrdom.[190]

And Paul was not alone. Multitudes were radically revolutionized by the post-resurrection appearances of Christ. James among them.[191] Before the appearances, James was embarrassed by his relationship to Christ;[192] afterward, he was willing to die for the notion that one of his kinsmen was God.[193]

No one summed up the consensus of both liberal and conservative scholarship better than did Professor Norman Perrin, the late New Testament scholar at the University of Chicago: "The more we study the tradition with regard to the appearances, the firmer the rock begins to appear upon which they are based."[194]

Transformation

What happened as a result of the resurrection is unprecedented. In the span of a few hundred years, a small band of insignificant believers succeeded in turning an entire empire upside down.

The Twelve (minus Judas, plus Paul)[195] were radically revolutionized. Peter, once afraid of being exposed as a follower of Christ, after Christ's resurrection became a lion of the faith.[196] Paul, the ceaseless persecutor, became the chief proselytizer of the Gentiles. Within weeks of the resurrection, not just a few, but an entire community of thousands of Jews, willingly transformed the spiritual and sociological traditions underscoring their national identity.[197]

Among the deeply entrenched traditions that were transformed is the Sabbath. In Genesis, the Jewish Sabbath was a celebration of God's work in creation.[198] In Deuteronomy, it expanded to a celebration of God's deliverance from the oppression of Egypt.[199] And in the New Testament epistles, it became a celebration of the "rest" that we have through Christ who delivers us from sin and the grave.[200] God himself provided the early church with a new pattern of worship through Christ's resurrection on the first day of the week, his subsequent Sunday appearances, and the Spirit's Sunday descent.[201] For the emerging Christian church, the most dangerous snare was a failure to recognize that Jesus was the substance that fulfilled the symbol of the Sabbath.

Like the Sabbath, the sacrificial system underwent radical transformation. Jews had been taught from the time of Abraham that they were to sacrifice animals as the symbol of atonement for their sin. After the resurrection, followers of Christ suddenly stopped sacrificing.[202] They recognized that the new covenant was better than the old covenant because the body and blood of Jesus Christ is better than the blood of animals.[203] They understood that Jesus was the substance that fulfilled the symbol—the sacrificial lamb that takes away the sin of the world.[204]

As with Sabbath and sacrifices, the Jewish rites of Passover and Baptism were radically transformed. In place of the Passover meal, believers celebrated the Lord's Supper. Jesus had just been slaughtered in grotesque and humiliating fashion, yet the disciples partook of the true body and true blood of Christ with great joy.[205] Only the resurrection can account for that. Baptism, too, was radically transformed. Prior to the resurrection, Gentile converts to Judaism were baptized in the name of the God of Israel.[206] After the resurrection, converts to Christianity were baptized in the name of Jesus.[207] In doing so, they equated Jesus with the God of Israel.[208]

Of one thing I have become certain—if twenty-first-century Christians would grasp the reality of resurrection like first-century Christians did, their lives would be totally transformed. Christ's resurrection was a historical event that took place in our space-time continuum. Likewise, your resurrection will be a historical event that takes place when Christ physically returns and transforms our mortal bodies. As there is a one-to-one correspondence between the body of Christ that died and the body that rose, our resurrection bodies will be numerically identical to the bodies we now possess. In other words, our resurrection bodies are not second bodies; rather, they are our present bodies gloriously transformed.[209]

Neither Ponce de León nor Alexander the Great ever discovered the fountain of youth they purportedly sought. It does exist, however. Jesus said, "I am the resurrection and the life. He who believes in me will live, even though he dies; and whoever lives and believes in me will never die."[210] All who put their trust in Jesus can be absolutely certain that they will eternally partake of the fountain of youth. Jesus promised that he would lay down his life and take it up again in three days. His fulfillment is the guarantee that there is life after life after life. Life after life in that the redeemed continue to exist in the presence of the Redeemer. Life after *life after life*, in that just as Jesus rose bodily from the grave, so too our bodies will rise immortal, imperishable, incorruptible. Proof of the greatest feat in the annals of recorded history is so certain that millions willingly lay down their lives, confident that they will take them up again.[211]

After looking at the evidence, I have become just as certain as they were. You likewise can be certain. Truly, for all who are in Christ, the fountain of youth awaits.

ANSWERS ON BIBLICAL AUTHORITY

Muslims point to the Qur'an to answer the question of authority. From the Muslim perspective, God spoke through the archangel Gabriel, who dictated the Qur'an to Muhammad over a period of twenty-three years. The miracle of the Qur'an, say Muslims, is that not even "one letter has been changed over the centuries."[212] Mormons likewise are certain that the Book of Mormon is "the most correct of any book on earth" and "the keystone" to their religion.[213] Joseph Fielding Smith, the sixth president of the Mormon Church, mirrors the Muslims in his assertion that "every letter was given to [founder Joseph Smith] by the gift and power of God."[214]

But has God *really* spoken through the Qur'an or the Book of Mormon? The answer quite obviously is no. The Qur'an is a hopelessly flawed document full of faulty ethics and factual errors. In Sura 4:3 Muhammad allegedly received a revelation from God allowing men to "marry women of [your] choice, two, three, or four." Also troubling is the fact that the Qur'an allows men to "beat" their wives in order that the women might "return to obedience" (4:34).

Factual errors are similarly problematic. A classic case in point involves the Qur'anic denial of Christ's crucifixion. The denial is explicit and emphatic: "They killed him not, nor crucified him, but so it was made to appear to them" (4:157).[215] As aptly documented, truth points in the opposite direction. The fatal suffering of Jesus as recounted in the New Testament is one of the most well-established realities of ancient history. In our age of scientific enlightenment, there is virtual consensus among credible scholars that Jesus did in fact die on a Roman cross.[216]

The Book of Mormon fares no better. While Mormons claim that Joseph Smith found golden plates containing the "fullness of the everlasting gospel" written in "reformed Egyptian" hieroglyphics,[217] facts say otherwise. Not only is there no archaeological support for a language such as "reformed Egyptian" hieroglyphics; there is no archaeological support for lands such as the "land of Moron."[218] Nor is there any archaeological evidence to buttress the notion that the Jaredites, Nephites, and Lamanites migrated from Israel to the Americas. On the contrary, both archaeology and anthropology demonstrate conclusively that the people, places, and particulars chronicled in the Book of Mormon are the products of a fertile imagination.[219]

Despite the deficiencies of their sacred texts, Muslims and Mormons brashly denigrate the Bible as a crooked stick that cannot be trusted. And they are not alone. According to critics such as Bart Ehrman, professor of religious studies at the University of North Carolina at Chapel Hill, the Bible is a dishonest book, littered with deceptions, errors, and outright lies.[220] Spinmeister Bill Maher is equally dismissive. He characterizes Christians who hold to the authority of the Bible as obscurantists who for all intents have lost their brains somewhere in the narthex of a church. "I believed all this stuff when I was young," says Maher. "I believed there was a virgin birth, I believed a man lived inside of a whale, and I believed that the Earth was five thousand years old. But then something very important happened to me—I graduated sixth grade."[221] Through media, manuscripts, and movies—and now most notably through the web—a procession of political pundits, professors, and public personalities are raising doubts in the minds of multiplied millions regarding the Bible as a reliable authority for faith and practice.

Since my book *Has God Spoken? Memorable Proofs of the Bible's Divine Inspiration* thoroughly counters the contentions of critics, I withhold further comment.[222] Instead, what follows is a memorable case for the absolute trustworthiness and authority of the biblical text. Here I use the acronym *M-A-P-S* to make memorable the four-part line of reasoning by which you can demonstrate that the Bible is divine as opposed to merely human in origin: **M**anuscript copies; **A**rchaeologist's spade; **P**rophetic stars; and **S**criptural synergy.

Manuscript Copies

The sheer volume of manuscripts undergirding sacred Scripture dwarfs that of any other work of classical history—including Homer, Plato, Aristotle, Caesar, and Tacitus.[223] Equally amazing is the fact that the Bible has been virtually unaltered since the original writing, as attested by scholars who have compared the earliest extant manuscripts with manuscripts dated centuries later.

The wisdom of God is evident through the way he protected the biblical text from tampering or ecclesiastical chicanery. By the time ecclesiastical power was centralized, the biblical manuscripts had long since been copied, distributed, and buried in the sands of time.[224] Nearly six thousand New Testament Greek manuscripts have now been uncovered. Not only is there a relatively short time interval between the earliest papyrus and parchment copies and their autographs, but there is less than a generation between those autographs and the events they chronicle. The sheer quantity and quality of manuscript copies assure us that the message and intent of the original autographs have been passed on to our generation without compromise.[225]

The eyewitness testimony of its authors is also powerful evidence for the absolute and irrevocable trustworthiness of Scripture. As the apostle Peter reminded his hearers, "We did not follow cleverly devised stories when we told you about the coming of our Lord Jesus Christ in power, but we were *eyewitnesses* of his majesty."[226] Luke, likewise, said that he gathered *eyewitness* testimony and "carefully investigated everything."[227] Internal evidence points to the reality that far from being inventors of internally inconsistent stories, the Gospel writers were inspired to faithfully narrate a core set of facts by which they had been radically transformed.

While internal evidence should be sufficient to establish the biblical manuscripts as authentic, reliable, and complementary, external evidence provides remarkable corroborating confirmation. From early external evidence provided by such credible historians as Suetonius (well known for gathering historical data from eyewitnesses and citing historical accounts without prejudice or partiality[228]), it is possible to piece together highlights of Christianity wholly apart from the internal evidence.[229] It is amazing that even historians such as the Jewish Josephus—an eyewitness to many of the details found in the manuscripts—provide ancient and authoritative attestation to the authenticity of the sacred text, but such is precisely the case.[230]

Archaeologist's Spade

Like the Book of Mormon, the Bible has been roundly denounced as a cleverly invented story. Unlike the Book of Mormon, however, the Bible is buttressed by history and evidence. While the archaeologist's spade continues to mount up evidence against the Book of Mormon, it has piled up proof upon proof for the trustworthiness of the biblical manuscripts. The pools notated in John's Gospel immediately spring to mind.

Until quite recently, skeptics viewed the existence of these pools to be little more than a religious conceit, a predilection on the part of Christians to believe that what they think is true *is* true solely because they *think* it's true.[231] Only fools believed in John's pools. All of that changed in June 2004 when workers in the Old City of Jerusalem unearthed the place where Jesus cured the man born blind. Today, you can step into the very pool of Siloam in which the blind man "washed, and came *back* seeing."[232] Likewise, you can rest your arms on the guardrail overlooking the excavated ruins of the pool of Bethesda, where Jesus cared for the physical and spiritual needs of a man who suffered there for thirty-eight years.[233] And, you can stand amazed that what was once secreted in soil accurately reflects that which is sealed in Scripture.[234]

Another gem unearthed by the archaeologist's spade involves the Assyrian Empire. From six hundred years before Christ until eighteen hundred years after him, Assyria and its chief city, Nineveh, lay entombed in the dustbin of history. Then the stones cried out. In 1845, Austen Henry Layard began digging along the Tigris River and unearthed Nineveh, diamond of Assyria, embedded in the golden arc of the Fertile Crescent midway between the Mediterranean and Caspian Seas. Among the stunning archaeological gems discovered there were Sennacherib's prism, which corroborates the Bible's account of Sennacherib's assault on the Southern Kingdom of Judah; the Black Obelisk of Shalmaneser, showing archaeology's oldest depiction of an Israelite; and the palace of Sargon, previously known only by a single reference in sacred Scripture (Isaiah 20). Together, Sennacherib's prism, the Black Obelisk, and the ruins of Sargon's palace provide weighty testimony to the reliability of the biblical record.[235]

In 1947, the shattering of parchment-preserving pottery led to one of the greatest archaeological discoveries of modern times. With the discovery of the Dead Sea Scrolls, we now have a virtual first-century Hebrew Old Testament library available at the click of a twenty-first-century mouse. Not only so, but the Dead Sea Scrolls predate the earliest extant Hebrew text (Masoretic) by a full millennium. Thus, everyone from scholar to schoolchild can determine whether the Old Testament scriptures have been corrupted by men or miraculously preserved by God. Additionally, the Dead Sea Scrolls provide significant insight into the text of the Old Testament and add considerable clarity to the text of the New Testament.[236]

The archaeologist's spade demonstrates time and time again that, in direct contrast to pagan mythology—from Mormonism to Mithras—the people, places, and particulars found in sacred Scripture have their roots in history and evidence. What was concealed in soil corresponds to what is revealed in Scripture.

Prophetic Stars

As with manuscript copies and the archaeologist's spade, prophetic stars in the constellation of biblical prophecy are powerful proofs for biblical authority. In the words of the Almighty, "I told you these things long ago; before they happened I announced them to you so that you could not say, 'My images brought them about; my wooden image and metal god ordained them.'"[237] Or as Jesus put it, "I have told you now before it happens, so that when it does happen you will believe."[238]

One of the most significant demonstrations that God has spoken is the undeniable reality that Daniel, writing six centuries before the advent of

Christ, was empowered by almighty God to do what no soothsayer or astrologer could. With awe-inspiring precision, he predicted a succession of nations from Babylon through the Median and Persian Empires. He also foretold the persecution and suffering of the Jews under the second-century Greco-Syrian beast Antiochus IV Epiphanes, including the despot's desecration of the Jerusalem temple, his untimely death, and freedom for the Jews under Judas Maccabaeus. Moreover, as Daniel looked down the corridor of time, he got a glimpse of a kingdom that will itself endure forever.[239]

The detail and dynamics of Daniel's prophetic prowess are such that anti-supernatural scholars have dogmatically declared Daniel to be written pseudonymously by a second-century author. Their argument is simple: a Jewish exile writing six centuries before Christ could not possibly have known what would happen to Jews living four centuries later during the tyrannical reign of the second-century Greco-Syrian despot Antiochus IV Epiphanes.

Such anti-supernatural bias is hardly warranted, however. Jewish historian Josephus correctly chronicled Daniel as a contemporary of Nebuchadnezzar.[240] Furthermore, Jews roundly regard the writings of Daniel as authentic and include them in the Jewish canon.[241] Moreover, the Jewish Jesus not only accepted Daniel as a genuine prophet but viewed his writings as genuinely prophetic. Indeed, Jesus looked back at "'the abomination that causes desolation' spoken of through the prophet Daniel" as the basis for prophesying that the temple that had been desecrated by the forces of Antiochus would ultimately be destroyed by the forces of Antichrist.[242]

While there are stars in the constellation of biblical prophecy, there is only one enduring superstar. Little wonder, then, that prophecies concerning him outnumber all others. His ancestry was marked, and his birthplace foretold. Circumstances surrounding his death were prophesied before crucifixion was invented. The date of his visitation was predicted within historically narrow time parameters. He would work extraordinary miracles and fulfill the law and the prophets. It would be too small for him to bring back only those of Israel; thus, he would be a light for the Gentiles so that salvation would go out to the ends of the earth. Only the hand of God could have etched a prophetic portrait of the Christ in the Old Testament. Only God could cause it to take on flesh in the New. Only Jesus of Nazareth—the unique Superstar—could emerge through the doorway of Old Testament prophecy.[243]

Pseudo-prophecy stars have one thing in common: they are consistently wrong. In illumined contrast, genuine prophecy stars are infallibly correct. And, unlike the pretenders, their prophetic prowess cannot be pawned off to good luck, good guessing, or deliberate deceit.

Scriptural Synergy

One more powerful proof that the Bible is divine rather than merely human in origin is what I prefer to refer to as *scriptural synergy*. Simply stated, scriptural synergy means that the whole of Scripture is greater than the sum of its individual passages. We cannot comprehend the Bible as a whole without comprehending its individual parts, and we cannot comprehend its individual parts without comprehending the Bible as a whole. As such, individual passages of Scripture are synergistic rather than deflective with respect to the whole of Scripture.[244]

The Bible contains myriad books, written by many authors, in multiple languages, over more than a millennium, on a multitude of different subjects—yet it remains unified and consistent throughout. How is that possible? The individual writers had no idea that their message would eventually be assembled into one Book, yet each work fits perfectly into place with a unique purpose as a synergistic component of the whole. The synergistic harmony of the Bible is a powerful testimony and an enduring reminder of biblical authority and trustworthiness.

In sum, I can say with certainty that my research into the great apologetic issues has been validated over time. Hundreds—thousands—of attendant questions have been answered in a variety of forums including *The Complete Bible Answer Book* and *The Creation Answer Book*.[245]

BIBLICAL INTERPRETATION

Removing the Veil

Explain the Scriptures by the Scriptures.

—CLEMENT OF ALEXANDRIA[1]

As the Christian Research Institute is deeply committed to providing answers, so, too, a core value of CRI is equipping Christians in the art and science of biblical *interpretation*. This continues to be crucial in that multitudes distrust the message of the Bible because they mistake its meaning.

It is all too common to hear professors on university campuses dogmatically assert that the Bible could not possibly be divine in that its first two chapters are clearly contradictory. In chapter 1 the creation of plants precedes the creation of animals, which precedes the creation of Adam. In chapter 2 the creation of Adam precedes the creation of plants and animals. Since Genesis purportedly contradicts itself within the span of several sentences, you allegedly cannot trust what follows. Worse, as you continue through the Bible, you encounter a Second Adam—called Christ—who mistakenly predicted that his generation would experience the end of the world. The Bible gets even more bizarre as you proceed toward its climax. In the last book, you discover the talking snake in the first book, reimagined as a fire-breathing dragon. Thus, when the Bible is so much as mentioned, it is not uncommon to see expressions of polite exasperation etched on modern faces. After all, the Bible is not only hopelessly contradictory, but it also suggests that slavery is okay.

To counter all such misinterpretations involves a discipline known as *hermeneutics*. In Greek mythology the task of the god Hermes was to appropriately interpret the will of the gods. In hermeneutics, the task is to accurately interpret the Word of God. Simply stated, hermeneutics is the art and science of biblical interpretation. It is a science in that rules apply; an art in that the more you apply the rules, the better you get at it.

Yet, as will be underscored in part two, no matter how skilled you and I become in the art and science of biblical interpretation, we must always be cognizant of the reality that the sacred commission of the Fathers was the proper transmission of Apostolic Tradition from one generation to the next—from Holy Fathers such as Athanasius who formally codified what today is universally accepted as the authoritative New Testament canon onward to every neighborhood church in every successive generation. Thus, while Holy Tradition could not add anything to Scripture, it was in actuality Scripture rightly understood. (I will say more about the significance of Holy Tradition with respect to biblical interpretation shortly.[2])

LITERAL PRINCIPLE

The *literal principle of biblical interpretation* helps to negate the dangers of hyperliteralism. Simply stated, the literal principle instructs us to interpret the Bible as we interpret other forms of literature—in the most obvious and natural sense. Thus, to interpret the Bible *literally* is to interpret the Bible as *literature*. When a biblical author uses a symbol or an allegory, we do violence to his intentions if we interpret literalistically.

Even a cursory reading of Genesis 1 and 2 should be sufficient to discern that the author has a different purpose in one chapter than he does in the other. Chapter 1 presents a *hierarchy* of creation memorably associated with days of the week. Chapter 2 focuses on the crowning jewels of God's creation mandated to be in right relationship with their Creator as well as with the whole of creation. As such, the land is depicted as barren until the first man arrives to cultivate it; and animals are depicted as being created and brought to Adam in order to help him realize his need for a suitable helpmate; which culminates in God's creation of woman. In both chapters, the depiction of a chronological order of creation events is a literary device employed to facilitate the author's primary concern—which is to reveal God's *purposes* in creation.[3]

What is crucial to recognize here is that a literalistic method of interpretation often does as much violence to the text as does a spiritualized interpretation that empties the text of objective meaning. To avoid either extreme, one must adeptly employ the literal principle of biblical interpretation, paying careful attention to *form, figurative language,* and *fantasy imagery.*

To interpret the Bible as literature presupposes that we consider the kind of literature we are interpreting. Just as a legal brief differs in form from a prophetic oracle, so, too, there is a distinct difference in form between Leviticus and Revelation. Recognizing this reality is particularly important when considering writings that are difficult to categorize, such as Genesis, which is largely a historical narrative interlaced with symbolism and repetitive poetic structure.

If Genesis were reduced to an allegory conveying mere abstract ideas about temptation, sin, and redemption—devoid of any correlation with actual events in history—the very foundation of our faith would be destroyed. Conversely, if we consider Satan to be a slithering snake, we would not only misunderstand the nature of fallen angels but may suppose Jesus triumphed over the work of the Devil by stepping on the head of a serpent.

Proper consideration of figurative language is similarly crucial. Such language differs from literal language in which words mean exactly what they say. Figurative language requires readers to use their imagination to comprehend what the author is driving at. When Jesus said, "I am the bread of life,"[4] he was obviously not saying that he was literally the "staff of life" (i.e., physical bread). Rather he was metaphorically communicating that he is the "stuff of life" (i.e., the essence of true life).

Scripture is replete with fantasy imagery as well. A red dragon with seven heads and ten horns immediately springs to mind. While fantasy images are unreal, they provide a realistic means by which to ponder reality. Christian writers from John Bunyan to J. R. R. Tolkien and C. S. Lewis have emulated the biblical use of fantasy imagery to underscore the cardinal truths of the Christian worldview. Puritan writer William Gurnall, for example, used the "otherworldly" image of a man's head on a beast's shoulders to highlight the reality that righteousness without truth is abhorrent. "An orthodox judgment coming from an unholy heart and an ungodly life is as ugly as *a man's head would be on a beast's shoulders*. The wretch who knows the truth but practices evil is worse than the man who is ignorant."[5]

In sum, to read the biblical text for all its worth, it is crucial to read the Bible as literature, paying close attention to *form, figurative language,* and *fantasy imagery.* And in doing so, you and I must ever be mindful that, though the Bible must be read as literature, it is not merely literature. Instead, the Scriptures were uniquely inspired by the Spirit. Thus, we fervently pray that the Spirit, who inspired the text, illumines our minds to riches buried within its tapestry.[6]

ILLUMINATION PRINCIPLE

Illumination is the grace by which the Holy Spirit sheds divine light upon the inspired text. While it is crucial to defend the Bible as divine in an age in which it is under siege, only the Spirit removes the veil so that the blind may truly see. Illumination does not end when the veil is lifted and the spiritually blind receive their sight. The spiritually sighted need illumination throughout the duration of their lives. We do not as yet know the treasures that may be mined from the biblical text. Such mining is not dependent upon degrees. It is directly proportional to diligence. As we dig, the Spirit continues to illumine our minds. "We have not received the spirit of the world," said Paul to the Corinthians, "but the Spirit who is from God, that we may understand what God has freely given us."[7] The Spirit of truth provides insights that permeate the mind as well as *illumination* that penetrates the heart.

Far from supplanting the scrupulous study of Scripture, the Holy Spirit provides us with insights that can only be discerned spiritually. Thus, we must learn to listen carefully as God speaks to us through the majesty of his Word. Like Samuel, we should say, "Speak, LORD, for your servant is listening."[8] Or as Jesus so memorably put it, "My sheep listen to my voice; I know them, and they follow me."[9]

One of the most amazing aspects of Scripture is that it is alive and active, not dead and dull. Indeed, God still speaks today through the mystery of his Word. The Holy Spirit illumines our minds to what is revealed in Scripture. As is well said, the Holy Spirit makes us "wise up to what is written, not beyond it."[10]

While we *listen*, we must also "test the spirits." As John, the apostle of love, warned, "Do not believe every spirit, but test the spirits to see whether they are from God, because many false prophets have gone out into the world."[11] Satan's foremost strategy is to disguise himself as an angel of light. His slickest slogan is, *Feel, don't think*. God's Spirit, on the other hand, illumines our minds so that we may understand what he has freely given us.[12]

GRAMMATICAL PRINCIPLE

When Jesus came to Caesarea Philippi, he asked his disciples the mother of all questions: "Who do you say I am?"[13] His disciples asked a similar question: "Who is this? Even the wind and the waves obey him!"[14] Jesus left no doubt as to the answer. He claimed to be God in human flesh. On one occasion, he was so direct, the belligerent crowd picked up stones. "But Jesus said to them, 'I have shown you many great miracles from the Father. For which of these do you stone me?' 'We are not stoning you for any of these,' replied the Jews, 'but for blasphemy, because you, a mere man, claim to be God.'"[15]

Jehovah's Witnesses, like first-century Jewish Sanhedrists, do not believe the claim of Christ. In their view he was created by God as the archangel Michael, during his earthly sojourn became a mere man, and after crucifixion was re-created an immaterial spirit creature. From their perspective, the tiny little letter *a* makes all the difference in the world. Jesus Christ is not God, they say—he was *a* god.[16] God created him as his *first-born*. He then became a junior partner in the creation of all *other* things.

The moment they commence their grammatical gyrations, our baloney detectors should register red. Is it really true that Jesus Christ was just *a* god? Does the designation *first-born* substantiate their contention? Does the word *other*—as in he is the creator of all *other* things—buttress their denial of unique deity? Such questions underscore the significance of the grammatical principle of biblical interpretation.

Thankfully, you and I were hardwired for language from birth. From infancy onward, speech patterns are unconsciously absorbed and then modified in accord with unspoken rules of grammar. Even at age three, children display grammatical genius that enables them to master complex speech constructions and internalize sophisticated laws of language. In time even complex grammatical constructions and multiple word meanings become second nature.

It shouldn't surprise us, then, that the basic principles of language that we unconsciously absorb in early childhood and consciously internalize from grade school onward are foundational to the grammatical principle of biblical interpretation. As with any literary work, a thorough understanding of the Bible cannot be attained without a grasp of the basic rules (grammar) that govern the relationships and usages of words, including *syntax*—the proper word order of sentences or the relationship of words in a sentence—and *semantics*—the science of meaning.[17]

Historical Principle

Apart from an understanding of the historical context of any given book in the Bible, we have little hope of grasping its meaning. Put another way, in order to properly evaluate biblical texts, we must consider their historical context. The book of Ezekiel provides a telling example.

Ezekiel prophesied during an extremely dark period in Judah's history.

He was born into the priesthood in Jerusalem around the time that Josiah found the Book of the Law in the temple (622 BC)—a time in which spiritual renewal broke out in the land. Reformation, however, was short-lived. By the time of Josiah's death (609 BC) the idolatrous practices of the past had returned with a vengeance. Thus, the ax of God's judgment fell. In short order, Ezekiel found himself on the dusty plains of Babylon, warning fellow exiles that the worst lay right around the corner. In 586 BC the gilded city and its golden temple were desecrated and destroyed.

Without the historical backdrop, we'd be hard pressed to understand Ezekiel's words. As affirmed in the text, Ezekiel was prophesying from the dusty environs of a refugee camp in the south of Babylon near the river Kebar. From there the priest looked into the eastern sky, longing for the glory of the Lord to return to a temple that had vanished into the rocks that surrounded it. He yearned for the promise of a temple whose glory would exceed even that of Solomon's temple. In the Spirit he looked forward to events that would take place a generation later, when Zerubbabel would rebuild the spiritual condition of the returning exiles and Nehemiah would challenge his fellow countrymen to arise and rebuild the shattered walls of Jerusalem.

The historical principle of biblical interpretation keeps one from supposing that Ezekiel longed for a third or fourth temple when the second had not yet arisen from the ashes of the first.[18]

TYPOLOGY PRINCIPLE

A *type* is a person, event, or institution in the redemptive history of the Old Testament that prefigures a corresponding but greater reality in the New. The greater reality to which a type points and in which it finds its fulfillment is referred to as an *antitype*.

Hebrews specifically employs the word *antitype* to refer to the greatness of the heavenly sanctuary of which the Holy Temple was merely a *type*. For example, the coming of Christ has forever rendered the notion of another earthly temple obsolete. It is the Savior and the saved who now form the sanctuary in which the Spirit of the living God resides. To suppose that the Shekinah glory will return to a shrine in Jerusalem is to regress from antitype or substance to type or shadow and to impugn the finished work of Christ.

The apostle Paul highlighted Jesus as the antitype of temple, priest, and sacrifice. As such, the sacred ashes of the red heifer, like the blood of bulls and goats, find ultimate antitypical fulfillment in the blood of Jesus Christ. In place of sacrificing holy cows, the redeemed are called to celebrate Holy Communion. All of the types and shadows of the old covenant, including the Holy Land, the Holy City, and the Holy Temple, have been fulfilled in the Holy Christ. As the typology principle of biblical interpretation informs us, it is Paradise, not Palestine, for which our hearts yearn. It is the Heavenly City, not a Holy City, on which we fix our gaze. It is the Master Teacher, not a majestic temple, that forever satisfies our deepest longings.[19]

SYNERGY PRINCIPLE

Synergy may rightly be deemed the principal imperative in the art and science of biblical interpretation. As stated previously, this means that the whole of Scripture is greater than the sum of its individual passages. You cannot comprehend the Bible as a whole without comprehending its individual parts, nor its individual parts without comprehending it as a whole.

Synergy demands that individual Bible passages may never be interpreted in such a way as to conflict with the whole of Scripture. As you seek to understand the Scriptures, keep in mind that all Scripture, though communicated through various human instruments, has but one Author. And that Author does not contradict himself. Nor confuse his servants.

Proper application of the biblical principle of scriptural synergy could have saved Professor Bart Ehrman from a world of confusion. When Jesus told the court that condemned him to death, "In the future you will see the Son of Man sitting at the right hand of the Mighty One and coming on the clouds of heaven,"[20] Ehrman supposes Jesus was predicting that his generation would experience the end of the world.[21]

In reality, even the most basic comparison of Scripture with Scripture reveals that "coming on clouds" is a common Old Testament metaphor pointing to God as the sovereign judge of the nations. Jesus, heir to the linguistic riches of the Old Testament prophets, and a greater prophet than them all, wielded the symbolism of "clouds" to warn his hearers that as judgment had fallen on such nations as Egypt, so too it would befall Jerusalem and its temple.[22]

When such prejudices are imposed on Scripture, its tapestry is undone and loose ends dangle ignominiously. When synergy takes precedence, the majesty of its tapestry is illumined.

Because truth matters, it is imperative to engage ourselves heart and soul in mining the Bible for all its wealth. Familiarity with the *literal* principle, *illumination* principle, *grammatical* principle, *historical* principle, *typology* principle, and *synergy* principle is axiomatic in the quest.[23]

Countering Counterfeit Religions

Contrast Is the Conduit to Clarity

I fear, lest somehow, as the serpent deceived Eve by his craftiness, so your minds may be corrupted from the simplicity that is in Christ. For if he who comes preaches another Jesus whom we have not preached, or if you receive a different spirit which you have not received, or a different gospel which you have not accepted—you may well put up with it!

—THE APOSTLE PAUL[1]

When you google "counterfeit money," one of the first hits that pops up is a Treasury Department posting titled "How to Detect Counterfeit Money." According to the article, you and I "can help guard against the threat from counterfeiters by becoming more familiar with United States money." How? "Compare a suspect note with a genuine note of the same denomination and series, paying attention to the quality of printing and paper characteristics. Look for differences, not similarities."[2]

What is true of counterfeit currency is likewise true of counterfeit religions. You and I must become so familiar with essential Christian doctrine that when counterfeits loom on the horizon, we recognize them instantaneously. "The way to show that a stick is crooked is not to argue about it or to spend time denouncing it, but to lay a straight stick alongside it."[3]

The straight stick is essential Christian doctrine. Essential Christian doctrine forms the line of demarcation between the kingdom of Christ and the kingdom of the cults. It is the North Star by which the course of Christianity is set and the foundation on which the gospel of Jesus Christ rests. Collectively they are the main and plain teachings of Christ and his church.

Because truth matters it is crucial to counter counterfeit religions—all of which compromise, confuse, or contradict authentic Christianity—beginning with the deity of Christ.

DEITY OF CHRIST

Counterfeit religions uniformly deny the unique deity of Jesus Christ. Jehovah's Witnesses claim Jesus is the archangel Michael;[4] Mormons say he is the spirit brother of Lucifer;[5] New Age gurus assert he is an avatar, or enlightened messenger.[6] Jesus, however, claimed to be God. As a result, the Jewish leaders tried to kill him because in "calling God his own Father," they said, Jesus was "making himself equal with God."[7] From that day to today, Judaism, in all its various permutations, has uniformly denied the unique deity of Jesus Christ.

When Jesus claimed the very words by which God revealed himself to Moses from the burning bush, the Jews "picked up stones to stone him." Why? Because in Judaism this is the epitome of blasphemy. For by saying "I am," Jesus was incontrovertibly claiming to be God.[8] Again, when Jesus said, "I and the Father are one," the "Jews picked up stones to stone him, but Jesus said to them, 'I have shown you many great miracles from the Father. For which of these do you stone me?' 'We are not stoning you for any of these,' replied the Jews, 'but for blasphemy because you, a mere man, claim to be God.'"[9]

On yet another occasion when Caiaphas the Jewish high priest asked, "Are you the Messiah, the Son of the Blessed One?" "I am," said Jesus. "And you will see the Son of Man sitting at the right hand of the Mighty One and coming on the clouds of heaven."[10] A biblically illiterate person might well have missed the import of Jesus' words. Caiaphas and the Jewish council, however, did not. They knew that in saying he was "the Son of Man" who would come on "the clouds of heaven" he was making an overt reference to Daniel's prophecy.[11] And in doing so, he was not only claiming to be the preexistent Sovereign of the universe but prophesying that he would vindicate his claim by judging the very court that was condemning him. Moreover, by combining Daniel's prophecy with David's proclamation in Psalm 110, Jesus was claiming that he would sit upon the throne of Israel's God and share God's very glory. To the Jews, this was the height of blasphemy; thus, "they all condemned him as worthy of death."[12]

Jesus not only claimed to be God but also provided many convincing proofs that he was indeed divine. To begin with, Jesus demonstrated that he was God in human flesh by manifesting the credential of sinlessness. Jesus himself went so far as to challenge his antagonists by asking, "Can any of you prove me guilty of sin?"[13] Furthermore, Jesus demonstrated supernatural authority over sickness, the forces of nature, fallen angels, and even death itself. Matthew 4 records that Jesus went throughout Galilee teaching, preaching, "and healing every disease and sickness among the people." Mark 4 documents Jesus rebuking the wind and the waves saying, "Quiet! Be still!" In Luke 4, Jesus encountered a man possessed by an evil spirit and commanded the demon to "Come out of him!" And in John 4, Jesus told a royal official whose son was close to death, "Your son will live." Plus, all four Gospels record how Jesus demonstrated ultimate power over death through the immutable fact of his resurrection.[14]

In addition to Christ's claims and credentials, the biblical text clearly asserts that Jesus is God. Three texts stand out above the rest. Not only are they clear and convincing, but their "addresses" are easy to remember—John 1, Colossians 1, and Hebrews 1.

In chapter 1 of his Gospel, the apostle John was emphatic concerning the deity of Christ. "In the beginning was the Word, and the Word was with God, *and the Word was God.*" Here we see that Jesus not only was in existence before the world began but is differentiated from the Father and explicitly called "God," indicating that he shares the same nature as his Father. Colossians 1 likewise informs us that "in him all things were created"; he is "before all things"; and "God was pleased to have all his fullness dwell in him." Only deity has the prerogative of creation, preexists all things, and personifies the full essence and nature of God. Hebrews 1 overtly tells us that—according to God the Father himself—Jesus is God: "About the Son he [the Father] says, 'Your throne, O God, will last for ever and ever.'" Not only is the entirety of Hebrews 1 devoted to demonstrating the true deity of Jesus, but in verses ten through twelve, the inspired writer quoted a passage from Psalm 102 referring to Yahweh and directly applied it to Christ. In doing so, these verses specifically declare Jesus ontologically equal with Israel's God.[15]

Many similar texts could be added to this list. For example, in Revelation 1, the Lord God said, "I am the Alpha and the Omega . . . who is, and who was, and who is to come, the Almighty." In the last chapter of Revelation, Jesus applied these same words—*Alpha* and *Omega*—to himself![16] Additionally, in 2 Peter 1, Jesus is referred to as "our God and Savior Jesus Christ." In these passages and a host of others, the Bible explicitly claims that Jesus *is* God.[17] As the panoply of Scripture makes plain, Jesus is the eternal Creator who spoke and the limitless galaxies leapt into existence.

The Judaist contention that Jesus was a liar and a blasphemer is clearly counterfeit—a counterfeit mercifully undone by the straight stick of biblical brilliance and historical evidence.

ORIGINAL SIN

In the grand meta-narrative of the biblical text, the doctrine of original (ancestral) sin looms large. God spoke to the apex of his creation, saying, "You are free to eat from any tree in the garden; but you must not eat from the tree of the knowledge of good and evil, for when you eat of it you will surely die."[18]

In reckless response, Adam sprayed the canvas of God's creation with the venom of his own self-will. He disobeyed, and the whole of humanity inherited his "broken gene"—an inclination toward sin—a disease leading inexorably to death.[19] In the words of the apostle Paul, "sin entered the world through one man, and death through sin, and in this way death came to all people, because all sinned."[20] Saint Athanasius left no doubt about the spreading gangrene of the first sin. In his *Four Discourses Against the Arians* he summed it up concisely, saying, "When Adam had transgressed, his sin reached unto all men."[21]

The very chapter that references the original sin also records the divine plan for restoration[22]—a plan that takes on definition with God's promise to make Abram a great nation through whom "all peoples on earth will be blessed."[23] Abram's call, therefore, constituted the divine antidote to Adam's fall. God's promise that Abram's children would inherit the promised land was but a preliminary step in a progressive plan through which Abram and his heirs would inherit "a better country—a heavenly one."[24]

The plan came into sharp focus when Moses led Abram's descendants out of the four-hundred-year bondage in Egypt. For forty years of wilderness wandering, God tabernacled with his people and prepared them for the land of promise. Like Abram, however, Moses saw the promise only from afar. The plan became a tangible reality when Joshua led the children of Israel into Palestine. Palestine, however, was but a preliminary phase in the patriarchal promise.

Not only would God make Abram the father of a nation, but Abram would become Abraham—"A father of *many* nations."[25] Abraham "would be heir of the world."[26] As such, the climax of the promise would not be Palestine regained, but paradise restored.

As God promised Abraham Palestine, so, too, he promised him a royal seed.[27] Joshua led the children of Israel into the promised land; Jesus will one day lead redeemed humanity into paradise restored. From Adam's rebellion to Abraham's royal seed, Scripture chronicles God's one unfolding plan for the redemption of humanity.[28]

The grand meta-narrative of Scripture is indeed a majestic masterpiece. But a masterpiece obscenely vandalized by counterfeit religions such as Islam. In Islam, there is no original sin—just an original act of heedlessness. Thus, while the biblical worldview highlights the severity of sin and its consequences, the Qur'anic worldview reduces the original sin to an original slip—a mere bout of forgetfulness. In short, *the* fall is reformulated *a* fall.

In the words of Muslim scholars Jane Idleman Smith and Yvonne Yazbeck Haddad, "the common Christian conception has been that Adam was expelled from paradise because of his sin, and due to this original act of disobedience the succession of humanity is tainted." But this, they assert, is quite simply wrong. "While the Qur'an contains the narrative of Adam's expulsion from the Garden, the expulsion is the result of satanic deception, immediately pardoned, rather than a progenitive act of disobedience with ramifications for the rest of humanity."[29]

According to the Islamic worldview, every newborn child is born in a state of *fitrah*—or a state of original Muslim purity.[30] "No babe is born but upon Fitra [as a Muslim]. It is his parents who make him a Jew or a Christian or a Polytheist."[31] Yusuf Ali left no doubt about the Muslim dictum of original goodness. In his highly touted Qur'anic commentary he said, "As turned out from the creative hand of Allah, man is innocent, pure, true, free, *inclined to right and virtue*."[32]

Even apart from the Bible, Muslims ought to know better than to think such a thing. If we are born innocent and pure, inclined to righteousness and virtue, why is it that parents strive mightily to instill virtue in their offspring? As the parent of twelve wonderful children, I can tell you firsthand that King David was right to cry out, "Surely I was sinful at birth, sinful from the time my mother conceived me."[33]

Social commentator Dennis Prager underscores this reality with an appropriate mix of humor and solemnity. "Babies are lovable and innocent, but they are not good: They are entirely self-centered—as they have to be in order to survive. 'I want mommy; I want milk; I want to be held; I want to be comforted, and if you do not do all these things immediately, I will ruin your life!'" Said Prager, "That's not goodness; that's narcissism. We are born narcissists, preoccupied with 'number one': ourselves. And if you've ever worked with kids, you know how cruel, how bullying, they can be. And don't parents have to tell their child tens of thousands of times, 'Say thank you'? Now, why is that? If we are naturally good, wouldn't feeling and expressing gratitude come naturally?"[34]

The history of humanity bears eloquent testimony to Prager's contentions as well as to the consequences of original sin. After Adam ate the forbidden fruit, the Tree of Life remained a memorial to paradise lost. Another tree, however, stands on Golgotha's hill. On it, Jesus stretched one hand toward the Edenic garden, the other toward the eternal garden. The immortality the first Adam could no longer reach, the Second Adam touched in his place. On that tree Jesus vanquished the power of evil, giving ultimate victory to the knowledge of good.[35]

When the straight stick of original sin is laid alongside the Muslim pretender, the latter's crookedness is made readily apparent.[36]

CANON

Open the Mormon canon and you immediately encounter these words: "The Book of Mormon is a volume of holy scripture comparable to the Bible. It is a record of God's dealings with the ancient inhabitants of the Americas and contains the fulness of the everlasting gospel."[37]

The Book of Mormon is the record of two great civilizations. The first, Jaredites, left the Tower of Babel and immigrated to the Americas twenty-two hundred years before Christ. The second migrated from Jerusalem around 600 BC and divided into two great nations: Nephites and Lamanites. The Lamanites were "white, and exceedingly fair and delightsome." However, due to hideous evils, "the Lord God did cause a skin of blackness to come upon them."[38] In contrast to the blackness of the Lamanites, the Nephites were brilliantly brave.

Of particular note is the famed Nephite military commander Moroni. Moroni, along with his famous father Mormon, used "reformed Egyptian" hieroglyphics to create the "most correct of any book on earth,"[39] and subsequently entombed it in the hill Cumorah. After being resurrected as an angel, Moroni "appeared to the Prophet Joseph Smith [1823] and instructed him relative to the ancient record and its destined translation into the English language."[40] In due course, Smith found golden plates along with a pair of magical eyeglasses that he used to translate the Egyptian into English. The result was a new revelation called the Book of Mormon, which chronicles "the personal ministry of the Lord Jesus Christ among the Nephites soon after His resurrection. It puts forth the doctrines of the gospel, outlines the plan of salvation, and tells men what they must do to gain peace in this life and eternal salvation in the life to come."[41]

But here's the problem: No archaeological evidence for a language such as "reformed Egyptian" in hieroglyphics. No archaeological evidence for the great civilizations chronicled in the Book of Mormon. No archaeological evidence for such lands as the "land of Moron" described in Ether 7:6. No anthropological evidence that the Nephites and Lamanites migrated from Jerusalem to Mesoamerica. Indeed, both archaeology and anthropology militate against the people, places, and particulars that are part and parcel of the Book of Mormon and demonstrate conclusively that it is little more than the product of a fertile and enterprising imagination.

In sharp contrast, archaeological discoveries add eloquent testimony to the historical validity of the biblical account. Case in point. Like Nephites, the Hittites—from whom Abraham purchased a burial plot for his wife, Sarah—have long been rendered the stuff of myths and fables. "In 1906, however, archaeologists digging east of Ankara, Turkey, discovered the ruins of Hattusas, the ancient Hittite capital at what is today called Boghazkoy, as well as its vast collection of Hittite historical records, which showed an empire flourishing in the mid-second millennium BC."[42]

Time and time again, comprehensive archaeological field work has affirmed the reliability of the Bible. One of the most well-known New Testament examples concerns the books of Luke and Acts. Sir William Ramsay, a biblical skeptic trained as an archaeologist, set out to disprove the historical reliability of this portion of the New Testament. But through his painstaking Mediterranean archaeological trips, he was converted to Christianity as, one after another, the historical allusions of Luke proved accurate.[43]

Archaeologists discovered a treasure trove of archaeological nuggets that provide a powerful counter to objections raised by scholars against the biblical account of Christ's crucifixion and burial. In *U.S. News and World Report*, Jeffrey Sheler highlighted the significance of the discovery of the remains of a man crucified during the first century—a discovery that calls into question the scholarship of counterfeiters who contend Jesus was tied rather than nailed to the cross and that his corpse was likely thrown into a shallow grave and eaten by wild dogs that roamed the execution grounds.[44]

Finds have also corroborated biblical details surrounding the trial that led to the fatal torment of Jesus Christ—including the burial grounds of Caiaphas, the high priest who presided over the religious trials of Christ. In 1990 a burial chamber dating back to the first century was discovered two miles south of the Temple Mount. "Inside the chamber, archaeologists found twelve limestone ossuaries. One of the boxes, elaborately decorated with six-petaled rosettes, contained the bones of a sixty-year-old man and bore the inscription *Yehosef bar Qayafa*—'Joseph, son of Caiaphas.'"[45]

These and a host of other illustrations serve to make the point. In direct contrast to the revelations of counterfeit religions such as Mormonism, the people, places, and particulars found in sacred Scripture have their roots in history and evidence. What was once concealed in soil corresponds to what is revealed in Scripture. When we compare the Christian canon with the Mormon canon, the contrast demonstrates that the Mormon canon is more than a little crooked.[46]

TRINITY

As noted in the *Dictionary of Pentecostal and Charismatic Movements*, "Oneness Pentecostalism is a religious movement that emerged in 1914 within the Assemblies of God of the early American Pentecostal movement, challenging the traditional Trinitarian doctrine."[47] According to Oneness Pentecostalism, the doctrine of the Trinity is pagan polytheistic philosophy.

Oneness is hardly unique in its strident denouncement of the Trinity. Virtually all counterfeit religions are extreme in their denials. Jehovah's Witnesses contentiously claim Satan to be the originator of trinitarian dogma, and the Muslim Allah not only misapprehends trinitarian doctrine but avers that trinitarians are guilty of blasphemy.[48]

What these and many other like-minded counterfeit religions have in common is that their unitarian gods, by definition, lack the moral perfection of love and, thus, on the basis of logic, must be morally defective. This is so because, for God to be a perfect being, he must of necessity also be a loving being. That implies that there is someone to love, because in accordance with modern cosmology,[49] the universe and the persons that inhabit it came into being a finite time ago.[50] Thus, independent of creation, these unitarian gods would not have had an object on which to lavish love. While moral imperfections apply to such counterfeit gods, they do not likewise apply to the authentic trinitarian deity of historic Christian faith.

Though the biblical God is a single being, there are subject-object distinctions within the Godhead. And the three centers of consciousness within the one true God have loved one another from all eternity.[51] Said C. S. Lewis, "All sorts of people are fond of repeating the Christian statement that 'God is love.' But they seem not to notice that the words 'God is love' have no real meaning unless God contains at least two Persons. Love is something that one person has for another person. If God was a single person, then before the world was made, He was not love."[52]

While the Trinity is incomprehensible, the doctrine of the Trinity is hardly incoherent. As Professor Donald Fairbairn has well said, "Christian monotheism affirms the presence of three eternal, divine persons who are united in such a way as to be a single God and whose love for one another is the basis for all of human life. These persons are not separate—that would imply that they were different gods—but they are distinct as persons, and this distinction is what makes it possible for God to share love within himself from all eternity."[53]

In short, the trinitarian platform contains three planks. The first underscores the reality that there is only one God. The second emphasizes that in hundreds of passages Father, Son, and Holy Spirit are each declared truly God. The third asserts that the Father, Son, and Holy Spirit are eternally distinct. It is likewise significant to reemphasize that when Christians speak of one God, the reference is to the nature or essence of God. And, when they speak of Persons or Subjects, it is a reference to "identity formed and completed on the basis of relationships" within the Godhead.[54] In other words—the one true God of the Bible is one *What* and three *Whos*.[55]

Early Christians, like their Old Testament counterparts, were willing to die for the unalterable truth that there is one and *only* one God. Deuteronomy 6:4 contains the Hebrew Shema—the most significant prayer of Old Testament Judaism—"Hear, O Israel: The LORD our God, the LORD is one." Isaiah 43:10 likewise codifies the Old Testament commitment to only one God. Here, as elsewhere, God called ancient Israel to "know," "believe," and "understand" this singular truth: "Before me no god was formed, nor will there be one after me." Ephesians 4:6, in the New Testament, is equally emphatic: there is "one God and Father of all, who is over all and through all and in all." The Bible contains scores of similar passages so that "you might know that the LORD is God; *besides him there is no other.*"[56]

Furthermore, the Bible declares that the Father is God in numerous passages including Ephesians 1:3; 1 Peter 1:3; and 2 Corinthians 1:3. The Son is declared God in the first chapters of John, Colossians, Hebrews, and Revelation. And the Spirit is unmistakably rendered God in such passages as Acts 5:3–4, in which lying to the Holy Spirit is equated with lying to God.

Finally, the Bible decrees Father, Son, and Holy Spirit eternally distinct. Jesus, for example, made a distinction between himself and the Father, saying that the Father and Son are two distinct witnesses and two distinct judges. Such self-distinctions within the Godhead are amplified through the annunciation of Christ's birth; his baptism; and his commission to baptize believers "in the name of the Father and of the Son and of the Holy Spirit."[57]

For Christians, defending the doctrine of the Trinity is hardly theoretical; it is eminently practical. For unlike the counterfeits, the true and living God invites us to participate in the loving relationships that Father, Son, and Holy Spirit have enjoyed throughout eternity.[58]

RESURRECTION

As I write these words, I grieve my mother's death. However, I do not "grieve like the rest of mankind, who have no hope. For we believe that Jesus died and rose again, and so we believe that God will bring with Jesus those who have fallen asleep in him."[59]

My mother, who fell asleep in Jesus, was designed to live forever. Death is, in reality, entrance into a brand-new sphere of existence. Like the caterpillar, my mother will be transformed. The analogy is breathtaking. For though the caterpillar dies, yet will it live. Its chrysalis is in essence a casket in which it experiences ruin and resurrection. Constituent parts devolve into a mysterious molecular mixture and then the miraculous occurs. Eyes that once could only distinguish between darkness and light are transformed into majestic orbs with a field of vision and color acuity that exceeds our own. Wings appear as if by magic. An incredibly complex reproductive system—wholly absent in the caterpillar—materializes mysteriously. An unimaginable straw-like proboscis emerges, allowing the resurrected creature to indulge in the nectar of a brand-new life. The transformed being that emerges is simply beyond belief.[60]

Correspondence to my mother's death and forthcoming resurrection is extraordinary. For like the caterpillar, she, too, will experience metamorphosis. To borrow the words of the apostle Paul, my mother is now "away from the body and at home with the Lord."[61] Disembodied, my mother no longer experiences *whereness* (extension in space); her *awareness*, however, has been greatly magnified.

As glorious as all this is, my mother is poised to experience yet another phase of existence. Jesus died and was physically resurrected. And so it will be with my dear mother. As Jesus rose, she, too, will rise. This does not necessitate that every atom will be resuscitated in resurrection; it does, however, underscore continuity between our earthly body and our eternal body. "The body that is sown is perishable, it is raised imperishable; it is sown in dishonor, it is raised in glory; it is sown in weakness, it is raised in power; it is sown a natural body, it is raised a spiritual body."[62]

When Jesus appears a second time, the nonphysical aspect of my mother's humanity will be reunited with a real, physical, flesh-and-bone body, perfectly engineered for "a new heaven and a new earth."[63] Like the butterfly, my mother will be changed. In a moment, in the twinkling of an eye, she will be transformed. As a caterpillar is transformed into a butterfly, so her resurrected body will be numerically identical to the body she once possessed. In other words, her resurrection body is not a second body; it is her present body transformed.

What is true of my mother is true for us all. Daniel likens the resurrection of saints to the glory of the stars. "Multitudes who sleep in the dust of the earth will awake: some to everlasting life, others to shame and everlasting contempt. Those who are wise will shine like the brightness of the heavens, and those who lead many to righteousness, like the stars for ever and ever."[64] The resurrection envisioned is clear and unambiguous. Daniel speaks not of the disembodied state that follows death but of the bodily resurrection that follows the disembodied state.

Isaiah, likewise, looks forward to the resurrection of the dead. "Your dead will live; their bodies will rise. You who dwell in the dust, wake up and shout for joy. Your dew is like the dew of the morning; the earth will give birth to her dead."[65] It is from the dust that God created humankind, it is to the dust humankind returns, and it is from the dust that our DNA emerges as the pattern for resurrected bodies.

Jesus left no doubt about this coming resurrection. "Do not be amazed at this, for a time is coming when all who are in their graves will hear his voice and come out—those who have done what is good will rise to live, and those who have done what is evil will rise to be condemned."[66] As documented in chapter 1, if Christ had not himself been resurrected, the promise that he will resurrect dry bones in scattered graves would be as empty as the tomb guaranteeing its fulfillment.

Despite the evidence—evidence we are commissioned to proffer—millions upon millions remain trapped in counterfeit religions such as scientism. Many more in various cultic constructs that compromise, confuse, or outright contradict the reality of resurrection.

As such, post-enlightenment thinkers enthralled by scientism (not science)[67] carelessly suppose that nothing created everything, that life came from nonlife, and that the life that came from nonlife produced morals. And this is not the only ruse. Eastern religions have long considered reincarnation—literally, rebirth in another body—to be the universal law of life. Millions of

Buddhists, Hindus, Sikhs, and Jains hold reincarnation to be inexorable truth. Consequently, it is not at all surprising to find a cow in Calcutta afforded more consideration than a child.

What is surprising is the vast rapidity with which belief in reincarnation has grown in the West, where asking about your past lives is about as common as asking whether you are a Leo or a Libra. Incredibly, being born again in another body is now the theology du jour of approximately one out of every ten church attendees.[68]

In step with Hindus, Hollywood is rife with the reincarnation narrative. As noted by *Time*, Shirley MacLaine and Sylvester Stallone both believe they were beheaded, "she by Louis XV, he during the French Revolution. Stallone thinks he may have been a monkey in Guatemala, and MacLaine is sure she was a prostitute in a previous life."[69]

While reincarnation has become prevalent on Main Street and in movies, it hardly comports with reality. To murder a mosquito, even in self-defense, is hardly equivalent to taking the life of a previous person. And Stallone was hardly monkeyed around—at least not in a previous life. Reality is that resurrection and reincarnation can never be reconciled. The former is a historical reality. The latter a Hindu fantasy.[70]

INCARNATION

The Christian Creed, affirmed by the ancient Council of Nicea, asserts that, "for us and for our salvation," Christ "came down from heaven and was incarnate of the Holy Spirit and the Virgin Mary and became man." Or, as the apostle John avowed, Jesus "became flesh and dwelt among us, and we beheld His glory, the glory as of the only begotten of the Father, full of grace and truth."[71]

This, according to Dan Brown, is patently false. Following the release of his wildly popular bestseller *The Da Vinci Code*[72]—in which the Gospels are caricatured as fabrications and the miracle of incarnation a fable—Brown was said to be a brilliant historian. *Library Journal* characterized his work as "a compelling blend of history and page-turning suspense," a "masterpiece" that "should be mandatory reading."[73] *Publisher's Weekly* called it "an exhaustively researched page-turner."[74] And bestselling author Nelson DeMille christened it "pure genius."[75]

For his part, Brown avers that his evisceration of the historic Christian faith is based on carefully researched material fact, and truth be known, "*nothing* in Christianity is original."[76] Indeed, everything from Christ's incarnation to his resurrection and ascension was "taken directly from earlier pagan mystery religions."[77] Simply stated, the incarnation is a rip-off.

As documented in *The Da Vinci Code—Fact or Fiction?* Brown's contention is hardly unique.[78]

> The past four decades have seen an outpouring of sensationalist books, motion pictures, and television specials in which Jesus and the true origins of Christianity are barely recognizable. We might call this phenomenon "The Jesus Game," and here is how it is played: Begin with a general sketch of Jesus on the basis of the Gospels, but then distort it as much as you please. Add clashing colors, paint in a bizarre background, and add episodes to the life of Christ that could not possibly have happened. If the end result still faintly resembles the Jesus of the New Testament, you lose. But if you come up with a radically different—and above all, sensational—portrait of Jesus, you win.[79]

"The Jesus Game has been played ever since the pagan philosopher Celsus first helped set up the rules in the second century AD, but it has never been played with such enthusiasm."[80] And for good reason. Not only are post-truth people increasingly historically illiterate, but as the authors of *Reinventing Jesus: How Contemporary Skeptics Miss the Real Jesus and Mislead Popular Culture* note, "The icing on the cake is ready access to unfiltered information via the Internet and the influential power of this medium. The result is junk food for the mind—a pseudointellectual meal that is as easy to swallow as it is devoid of substance."[81]

Such is the case with pseudointellectual fast-food pontification that the incarnation of Jesus Christ is but a pathetic facsimile of earlier pagan mystery religions. A case in point may be found in the assertion—made famous by

Nobel laureate W. B. Yeats—that the incarnation of Christ directly parallels the Greek mythology of Leda and the swan.[82] As Zeus, having taken on the form of a swan, had intercourse with the virgin Leda, so the Spirit overshadowed Mary in the form of a dove. "In both scenes, according to Yeats, divinities, by impregnating mortal women, intervene in and transform cultural history."[83]

Purveyors of this sort of mythology employ biblical language and then go to great lengths to concoct commonalities. The alleged similarities as well as the terminology used to communicate them are clearly exaggerated. Parallels between the incarnation of Helen of Troy and the incarnation of Jesus Christ, as well as the terminology used to communicate such parallels, are an obvious stretch. And sadly, for the mystery religions this is as good as it gets.

In fact, the reason the mystery religions are so named is that they directly involve secret esoteric practices and initiation rites. Far from being rooted in history and evidence, the mysteries reveled in hype and emotionalism. Adherents not only worshiped various pagan deities but also frequently embraced aspects of competing mystery religions while continuing to worship within their own cultic constructs. Not so with Christianity. Converts to Christ placed their faith solely in "the one and only Son, who came from the Father, full of grace and truth."[84]

Those with a truly open mind should resist rejecting the incarnation *a priori*. Why? Because miracles such as the incarnation are not only possible but necessary in order to make sense of the universe in which we live. According to modern science, the universe not only had a beginning, but is unfathomably fine-tuned to support life. Not only so, but the origin of life, information in the genetic code, irreducible complexity in biological systems, and the phenomenon of the human mind pose intractable difficulties for merely natural explanations.

Thus, reason forces us to look beyond the natural world to a supernatural Designer who miraculously intervenes in the affairs of his created handiwork. In other words, if we are willing to believe that God created the heavens and the earth, we should have no problem accepting his incarnation in time and space. While many issues surrounding incarnation, such as the precise modes of interaction between Christ's divine nature and his human nature, transcend human understanding, the doctrine of the incarnation does not transgress the laws of logic.

To understand the logical coherence of incarnation, one must first consider human beings as icons of God. Because God created humanity in his own image, the essential properties of human nature are not inconsistent with his divine nature. While the notion of Zeus becoming a swan is self-evidently absurd, the reality that God became man is not.[85]

Moreover, it is more than intoxicating to reflect on the reality that as Christ is incarnate in the image of humankind, so humanity in Christ is being refashioned in the image of God. Those in Christ become by grace what the Son of God is by nature—"Children of God."[86] His divinity interpenetrating our humanity (see part two).

Suffice it to say, when we encounter those who cast aspersions on the miraculous nature of Christ's coming in the flesh, we would do well to remember that it is our responsibility to use well-reasoned answers as springboards or opportunities to demonstrate that the historical account of Christ's incarnation is not blind faith but rather faith founded on irrefutable fact.

NEW CREATION

As Christ is incarnate in the image of humankind, so those who are redeemed are being refashioned as new creations. "If anyone is in Christ, the *new creation* has come: The *old* has gone, the *new* is here!"[87]

Such a passage is conspicuous by its absence in such counterfeit religions as Islam. It is sheer absurdity to so much as suggest that someone can be a new creation in *Muhammad*. A Muslim might imitate Muhammad or idealize Muhammad, but the notion that they could be *in* Muhammad is self-evidently absurd.[88]

Not so with Christ. The Father's greatest gift to those saved through the death of his dear Son is the impartation of a new order of life. An order of life that is of the same quality as the life of Christ. For that is precisely what it is—the ingrafting of the life of Christ. Thus, to be *in* Christ is more than a changed life; it is an exchanged life—an impartation of life by which the incarnation continues.[89] To reiterate the words of the Apostle to the Gentiles, "If anyone is in Christ, the new creation has come: The old has gone, the new is here!"

Such newness is not relegated to the felicity of forgiveness and purification—though it is most certainly that. It encompasses the great and glorious grace by which the forgiven now live in intimate union with the triadic One.[90] This is not merely an objective truth to be cognitively apprehended. "Life in the Trinity" is a living reality to be comprehended experientially.[91]

The descent of the ineffable in incarnation provides the ladder of divine ascent by which fallen humanity may rise up to union with God—*and as such become new creations in Christ.* Those who are in Christ have been transformed into new creations. The image and likeness of God, once ruinously marred, is being miraculous restored.

It is not a famous counselor or teacher who is changing the sensibilities of the redeemed from one thing to another. No! It is Jesus himself turning the tin man into a true man. Yes, he is God. The One who spoke and the limitless galaxies leapt into existence. But he is also very much a man. Not one who is dead, but one who is alive forevermore. Not only alive, but actively transforming you and me into a likeness of himself.

"It is a root and branch change," proffered Charles Haddon Spurgeon, the prince of preachers. "It is not a new figuring of the visible tapestry, but a renewal of the fabric itself. Regeneration is a change of the entire nature from top to bottom in all senses and respects, and such is the new birth! Such is it to be *in* Christ and to be *renewed* by the Holy Spirit. . . . It is as though the former creature were annihilated and put away, and a something altogether new were formed from the breath of the eternal God."[92]

The theology of "New Creation" is unique to the historic Christian faith. Search as you may, you will not find it in counterfeit religions. Certainly not in Islam. There, one cannot be in Christ, for Christ is not God. Nor is there any need or room for the atonement of the cross. All you can hope for is that your good deeds outweigh the bad, that perhaps Muhammad may intercede on your behalf, or that based on an arbitrary judgment you may be granted forgiveness.[93]

How odious the crooked stick when laid next to the straight stick of Scripture. How crucial to counter counterfeits with the glorious reality that we may be transformed into new creations through Christ's coming in flesh.

ESCHATOLOGY

Eschatology is an intimidating word with a simple meaning—the study of end times. While the meaning of eschatology is simple to grasp, its importance is difficult to overemphasize. Far from being a mere branch in the theological tree, eschatology is the root that provides life and luster to every fiber of its being. Put another way, eschatology is the thread that weaves the tapestry of Scripture into a harmonious pattern. It is the study of everything we long and hope for!

Like eschatology, the word *exegetical* may at first sound daunting. Its meaning, however, is easy to comprehend. *Exegesis* is the method by which a student seeks to uncover what an author intended an original audience to understand. (In sharp contrast *eisegesis* is reading into the biblical text something that simply isn't there.)

I coined the phrase *Exegetical Eschatology* in my book *The Apocalypse Code: Find Out What the Bible Really Says About the End Times ... and Why It Matters Today* to underscore that above all we must be deeply committed to a proper method of biblical interpretation rather than to any particular model of eschatology.[94] The plain and proper meaning of a biblical passage should always take precedence over any particular eschatological presupposition or paradigm.

To highlight the significance of proper methodology, I use the symbol e^2 interchangeably with the phrase *Exegetical Eschatology*. In mathematics, the squaring of a number increases its value exponentially. Likewise, in eschatology, perceiving the text through the prism of proper exegesis increases its value exponentially. More to the point, e^2 precludes fanciful eschatological interpretations that continue to subvert the faith of multiplied millions worldwide.

The writings of Bart Ehrman, professor of religious studies at the University of North Carolina, Chapel Hill, provide a sober illustration. In books and in lectures, on TV and in classrooms, Professor Ehrman depicts the historical Jesus as a false apocalyptic prophet who wrongly predicted that his generation would experience the end of history: "Jesus expected this cataclysmic end of history would come in his own generation, at least during the lifetime of his disciples. It's pretty shocking stuff, really. And the evidence that Jesus believed and taught it is fairly impressive."[95]

Inconceivably—particularly for a highly touted scholar—Ehrman uses the words spoken by Jesus as he sat on the Mount of Olives surrounded by his disciples as evidence of "a judgment that is universal," which "would affect everyone and everything." Said Ehrman, "This effect is spelled out in language that heightens its cosmic nature: 'the sun will be darkened, and the moon will not give its light, and the stars will be falling from heaven and the powers in the heavens will be shaken.'"[96]

Had Ehrman considered the language of the prophets, he may not have so imprudently accused Christ of being a false apocalyptic prophet. In comparing Scripture with Scripture, it is more than obvious that Jesus used the imagery of sun, moon, and stars to predict his coming in judgment, not his coming at the end of time. The prophets all spoke similarly. Using the metaphorical imagery of cosmic disturbances, they also predicted judgment in their generations. Take, for example, the words of Isaiah: "See, the day of the LORD is coming—a cruel day, with wrath and fierce anger—to make the land desolate and destroy the sinners within it. *The stars of heaven and their constellations will not show their light. The rising sun will be darkened and the moon will not give its light.*"[97] To those unfamiliar with apocalyptic prose, these words may well be taken to mean that the end of the world was at hand. In reality, Isaiah was using apocalyptic prose to predict that the Medes were about to put an end to the glories of the Babylonian Empire.[98]

The point here is that far from being undressed as a false prophet who mistakenly believed that the world would end within the generation of his disciples, Jesus rightly prophesied that their generation would see the destruction of Jerusalem and its temple. As heir to the linguistic riches of the Old Testament prophets, our Lord simply used familiar cosmic metaphors to pronounce judgment on Jerusalem, just as Isaiah had done to pronounce judgment on Babylon.

Ehrman, of course, is not unique in misconstruing the language of the prophets. Long before Ehrman's reckless pontifications, world-class philosopher Bertrand Russell communicated a similar sentiment in an essay titled "Why I Am Not a Christian." Jesus "certainly thought that His second coming would occur in clouds of glory before the death of all the people who were living at that time."[99]

Like Ehrman, if Russell had prudently considered the context of Scripture, he may not have presumptively pronounced Christ a false prophet. When Jesus spoke of "coming on the clouds of the sky, with power and great glory,"[100] he spoke of coming judgment. "Clouds" quite obviously are a common Old Testament symbol pointing to God as the sovereign judge of the nations. In the words of Ezekiel, "The day of the LORD is near—a day of *clouds*, a time of doom for the nations."[101] Or as Joel put it, "The day of the LORD is coming. It is close at hand—a day of darkness and gloom, a day of *clouds* and blackness."[102] Isaiah spoke similarly. "See, the LORD rides on a swift cloud and is *coming* to Egypt. The idols of Egypt tremble before him, and the hearts of the Egyptians melt within them."[103]

Certainly no one is so benighted as to think that *coming on clouds* in these examples is anything other than judgment language. Why then would anyone suggest that Christ's *coming on clouds* in the context of the Olivet Discourse is any different? We must inevitably ask ourselves whether it is indeed credible to suppose that Jesus, "heir to the linguistic and theological riches of the prophets, and himself a greater theologian and master of imagery than them all, should ever have turned their symbols into flat and literal prose."[104]

Common sense alone should have been sufficient to convince Russell that redefining the word "coming" to mean "second coming" and the phrase "end of the age" to mean "end of the world" is at best misguided. When Jesus said, "I tell you the truth, this generation will certainly not pass away until all these things have happened,"[105] his disciples did not for a moment think he was speaking of his second coming or the end of the cosmos. As conflicted as they may have been about the character of Christ's kingdom or the scope of his rule, they were well aware that with these words, Jesus was pronouncing judgment on Jerusalem and its temple.

In sum, Jesus, like the prophets before him, used the imagery of sun, moon, and stars to refer to the near-future judgment of Jerusalem. And while the judgment imagery of coming on clouds finds ultimate fulfillment in Christ's second coming, it was inaugurated in the holocaust of AD 70, precisely as Jesus had prophesied. When false eschatological paradigms are imposed on the text, its tapestry is undone and the loose ends dangle ignominiously. Ehrman, Russell, and a host of others have done just that. They have imposed fallacious meanings on eschatological passages, blemishing their tapestry and besmirching the prophetic legacy of Jesus Christ.

While it is fair to debate secondary aspects of eschatology, we must as Christians resist the teachings of all those who relegate Christ and his teachings to falsities. For as Christ came in judgment on Jerusalem, so too he will appear a second time to judge blasphemers. On that day, the righteous will be resurrected to eternal life and the unrighteous to eternal separation from the goodness and glory of God. Paradise lost will become paradise restored and the problem of sin and Satan will be fully and finally resolved.[106]

No Life Without Truth— No Truth Without Life

What we have seen thus far is that truth matters. Truth really, really matters! You and I have been commissioned to "always be prepared to give an answer to everyone who asks you to give the reason for the hope that you have." And to do "this with gentleness and respect."[107]

Moreover, we have been called to educate ourselves and our children in the art and science of biblical interpretation, to communicate that the Bible rightly understood is an immovable bulwark fueling our faith and shattering

the waves of skepticism and doubt. For "if," as Daniel Webster wisely proffered, "we abide by the principles taught in the Bible, our country will go on
prospering and to prosper; but if we and our posterity neglect its instructions
and authority, no man can tell how sudden a catastrophe may overwhelm us
and bury all our glory in profound obscurity."[108]

We have also come face-to-face with the criticality of countering counterfeit religions. Wrongly apprehended, this discipline might rightly be regarded
a never-ending tedium. Satan packages and repackages his lies in a wide variety of ways. Thus, rather than attempt to absorb every deviation of every
counterfeit, we are far better served to become so familiar with the main and
plain things of Scripture that when counterfeits loom on the horizon, we spot
them instantaneously.

Yet, being intellectually equipped is hardly sufficient. The Father's greatest gift to those who have been saved through the death of his Son is the
impartation of a new order of life, an order of life that is of the same quality
as the life of Christ. For that is precisely what it is. The impartation of the life
of Christ by which the incarnation continues. The descent of the ineffable in
incarnation provides the ladder of divine ascent by which humanity may rise
up to union with God. To "participate," as Peter put it, "in the divine nature."[109]

If we relegate the Christian experience to a headful of knowledge—
mental assent to logical truth propositions—we are in danger of devolving
into a transactional rather than transformational relationship with the
Lover of our souls. A transaction that offers heaven and avoidance of hell
yet strangely devoid of the transformational intimacy that Christ offers his
apprentices right here, right now. Not a mere headful of knowledge but active
participation in the kingdom of God. Entrance into the divine life of the Holy
Trinity. Union with the triadic One.

In *The Divine Conspiracy*, Dallas Willard recounts growing up in an area
of Missouri, devoid of electricity. During his senior year in high school, when
the transformational power of electricity became available, residents had
the choice to believe and rely on electricity or to continue living as before.
To "turn from their kerosene lamps and lanterns, their iceboxes and cellars,
their scrubboards and rug beaters, their woman-powered sewing machines

and their radios with dry-cell batteries." Incredibly, some refused to turn and "enter the kingdom of electricity." They "didn't want to change." They refused to believe in the reality of electricity.[110]

I found myself in a similar situation. I believed truth mattered, but the notion that I could participate in the divine nature was essentially lost on me. Electricity had come, but I continued to muddle along apart from its transformational reality. In a tragic twist, said Willard, "the souls of human beings are left to shrivel and die on the plains of life because they are not introduced into the environment for which they were made, the living kingdom of eternal life."[111]

And yet . . . and yet by the grace of God my shriveled condition was dramatically transformed as a result of hearing a three-word phrase on the way to a restaurant in Southern California.

PART 2

LIFE MATTERS MORE

After the Fall, human history is a long shipwreck awaiting rescue: but the port of salvation is not the goal; it is the possibility for the shipwrecked to resume his journey whose sole goal is union with God.

—VLADIMIR LOSSKY[1]

When I first heard the phrase "Life Matters More," I instinctively recoiled. "Truth Matters" was our DNA. For decades I had been providing *answers* on the *Bible Answer Man* broadcast because truth matters; teaching Christians the art and science of *biblical interpretation* because truth matters; countering *counterfeit religions* because truth matters. And now someone was telling me that life mattered more. The very notion sounded foreign—perhaps even offensive.

Yet these were the very words I heard as I walked toward a restaurant in Southern California with my dear Singaporean friend Elijah Widjaja. On my wrist I wore a blue band. Prominently etched on the band in white lettering was the motto of our ministry—"*. . . because Truth Matters.*" As we neared the restaurant, I slipped off the band and handed it to Elijah, thinking that if anyone would appreciate the significance of the white lettering on the bright blue backdrop, he would. Yet when I handed the blue band to Elijah he did not accept it as a gift. Instead, he handed it back to me along with three words. Words that would long haunt me. Words forever carved into the canvas of my consciousness. They struck with the force of a freight train. I still remember wondering how someone I respected so deeply could say something so outrageous. *Life matters more?!* Certainly not!

Elijah, however, is not easily dismissed. Time and time again he has spoken precisely the right words, in precisely the right circumstances. A treasure I do not take lightly. As Solomon wisely proffered, "Gold there is, and rubies in abundance, but lips that speak knowledge are a rare jewel."[2] Thus, I pondered the words *life matters more* in my heart.

In time, the meaning began to dawn on me. What Elijah wanted me to grasp as we walked toward the restaurant was that the meal mattered more than the menu. That the menu was necessary but wholly insufficient. That the menu was ultimately designed to direct me into an experience with food.

Elijah was not saying that truth was insignificant. Far from it. Time and time again I have witnessed his deep love for truth. Often when I bring a biblical passage into our conversations, he finishes it along with me. What he rightly identified was a far deeper reality. As a faithful friend, he knew that I was steeped in truth—that I could debate truth, defend truth, define truth—but that I was not experiencing life that is life to the full. The life that Jesus promised in saying, "I have come that they may have life and may have it abundantly."[3]

Furthermore, I had little or no concept of what the life that mattered more might entail. The very notion that it might involve what the early church designated as deification or union with God existed outside of my conceptional framework. And therein lies a problem that may well apply equally to you. Our personal paradigms function as *frames* and *filters*. A set of blinders, limiting our peripheral vision and screening out data incompatible with our existing conceptual structures and values.

In the deep-seated psychological need for meaning and security, we often allow immature and even tribal paradigms to become petrified—a hardening of the categories. We cling desperately to mental models of reality because of the terrifying uncertainty and sense of vulnerability that lurk outside the sanctuaries of our carefully constructed and defended theoretical systems. As such, we often confuse *translation* with *transformation*. Translation is *horizontal* growth (expanding knowledge at a particular level of personal development). Transformation is *vertical* growth—either breaking through to new heights of perspective or to new depths of understanding. The latter is often the result of paradigm shifts that trigger not just new sights but also new ways of seeing. New ways of looking at the world.[4]

For example, throughout most of human history, earth was believed to be the center of the universe. In recent centuries the notion of a heliocentric universe emerged. Now we know that the universe comprises trillions of galaxies, each replete with hundreds of billions of stars. What is more, we once perceived atoms to be indivisible. At present we know that they are composed of constituent parts—electrons, protons, neutrons, and the like. And even that has been called into question. Everything in the physical universe may well be reducible to fermions and bosons—the former what matter consists of; the latter what fields of force are composed of.[5] We once believed in the solidity of matter. It now appears that solidity is myth. All that appears solid is but empty space dotted with bundles of energy—wavelets of information.[6]

The point here is that our perceptual lenses are in desperate need of cleansing. As telescopes and microscopes uncovered truths about the universe previously unimaginable, so the transfiguration of Jesus unveiled realities concerning participation in the divine nature previously unthinkable. As modern technology has uncovered truths concerning the nature of matter, so Mount Tabor served to disclose new heights of perspective and new depths of understanding. When the disciples saw the face of Jesus shining like the sun, they came face-to-face with the poverty of their own paltry paradigms. Indeed, the notion that they might be transfigured like unto their Lord was as remote to them as nuclear physics to a nineteenth-century scientist.

Seeing the effulgence of his glory on Mount Tabor produced nothing less than a mega shift in perception. John became acutely aware that the glory God had given to Jesus, Jesus had "given to them."[7] As with the uncreated light that transfigured his Lord, John perceived that he, too, might be the repository of immaterial fire. In like fashion, Paul perceived that "we, who with unveiled faces all reflect the Lord's glory, are being transformed into his likeness with ever-increasing glory, which comes from the Lord."[8]

Before explicating life that is life in its fullest measure, I hasten to note that in saying life matters more, Elijah did not set up a false dichotomy. After all, Jesus not only declared himself to be the way to the Father but "the truth *and* the life."[9] Vladimir Lossky said it best: "Outside the truth kept by the whole Church personal experience would be deprived of all certainty, of all objectivity. It would be a mingling of truth and of falsehood, of reality and of illusion." Why? Because "the teaching of the Church would have no hold on souls if it did not in some degree express an inner experience of truth, granted in different measure to each one of the faithful."[10]

The point is this: there can be no life without truth, but above all, no truth without life.

The life that matters more is a realm largely inaccessible to our human apprehensions of truth. It involves a *mysterium* that is to be experienced rather than explained. While the divine incomprehensibility of the life that matters more is not a prohibition upon knowledge, it is the transcending of knowledge. The transcending of all philosophical speculation. Said Lossky, "Christian theology is always in the last resort a means: a unity of knowledge subserving an end which transcends all knowledge. This ultimate end is union with God or deification."[11]

DEIFICATION

Becoming gods by Grace

Just as the word of God became flesh, so it is certainly also
necessary that the flesh become word. For the word becomes
flesh precisely so that the flesh may become word. In other
words: God becomes man so that man may become God.

—MARTIN LUTHER[1]

I first wrote on deification in the early nineties in *Christianity in Crisis*. In a
chapter titled "Deification of Man," I noted that ever since the dawn of time
Satan has tried to peddle the lie that men can become gods. That his seductive
hiss "You will be like God" has reverberated across the ages with sensuous
frequency.[2] That he packages and repackages the lie in whatever size or shape
is needed to make it sell. I went on to provide distortions of deification in the
kingdom of the occult, the kingdom of the cults, and in corruptions within
Christianity.[3]

Some may well remember Shirley MacLaine's proclamation in the TV
movie *Out on a Limb*. With arms thrust skyward her cry echoed over pounding surf, "I am God! I am God!"

In *The Road Less Traveled*, M. Scott Peck, a psychologist popular in both cultic and Christian circles, put words into the mouth of the Creator. "God wants us to become Himself (or Herself or Itself). We are growing toward godhood. God is the goal of evolution."[4]

Well-known witch Margot Adler took it a step further. Quoting the Whole Earth Catalog, she said, "We are as gods and might as well get good at it."[5]

Notorious cult leader Rajneesh, who in Poona, India, took on the title Bhagwan Shree (meaning Sir God), had the temerity to announce, "When you call Jesus, really you have called me. When you call me, really you have called Jesus."[6]

Maharishi Mahesh Yogi, of Transcendental Meditation fame, sabotaged Scripture slipping in the word "you" for "I," and then proclaimed, "Be still and know that you are God."[7]

And the infamous Jim Jones, who personally led almost a thousand men, women, and children to violent deaths in Jonestown, Guyana, infamously avowed, "I'm a god and you're a god. And I'm a god, and I'm gonna stay a god until you recognize that you're a god. And when you recognize that you're a god, I shall go back into principle and will not appear as a personality. But until I see all of you knowing who you are, I'm gonna be very much what I am—God, almighty God."[8] Tragically, devotees drank the Kool-Aid.

In more conservative circles, Kenneth Copeland, then at the apex of his career, sought to convince devotees that "God's reason for creating Adam was His desire to reproduce Himself." Said Copeland, Adam "was not a little like God. He was not almost like God. He was not subordinate to God even."[9] Moreover, according to Copeland, God is "a being that stands somewhere around six-two, six-three, that weighs somewhere in the neighborhood of a couple of hundred pounds, little better, [and] has a [hand] span of nine inches across."[10]

Eventually, teachings on deification by Copeland and a host of similar prosperity preachers became so blasphemous, so bizarre, that even cultists pushed back. Mormon scholar Stephen E. Robinson (whose founder Joseph Smith declared that "God himself was once as we are now, and is an exalted man, and sits enthroned in yonder heavens"[11]) was among them: "Now, in fact, the Latter-day Saints would not agree with the doctrine of deification as understood by most of these evangelists, for in the LDS view we receive the full divine inheritance only through the atonement of Christ and only after a glorious resurrection."[12]

But here's where it got interesting. After cataloging heretical views on deification—and prior to providing a response—I wrote that just as there are counterfeits of deification, so, too, there is an authentic expression. I proceeded to underscore Eastern Orthodoxy as a case in point.[13]

Predictably, my affirmative reference to the Eastern Orthodox perspective on deification met with significant resistance from scholars within the Christian community, among them the brilliant Recovery theologian Kerry S. Robichaux. In an article titled "Can Human Beings Become God?" Robichaux provided the following corrective: "While many modern writers understand that Eastern Orthodoxy teaches deification as its central characteristic of salvation and find little fault with it, few admit that the doctrine relies solidly on [the] distinction between the essence and the energies of God."[14] Robichaux went on to cite me as a prime example.

Following an excerpt from what Robichaux described as my "very popular book *Christianity in Crisis*," he wrote: "Unfortunately, Mr. Hanegraaff's characterization of Orthodox deification is extremely evangelical in composure and does not do full justice to what Orthodox theology actually teaches."[15] (Or as Andrew Louth observed in a similar context, "Western attempts to understand [deification] have consequently assimilated it into an alien framework, and not surprisingly, it fits very awkwardly."[16])

As it turned out, Robichaux's clarification was not only instructive but along with Elijah's moniker—*Life Matters More*—proved to be providential! The title question posed by Robichaux—"Can Human Beings Become God?"—along with his dedication ("to the believer in Christ who suspects that there is *more* to Christian experience than modern Christianity lets on to")[17] piqued my interest to such an extent that I have since immersed myself in seeking a more adequate understanding of deification—which is in essence, "the experience of life."

Today a full decade and a half after my providential reading of Kerry

Robichaux's corrective, the priorities of my life have been radically re-arranged. To reframe what I wrote in the introduction, deification is God's greatest gift. It is the high peak truth of redemptive revelation, the Everest of experiential epistemology. It encompasses the great and glorious grace by which the forgiven now live in intimate union with the triadic One.

Robichaux said it well. "If our view of God's salvation is merely judicial, our experience is merely judicial; if it is merely ethical or moral, our daily Christian life is limited to a merely ethical or moral human life." However, "if we see salvation as becoming God in life, nature, image, and expression, our aspiration, our standard, and ultimately our experience will follow, and we will be, on this earth among our peers, God expressed. There will never be another God beside the unique and marvelous Triune God; that much is eternally true. But there will be for eternity to come an expression of Him that *is* Him, and the whole meaning and purpose of humankind will be achieved."[18]

Perhaps you have suspected "that there is more to Christian experience than modern Christianity lets on." If so, you are absolutely right. Recall the words of Orthodox theologian Vladimir Lossky. "After the Fall, human history is a long shipwreck awaiting rescue: but the port of salvation is not the goal; it is the possibility for the shipwrecked to resume his journey whose sole goal is union with God."[19]

The goal is not for the saved to remain within the port of salvation. Rather it is to continue on a journey whose sole goal is deification. It is to experience fellowship in the Trinity. As my friend Elijah has made plain over the years, deification is far greater than knowing about God as a logical truth proposition. It *is* the experience of life. All attempts to understand the Christian message from a solely rational perspective remain partial and inadequate.

As the esteemed professor of Patristic and Byzantine Studies at the University of Durham, England, Father Andrew Louth has well said, "deification has to do with human destiny, a destiny that finds its fulfillment in a face-to-face encounter with God, an encounter in which God takes the initiative by meeting us in the Incarnation, where we behold 'the glory as of the Only-Begotten from the Father' (Jn 1:14), 'the glory of God in the face of Jesus Christ' (2 Cor 4:6)."[20] Louth goes on to illustrate this existential reality in terms of two arches. A greater arch stretching from creation to deification and a lesser arch extending from the fall to redemption.

"The loss of the notion of deification leads to lack of awareness of the greater arch from creation to deification, and thereby to concentration on the lower arch, from Fall to redemption; it is, I think, not unfair to suggest that such a concentration on the lesser arch at the expense of the greater arch has been characteristic of much Western theology."[21] Deification, rightly regarded, preserves the reality that "God created the world to unite it to himself; it preserves the sense that the purpose of creation is to achieve union with God."[22]

Rightly understood, the arch of deification entails participation in the kingdom of heaven—likened by Jesus to "treasure hidden in a field. When a man found it, he hid it again, and then in his joy went and sold all he had and bought that field. Again, the kingdom of heaven is like a merchant looking for fine pearls. When he found one of great value, he went away and sold everything he had and bought it."[23] That treasure is divine life.

As respected apologist and author Dr. Scott Hahn put it, "Salvation is much more than most people believe and hope it could be. For we are not merely saved *from* sin; we are saved *for* sonship, to be divinely adopted sons and daughters of God. Forgiveness is the precondition for God's greater gift, the gift that will last beyond our death: the gift of divine life."[24]

Dr. Hahn went on to point out that "the early church Fathers were so bold as to call this process 'divinization' and 'deification,' because it is the means by which we enter the life of the Trinity." That sadly "this primal language of salvation has fallen into disuse in the Western Church." That "its decline began in the late Middle Ages, with the nominalist corruption of philosophy and then theology." That it is "present, though faintly, in the works of the Protestant reformer Martin Luther." And that "it is identifiable, but barely, in Luther's later contemporary, John Calvin; but that it vanishes entirely in subsequent generations of Protestantism."[25]

Hahn added that "even in the Catholic Church, the idea of divinization got lost amid all the post-Reformation disputes over the relationship of faith, works, and justification." That "Catholic and Protestant theologians alike focused so narrowly on these controversies that they obscured the central fact of Christian salvation." And that by the late nineteenth century, deification was not only dismissed as a pagan corruption, but that "the Bible's pristine and primitive message" was reduced "to the Fatherhood of God and the brotherhood of man."[26]

This, then, is why it is so crucial to refocus our attention on the great and glorious reality that as Christ participated in our humanity, so we participate in his divinity. This is the great exchange. "In the Incarnation the Son lowers himself to humanity so as to elevate humans to divinity. *In his kenosis is our theosis.*"[27] In his emptying is our filling.

In a fantastic resource titled *Life in the Trinity*, Donald Fairbairn described *theosis* as "the link between divine life and human life."[28] *Theosis*, translated "deification" in English, is also the word that I will use as my acronym in the pages that follow to explicate the meaning of deification in memorable fashion—beginning with the "T" in **T**-H-E-O-S-I-S, which will serve to remind us of *Theotokos*, who in her person exemplifies the quintessence of deification. Indeed, the *kenosis* of the new Adam presupposes the *theosis* of the new Eve.

The first Eve was deceived and became a sinner; the last Eve conceived and brought forth a Savior. She is the first to have achieved deification—and that, in an incomparable and impeccable way. St. Gregory Palamas well described our Panagia as "the boundary of created and uncreated"[29]—one who "has crossed the frontier which separates us from the age to come."[30] As such, the last Eve who bore in her body the last Adam is forevermore exalted as "more honorable than the Cherubim and incomparably more glorious than the Seraphim."[31]

She is the starting point of any proper explication of deification and the greatest exemplar of union with God there is, was, or ever will be.

THEOTOKOS—MOTHER OF GOD

Allow me to begin with a confession. For most of my Christian life, I lacked an appropriate appreciation for the grandeur and glory of the mother of my

Savior. My sin in this regard involved not merely a dearth of enthusiasm but consummate error as well.

When questions arose regarding the Virgin Mary, I would inevitably append my remarks by reminding my audience that she was a sinner just as we are—after all, did not Mary in her Magnificat overtly refer to Christ as "my Savior"?[32] In distinct contrast, when Elizabeth spoke of Mary following the Annunciation, she cried out in a loud voice saying, "Blessed art thou among women, and blessed is the fruit of thy womb. And whence is this to me, that the mother of my Lord should come to me?"[33]

More serious than dearth of enthusiasm was my denial of the perpetual virginity of the mother of our Lord. Whenever the occasion arose, I pointed out that the Bible explicitly tells us that Jesus had brothers and sisters. That Matthew's Gospel records the rhetorical questions of those acquainted with Jesus' immediate family: "Isn't this the carpenter's son? Isn't his mother's name Mary, and aren't his brothers James, Joseph, Simon and Judas? Aren't all his sisters with us?"[34] That there's no biblical precedent for rendering the Greek word *adelphós* (brother) or its feminine form *adelphae* (sister) as cousin. And had the New Testament writers wanted to designate Jesus' siblings as cousins, they would have used the word *anepsios*.

This, I now freely confess, was an egregious error. Both in Hebrew and in Greek the designation "brother" (or "sister") is appropriately used to refer to relatives as well. Jacob and Laban are called brothers, though Laban was in fact the uncle of Jacob.[35] And Abraham and Lot are called *adelphoì* (brothers) in the Septuagint or Greek rendering of the Old Testament used by New Testament apostles.[36] Therefore, there *is* a biblical precedent for viewing the Greek word *adelphós* as referring to a relative rather than brother.

I also wrongly argued that because Matthew tells us that Joseph did not have sexual relations with Mary *"until* she gave birth to a son"[37] we are justified in believing that Mary *did* have sexual relations with Joseph *after* the birth of Jesus. This was quite simply wrongheaded. In 2 Samuel 6:23 (2 Kingdoms 6:23) we read that "Michal the daughter of Saul had no child *till* the day of her death."[38] Quite obviously this is not meant to imply that Michal had children following her death. Many such examples could be given. But I'm sure you get the point. There is no warrant, apart from theological prejudice, for holding that Mary and Joseph had sons and daughters following the birth of our Lord and Savior Jesus Christ.

Whether Joseph was a widower who had children by a previous marriage and therefore the sons and daughters referred to in Scripture were stepchildren,[39] or the children referenced in the sacred text were the children of Joseph's brother Cleopas, who died and left them in the care of Joseph,[40] I cannot say with certainty. What can be said with a great deal of confidence is that if Mary and Joseph had had other biological children, Jesus, in concert with Mosaic Law, would have commended his sacred mother into their care. Instead, as Mary stood by the cross, the Son of the promise entrusted the ever-Virgin Mary to the care of his beloved disciple John—"And from that hour that disciple took her to his own home."[41]

Martin Luther once exclaimed, "a new lie about me is being circulated. I am supposed to have preached and written that Mary, the mother of God, was not a virgin either before *or after the birth of Christ*, but that she conceived Christ through Joseph *and had more children after that*."[42] In the case of Luther, it *was* a lie. In my case, it is true. While I have never supposed that Mary was not a virgin *before* the birth of Christ, I have both preached and written that Mary conceived children *after* the birth of Christ. And for that I am truly sorry.

The church has historically referred to Mary as "Our All-holy, immaculate, most blessed and glorious Lady, the Theotokos and Ever-Virgin Mary"—not to provoke us to worship the creature in place of her Creator, but to affirm the ever-Virgin mother of our Lord as the new Holy of Holies, in which the Shekinah glory of God dwelt in human form. Moreover, Mary is conceived of as the "new Ark of the Covenant, a created thing which somehow contained the uncontainable God." Thus, "the reason that St. Joseph the Betrothed (as tradition names him) did not enter into marital relations with her is that he understood her as one would understand the Ark, that she had been set aside for use by God, and that her womb had in some sense been made into a temple."[43]

The titles afforded the ever-Virgin Mother of God must never be dismissed cavalierly. Nor taken for granted. For within Mary is contained the history of God's economy. As Saint Dimitri of Rostov, well-known for his translation and publication of *The Lives of the Saints*, has aptly written, "One could ask why the Word of God delayed His descent to the earth and His incarnation to save fallen humanity." It is because from the fall of Adam, "it was not possible to find a virgin pure in body as well as in spirit. There was only one such, unique by her spiritual and bodily purity, who was worthy to become the Church and the temple of the Holy Spirit."[44]

From the fall of the first Eve, history awaited the fruit of the last Eve. The very passage that references humanity's fall provides—in embryo—the prophetic antidote. As the woman fell, so too a woman would bear a Second Adam through whom sin and Satan would be vanquished. Through whom we may experience what it is to be truly human. To share in the divine life. To walk again with God as a friend in the cool of the day. "The woman [Eve] was deceived and became a sinner."[45] The woman (Mary) conceived and brought forth a Savior.

The entire history of the old covenant, from the first Adam and Eve onward, is preparation for the incarnation of the last Adam conceived through the final Eve. While "the dogma of the immaculate conception is foreign to the Eastern tradition," the nature of the Mother of God was wondrously "purified by the Holy Spirit," thus throwing "open the way of deification to the whole creation."[46] Saint Gregory Palamas, who may well be dubbed the "doctor of deification," described Mary as "all-beautiful." In her God "brought together all the partial beauties which he distributed amongst other creatures, and has made her the ornament of all beings, visible and invisible; or, rather, He has made her a blending of all perfections—divine, angelic, and human; a sublime beauty adorning two worlds, lifted up from earth to heaven, and even transcending that."[47]

At times the honor given to the mother of our God quite naturally stretches into hyperbole. And not surprisingly so. If I describe my recently deceased earthly mother with a rhetorical flourish that exceeds the bounds of reality, how much more will I be prone to doing so when searching for adequate ways to describe "the first-fruits of the glorified Church"?[48]

HOLY FATHERS

As with the Holy Mother of God, I confess that I have not always had a sufficient appreciation for the Apostolic and Holy Fathers of the church. In *Resurrection*, I wrote about the apostles who faced the tyrant's brandished steel, the lion's gory mane, the fires of a thousand deaths because they knew that like their Master, they would rise from the grave in glorified, resurrected bodies.[49] Regrettably, I have written precious little about their successors.

Those like Polycarp of Smyrna and Ignatius of Antioch who surrendered their lives for the faith "once for all delivered to the saints."[50] Holy Fathers of the church who faithfully transmitted the teachings of the apostles. Expositors. Witnesses to life and truth. Deification. Fathers without whom we would not so much as have our treasured Bibles.

Apostolic Fathers such as Irenaeus who in his youth had listened to and learned from the teachings of Polycarp. Polycarp who in turn sat at the feet of the beloved apostle John. Apostolic Fathers who followed the Holy Tradition of apostles willing to sacrifice their all for the perpetuation of the faith once for all delivered to the saints. Fathers who counted their lives not worthy even to the point of shedding their own blood.

Upon the urging to the Roman proconsul to renounce Christ so as to save his life, Polycarp did not so much as blanch: "Eighty-six years have I served Him, and He has never done me wrong. How then will I now renounce the King who saved me?"[51] In the midst of a fiery death, Polycarp remained faithful to what he had received from those who had actually "looked upon and touched the Word of Life."[52]

Ignatius, friend of Polycarp and a disciple of Peter and John, upon approaching his own martyrdom, surrendered his body as "the wheat of Christ, ground by the teeth of beasts to become pure bread."[53] In life he experienced the Eucharist as the "medicine to immortality."[54] In death he experienced the congruent vicissitudes of victim and of victor. Like Polycarp, Ignatius resolutely passed forward the faith as Christ-bearer and "[partaker] of the divine nature."[55]

Irenaeus of Lyons, greatly influenced by Polycarp and contemporary of Ignatius, was likewise willing to lay down his life for the faith.[56] As the prodigious author of *Against Heresies*, Irenaeus clinically unmasked the dark underbelly of Gnostic heresy. "Like a surgeon performing a major operation, Irenaeus through his writings laid bare the nerves and sinews so as to take his reader to the very heart of a heresy with the sole purpose of healing the Church from such disease."[57]

For Irenaeus the sacred commission of the Apostolic Fathers was the proper transmission of Apostolic Tradition from one generation to the next—from the Holy Fathers onward to the eucharistic assembly of every local church in every successive generation. In the vernacular of Vincent of Lérins, *"we must hold what has been believed everywhere, always, and by all."*[58]

The Holy Tradition of the Apostolic Fathers was not "an independent instance, nor was it a complementary source of faith. Ecclesiastical understanding could not add anything to the Scripture. But it was the only means to ascertain and to disclose the true meaning of Scripture. Tradition was, in fact, the authentic interpretation of Scripture. And in this sense it was coextensive with Scripture. Tradition was actually Scripture rightly understood."[59]

Heretics have no key to the mind of Scripture. Thus, they turn it into a wax nose. They purpose, said Irenaeus, "to weave ropes of sand," and in so doing "dismember and destroy the truth." The manner of the heretic is "just as if one, when a beautiful image of a king has been constructed by some skillful artist out of precious jewels, should then take this likeness of the man all to pieces, should re-arrange the gems, and so fit them together as to make them into the form of a dog or of a fox, and even that but poorly executed." Worse yet, by drawing attention to the authenticity of the jewels, they "deceive the ignorant who had no conception what a king's form was like and persuade them that the miserable likeness of the fox was, in fact, the beautiful image of the king."[60]

In countering the devious rearrangement of incarnational jewels by the heretics of his day, Irenaeus offered up an authentic image of salvation—an image rightly portraying the glory of Christ's coming in flesh. In doing so, Irenaeus became the first of the Fathers to systematize what is known in Christian parlance as "the exchange formula" of salvation.[61] "The Word of

God, our Lord Jesus Christ, who did, through His transcendent love, become what we are, that He might bring us to be even what He is Himself."[62]

In contrast to the innovations of heretics, the Fathers were faithful perpetuators of life and truth. Thus, as the Holy Theotokos is, and forever will be, the greatest exemplar of deification, the Holy Fathers were the great expositors of this glorious experiential reality. Against the Gnostics who maintained that Jesus was merely a man, Irenaeus deftly employed the sacred text: "I said, Ye are all the sons of the Highest, and gods; but ye shall die like men." These words, said Irenaeus, apply "to those who have not received the gift of adoption, but who despise the incarnation of the pure generation of the Word of God, defraud human nature of promotion into God, and prove themselves ungrateful to the Word of God, who became flesh for them."[63]

Like Irenaeus, Origen of Alexandria (d. 254) deftly employed the biblical text to explicate the deification of the saints through participation in the divine nature. In his *Commentary on Romans,* Origen pointed directly to 2 Peter 1:4 to ensure the saints of their "participation in the divine nature" through "the fullness of love furnished through the Holy Spirit."[64]

To the extent that there are ambiguities in the writings of Origen,[65] there are none in the compact and memorable formulation of Athanasius of Alexandria who unambiguously asserted that *God* "was made man that we might be made God."[66] And this was not an isolated declaration. In refuting the Arian heresy, Athanasius adroitly employed "the terminology of deification in a new context—namely, to defend the full divinity of the Son and Spirit. He *assumes* that human destiny is to share in the divine nature and uses this to argue that the Son and Spirit *must be* divine if they genuinely give us a share in the divine nature."[67] Drawing on that which had been passed down from Origen, Athanasius reinforced deification as the "lynchpin that brings together the doctrine of the Trinity, the Incarnation of the Son, and our share in the Son through the Spirit given through baptism."[68]

It is instructive to note that though Athanasius will forever be linked to the famed aphorism—"God was made man that we might be made God"—this distinguished Alexandrian doctor valiantly defended such essentials of the historic Christian faith as the incarnation of our Lord and Savior Jesus

Christ. Moreover, Athanasius (in 367) was first to formally codify what today is universally accepted as the authoritative new covenant canon.[69] As Dr. Robichaux rightly reminded us, "Athanasius is far more than a minor figure in the Christian church; through his service our basic faith was unambiguously defined and thoroughly protected, and what we hold today as the normative documents of our faith were clearly identified under his leadership."[70]

As with Athanasius, St. Gregory of Nyssa is witness par excellence to the reality of deification.[71] In his *Great Catechism*, the esteemed Cappadocian Father notes that God left the heights of glory and "mingled with our nature in order that, by virtue of its mingling with the divine, our nature might become divine."[72] Saint Gregory carefully qualified deification by explaining that though human beings partake "of the properties of divinity," they never attain to God's "identity of nature."[73] "The archetype, the 'uncreated,' is 'unchanging by nature,' whereas the image, the 'created,' 'having existence from a change, is subject to alteration and does not remain absolutely in existence.'"[74] The bishop of Nyssa underscored the Eucharist as a principal means by which the believer becomes a partaker of the properties of deity.[75] By which the seed of divinity is sown into the corporate body of Christ. By which the body may exude with Solomon, "I am my beloved's and my beloved is mine."[76] And by which members of the body may as yet experience the "life that is life to the full."[77]

To do justice to the centrality of deification in the teachings of the Holy Fathers would require an entire volume in itself. This is so because deification was central to their message. In an instructive volume titled *The Divinization of the Christian According to the Greek Fathers*, Jules Gross "presents an extensive collection of citations from thirty-three Greek fathers of the early church (from a total of 184 works) in which they express their belief that human beings are deified in salvation. Gross's book reads almost like a general survey of the Greek-speaking church of the first eight centuries, for every significant teacher is quoted on the subject of deification, and the quotations are not insignificant asides by these writers but central statements of how they perceived salvation."[78]

The central theme of deification appears not only in the writings of

St. Gregory of Nyssa but in the works of all three Cappadocian Fathers. St. Basil conceives of the life that is life to the full as one of enduring and ever-increasing deification. "What is most desirable," wrote Basil, is "being made God."[79] Being transformed into God, according to St. Basil, is "a little like iron, which placed in the midst of fire, becomes fiery through the most intimate contact with it. Without ceasing to be of iron, it 'receives in itself the whole nature of fire and changes into fire as to color and activity.'"[80]

In concert with Basil the Great, Gregory of Nazianzus—preeminent theologian among the Cappadocians—clearly testifies to the reality of deification. Though going beyond his predecessors in the persistent application of deification, Gregory was ever careful to underscore that "deified, humankind could never cross the barrier which separates them from the Trinity."[81]

Often overlooked in elaborations on deification is the famed bishop of Hippo. Though his life and legacy are arguably best known of all the Holy Fathers, the articulate Augustine is least cited in elaborations concerning the grace of deification. And yet it was Augustine who memorably noted that "our first parents could not have been persuaded to sin unless they had been told, *You will be like gods*."[82] And that this "deifying union for which we have been made was the only promise able to entice our otherwise perfect protoparents. In one way, Augustine admits, the Enemy did not lie here at Genesis 3:5—for we shall be like gods—but the deception came through his feigning that such divinity was his to give."[83]

In an insightful article titled "No Longer a Christian but Christ," Father David Meconi, professor of patristic theology at St. Louis University, fleshes out Augustine's contention that we were not created "to be 'merely' human but in time to be invited to become even more than human (*ultra homines*) as the divine image and likeness in humans was fulfilled. In other words, Augustine's famous 'restless heart' points us to a human creature who remains incomplete and unsteady, stressed and stretched, until he realizes union with God."[84] For, said Augustine, "God wishes not only to vivify, but also to deify us."[85]

As the beloved John reminds us, the Father will forever have but one Son by nature; however, he has provided us with myriad graces by which we may genuinely become "children of God."[86] And, says Augustine, "If we are made

God's children, we are made gods: but this is through the grace of the one who adopts and not through the nature of the one who begets. For there is only one Son of God: our Lord and Savior Jesus Christ."[87]

As with Augustine, who exhorts us to imitate the love of God so as to truly become gods by grace, Maximus the Confessor exalts love as the enigmatic key to deification. "For nothing is more truly godlike than divine love, nothing more mysterious, nothing more apt to raise up human beings to deification."[88] Echoing Augustine, Maximus sees love as the vehicle by which "the whole of the human being is interpenetrated by the whole of God and becomes all that God is, excluding identity of essence. The human being receives to itself the whole of God and, as a prize for ascending to God, inherits God himself."[89]

The patristic scholar and prolific author Norman Russell has aptly noted that the Confessor's teachings on deification represent "the true climax of the patristic tradition."[90] And that "the Irenaean and Alexandrian principle that God became man in order that man might become god receives in his hands its greatest elaboration and most profound articulation."[91]

Like the Holy Fathers who preceded him, Maximus the Confessor suffered mightily for his fidelity to the faith. Not only did he endure imprisonment, but this sainted theologian was subjected to the unimaginable cruelty of having his tongue and right hand cut off. His legacy, however, has remained immutable. For long before his tongue was rendered mute and the eloquence of his right hand maliciously stunted, Maximus communicated Christ as the "origin, middle, and end of all time." That "the time preceding Christ is that of preparation for the incarnation, the time subsequent to Christ is that of the divinization of humankind."[92]

God became incarnate in the form of humanity that humanity might rise up to union with God. This, wrote the Confessor, is the very purpose for which God has created us, "that we may become partakers of the divine nature, in order that we may enter into eternity, and that we may appear like unto Him, being deified by that grace out of which all things that exist have come, and which brings into existence everything that before had no existence."[93]

Essence and Energies

Seven centuries after Maximus, Saint Gregory Palamas, archbishop of Thessalonica—who, like Maximus, was imprisoned for his unwavering commitment to truth—underscored the criticality of apprehending the ineffable distinction between the *essence* and the *energies* of the triune God. As the Trinity is simultaneously one and three, proffered Saint Gregory, "the divine nature must be said to be at the same time both exclusive of, and, in some sense, open to participation. We attain to participation in the divine nature, and yet at the same time it remains totally inaccessible. We need to affirm both at the same time and to preserve the antinomy as a criterion of right devotion."[94]

It may be helpful to reread the previous sentence—perhaps even more than once. While admittedly Saint Gregory's words are difficult, it is necessary to understand them. As I have consistently said throughout the course of my ministry, *virtually every single theological heresy begins with a misconception of the nature of God*. Theology is, after all, *the study of God*. Thus, to paraphrase the sentiment of Maximus in concert with Palamas and the Holy Fathers, "to know the mystery of the Trinity in its fullness is to enter into perfect union with God and to attain to the deification of the human creature: in other words, to enter into the divine life, the very life of the Holy Trinity, and to become, in St. Peter's words, 'partakers of the divine nature.'"[95]

What must be understood here is that we who take the sacred name of Christ upon our lips are compelled to recognize in God an ineffable distinction—a distinction other than that between his Oneness and his Triunity. This distinction, as Vladimir Lossky has explained, is the distinction between the essence of God and the energies by which he goes forth from himself, and by which he gives himself. "If we were able at a given moment to be united to the very essence of God and to participate in it even in the very least degree, we should not at the moment be what we are, we should be God by nature. God would then no longer be Trinity, but 'of myriads of hypostases'; for He would have as many hypostases as there would be persons participating in His essence. God, therefore, is and remains inaccessible to us in His essence."[96]

The energies that flow forth are therefore God himself but not according to his essence. Said Maximus, "God is communicable in what He imparts to us; but He is not communicable in the incommunicability of his essence."[97] Just as we make a distinction between the persons and the essence of the triadic One, so we rightly distinguish between his energies and his essence.[98]

In an attempt to make this comprehensible, the Holy Fathers illustrate the energies of God as "rays of divinity" penetrating the created realm—God being altogether existent in each ray of his divinity. Even apart from the existence of the universe, "God would none the less manifest Himself beyond His essence; just as the rays of the sun would shine out from the solar disk whether or not there were any beings capable of receiving their light."[99]

God needs no witness to the effulgence of his glory, yet "in His mercy and His infinite love He desires to communicate His blessedness, to create for Himself beings capable of sharing in the joyfulness of His glory."[100] As Lossky went on to elucidate, "this is the glory in which God appeared to the righteous in the Old Testament; the eternal light which shone through the humanity of Christ and manifested His divinity to the apostles at the Transfiguration. This is the uncreated and deifying grace, the portion of the saints of the Church in their life of union with God; this is the Kingdom of God where the righteous will shine forth as the sun (Matt. xiii, 43)."[101] Or in the prophetic prose of Habakkuk, "God comes from Teman, and the Holy One from Mount Paran [i.e., God arises from the east]. His splendor covers the heavens, and the earth is full of His praise. His radiance is like the sunlight; He has rays flashing from His hand."[102]

Such rays are not a mere abstraction—for the saints who experience deification participate in the life of God himself. As such, the energies of God manifest in our lives and are the divine life itself. "It is no longer I who live," said the Apostle to the Gentiles, "but Christ lives in me."[103] And this is the life that matters more.

In one vibrant image, St. Gregory likened the deified life to the vivid image of an earthen pot in a kiln:

> When a pot is in the kiln, it shares in the very life of the fire, taking on its hot and burning qualities, becoming capable of transferring that very "energy" to

something else. When removed from the fire, the pot still participates in the fire's effects . . . but it no longer participates in the "energies" of the fire itself. The participation in the "energies" of the fire is the truer participation than the participation in the effects. Thus, while all creatures participate in the effects of their creator, not all participate in God's very life; that is reserved for the saints, who have God not only as "maker," but also as "Father," through divine adoption.[104]

Through divine adoption we become by grace what the Son of God is by nature—"Children of God."[105] Gods by grace. Gods by participation in the divine nature. As I have noted previously, this scintillating truth has been historically illustrated by the thrusting of a sword into the red-hot flames of a furnace. As with a pot in a kiln, the steel of the sword takes on the properties of fire, such that gray steel turns fiery red; the sword never becomes the fire nor the fire the sword. This verity may likewise be illustrated by way of water and sponge. Though the sponge absorbs the ineffable waters of God's inexhaustible energies, it yet remains a sponge. The sponge does not become the water, nor the water the sponge.[106] Again, to be in Christ—to experience his divine life—is to experience his *energies*, not to partake of his *essence*. For no one can see God and live.[107]

A millennium before St. Gregory, St. Basil elaborated the self-same antinomy. "The energies are various, and the essence simple, but we say that we know our God from His energies, but do not undertake to approach near to His essence. His energies come down to us, but His essence remains beyond our reach."[108] As with the grasping of an unsheathed electric wire, seeking to grasp the essence of God is a prescription for certain death—for no one can see God and live; yet, the self-same wire covered and connected to a lamp is an energetic force by which we are empowered to experience illumination. The very illumination and life that Adam and Eve were created to experience in Paradise.[109]

OLD AND NEW TESTAMENTS

Over the span of my ministry, I have often referred to Genesis as a literary masterpiece. With inspired brilliance, Moses interlaced a historical narrative with symbolism and repetitive poetic structure. He employed the powerful elements of story (character, plot, tension, resolution) to set the foundation for the rest of redemptive history. Genesis opens with a literary mnemonic by which we are reminded daily of God's creative prowess. The first six days outline a hierarchy of creation culminating in humanity as its crowning jewel. On the seventh day, the Creator, in whom we ultimately find our sabbath, rests. As such, the history of creation is remembered and recalled through its association with the continuous seven-day cycle of life.

The rest of Genesis is structured in a way that it may be remembered using our ten fingers. With one hand we recall primeval history: the accounts of the heavens and the earth, Adam, Noah, Noah's sons, and Shem—father of the ancient Near East. With the other five fingers, we remember the accounts of Terah (father of Abraham), Ishmael, Isaac, Esau, and Jacob—who was renamed Israel. *What the genius of Genesis does not permit is for us to render its majestic tapestry as flat and literal prose.*[110]

No one understood that more clearly than did St. Ephrem the Syrian. In his *Commentary on Genesis*, Ephrem depicted "the paradise narrative as a paradigm of deification, an interpretive framework for the history of redemption, and a spiritual geography for the conceptualization of deifying union with God as the goal of the Christian life."[111]

In a brilliantly concise distillation, Dr. Thomas Buchan pointed out that in the writings of Ephrem, "paradise occupies and operates as a liminal space: it is the part of the created cosmos intended to serve as the venue for divine and human communion and as such it is special and set apart in relation to the rest of creation."[112] Ephrem imagines the Edenic garden as a mountain like unto Mount Zion—a mountain dwarfing all others. Its paradisiacal peak reaching to the very habitation of God. He "imagined that the Tree of Knowledge was planted halfway up the mountain, while the Tree of Life was located, with the Shekinah, at the mountain peak."[113]

If Adam and Eve had rejected the serpent, they "would have eaten from the tree of life and the tree of knowledge would not have been withheld from them; from the one they would have gained infallible knowledge and from the other they would have received immortal life. They would have acquired divinity with their humanity."[114] Instead they were exiled from the Edenic garden and from traversing the slope leading upward toward the peak of deification.

But "the rest of the story," as famed radio broadcaster Paul Harvey would have it, is that of a Second Adam who "clothed" himself in fallen humanity. "In his temptation and obedience on the mountain in the wilderness, Christ rehearsed the events and reversed the effects of Adam's temptation and disobedience on the mountain of paradise, rehabilitating human free will and reiterating the proper paradigm for its use." And, "it was above all in his death on the cross and resurrection from the dead that Christ returned Adam/humanity to the life of Eden."[115]

The wisest man who ever lived[116] rendered *wisdom*, "the fruit of the righteous," and "longing fulfilled," the proverbial "tree of life."[117] A tree that finds ultimate root in two gardens. In the ante-historical state, the Tree of Life stood at the apex of the Edenic garden. In the post-historical state, the Tree of Life is rooted in an eternal garden—a memorial to Paradise regained. "To him who overcomes," said Jesus, "I will give to eat from the tree of life, which is in the midst of the Paradise of God."[118] To experience deification throughout eternity.

And yet there is a Tree of Life of which we may presently partake. It stands on Golgotha's hill as the fulcrum of history. On it, Jesus stretched one hand toward the Edenic garden, the other toward the eternal garden. The deification the first Adam could no longer reach, the Second Adam touched in his place.[119] As such, the cross of Christ is the way forward toward deification. For on it hangs the eucharistic bounty. "The assembly of saints bears resemblance to Paradise," sang Ephrem, "in it each day is plucked the fruit of Him who gives life to all; in it, my brethren, is trodden the cluster of grapes, to be the Medicine of Life."[120]

While the Genesis narrative prefigures the prodigious arc reaching from creation to deification, Exodus provides the prototypical archetype. There God speaks "to Moses face to face, as a man speaks to his friend."[121] There it is that Moses scales Mount Sinai and reaches the summit of divine ascent. There it is, as St. Dionysius, convert of the apostle Paul, would have it, Moses "shuts his eyes to all apprehensions that convey knowledge, for he has passed into a realm quite beyond any feeling or seeing. Now, belonging wholly to that which is beyond all, and yet to nothing at all, and being neither himself, nor another, and united in his highest part in passivity with Him who is completely unknowable, he knows by not knowing in a manner that transcends understanding."[122]

Moses is, said the erudite Norman Russell, "lost in the vertiginous darkness of the presence of God—or rather of 'the place where he is' for God's presence eludes him." This is "the paradoxical nature of the soul's union with God. The soul is simultaneously separated from God and united with him, disoriented and cut off from all sensation and thought, yet belonging wholly to something that transcends even being."[123]

In Moses, we realize the earnest of the perfect man. A man ruling over his passions, having a share in the cosmic commandments of God. A man deemed worthy of divine rank because he is a friend of God.[124] A mediator between the human and the divine.[125] A man explicitly called a god unto Pharaoh.[126] A man whose face shone after talking with God.[127] A man who in life was transformed by the energies of God on Mount Sinai and in life after life was an eyewitness to the dazzling transfiguration of Christ on Mount Tabor.[128] A man who is the earnest of all who with unveiled faces will behold the glory of the Lord. Those, even now, being transformed into the same image from glory to glory by the Spirit of the Lord.[129]

As we make our way through the Old Testament, we encounter the vivid imagery of Israel as a bride prepared for union with her bridegroom. In divine embrace, the bride shares in the very life of the groom. A foretaste of the time when God breaks into history perfectly uniting divinity and humanity within himself. The time in which Jesus is revealed as the new Moses. The Moses who carries his beloved bride over the threshold of Jordan into the New Jerusalem coming down out of heaven from God.[130]

The culmination of the old covenant is found in the New Testament where Jesus, the quintessential Moses, authorizes his disciples to do the unthinkable—to address God as Father—thus revealing their adoption as sons.[131] The apostle John makes this explicit by rendering all those who have life in the incarnate Word "children of God"[132]—"Sons of light."[133] Such sonship is "born, not of blood, nor of the will of the flesh, nor of the will of man, but of God."[134]

Therefore, our adoption as sons and daughters is not a matter of genealogy, nor of natural birth, nor even of the will of humanity. But rather is a reflection of God's eternal purposes from the creation of the first man onward. Through adoption God's children become what they were designed to be—gods by grace. Not surpassing what it means to be human but satisfying what it means to be human—*becoming truly human.*[135] Thereby entering into a mystery, beyond all comprehension. As a sword thrust into the flames takes on properties of fire, so the nature of our humanity permeated by divinity takes on the properties of the divine nature.

This is the great exchange emphasized again and again in the New Testament. In incarnation, the Son of God becomes what we are so that we might become what he is. He emptied himself of heavenly glory to join humanity to his divine nature.[136] As the apostle Paul made plain to the Corinthian Christians, the grace of the Lord Jesus Christ was made manifest in that "though He was rich, yet for your sakes He became poor, that you through His poverty might become rich."[137] His *kenosis* is our *theosis.*[138] His poverty our riches.

The apostle Peter put an exclamation point on deification by designating new covenant Christians "partakers of the divine nature" as he himself is a "partaker of the glory that will be revealed."[139] Gods by grace, adopted sons and daughters, Christ-bearers. His divinity interpenetrating our humanity. His love, his strength, his glory. His righteousness.

Those who participate in the divine nature are destined to partake of the Tree of Life in the paradise of God. "Blessed are those who wash their robes, that they may have the right to the tree of life and may go through the gates into the city."[140] In the middle of that great city stands the Tree of Life, "bearing twelve crops of fruit, yielding its fruit every month. And the leaves of the tree are for the healing of the nations. No longer will there be any curse. The throne of God and of the Lamb will be in the city, and his servants will serve him. They will see his face, and his name will be on their foreheads."[141]

This, then, is the great arc of the biblical narrative. From the Old Testament to the New. From Genesis to Revelation. Creation to deification.

SEVEN ECUMENICAL COUNCILS

The great arch from creation to deification is at once an exemplar of truth and the experience of life. There can be no life without truth and no truth without life. In contrast to the gnostic, for whom knowledge is an end in itself, knowledge for the Christian is the means by which to experience a life transcendent to truth. A life of deification—of fellowship in the Trinity.

As Vladimir Lossky has aptly written, the battles for truth down through the ages were "dominated by the constant preoccupation which the Church has had to safeguard, at each moment of her history, for all Christians, the possibility of attaining to the fullness of the mystical union. So the Church struggled against the gnostics in defence of this same idea of deification as the universal end: 'God became man that men might become gods.'"[142]

In the first ecumenical council, the Council of Nicea (325), the church affirmed—against the Alexandrian priest Arius—"The dogma of the consubstantial Trinity; for it is the Word, the Logos, who opens to us the way to union with the Godhead; and if the incarnate Word has not the same substance with the Father, if he be not truly God, our deification is impossible."[143]

In the second ecumenical council, the Council of Constantinople (381), the church affirmed—against Macedonius, the Arian bishop of Constantinople—the equality and single essence of God the Holy Spirit with God the Father and God the Son. For if the Holy Spirit, as Macedonius contended, is a created power, and therefore subservient to God the Father and God the Son, our deification is rendered moot. Why? Because the "doer" in deification is the Holy Spirit with whom deified humanity joins its will so as to experience union with God. In addition to its significance respecting deification, the Council of Constantinople supplemented Nicea with five articles in which are set forth the theology concerning the Holy Spirit, the church, the mysteries, the resurrection of the dead, and the life of the age to come.[144] As such, the first two ecumenical councils formulated the Niceno–Constantinopolitan Creed, which serves as a template to the church for what "has been believed everywhere, always, and by all."[145]

In the third ecumenical council, the Council of Ephesus (431), the church affirmed—against *Nestorius,* archbishop of Constantinople—that the Virgin Mary is, and forever will be, *Theotokos*—bearer of God—as opposed to the heretical notion that she was merely *Christotokos*—bearer of Christ, a *man* in whom God dwelled as if in a temple. Without equivocation, the Council affirmed the apostolic truth that Jesus is true God and true Man. And that, therefore, the Virgin Mary is truly *Theotokos,* the Mother of God. For if Christ were not truly the God-man, we could not become gods by grace—"God in life and in nature, but not in the Godhead."[146]

In the fourth ecumenical council, the Council of Chalcedon (451), the church affirmed—against *Eutyches,* abbot of a monastery outside Constantinople—that Christ is one person with two natures in opposition to the heresy that the human nature of Christ was swallowed up by the divine nature "like a drop of wine in the sea."[147] As such, the church "rose up against" the "Monophysites ['one nature'] to show that, since the fullness of true human nature has been assumed by the Word, it is our whole humanity that must enter into union with God."[148]

In the fifth ecumenical council, the Council of Constantinople II (553), the church reaffirmed—against *Nestorius* and *Eutyches*—that Christ is forever one person with two natures. For if, in incarnation, Christ did not take on our humanity, we could not attain to the great and glorious promise of "participating in the divine nature."[149] Moreover, in concert with the first four councils, the Council of Constantinople II ratified the trinitarian and christological creeds that are yet regarded as normative by the major Christian confessions of both East and West. Even today—especially today—we may well say in concert with St. Gregory the Great: "Just as the four books of the holy gospel, so also I confess to receive and venerate four councils."[150]

In the sixth ecumenical council, the Council of Constantinople III (680), the church affirmed—against *Sergius,* ecumenical Patriarch of Constantinople—that Christ has two wills, the human will freely subject to the divine will. The church resisted the Monothelites ("one will") because "apart from the union of the two wills, divine and human, there could be no attaining to deification—'God created man by His will alone, but He cannot save him without the co-operation of the human will.'"[151] The significance of Constantinople III is embodied by Maximus the Confessor, who did not live to see his convictions vindicated. For in 662, some twenty years prior to Constantinople III, he was dismembered and died at the hands of a Monothelite emperor.

In the seventh and last of the great ecumenical councils, the Council of Nicea II (787), the church affirmed—against Byzantine Emperor *Leo III* and the iconoclasts (icon-smashers)—that far from violating the second commandment, icons are "the expression through a material medium of the divine realities—symbol and pledge of our sanctification."[152] The second council of Nicea convened by Empress Irene (widow of Emperor Leo IV, grandson of Leo III) not only exonerated iconodules (venerators of icons) but afforded icons their rightful place as windows into another world. A world of Christ and the cross. A world of saints and martyrs. An iconographic world of those deified by graces dispensed within the spiritual gymnasium, which is the body of Christ. As with other heresies condemned by the councils, the iconoclastic heresy exposed a false christology. For the invisible Word, who took on flesh, also sanctified visible realities—iconographic images of "the faith once for all entrusted to the saints."[153]

The Fathers of the Seven Ecumenical Councils never lost sight of our union with God. Under the guidance of the Holy Spirit they testified to the transcendence of trinitarian and christological truths—in harmony with the Scripture, and as they themselves had received them through Apostolic Tradition. Their authority was grounded in the church of the living God— "The pillar and foundation of the truth."[154] For, said Lossky, our deification "becomes impossible if one separates the two natures of Christ, as Nestorius did, or if one only ascribes to Him one divine nature, like the Monophysites, or if one curtails one part of human nature, like Apollinarius, or if one only sees in Him a single divine will and operation, like the Monothelites." For, "'What is not assumed, cannot be deified'—this is the argument to which the Fathers continually return."[155]

INCARNATION

All commentary on deification must inevitably fall prostrate before the greatest of all mysteries—the mystery of incarnation. When recapitulating the most famous patristic aphorism respecting the doctrine of deification— the Athanasian aphorism—great consternation is often appended to its conclusion. "God became man that *man might become God*."[156] In truth, the *mysterium tremendum et fascinans*[157] is more properly appended to the first clause in the aphorism. *God became man.*[158]

The more one contemplates the mystery of God becoming man, the more staggered the imagination. The thought that the One who spoke and trillions of galaxies leapt into existence should cloak himself in our humanity is, well, beyond all comprehension. To imagine that the One who knit me together in my mother's womb would himself inhabit Mary's temple boggles the mind. Yet this is precisely what Christianity proffers—a Creator beyond all comprehension who has revealed himself in incarnation. In the words of the Beloved Apostle, the Christ who was with God and who is God "became flesh, and dwelt among us, and we saw His glory, glory as of the only begotten from the Father, full of grace and truth."[159]

To Epicurean and Stoic philosophers, this was the height of absurdity. To Muslim philosophers, blasphemous. God "begetteth not, nor is He begotten."[160] Modern thinkers are similarly persuaded. *New York Times* columnist Nicholas Kristof sees the incarnation as reflective of the way "American Christianity is becoming less intellectual and more mystical over time." "The heart is a wonderful organ," said Kristof, "but so is the brain."[161] Smirking at incarnation, he swallows the odd predilection that nothing created everything.

Those who have a truly open mind must resist such obscurantism. Miracles such as incarnation are not only possible but necessary to make sense of the universe. Thinking otherwise is tantamount to the implausible contention that life sprang from nonlife. That the life that sprang from nonlife produced metaphysical realities including mind and morals. That the universe in all of its incomprehensible magnitude is but a function of time and happenstance.[162] And that, as evolutionary behemoth Carl Sagan once put it, "we live on an insignificant planet of a humdrum star lost in a galaxy tucked away in some forgotten corner of a universe in which there are far more galaxies than people."[163] Or to put it in the vernacular of Bill Nye, the ever-popular "science guy," "I'm a speck on a speck orbiting a speck among other specks amongst still other specks in the middle of specklessness. I am insignificant! I suck."[164]

For Sagan and his naturalistic offspring, our significance is a mirage. "Our posturings, our imagined self-importance, the delusion that we have some privileged position in the Universe, are challenged by this point of pale light. Our planet is a lonely speck in the great enveloping cosmic dark. In our obscurity, in all this vastness, there is no hint that help will come from elsewhere to save us from ourselves."[165]

But there is a hint. Far more than a hint. The heavens quite literally shout. "The heavens declare the glory of God; the skies proclaim the work of his hands. Day after day they pour forth speech; night after night they display knowledge. There is no speech or language where their voice is not heard. Their voice goes out into all the earth, their words to the ends of the world."[166]

Far from impinging on our significance, the vastness of the universe intensifies our significance. Your significance, my significance, our significance is found in the reality that Christ took on our humanity. That "God was pleased to have all his fullness dwell in him, and through him to reconcile to himself all things, whether things on earth or things in heaven, by making peace through his blood, shed on the cross."[167] "The image of the invisible God, the firstborn over all creation." He, by whom "all things were created: things in heaven and on earth, visible and invisible," created the vastness of the universe for us.[168] For us to explore throughout eternity. If the length of our days were a mere seventy or eighty years, we might rightly say that we are but "specks in the middle of specklessness." But we are created for eternity. An eternity of continuous new horizons, constant growth, and incomprehensible development.

By nature, we are finite, and that is how it always will be. Thus, we will never come to an end of learning; an end of exploration; an end of exhilarating new horizons. New galaxies. Moreover, what we now merely apprehend about the incarnate Christ, we will spend an eternity seeking to comprehend. Imagine forever exploring the depths of God's love, wisdom, and holiness. Imagine forever growing in our capacities to fathom his immensity, his immutability, his incomprehensibility, and his ineffability.[169] Imagine that we all "with unveiled faces" will forever "contemplate the Lord's glory," as we are "transformed into his image with ever-increasing glory."[170] Imagine! Imagine! Imagine!

A contrary refrain is no doubt stuck in your head as it is in mine. That of John Lennon who *imagined* a world of people living only for today.[171] We might, however, imagine a far more intoxicating reality. Imagine a universe "liberated from its bondage to decay."[172] Imagine learning and growing and developing without error. Imagine exploring the inexhaustible. *Imagine there is a heaven; it's easy if you try!*

Those who tout our "specklessness"—those who tout the "great enveloping cosmic dark"—are like children addicted to virtual reality. While all around there is a world full of realism and relationships left begging to be explored. Post-enlightenment thinkers have become "wretched flatlanders."[173] Stuck in the pyschoepistomological cocoons of their own fundamentalism. Far from considering the possibility that they might step through the wardrobe into Narnia, they mindlessly mouth Sagan's mantra: "the Cosmos is all that is or ever was or ever will be."[174]

Imagine this. God became man that man might become god! The echo of the Holy Fathers pounds at our psyches seeking to rid us of our obscurantism. Christ invaded time and space. He took on our humanity. That we might experience "the *perichoretic* movement" inherent to the "divinization of Christ's flesh." A movement "undeniably commenced by the divine nature of the Logos who 'united our nature to himself in a single hypostasis, without division and without confusion.'"[175] In "reciprocal movement, 'the image returns to the archetype,' who, in turn, imparts to it the divine life.'"[176] For Maximus, as for Athanasius, Irenaeus, and a great crowd of witnesses that even now surround us, "the whole of the human being is interpenetrated by the whole of God and becomes all that God is, excluding identity of essence. The human being receives to itself the whole of God and, as a prize for ascending to God, inherits God himself."[177]

The movement of all creation from the moment that God made the heavens and the earth to the moment he created man in his own image and likeness is a movement toward this goal. "For to this end did He make us," exuded the Confessor, "that we should become partakers of the Divine nature and sharers of His eternity; and that through deification, which proceeds from Grace, we might prove like unto Him. It is for the sake of deification that all existing things are constituted and abide, and all non-existing things are brought into being and come into being."[178]

While eternity awaits the effulgence of our deification, even now we may take hold of the life that is truly life. And in doing so experience the life that matters more.

SALVATION

I find it a glorious providence that I am typing these words on the eve of the annual Christmas celebration. And as I do, I cannot help but think of our Lord's words concerning the reason he condescended to cloak himself in human flesh. "The Son of Man came to seek and to save what was lost."[179] Salvation is what Jesus embodies. The Greek form of the Hebrew *Joshua*, meaning "Yahweh is salvation." Said Paul, "Christ Jesus came into the world to save sinners—of whom I am the worst."[180] Words I will repeat in liturgy a few hours from now before I partake of the pure body and precious blood of our Savior. "I believe and confess, Lord, that you are the Christ, the Son of the living God, who came into the world to save sinners, of whom I am the first."

As previously expressed, salvation means far more than being "saved *from* sin; we are saved *for* sonship, to be divinely adopted sons and daughters of God. Forgiveness is the precondition for God's greater gift, the gift that will last beyond our death: the gift of divine life."[181] Thus, it may be said with a certainty that, for we who were shipwrecked, the port of salvation is not the sole goal. The goal is the resumption of a "journey whose sole goal is union with God."[182] You and I are destined for fellowship in the Holy Trinity. Sharing in the life of God, as God has shared in our humanity. This, then, is the life that matters more.

The reason we rejoice is that the baby born to Mary on the first Advent was no ordinary child. As Matthew records, this baby was the ultimate fulfillment of Isaiah's prophecy of *Immanuel*—"God with us."[183] For Maximus as for the Fathers, "Incarnation and deification correspond to one another; they mutually imply each other. God descends to the world and becomes man, and man is raised towards divine fullness and becomes god, because this union of two natures, the divine and the human, has been determined in the eternal counsel of God, and because it is the final end for which the world has been created out of nothing."[184]

In order to achieve the salvation for which we are destined, it is "necessary to break through a triple barrier."[185] The "triple barrier" of which Nicholas Cabasilas (a contemporary of Gregory Palamas) wrote in a remarkable work titled *Life in Christ*. "The Lord allowed men, separated from God by the triple barrier of *nature, sin* and *death*, to be fully possessed of Him and to be directly united to Him by the fact he has set aside each barrier in turn: that of nature by His incarnation, of sin by His death, and of death by His resurrection."[186]

Perhaps in the noise surrounding modern-day Christmas celebrations, you still hear the faint echo of Isaiah's earth-shattering pronouncement. "The virgin will be with child and will give birth to a son, and will call him Immanuel."[187] And, "he will save his people from their sins."[188] Isaiah's prophetic words foreshadow the first broken barrier. The barrier of nature forever shattered by incarnation. The context of the prophecy is fraught with intrigue.

Ahaz, monarch of the tiny kingdom of Judah, is "shaken, as the trees of the forest are shaken by the wind."[189] He is in mortal terror of kings Rezin of Syria and Pekah of Israel who plot his ruin. Isaiah exhorts Ahaz to trust the Lord with all his heart and lean not on his own understanding (see Proverbs 3:5). "Keep calm and don't be afraid. Do not lose heart because of these two smoldering stubs of firewood."[190] Though faithless Ahaz greatly tried God's patience, the ever-faithful Almighty provided a sign guaranteeing Rezin and Pekah would come to ruin. "The virgin will be with child and will give birth to a son and will call him Immanuel," promised Isaiah. And "before the boy knows enough to reject the wrong and choose the right, the land of the two kings you dread will be laid waste."[191]

What God promised came to pass. Isaiah "went to the prophetess, and she conceived and gave birth to a son." Before the boy knew how to say "My father" or "My mother," Syria and Samaria were laid waste by superior Assyrian forces.[192] Despite God's providential care, Ahaz sought favor from King Tiglath-Pileser III of Assyria with resources pilfered from the temple treasury. Worse still, he abandoned temple sacrifice, going so far as to sacrifice his own sons to Assyria's pagan gods. As a consequence of sin, the salvation Ahaz experienced was only temporary. Ahaz was reduced to a mere puppet king, his every move controlled by the evil Assyrian Empire. One hundred and fifty years later, the temple itself suffered destruction and all Jerusalem lay in ruin. Yet God was not done with the people of the promise. Seven hundred years after faithless Ahaz, Matthew saw the temporary salvation of Judah as a type of the eternal salvation the people of God would experience through Jesus.

In his Gospel, Matthew elegantly unveiled the historical pattern of events surrounding the birth of Isaiah's son, which find fulfillment in the corresponding historical pattern surrounding the birth of Messiah. For although Isaiah's wife gave birth to Maher-Shalal-Hash-Baz in a fashion common to all humanity, the pattern reaches its climax in the miraculous virgin birth of Messiah. While Isaiah's wife did *not* give birth as a virgin, Mary most certainly *did*.[193] The first barrier then—that of a "flaming sword flashing back and forth to guard the way to the tree of life"[194]—is removed by Christ's virgin birth.

Furthermore, as Christ set aside the first of the triple barriers by his incarnation, so too he set aside the second by his death. As with the first barrier, it is Isaiah who commands our attention—this time in riveting our gaze on the canvas of Christ's death. "He was pierced for our transgressions, he was crushed for our iniquities; the punishment that brought us peace was upon him, and by his wounds we are healed."[195]

Isaiah portends Christ as a "tender shoot" coming forth from the stump of Jesse. "Despised and rejected by men," he "took up our infirmities and carried our sorrows." For "though he had done no violence, nor was any deceit in his mouth," the Lord "laid on him the iniquity of us all," "the punishment that brought us peace was upon him, and by his wounds we are healed." "Led like a lamb to the slaughter," the Servant of the Lord "bore the sin of many, and made intercession for the transgressors."[196]

Isaiah here foreshadows the suffering and death of Christ as the aim and the end of all Old Testament sacrifices—the antitype of the sin offering, the trespass offering, the Passover Lamb itself—silent before its shearers. Peter builds on the fulfillment of Isaiah's prophecy in asserting that Christ "himself bore our sins in his body on the tree, so that we might die to sins and live for righteousness; by his wounds you have been healed. For you were like sheep going astray, but now you have returned to the Shepherd and Overseer of your souls."[197] Zechariah adds this to the portrait: "They will look on me, the one they have pierced, and they will mourn for him as one mourns for an only child and grieve bitterly for him as one grieves for a firstborn son."[198]

As Theanthropos ("God-Man"), the spotless "Lamb of God" lived a perfectly sinless human life and died a sinner's death to sufficiently atone once for all for the sins of humanity. Without both natures, Christ's payment would have been insufficient. As God, his sacrifice was sufficient to provide redemption for the sins of humankind. As man, he did what the first Adam failed to do. For, "as in Adam all die, so in Christ all will be made alive."[199] Thus, through his death the second barrier—the barrier of sin—is forever set aside.

Finally, the sting of death itself, the third and final barrier, was forever voided through resurrection. Through the resurrection "the sting of death" has been "swallowed up in victory."[200] Here, as with the first two barriers, Isaiah prophetically looks forward toward the resurrection of "a man of sorrows, and familiar with suffering,"[201] as the earnest of our resurrection on the last day. "After the suffering of his soul," exudes Isaiah, "he will see the light of life and be satisfied."[202] In like fashion, our bodies will be resurrected from the dust of the ground. The mortal will be clothed with immortality.[203]

Isaiah's prophecy is pregnant with the promise of new birth: "Your dead will live; their bodies will rise. You who dwell in the dust, wake up and shout for joy. Your dew is like the dew of the morning; the earth will give birth to her dead."[204] It is from the dust that God created humankind;[205] it is to the dust humankind returns;[206] yet it is also from the dust that our DNA emerges as the pattern for resurrected bodies. The restoration of Israel points forward to the restoration of true Israel, and the restoration of true Israel is the earnest of every individual who realizes in Immanuel the promise of resurrection from the dead.

The typological relationship between the resuscitation of Israel and the resurrection of true Israel is seen with stunning clarity in Ezekiel's vision of dry bones scattered in a valley. Dry and discarded, the bones were in danger of disintegrating into dust. A poignant picture of the people of the promise—wasted and dead in exile and sin. Ezekiel prophesied as he was commanded and suddenly "there was a noise, a rattling sound, and the bones came together, bone to bone. I looked," said Ezekiel, "and tendons and flesh appeared on them and skin covered them, but there was no breath in them."[207] Again Ezekiel prophesied as he was commanded, and breath entered the bodies; "they came to life and stood up on their feet—a vast army."[208]

The interpretation leaves little to the imagination. God would open the graves and restore Israel. "I will put my Spirit in you and you will live, and I will settle you in your own land. Then you will know that I the LORD have spoken, and I have done it, declares the LORD."[209] The resurrection of Israel to the land, of course, is but a type of resurrection that finds ultimate fulfillment in the resurrection of the Lord—who is the locus of the land.

As such, Ezekiel's resurrection imagery finds ultimate resolution in the resurrection of Christ and the resurrection of *Christ*-ians. The antitype that fulfills the entire mosaic of Old Testament resurrection prophecies left no doubt about this coming resurrection: "Do not be amazed at this, for a time is coming when all who are in their graves will hear his voice and come out— those who have done good will rise to live, and those who have done evil will rise to be condemned."[210] If Christ had not himself been resurrected, the promise that he will resurrect dry bones in scattered graves would be as empty as the tomb guaranteeing its fulfillment.[211]

Lossky summed up our salvation in deification with typical eloquence and erudition:

> The way to union will henceforth be presented to fallen humanity as *salvation*.
> This negative term stands for the removal of an obstacle: one is saved from

something—from death, and from sin—its root. The divine plan was not fulfilled by Adam; instead of the straight line of ascent towards God, the will of the first man followed a path contrary to nature, and ending in death. God alone can endow men with the possibility of deification, by liberating him at one and the same time from death and from captivity to sin. What man ought to have attained by raising himself up to God, God achieved by descending to man. That is why the triple barrier which separates us from God—death, sin, nature—impassable for men, is broken through by God in the inverse order, beginning with the union of the separated natures, and ending with victory over death.[212]

Theotokos—the exemplar of deification
Holy Fathers—the expositors of divinization
Essence/Energies—an ineffable distinction
Old and New Testaments—the foundation
Seven Ecumenical Councils—the bulwark
Incarnation—in his *kenosis* is our *theosis*
Salvation—the bridge toward union with God

5

ECCLESIA

The Church as the Source of Life

No one can have God for his Father, who does not have the
Church for his mother.

—CYPRIAN OF CARTHAGE[1]

It must surely be the most iconic image in all of sports. It has been displayed
in thousands of venues. Corporate offices. Sports bars. Locker rooms. Even
palaces. If the picture is nowhere nearby, golf lovers need only close their eyes
and it will appear as if by magic on the canvas of their consciousness.

The portrait is that of Ben Hogan striking the shot heard around the world. The
pose is regal. The balance impeccable. Hogan's body elegantly uncoiled toward
the target. His club painting a perfect parallel across the horizon. Everything in
symmetry and equilibrium. Surreal—bordering on the miraculous.

What makes it all the more astounding is that the club Ben Hogan wields
is a one-iron. The most difficult of all golf clubs to master. As golfing great Lee
Trevino quipped (after actually being struck by lightning), "If you are caught
on a golf course during a storm and are afraid of lightning, hold up a 1-iron.
Not even God can hit a 1-iron."[2]

Only the rarest of golfers even countenance taking a one-iron to the course. Yet that is precisely the club Hogan wielded to perfection during one of the most epic moments in golf history. The story behind the story makes Hogan's one-iron wizardry all the more impressive. Scarcely a year before that spectacular strike toward the eighteenth green of the famed Merion East Course in Ardmore, Pennsylvania, Hogan was fighting for his life in an El Paso hospital.[3]

The year was 1949 and Hogan had arrived at the pinnacle of golfing fame. He had just won the PGA championship in Southern California and was looking forward to stepping into his dream home in Texas. As Hogan and his bride expectantly wove their way toward Fort Worth on a foggy February morning, a Greyhound bus passing a cargo truck on a narrow bridge collided with Hogan's Cadillac at fifty plus miles an hour.

Mere seconds before the impact, Hogan launched his body toward the passenger seat in a heroic effort to save the life of his wife. And in that instant saved his own. The steering column that would have impaled him throttled through the empty driver's seat instead.

Miraculously, Valarie walked away from the carnage without injury. Ben, however, was not as fortunate. His pelvis was severely splintered, his collarbone shattered, his ribs smashed, and his left ankle hideously broken. In acute agony, Hogan lapsed in and out of consciousness arriving in an emergency ward in life-threatening condition. For weeks he hung in the tenuous balance between life and death.

And then, against all odds, Hogan survived. After two torturous months in a hospital bed, he was finally wheeled into his dream home. Walking was but a distant memory. Playing even recreational golf, impossible. Competing for major championships, out of the question.

Yet, Hogan did walk again. And in 1950, scarcely a year following the near-fatal head-on collision, Hogan not only walked but won the prestigious U.S. Open Championship at Merion in almost miraculous fashion. Again and again his severely wounded legs seized up as he attempted to traverse Merion's brutally undulating fairways. Yet with iron will he persevered. And on June 10, on the final hole of regulation play, he hit that famous golf shot that graces countless walls around the world.

The point here is one of seismic proportions. Hogan's view of the near-miraculous one-iron to Merion's tightly guarded eighteenth green was vastly different from that of his most ardent admirers. In his words, "They are inclined to glamorize the actual shot since it was hit in a pressureful situation. *They tend to think of it as something unique in itself, something almost inspired,* you might say, since the shot was just what the occasion called for. I don't see it that way at all." Why? Because "I didn't hit that shot then—that late afternoon at Merion. *I'd been practicing that shot since I was twelve years old. After all, the point of tournament golf is to get command of a swing which, the more pressure you put on it, the better it works.*"[4]

From age twelve, Hogan committed himself to strict training. His over-all way of life prepared him to hit the iconic shot that crowned him a U.S. Open champion for life. Almost two thousand years prior to Hogan's feat, the apostle Paul drew a parallel between the kind of dedication displayed by Hogan in the kingdom of golf and that which must be displayed in the kingdom of God. "Everyone who competes in the games goes into strict training," said the Apostle to the Gentiles. "They do it to get a crown that will not last; but we do it to get a crown that will last forever. Therefore I do not run like a man running aimlessly; I do not fight like a man beating the air. No, I beat my body and make it my slave so that after I have preached to others, I myself will not be disqualified for the prize."[5]

Such was the kind of spiritual training manifest in the life of Polycarp. Like Hogan, he trained himself for the moment of truth. A moment that arrived in his eighty-sixth year. It was the second century of the Christian church and Asia was awash in persecution. With blinding rapidity, Roman scourges tore through the arteries of heroic martyrs. Martyrs stretched across sharp spikes. Fed to ferocious beasts. The blood lust of the pagan hordes seemed insatiable. But what they craved most was the torture of the man appointed by the apostles as bishop of the church of Smyrna.[6]

When they finally laid hands on him, they afforded Polycarp opportunity to blaspheme Christ. To worship Caesar as Lord and Savior. To repeat an invocation to the deities of pagan Rome. Polycarp, however, remained resolute. "Eighty-six years I have served him, and he never did me any wrong. How can I blaspheme my King who saved me?"[7]

Enraged, the proconsul threatened to throw Polycarp to the wild beasts. To have his ravaged body lit ablaze. Polycarp, however, remained unfazed. "You threaten a fire that burns for a time and is quickly extinguished. Yet a fire that you know nothing about awaits the wicked in the judgment to come and in eternal punishment."[8]

In fevered response, the pagan hordes gathered up logs and torches and forthwith ignited the blaze that consumed Polycarp's mortal body.

EUCHARISTIC ASSEMBLY

Like Hogan, Polycarp prevailed when it mattered most. But he did not do so in isolation. Rather, the pattern of his life was forged within the eucharistic assembly. In concert with Ignatius, who was likewise martyred,[9] he conceived of the church as an organic body. A body that "only realizes its true nature when it celebrates the Supper of the Lord, receiving His Body and Blood in the sacrament."[10] This, he believed, could happen only locally. "At every local celebration of the Eucharist it is the *whole* Christ who is present, not just a part of Him. Therefore each local community, as it celebrates the Eucharist Sunday by Sunday, is the Church in its fullness."[11]

The word *church*, as conceived of by Polycarp, meant far more than an organization. It is a life. This is precisely why I titled this chapter *Ecclesia*. The word *church* today has a decidedly pejorative meaning. Indeed, it may well conjure up crass images of pagan consumerism. The glory of ecclesia—*church life*—transposed by the glory of extravaganzas. The triumph of technique over truth. Style over substance. A novel brand of Christianity perfectly suited for a feel-good generation. The antithesis of what Christ had in mind when he said that "the gates of hell" would "not prevail against it."[12]

Even as I write I am reminded of a description of church encountered in a book titled *The Divine Commodity*. In it, author Skye Jethani vividly portrayed his experience in an all-too-typical modern-day church. "Wherever I looked flat-panel displays crammed my field of vision with presenters flashing their high-definition smiles. And the stage was alive, a mechanical beast to behold. It was moving fluidly, breathing smoke, and shooting lasers through its digital chameleon skin. The band members were spread across the platform as jagged teeth in the beast's mouth, and the drummer was precariously suspended from the ceiling like a pagan offering." As Jethani exited this expression of church, he was left to wonder whether this was "what Jesus envisioned. *Is this why he came, and suffered, and died? Is this why he conquered death and evil, so that we might congregate for multimedia worship extravaganzas in his name?*"[13] The answer is a resounding no! Church is not meant to be an extravaganza. It is a life. It is "the sphere wherein the union of human persons with God is accomplished."[14]

This sacred sphere—this unity of God and humanity—is inextricably woven together in the fabric of one cloth. As Saint Cyprian succinctly put it in *On the Unity of the Church*, "No one can have God for his Father, who does not have the Church for his mother."[15] This ought to be a self-evident truth. Why? Because it is through the church that God's saving power is mediated to the whole of humanity. Thus, "outside the Church there is no salvation, because *salvation is the Church*."[16] Christianity knows nothing of lone ranger Christians. To be baptized is to be born anew into a body of which Christ is the head.

Ecclesia is thus "the centre of the universe." The "sphere within which union with God takes place in this present life, the union which will be consummated in the age to come, after the resurrection of the dead."[17] It is the reincarnation of Eden. The place in which you and I may access the Tree of Life replete with its eucharistic bounty. A bounty by which our nature is unified with Christ and with other *Christ*-ians.

The Central Mystery of Ecclesia

The Eucharist (thanksgiving meal)—variously called Communion (union with Christ), Mass (mission), or the Lord's Table (1 Cor. 10:21)—is the central mystery of ecclesia. The central sacrament of the church. The source and the zenith of church life. By it we are changed from human multiplicity to one body in Christ, the temple of the Holy Spirit. As the revered doctor of the church Saint John of Damascus would have it, "if union is in truth with Christ and with one another, we are assuredly voluntarily united also with all those who partake with us."[18]

Within the eucharistic assembly, the church, "divine life flows into us and penetrates the fabric of our humanity. The future life is infused into the present one and is blended with it, so that our fallen humanity may be transformed into the glorified humanity of the new Adam, our Lord and Saviour Jesus Christ."[19] As such, Ignatius christened the Eucharist our "medicine of immortality and the antidote against death, enabling us to live forever in Jesus Christ."[20]

Far from a sacred drama, a mere representation of past events, the medicine of immortality "constitutes the very presence of God's embracing love, which purifies, enlightens, perfects, and deifies (2 Pet 1.4) all those who are invited to the marriage supper of the Lamb (Rev 19.9), all who through baptism and chrismation [Greek *chrismatis*, "anointing"] have been incorporated into the Church and have become Christ-bearers and Spirit-bearers."[21] Like the burning bush encountered by Moses, the Eucharist introduces into our being the fire by which we are inflamed yet not consumed. The fire by which we experience Pentecost in the present.

As in early ecclesia, so in the present, the Holy Spirit changes the bread and the wine into the pure body and precious blood of Christ—not physically but mystically. "In the Eucharist we are offered Christ's deified flesh, to which we are joined, without confusion or division, in order to partake of divine life."[22] As Palamas so poignantly put it, by the Eucharist, the church "is raised to heaven; that is where this Bread truly dwells; and we enter into the Holy of Holies by the pure offering of the Body of Christ."[23] By it, *the body of Christ* partakes of *the Body of Christ* and experiences life in the fellowship of the divine Trinity.[24]

Though a mystery, this is nevertheless grounded in the certainty of Christ. During the Last Supper, he took the bread and said, "Take, eat; this is My body." Thereafter, "He took the cup, and gave *thanks* [Greek, *eucharistēsas*], and gave it to them, saying, 'Drink from it, all of you. For this is My blood of the new covenant, which is shed for many for the remission of sins,'"[25]

For the first thousand years of church history, when the body of Christ was as yet undivided, the eucharistic assembly humbly took him at his word. "This is My body"; "this is My Blood." How this was so, no one could tell. The church simply confessed the real presence of Jesus Christ to be a great and glorious sacramental mystery.

Even after the Great Schism (1054), when the Eastern and Western churches were divided at the Table, the Eucharist was unanimously believed to be the *real presence of Christ*. This was likewise the conviction of Martin Luther. Though he was at the center of a second Great Schism—one that fissured the Western half of the church—he nonetheless remained unified with the ancient church respecting the matter of *real presence*.

Indeed, Luther went so far as to liken the presence of the sun in creation to the presence of the Son in Communion: "At Creation God ordained that the sun must daily rise and shine and give light and warmth to creatures. Just so the Lord Christ also ordained and commanded that in His church His essential body and blood are to be present in the Lord's Supper, not merely in a spiritual but also in a bodily and yet incomprehensible manner."[26]

The incomprehensibility of Christ's real presence was of little consequence to Luther. In a 1528 exposition on the Eucharist, he likened the enigma to the mysterious reality of Christ's incarnation.[27] For Luther, as for the early church fathers, the explanation was far less significant than the experience. Experiencing the real presence of Christ was tantamount to becoming one with Christ—and oneness with Christ was tantamount to oneness with the Father and the Spirit.

What this means from a practical perspective is nothing less than the *theosis* discussed in the previous chapter. In the words of distinguished fourth-century theologian Cyril of Jerusalem, "We become Christ-bearers, since His body and blood are distributed throughout our limbs. So, as blessed Peter expressed it, we are made partakers of the divine nature."[28] Cyril's words aptly codify the faith of the Fathers. As the venerable patristic scholar J. N. D. Kelly has well said, "the eucharist for the fathers was the chief instrument of the Christian's divinization."[29]

It should be noted here that while the first Great Schism split the body of Christ from East to West, it did little to fissure the centrality and substance of the Lord's Table. Not so the second Great Schism five hundred years after the first, which quite literally deformed the sacred sacrament. While Luther held fast to the real presence of Christ in the Eucharist, fellow Protestants such as Swiss reformer Huldreich Zwingli moved in an entirely different direction. In his infamous dialogue with Luther at the Marburg castle in Germany in 1529, Zwingli argued that the eucharistic meal was a mere commemoration of Christ's sacrifice and that the bread and the wine were purely symbolic.[30]

Luther considered Zwingli's rhetoric to be a gratuitous alteration of the words of our Lord, the writings of the apostles, and the witness of ancient ecclesia. Moreover, for Luther, taking our Lord at his word was far from unreasonable. "Why should not Christ be able to include his body within the substance of bread?" asked Luther. "Fire and iron, two different substances, are so mingled in red-hot iron, that every part of it is both fire and iron. *Why may not the glorious body of Christ much more be in every part of the substance of the bread?*"[31]

So certain was Luther of the real presence of Christ in Communion that he enjoined hearers to "let a hundred thousand devils, with all the fanatics, come forward and say, 'How can bread and wine be Christ's body and blood?' Still I know that all the spirits and scholars put together have less wisdom than the divine Majesty has in his little finger. Here is Christ's word: 'Take, eat, this is my body.' 'Drink of this, all of you, this is the New Testament in my blood.' Here we shall take our stand and see who dares to instruct Christ and alter what he has spoken."[32]

Despite biblical acumen and brilliant articulacy, the father of the Protestant Reformation largely lost in the battle for the real presence of Christ. While Zwingli was clearly dwarfed at Marburg, in the end his influence towered over the masses. Zwingli's categorical denial of the real presence of Christ spread like wildfire and is now the predominate position of Protestantism. Even within modern-day Lutheranism the real presence of Christ in the sacraments is broadly denied. Philipp Melanchthon, disciple of Luther, who at one time went as far as to advocate the death penalty for anyone who denied the real presence of Christ, in the end relegated the ubiquitous practice of the ancient church to be mere "bread worship."[33]

What Melanchthon uncharitably described as bread worship has now tragically devolved into bread neglect. And therein is the heart of the problem. Communion is not a moral tale; it is a miraculous truth—one by which the body of Christ is empowered to turn the world right side up.

As our Lord so plainly put it: "He who abides in Me, and I in him, *bears much fruit*; for without Me you can do nothing."[34] Life flows from the One True Vine to its outstretched branches. As such the branches are empowered to bear fruit. A branch cannot bear fruit separated from the vine. Nor can it bear fruit cut off from the other branches. "Whoever eats my flesh and drinks my blood *remains* in me, and I in him. Just as the living Father sent me and I live because of the Father, so the one who feeds on me will live because of me. This is the bread that came down from heaven. Your forefathers ate manna and died, but he who feeds on this bread will live forever."[35]

The unambiguous point here is that in order to remain alive spiritually one must *continuously* feed on the body and blood of Christ. Although the Gospel of John does not record the institution of Holy Communion, as do the other Gospels, his report of our Lord's words offer the clearest and most profound biblical understanding of the living power inherent in the real presence of Christ. When we partake of the Mystical Supper instituted by our Lord, we live in him and he lives in us. When we do not, we have no life. The words of our Lord are emphatic: "Most assuredly, I say to you, unless you eat the flesh of the Son of Man and drink His blood, *you have no life in you*."[36]

While there are other graces by which we may partake of the divine nature, there is nothing more needful to sustain the church in the wasteland of a warped and wicked world than the supernatural manna dispensed to us through the Eucharist. This manna is "appropriately called food of the soul, for it nourishes and strengthens the new creature. For in the first instance, we are born anew through Baptism. However, our human flesh and blood have not lost their old skin. There are so many hindrances and attacks of the devil and the world that we often grow weary and faint and at times even stumble. Therefore the Lord's Supper is given as a daily food and sustenance so that our faith may be refreshed and strengthened and that it may not succumb in the struggle but become stronger and stronger."[37]

Spiritual Gymnasium

While Ecclesia is principally the eucharistic assembly, it is not exclusively so. The church is simultaneously a spiritual gymnasium wherein which we are called to "gymnasize" ourselves unto godliness. Said Paul, "*Gymnasize* yourself to be godly. For physical training is of some value, but godliness has value for all things, holding promise for both the present life and the life to come."[38]

To execute the shot Ben Hogan hit in the white-hot glare of competition requires life practices honed far from the bright lights of fame. In like fashion, the selfless instinct to save the life of a loved one does not emerge in a vacuum. It reveals character trained and disciplined in the crucible of life. While millions may well dream of winning a U.S. Open, far rarer is the one willing to discipline body and mind for the moment of truth.

Hogan chose a particular way of life—a regimen of diet and discipline—that prepared him to reach the pinnacle of fame and fortune. Those who wish to emulate Hogan do not become Hoganesque by simply dressing like Hogan or imitating his mannerisms. Instead, they become Hoganlike through mental and physical discipline. Similarly, those who wish to emulate Jesus Christ do not become Christlike by simply taking on the trappings of Christianity, nor do they win the good fight by merely mouthing Christian slogans.[39] Instead they become Christlike by offering themselves to God as "living sacrifices."[40] Prayer, study, and fasting characterized the life of Christ. In like fashion, such spiritual disciplines honed in the spiritual gymnasium must characterize the lives of those who sincerely desire to become Christlike.

Spiritual disciplines are, in effect, spiritual exercises. As the physical disciplines of weightlifting and running promote strength and stamina, so the spiritual disciplines promote righteousness. Tom Landry, former coach of the Dallas Cowboys, is often quoted as saying, "The job of a football coach is to make men do what they don't want to do in order to achieve what they've always wanted to be."[41] In much the same way, said Donald Whitney, "Christians are called to make themselves do something they would not naturally do—pursue the Spiritual Disciplines—in order to become what they've always wanted to be, that is, like Jesus Christ."[42]

To reduce the spiritual gymnasium to the crass specter of pagan consumerism is to give birth to an unholy church. Such an ecclesia is "an abomination, hell's laughter, heaven's abhorrence. And the larger the church, the more influential, the worse nuisance it becomes when it becomes unholy. The worst evils which have ever come upon the world have been brought upon her by an unholy church."[43]

In C. S. Lewis's *The Screwtape Letters*, Uncle Screwtape is displeased with Wormwood because his patient has become a Christian. However, says Screwtape, "There is no need to despair: Hundreds of the adult converts have been reclaimed after a brief sojourn in the Enemy's camp and are now with us. All the *habits* of the patient, both mentally and bodily, are still in our favour."[44] Screwtape knew full well that converts who failed to embrace the spiritual gymnasium would likewise fail to become Christlike. Put another way, unless and until a convert embraces the spiritual disciplines, there is no need for the forces of darkness to be alarmed.[45]

In his classic *The Spirit of the Disciplines*, Dallas Willard noted that "one of the greatest deceptions in the practice of the Christian religion is the idea that all that really matters is our internal feelings, ideas, beliefs, and intentions. It is this mistake about the psychology of the human being that more than anything else divorces salvation from life, leaving us a headful of vital truths about God and a body unable to fend off sin."[46]

Western Christians have majored on believing right things about Christ, but many have sadly neglected to become his imitators. How is it that multiplied millions can take the sacred name of Christ upon their lips and yet fail to transform the world? If a cup of salt can transform a quart of water, cannot a majority of Christians transform the masses?[47] The problem I fear is that the salt submerged in the water is as yet in ziplock bags. Closed communities in which we profess faith in the death of Christ but have little concept of the power inherent in his life.

Paul put the emphasis where it rightly belongs: "If, while we were God's enemies, we were reconciled to him through the death of his Son, how much more, having been reconciled, shall we be saved through his life!"[48] What that means practically speaking is that we are to embrace all of the practices that Christ modeled during his earthly sojourn. To make his overall way of living our own. Thus, if Jesus often withdrew to lonely places to pray, we must do so as well. If Jesus studied the scroll of Isaiah, so must we. If Jesus abstained from the pleasures of food and drink for a season so as to feast on uncreated energy, we must follow in his train. In short, the practices of Christ's life must become our very own.

A word of caution is in order before looking at some of the life practices by which we may experience the *dunamis* (power) of God. Such practices must never be relegated to external demonstrations of religiosity. For when they are, they become little better than the practices of Pharisees and teachers of the law. "Everything they do," said Jesus, "is done for people to see: They make their phylacteries wide and the tassels on their garments long."[49] God forbid that we should emulate their practices. The goal of spiritual disciplines is internal transformation. Only this can truly satisfy.

While myriad disciplines beg our attention, none is more vital than prayer. But before I delve into this discipline, let me begin with some true confessions.

PRAYER

To begin with, let me confess a primary fear. Starting with prayer as the foremost of life practices may tempt some to tune out. To skip forward to a spiritual discipline that seems more intriguing. Less common. Perhaps abstinence, which is perceived to be not nearly as pedestrian as prayer. Please don't do it! Prayer is primary to life practices in that it marshals us into continuous communion with the Lover of our souls. It is the principal practice through which we experience being filled with the presence and power of God. Nothing is more transformational!

Here's another confession. Whenever I write on the subject of prayer, I feel a certain sense of inadequacy. Not because I do not know the subject well, but because I have not always been as vigilant in personal prayer as is prudent. In truth, I often feel like the man who complains about prayer being involuntarily taken out of the schoolhouse all the while voluntarily neglecting it in my own house.

And while I'm at it, one more confession (I'm sure there are others). In encountering examples of great women and men of prayer, I am often discouraged rather than encouraged. Why? Because of how unlike them I am! When I wake up in the morning and the responsibilities of yet another pressure-packed day rush through my mind like a menacing avalanche, I simply grit my teeth and strap on my boots and power through the day imbued by my own fragile energies.

Little by little, however, there has been change. I am succumbing to a power—an energy—beyond my own. The roaring of the avalanche is being muted by a mighty rushing wind. The "tin man," to use a C. S. Lewis illustration, is being turned into a real man. Dare I say it? I am being transfigured into a "son of God." Said Lewis, "The real Son of God is at your side. He is beginning to turn you into the same kind of thing as Himself. He is beginning, so to speak, to 'inject' His kind of life and thought, His *Zoe*, into you; beginning to turn the tin soldier into a live man."[50]

It is not a famous counselor, pastor, or teacher that is changing my sensibilities from one thing to another. No! This is Jesus himself turning the tin man into a true man. Yes, he is God. The One who spoke and the limitless galaxies leapt into existence. But, he is also very much a man. Not one who is dead, but one who is alive forevermore. And not only alive, but active. Actively transforming you and me into a likeness of himself.

Lewis pulls no punches. Christ, he said, is turning you into "a different sort of thing; into a new little Christ, a being which, in its own small way, has the same kind of life as God; which shares in His power, joy, knowledge and eternity."[51] How? To begin with, through prayer. To pray is to experience union with God. Like a branch united to the vine. As the apostle Paul put it, "anyone united to the Lord becomes one spirit with him."[52] Such union is a "profound mystery."[53] When we are joined with Christ, we have life. When we are not, we experience a kind of spiritual death. Thus, saints in the faith hall of fame (Hebrews 11) would more gladly experience physical decapitation than spiritual separation. And yet without the primacy of prayer, spiritual separation is as inevitable as is nighttime following day.

In light of the majesty of union with God through prayer, allow me to offer a pattern of prayer that has been revolutionary in my personal union with God. Each day afresh I begin with the prayer that our Lord taught his disciples to pray. Following the Lord's Prayer—or what I prefer to call the Prayer of Jesus—I transition into a prayer pattern I have dubbed the Facts Prayer Guide. Thereafter I "continue steadfastly in prayer"[54] by means of the Jesus Prayer, which has empowered me to discipline my wandering and often anxious mind.

The Prayer of Jesus

Perhaps you recall the scene. The disciples gathered around Jesus, urgency sketched on their faces. They had watched him withdraw to secluded places and marveled at his serenity in the aftermath. They did not know what caused their Master's face to glow. But one thing they did know. Whatever it was they wanted it. And they wanted it *now*.

One of them, perhaps Peter, assumed the role of spokesman. Impetuously he blurted out, "Lord, teach us *now* to pray."[55] And that is precisely what Jesus did. He taught his disciples a prayer that is deftly divided into two parts. The first is focused on God's glory. Thus, we pray, "Hallowed be your name, your kingdom come, your will be done."[56] The second is focused on our requests. In the words of the great early church ecclesiastical writer Tertullian: "How gracefully has the Divine Wisdom arranged the order of the prayer; so that *after* things heavenly—that is, after the 'Name' of God, the 'Will' of God, and the 'Kingdom' of God—it should give earthly necessities also room for a petition!"[57]

Following the heavenly petitions, Jesus taught his disciples to pray, "Give us today our daily bread"—everything necessary to sustain us body and soul. "Forgive us our debts [trespasses], as we also have forgiven our debtors [those who trespass against us]"—a daily acknowledgment of the infinite price that was paid so that we might be forgiven. "And lead us not into temptation, but deliver us from the evil one."[58] The last petition a reminder that God is in control of all things, including the temptations of Satan. While our "enemy the devil prowls around like a roaring lion looking for someone to devour,"[59] he is, after all, a lion on a leash the length of which is determined by the Lord.

Jesus made every word count. The prayer he taught his disciples to pray is a treasure of incalculable value. The words beckon those snorkeling with burnt backs to descend into its glorious depths. There await unfathomed resources and riches that can scarcely be described to those paddling on the surface.[60] While the Prayer of Jesus must never be regarded as a prayer mantra, it is a prayer manner beginning with the glorious privilege of addressing the Creator of the universe as "Father."

Our Father in heaven. To the disciples, the very phrase must surely have bordered on the scandalous. They were not even permitted to utter the name of the One who dwells in unapproachable light, much less refer to him as "Father." Yet this is precisely how Jesus teaches his followers to address God. There is, of course, a catch. As John explained, only those who receive Jesus and believe on his name have the right to refer to God as "Father."[61] In one sense, Jesus is the only one who can legitimately address God as Father, for he is uniquely God by nature. Nonetheless, as the apostle Paul explained in Romans 8, we who are led by the Spirit of God are not illegitimate children but actual members of his family by grace. By grace, we are becoming what God is by nature. Thus, we who have received "the Spirit of adoption" may cry out, "Abba, Father."[62] Quite literally "Papa, Father." Said Paul, "we are God's children. Now if we are children, then we are heirs—heirs of God and co-heirs with Christ."[63] Daily I thank our Father in heaven that while he is far beyond my comprehension, he has granted me the privilege to call him Father, and not only my Father but "our Father."[64] For by his grace I am a member of the Father's family, a living stone in a spiritual house of which our Lord is the head.[65]

Hallowed be your name. To pray "hallowed be Your name"[66] is to put the emphasis exactly where it belongs. Our daily lives must radiate a far greater commitment to God's nature and holiness than even our own needs. Thus, to pray "hallowed be Your name" is to ask that our heavenly Father be given the unique reverence his holiness demands; that his Word be preached without corruption; that our churches be led by faithful pastors and priests, and preserved from false prophets; that we be kept from language that profanes his holiness; that our thought lives remain pure; and that we cease from seeking honor for ourselves and instead seek that his name be glorified.

In the words of Saint Augustine, "This is prayed for, not as if the name of God were not holy already, but that it may be held holy by men; that God may so become known to them, that they shall reckon nothing more holy, and which they are more afraid of offending."[67]

> Today, once again, I thank you, dear Father, that I may be among those through whom your name is made holy, not just for today, but for the ages of ages.

Your kingdom come. In teaching us to pray, "Your kingdom come,"[68] Jesus is teaching us to petition our heavenly Father to expand his rule over the territory of our hearts. He is calling us to renounce our deal with the Devil and pledge our allegiance to expand his kingdom rather than our own. To pray "Your kingdom come" is to pray that God would use our witness for the expansion of his kingdom. C. S. Lewis was right. This world is "enemy-occupied territory" and "Christianity is the story of how the rightful king has landed, you might say landed in disguise, and is calling us all to take part in a great campaign of sabotage."[69] Christ has already won the war, but the reality of his reign is not yet fully realized.

At present you and I are sandwiched between the triumph of the cross and the termination of time—between D-day and V-day. "D-day was the first coming of Christ, when the enemy was decisively defeated; V-day is the Second Coming of Christ, when the enemy shall totally and finally surrender."[70] History is hurdling toward a glorious and climactic end when the kingdoms of this world will become the kingdoms of our Lord.

> O, Lord Jesus. O, Lord Jesus. O, Lord Jesus. Thank you that you are preparing the church as a bride beautifully dressed for her husband. And that one day the veil that separates your habitation from ours will be removed. What a grace to know that you will be available to us physically, as even now you are available to us spiritually. Your kingdom come!

Your will be done. In teaching his disciples to pray "Your will be done,"[71] Jesus focused their attention—and vicariously ours—on the sovereign wisdom of our Father in heaven. Truth is, we simply do not know how to reconcile all the converging factors of life. Thank God this world is under his control, not ours! One of the most comforting thoughts that can penetrate a human mind yielded to the will of God is that he who has created us also knows what's best for us. Thus, if we walk according to his will rather than trying to command him according to our own wills, we will have as he promised—not a panacea, but peace in the midst of the storm.

In the yielded life there is great peace in knowing that the One who taught us to pray "Your will be done" has every detail of our lives under control. We can rest assured that even in sickness and tragedy all things work together for good to those who love God and are called according to his purpose.[72] God will not spare us from trial and tribulation; rather, he will use the fiery furnace to purge the impurities from our lives.

Charles Haddon Spurgeon was severely afflicted with gout, a condition that brings on excruciating pain. In a sermon published in 1881 he wrote, "Were you ever in the melting pot, dear friends? I have been there and my sermons with me.... The result of melting is that we arrive at a true valuation of things [and] we are poured out into a new and better fashion. And, oh, we may almost wish for the melting pot if we may but get rid of the dross, if we may but be pure, if we may but be fashioned more completely like unto our Lord!"[73]

> *Dear Jesus, you know what is best for me; help me to trust you more today. To know that your way is the best way. Your will be done!*

On earth as it is in heaven. As previously noted, the Prayer of Jesus is divinely divided into two parts. The first is focused on God's glory. Thus, we pray, "hallowed be your name, your kingdom come, your will be done." The second is focused on our needs. And this is precisely how it should be. Jesus taught us to first reverence the realm of heaven and only then to turn our petitions toward earthly things.

The phrase "on earth as it is in heaven"[74] is a glorious reminder that the Shekinah glory that once filled Solomon's temple will of a certainty fill the new heavens and the new earth. "The earth will be filled with the knowledge of the glory of the LORD as the waters cover the sea."[75] Bethel, an ordinary place, became sacred space when Yahweh, the Creator of the heavens and the earth, appeared to the father of true Israel. Suddenly that which was ordinary became extraordinary. Bethel was transformed into the sacred space of God. "Surely . . . ," exuded Jacob, "this is none other than the house of God; this is the gate of heaven."[76]

Mount Sinai likewise became sacred space when Moses there encountered God's glory. "To the Israelites the glory of the LORD looked like a consuming fire on top of the mountain,"[77] for a glimpse of glory had been unveiled. Joshua encountered sacred space when he neared Jericho. Thus, the commander of the Lord's army said to him, "Take off your sandals, for the place where you are standing is holy."[78] The garden of Eden was the quintessential sacred space. For there it was that God walked with the parents of humanity in the cool of the day.

All of this is but a portrait of what will be when the veil between where God is and where we are is permanently removed. Moses trembled in fear when he encountered the presence of God within the burning bush.[79] Likewise, when the prophet Isaiah, the holiest man in Israel, "saw the LORD, high and exalted, seated on a throne; and the train of his robe filled the temple," he cried out, "Woe to me! I am ruined! For I am a man of unclean lips and I live among a people of unclean lips, and my eyes have seen the King, the LORD Almighty."[80] Yet when God's space and ours merge, all such terror will be no more. Our lips will be cleansed. Our hearts will be purified. We will touch the sacred mountain, the heavenly Jerusalem, without as much as a tinge of fear. We will "come to thousands upon thousands of angels in joyful assembly, to the church of the firstborn, whose names are written in heaven. [We will] have come to God."[81]

> *Lord Jesus Christ, Son of God, may your kingdom be established on earth as it is in heaven. And may I even now partake of the heavenly fruit so as to become one with you, saturated body and spirit in your divine life.*

Give us today our daily bread. As God dwells within us, filling us with his life and nature, so too he provides all that is necessary for the sustenance of our physical bodies and more. When we ask our heavenly Father to "give *us* today our daily bread,"[82] we pray in plural. Not only are we praying for our needs and those of our immediate family, but we are praying for the needs of our extended family as well. We do not pray as mere rugged individualists but as members of a community of faith. All we need do is turn on the television to see that our sisters and brothers around the world suffer daily from maladies ranging from drought to deadly diseases. Yet all too quickly these images fade before the next commercial interruption.

In Luke 12, Jesus told a "there are no moving vans following hearses" story. God had richly blessed a man whose priorities remained out of whack. His rhetoric was laced with self-interest—*my* grain, *my* goods, *my, my, my.* There was nothing wrong with how he had gained his wealth. No hint of impropriety. The problem was that he had purposed in his heart to "take life easy; eat, drink and be merry," and in the process he had become insensitive to the needs of others. The condemnation of our Lord was not only crisp and clear, it was downright chilling. "You fool!" he said. "This very night your life will be demanded from you."[83]

> *Oh, what a grace to live with eternity in mind. Lord Jesus, may we evermore be reminded that the bread we partake of, like the bread we dispense to those who are hungry, is symbolic of you, "the bread of life."[84] While the elements are physical, they are a spiritual reminder that we who may now partake of the divine nature will in eternity sit at the eternal banquet table with the very One who is the bread of life.*

Forgive us our debts, as we also have forgiven our debtors. As we pray, "forgive us our debts, as we also have forgiven our debtors,"[85] we may well be reminded of one of the most riveting parables Jesus ever communicated to his disciples. It was the story of two debtors. The first owed his master about twenty million dollars—more than he could pay if he lived to be a thousand. The second debtor owed the first debtor less than a twenty-dollar bill.

When the day of reckoning came, the master forgave the multimillion-dollar debtor every last penny. Instead of being overwhelmed with gratitude, the man who was forgiven much tracked down the man who owed little, grabbed him by the throat, and dragged him away to debtors' prison. When the master heard all that had happened, his condemnation was swift and severe. The ungrateful servant was thrown into prison to be tortured until he could repay his debt in full.

When Jesus finished telling the story, he turned to his disciples and said, "This is how my heavenly Father will treat each of you unless you forgive your brother or sister from your heart."[86] The words of Christ leave no room for ambiguity. "If you forgive other people when they sin against you, your heavenly Father will also forgive you. But if you do not forgive others their sins, your Father will not forgive your sins."[87] The debts we owe one another are like mere twenty-dollar bills compared to the infinite debt we owe our heavenly Father. Since we have been forgiven an infinite debt, it is a horrendous evil to even consider withholding forgiveness from those who seek it. If for a moment we might wonder whether to forgive our debtors, may this parable soften our hearts and illumine the darkness of our minds.

> *O Lord Jesus, may we ever be mindful that it was you who hung on the cross so that we might experience reconciliation in time and for eternity.*

And lead us not into temptation, but deliver us from evil. When you pray, "lead us not into temptation, but deliver us from evil,"[88] you should immediately remember to "put on the full armor of God, so that you can take your stand against the devil's schemes."[89] Clothed in the armor you are invincible. Without it, you are a guaranteed casualty.

From the primordial Garden to the present generation, the Devil and his hellish hordes have honed the craft of temptation. He knew just what to say to tempt Eve to fall into a life of constant sin terminated by death. And twice, the tempter found David's Achilles' heel and sent flaming arrows deep into his soul.

When we pray *"lead* us not into temptation, but deliver us from evil," we are acknowledging that God is sovereign over all things, including the temptations of Satan. Tertullian rightly characterized the evil one as the ape of God.[90] Likewise, Luther called the Devil, "God's devil."[91]

It is significant to note that Jesus was "led *by the Spirit* into the wilderness to be tempted by the devil."[92] Thus, while Satan was the *agent of the temptation*, God was *the author of the testing*. Satan used the occasion to tempt Christ to sin; God used the occasion to demonstrate that he could not sin.

The very fact that Jesus withstood the temptations in the wilderness is our guarantee that one day soon the kingdom will be ours. The tempter will be thrown into the lake of burning sulfur,[93] and temptations will be no more. We will enter the Golden City with divine assurance that "nothing impure will ever enter it, nor will anyone who does what is shameful or deceitful, but only those whose names are written in the Lamb's book of life."[94]

> *Dear heavenly Father, may I stand firm with the belt of truth buckled around my waist, with the breastplate of righteousness in place, and with my feet fitted with the readiness that comes from the gospel of peace. May I take up the shield of faith, with which to extinguish all the flaming arrows of the evil one. The helmet of salvation and the sword of the Spirit, which is the Word of God. And may I be empowered to pray in the Spirit on all occasions with all kinds of prayers and requests. For yours is the kingdom and the power and the glory forever. Amen!*

I'll say it again: the Prayer of Jesus is not a prayer mantra. It is a prayer manner. A means by which we may step out of the shallow tide pool of our hearts and plunge into an unbounded ocean of uncreated energy. A means by which we may transcend surface things and experience union with God. The Prayer of Jesus provides the doorway into an ever-deepening experience with the divine. Going deep involves making a major paradigm shift in our perceptions of prayer. Rather than a technique through which we can get God to meet our perceived needs, the Prayer of Jesus is a means by which we may attain a level of intimacy we may never before have imagined.

The Bible never encourages us to stamp out the self as the Buddhists do. It does, however, exhort us to stamp out selfishness. Genuine prayer is not found in our noisy askings and gettings; it is experiencing intimacy with the

Lover of our souls. Submersion into the divine nature. And our precious Lord provided the archetypal entreaty for doing that very thing.

> It is a model prayer and, as such, commends itself to the most superficial glance—approves itself at once to the conscience of man. It is beautiful and symmetrical, like the most finished work of art. The words are plain and unadorned, yet majestic; and so transparent and appropriate that, once fixed in the memory, no other expressions ever mix themselves up with them; the thought of substituting other words never enters the mind. Grave and solemn are the petitions, yet the serenity and tranquil confidence, the peace and joy which they breathe prove attractive to every heart.

> The prayer is short, that it may be quickly learned, easily remembered, and frequently used; but it contains all things pertaining to life and godliness. In its simplicity it seems adapted purposely for the weakness of the inexperienced and ignorant, and yet none can say that he is familiar with the heights and depths which it reveals, and with the treasures of wisdom it contains. It is calm, and suited to the even tenor of our daily life, and yet in times of trouble and conflict the church has felt its value and power more especially, has discovered anew that it anticipates every difficulty and danger, that it solves every problem, and comforts the Disciples of Christ in every tribulation of the world.

> It is the beloved and revered friend of our childhood, and it grows with our growth, a never-failing counselor and companion amid all the changing scenes of life. And as in our lifetime we must confess ourselves, with Luther, to be only learning the high and deep lessons of those petitions, so it will take eternity to give them their answer.[95]

I remember all too well the days in which praying for even ten minutes was unthinkable. I hurried into God's presence and, before my knees had even touched the ground, I was already thinking about getting back to my frenzied lifestyle. How things have changed. While there is so much more beauty to be explored, I now find myself losing all track of time in the presence of my Lord. And while the Prayer of Jesus is frequently the entryway, it is not the only way.

The F-A-C-T-S Prayer Guide, to which we now turn, has been a glorious shaft into the depth of an encounter with the divine.

The F-A-C-T-S Prayer Guide

The word *facts* serves as a marvelous structure for my daily prayer time. In place of merely snorkeling in the surface waters of prayer, *F-A-C-T-S* provides me a means by which I can dive deep beneath the tumult and turbulence of the ocean surface to a place that is silent and serene.[96] A place in which my harried requests may give way to the quiet of union with the Lover of my soul. Deep is where I can step out of the shallow tide pool of my own heart into the boundless ocean of God's power and presence. It is where I can go beyond surface things and plunge into a profound experience with my Creator.

To be honest, I learned to pray backward. I rushed into God's presence with a laundry list of prayer requests and then rushed back into my frenzied lifestyle. I treated my Lord with even more impatience than treasured loved ones.

In short, I was in desperate need of a paradigm shift. To begin with, I needed to make prayer a priority. To realize that prayer is a power source without which I would soon go dark.

Thereafter, I desperately needed a secret place. A place where I could withdraw from the invasive sounds of the world and tune in to the sounds of another dimension. Jesus was the ultimate example. Scripture says that he often "withdrew to lonely places and prayed."[97] Jesus longed to be alone with his Father in secret.

This raises an obvious question: Do you have a secret place? A place where you can drown out the static of the world and hear the voice of your heavenly Father? If not, consider finding one. My wife's place is in the sauna. Mine is walking. The issue is not location but motivation. We are all unique creatures of God. Thus, your secret place will likely be different from mine. The point is that we desperately need a place away from the frenetic static of this world so that we can tune in to the sounds of another place—another voice.

Once you have found your secret place (no need to be rigid), you are poised to begin your experience with God by focusing on the first letter of the acronym F-A-C-T-S, which will serve to remind you of the word *faith*. This for me is another wonderful entryway into prayer.

Faith. So here's how I typically begin: "*O, Lord Jesus. O, Lord Jesus. O, Lord Jesus! Once again, this morning, I place my entire trust in you. No place is safer than in your loving arms. I thank you, dear Lord, that you are always there as my refuge in the midst of life's storm . . .*" These words are not memorized. Nor do I begin each morning with the exact same phrases. I do, however, begin each day afresh with an expression of my faith in the One to whom I am praying. This is my constant daily reminder that faith is only as good as the object in whom it is placed.

Faith is ultimately rooted and grounded in the nature of God himself. And nothing is more crucial to a praying person than a proper perception of who God is. In Christian theology, he is portrayed as the Sovereign of the universe. He is described as spirit, perfectly wise, self-sufficient, omnipotent, and omniscient. The Bible depicts him as the One who sees all and knows all from all eternity, the One who wields supreme and absolute authority. Thus, in biblical vernacular, faith is *a channel of living trust—an assurance*—which stretches from a human being to their God. As such, it is the object of faith that renders faith faithful.

The greatest demonstration of faith is trusting God even when we do not understand. It is the sort of confidence exemplified by Job as he persevered in the midst of affliction, trusting God despite the whirlwind that threatened to blow his life into oblivion. Emotionally, he was on a roller coaster, his mind desperate for answers. Yet in the end he personified extreme faith by staking his fate and fortune on the trustworthiness of God. His eternal perspective forever enshrined in the words, "Though he slay me, yet will I hope in him."[98]

Faith is likewise demonstrated in the life of the apostle Paul, who not only fought the good fight but also finished the race and kept the faith. His faith, like that of Job, was fixed not on his temporary circumstances but on the trustworthiness of his Creator. The faith hall of fame in Hebrews 11 is filled with men and women who had faith in God even when they did not understand. Those who like Gideon, Barak, Samson, Jephthah, David, Samuel, and the prophets through faith conquered kingdoms; who have been tortured, jeered, and flogged; who have been chained and put in prison; stoned and put to death; destitute, persecuted, and mistreated; yet were commended for their faith—because their faith was fixed on God.

The faith that serves to protect us in the midst of life's storms is not to be confused with mere knowledge. Millions know that the biblical worldview corresponds to reality. Moreover, they acknowledge that it has served as the backbone of Western civilization. Yet they do not trust in what they know and acknowledge. Thus, they do not experience transformation.

People with pneumonia may know about penicillin. They may even agree that penicillin has saved millions. But until they take it, they demonstrate that they do not genuinely believe in it. And so it is with faith. Faith is more than mere *knowledge* and *agreement*; it involves living *trust*. Not faith in your own faith. But dependence on the Lover of your soul.

Nowhere is such faith in God expressed more beautifully than in the 139th Psalm (Psalm 138 in the Orthodox Old Testament). It ever reminds you that God has every detail of your life under control. "Even the very hairs of your head are all numbered. So don't be afraid."[99] I cannot tell you how often during dark times the words of this psalm flow through my mind like the balm of Gilead.

> O LORD, you have searched me
> > and you know me.
> You know when I sit and when I rise;
> > you perceive my thoughts from afar.
> You discern my going out and my lying down;
> > you are familiar with all my ways.
> Before a word is on my tongue
> > you know it completely, O LORD.
> You hem me in—behind and before;
> > you have laid your hand upon me.
> Such knowledge is too wonderful for me,
> > too lofty for me to attain.
> Where can I go from your Spirit?
> > Where can I flee from your presence?

If I go up to the heavens, you are there;

if I make my bed in the depths, you are there.

If I rise on the wings of the dawn,

if I settle on the far side of the sea,

even there your hand will guide me,

your right hand will hold me fast. (Ps. 139:1–10)[100]

Even now you may wish to pull out your Bible and finish this psalm of faith. Verses 15 and 16 are extraordinarily precious. "My frame was not hidden from you when I was made in the secret place. When I was woven together in the depths of the earth, your eyes saw my unformed body. All the days ordained for me were written in your book before one of them came to be."[101]

Knowing that God has every detail of my life under control—that he will "lead me in the way everlasting"[102]—provides a sense of faith. A sense of security and trust that makes life work. Faith in the arm of flesh is foolishness. Faith in the arms of our heavenly Father unfailing.

Such faith naturally leads to prayerful expressions of *adoration*.

Adoration. Prayer without adoration is like a body without a spirit. Not only is it incomplete, it just doesn't work. Through adoration we naturally express our genuine, heartfelt love and longing for God. Simply put, adoration is passionate admiration that culminates in awe, in reverence, and in the worship of God. As with our expression of faith, the way in which adoration is felt is new every morning. At times, our adoration involves the inexpressible experience of the presence of God—a mystery inexplicable to anyone else. Sometimes it is a function of what we experienced the previous day or even the previous moment. At yet other times it is fueled by an experience in the treasure store of Scripture.

The beauty of adoration is that it unshackles us from preoccupation with self and places our focus directly on the Sovereign of our souls. What is most marvelous about this is that in abject adoration of the Almighty we discover ultimate pleasure. Why? Because the greater the object of our worship, the more intense our enchantment. What I have personally found to be most helpful in expressing worship, praise, and adoration are the Psalms.

In them the ineffable glories of God spring forth in inspired and majestic adoration.

Psalm 145 stands out above the rest. It is memorably arranged in the Hebrew from *aleph* to *taw*—or as we might say in English, "from A to Z." This psalm (Psalm 144 in the Orthodox Old Testament) is literally an explosion of adoration. As with its memorability it quite naturally lends itself toward personalization. "*I* will exalt you, my God the King; *I* will praise your name for ever and ever. *Every day I will praise you* and extol your name for ever and ever."[103] God does not need our adoration. It is we who desperately need to adore him. Adoration propels us into participation in the divine nature. And to "participate in the divine nature," as Peter put it, is to "escape the corruption in the world caused by evil desires."[104]

In adoration, we escape tediousness and experience transcendence. This is particularly needful in an era in which we have experienced what William Placher has well titled "the domestication of transcendence."[105] Far from aiming at the domestication of God, we do well to adore the dominion of God—as King David exuded, "your dominion endures through all generations."[106] Oh, to know the unfathomable experience of union with God! "Great is the LORD and most worthy of praise; his greatness no one can fathom. One generation will commend your works to another; they will tell of your mighty acts. They will speak of the glorious splendor of your majesty, and *I* will meditate on your wonderful works."[107]

In our fast-food culture, we are forever looking for instant gratification. A cacophony of voices promises quick fixes and instant cures. In reality there are none. The secret to a successful marriage is found in the time spent developing a relationship with your spouse. The secret to raising kids is a function of the quality and quantity of the time spent interacting with them. The secret to a successful portfolio is directly related to understanding the fundamentals of the company in which you invest. The secret to a perfectly sculpted body is proper eating and exercise. And the secret to prayer is adoration. There we are lifted above the mundane and experience the supernatural.

To memorize a psalm of adoration, such as Psalm 145—and there are many such treasures in Scripture—takes effort. The reward, however, is nothing short of an experience with the living God. It is to experience life and to experience it more abundantly. If you do nothing else but incorporate this psalm into your prayer time, you *will* experience a spiritual revolution.

Confession. It is quite natural for your prayers to transition from adoration of God to confession of guilt. Indeed, one inevitably leads toward the other. When we touch the transcendence of God, we are inevitably reminded of our own unworthiness. This was precisely the case with King David. The story is poignant and profound.

In the days during which kings went to war, David stayed in the palace and lusted after another man's wife. After he had slept with Bathsheba, he sent orders to have Uriah killed so that he might have his wife. Thereafter he lived with Bathsheba in blissful denial. No accountability. His sin so covered up that only God could see.

Thus, the One whose eyes roam to and fro throughout the earth (2 Chronicles 16:9)—the One who sees all and knows all from all eternity—sent Nathan the prophet to the palace with a parable. There was a rich man who had an abundance of flocks and herds. And a poor man with but one little lamb—a lamb that he loved and cherished as though it were a daughter to him. One day the rich man stole that precious lamb and sacrificed it in feigned hospitality to a traveler.

When David heard of the rich man's debauchery, his anger was aroused. He demanded that the rich man restore fourfold what he had stolen and then be put to death. Nathan's response snapped David out of deep-seated denial. "You are the man who did this!" Though David had everything a man could ever want, Nathan continued, "you struck down Uriah the Hittite with the sword; you took his wife to be your wife, and you killed him with the sword of the sons of Ammon. Now, therefore, the sword shall never depart from your house."[108]

David's response is instructive. Shaken out of a deep sense of self-absorption, he confessed his sin beginning with the words, "Have mercy on me, O God."[109] As you read on, one thing becomes patently clear. Though God responded in forgiveness, the sword never left David's home. The consequences of his sin followed inexorably as night follows day. The message here must not be minimized. Though confession may cleanse our conscience, corruption carries its own consequences. Thus, we must never suppose that because we are being redeemed by the blood of the Lamb, we may as yet sin with impunity.

Like David, you and I are prone to live in denial. There are no doubt hundreds of sins of which we remain blithely unaware. Therefore, our need for confession remains great. Each morning afresh, the sins of the previous day must drive us from adoration to confession. Oh, what a grace! "If we confess our sins, he is faithful and just and will forgive us our sins and purify us from all unrighteousness." But "if we claim we have not sinned, we make him out to be a liar and his word is not in us."[110]

The sins of David, though egregious, yet have become a template for confession. In Psalm 51 he begs for the Lord's mercy, professes his sins, prays for cleansing, petitions for a pure heart, and pleads for a willing spirit to sustain him. If ever there was a passage to commit to memory, this is it! Perhaps you can pause for a moment even now and read it aloud.

Now imagine every verse followed by what is popularly referred to as "the Jesus Prayer": "Lord Jesus Christ, Son of God, have mercy on me a sinner." The Jesus Prayer is variously derived from such biblical pleas as that of the Gentile woman who so identified with the sufferings of her daughter that she cried out, "Have mercy on me, O Lord."[111] The ten lepers who lifted up their voices saying, "Jesus, Master, have mercy on us."[112] And the blind man who implored, "Jesus, Son of David, have mercy on me."[113]

While I will have more to say concerning the power and relevance of the Jesus Prayer later on, for now it is sufficient to echo the words of Frederica Mathewes-Green who has rightly proclaimed it "a spiritual discipline" akin to the repetitive practice of musical scales: "For a cellist, the tedium of practicing scales must appear so distant from the final goal, when that beautiful, dark music will spill forth fluidly. Yet, one day, the cellist will pick up her bow, and she and the instrument will have become *one*."[114]

Did you catch that? *One!* Union with God! Unction! Unbounded reservoirs absorbed as with a sponge! "Participation in the divine nature." Prayer no longer a burden. Or a duty. But a pleasure beyond compare. The cellist and the Creator become one. If you have never done so before, perhaps this very moment you can experience the first step in a lifelong journey toward oneness with Christ. For when you confess your sins as David did, God will purge your iniquities and infuse grace into your inner being:

"Have mercy on me, O God, according to your unfailing love; according to your great compassion blot out my transgressions."

Lord Jesus Christ, Son of God, have mercy on me a sinner.

"Wash away all my iniquity and cleanse me from my sin."

Lord Jesus Christ, Son of God, have mercy on me a sinner.

"For I know my transgressions, and my sin is always before me."[115]

Lord Jesus Christ, Son of God, have mercy on me a sinner.

As you continue in this way through the entirety of the fifty-first psalm, you may well discover that intolerance for prayer may soon become intoxication. If you will but confess in humility—with godly sorrow—not hiding your sin but purposing to amend your life, God *will* forgive and restore. If you have sinned a thousandth time, you have not come close to exhausting his grace.

Like the prodigal son, confess, "Father, I have sinned against heaven and against you. I am no longer worthy to be called your son." And the Father will as yet cry out, "Quick! Bring the best robe and put it on him. Put a ring on his finger and sandals on his feet. Bring the fattened calf and kill it. Let's have a feast and celebrate." Why? "For this son of mine was dead and is alive again; he was lost and is found."[116]

All is now thanksgiving. As you take stock of your life, confess your sins, and again partake of the Lord's Table, you may thank God for the grace that allows you to again participate in the life of an overcomer. *Thanks be to God!*

Thanksgiving. *Faith* is the entry way to prayer; *adoration* unshackles us from preoccupation with self; *confession* is the key to forgiveness; and *thanksgiving* is the gateway to righteousness. "Open for me the gates of the righteous; I will enter and give thanks to the LORD. This is the gate of the LORD through which the righteous may enter. I will give you thanks, for you answered me;

you have become my salvation."[117] As William Hendriksen has well said, "Prayer without thanksgiving is like a bird without wings."[118]

Scripture exhorts us to "enter his gates with thanksgiving."[119] Failure to do so is the stuff of pagan babblings and carnal Christianity. Pagans, said Paul, know about God, but "they neither glorified him as God *nor gave thanks to him*."[120] Carnal Christians likewise fail to thank God daily for his many blessings. They suffer from what might best be described as selective memories. They are prone to forget the blessings of yesterday as they thanklessly barrage the throne of grace with new requests every day. Oh, may we not follow in their path. May you and I, instead, be one of ten.

As he was on his way to Jerusalem, Jesus encountered ten men suffering the ravages of leprosy. "They stood at a distance and called out in a loud voice, *'Jesus, Master, have pity on us!'*" Having great compassion for their condition, Jesus healed them all. Yet only one of ten, upon recognizing his healing, "threw himself at Jesus' feet and thanked him." Immediately Jesus asked, "Were not all ten cleansed? Where are the other nine?"[121]

This may well be the question of the ages. Every day we experience the grace of God. Yet how many of us daily throw ourselves at the feet of Jesus and thank him? I personally am tremendously convicted even as I write these words. How many times has God answered my prayers? Directly! Specifically! Yet how few times I have thanked him!

Each new day we ought to approach God "overflowing with thankfulness" as we devote ourselves "to prayer, being watchful and thankful."[122] Such thankfulness is an action that flows from the sure knowledge that our heavenly Father knows exactly what we need and will supply it.[123] Thus, said Paul, we are to "rejoice always, pray continually, give thanks in all circumstances; for this is God's will for you in Christ Jesus."[124]

As with *faith, adoration,* and *confession,* I have found the Psalms to be a rich reservoir for my daily prayers of *thanksgiving.* While many psalms are tremendous templates for thanksgiving, Psalm 118 provides a particularly powerful treasury for giving thanks. As in the examples above, I often combine the Jesus Prayer with my prayer of thanksgiving. And as I do, I sense the connection of power cord and socket. As such, I experience "all his energy, which so powerfully works in me."[125]

Supplication. It is proper and right that our supplications tend toward the end rather than beginning of our prayers. For it is only in the context of a relationship with God that our requests make any sense at all. Imagine asking a complete stranger to pay for your dinner. Or imagine importuning a friend for help despite an obviously neglected relationship. Supplication only makes sense in the context of connection. It is akin to a child turning to her father with full confidence in his loving-kindness.

As Paul put it, "Do not be anxious about anything, but in everything by prayer and supplication with thanksgiving let your requests be made known to God. And the peace of God, which surpasses all understanding, will guard your hearts and your minds in Christ Jesus."[126] No anxiety, only peace. The purpose of supplication is not to pressure God into providing us with provisions and pleasures, but rather to conform us to his purposes. As we read in 1 John 5:14–15, "This is the confidence we have in approaching God: that if we ask anything *according to his will*, he hears us. And if we know that he hears us—whatever we ask—we *know* that we have what we have asked of him."

Note carefully that I have emphasized the words *"according to his will."* It is quite popular in contemporary Christian circles to disdain such a phrase. One Christian superstar went as far as to say, "Never, ever, ever go to the Lord and say, 'If it be thy will . . .' Don't allow such faith destroying words to be spoken from your mouth. When you pray 'if it be your will, Lord,' faith will be destroyed. Doubt will billow up and flood your being. Be on guard against words like this which will rob you of your faith and drag you down in despair."[127] Such teachings are spoken in the context of an ideology in which faith is a force, words are the containers of the force, and by your words you create your own reality.[128] This, however, is far from true. As noted previously, faith is only as good as the object in which it is placed. If faith is in faith, it is mere credulity. If, on the other hand, faith is placed in the providence of the supreme Sovereign of the universe, it is more than certain.

In what is perhaps the greatest literary masterpiece of all time—the majestic Sermon on the Mount—Jesus taught his disciples (and vicariously us) to pray, "*Thy will be done.*"[129] In the Garden of Gethsemane, he himself prayed, "My Father, if it is possible, may this cup be taken from me. *Yet not as I will, but as you will.*"[130] James, likewise, warned those who are prone to boast and brag that they ought to pray instead, "*If it is the Lord's will*, we will live and do this or that."[131] The apostle Paul earnestly prayed that "by God's will" he might have the opportunity to visit the believers in Rome.[132] Indeed, he encouraged the faithful in Rome to pray that "*by God's will*" he might join them in their city.[133]

As you and I pray, we must ever be mindful that the sovereignty of God is an overarching principle of Scripture.[134] We may genuinely be thankful that this world is under his control, not ours. We would be in deep trouble if God gave us everything we asked for! The truth is that we often don't know what is best for us. Years ago, Billy Graham's wife, Ruth Bell Graham, drove the point home emphatically. "If God had answered every prayer of mine, I would have married the wrong man seven times."

Indeed, one of the most comforting thoughts to a human mind yielded to the will of God is that he who has created us also knows what is best for us. If we walk according to his will rather than trying to command him according to our own, we will enjoy not a counterfeit panacea but what he promised: peace in the midst of the storm.

When you pray earnestly as Christ did, "Nevertheless not my will but thy will be done,"[135] we can rest assured that even in sickness and tragedy all things work together for good to those who love God and are called according to his purpose.[136]

Each new morning as I lay my requests before my God, I am reminded that he is indeed my Father, and that as my Father he cares deeply about every detail of my life.[137]

The Jesus Prayer

In 2000 I began writing *The Prayer of Jesus*.[138] It was published a year later and in 2002 rose to number one on the Christian Marketplace bestseller list. More importantly, it transformed my *personal* prayer life. Today, as I write—some fifteen years later—another prayer has become transformative. But in a different way. The Prayer of Jesus has become my entryway into God's presence every day. The Jesus Prayer is the means by which I remain *constant* in prayer throughout the day.

It is rooted in the notion that we are to pray constantly. In the words of Paul to the Thessalonians, "pray without ceasing."[139] To the Ephesians, "pray at all times."[140] To the Colossians, "continue steadfastly in prayer."[141] To the Romans, be "devoted to prayer."[142] The goal is to nurture nearness to God. It is to experience the presence of God as Moses did in the flames of fire within a bush that was not consumed. Said Moses: "The LORD our God is near to us whenever we pray to him."[143] Jeremiah said much the same. When he called upon the name of the Lord, the Ineffable "came near," saying, "Do not fear."[144] Zephaniah noted that the meek and the humble, those who trust in the name of the Lord, will have their lips purified so "that all of them may *call on the name of the* LORD and serve him shoulder to shoulder."[145]

Witness Lee, from whose progeny I first learned the practice, spoke often of the surpassing peace and joy that flows out of the habit of calling upon the name of the Lord.[146] It is food for the soul. Sustenance for the Spirit. A means by which, as Peter put it, we may partake of the divine nature.[147] Or in the wisdom of Paul, experience being "in Christ" and experience Christ being "in me."[148]

When we sin, we sever the power cord that connects us to our Maker. Calling on the name of the Lord repairs the severed cord. It reconnects us with the Lord of life and light. David's fevered cry, "Have mercy on me, O God,"[149] reconnected him to the Lover of his soul. And that cry echoed throughout the New Testament text is to be our cry as well. Recall the lepers who shouted, "Jesus, Master, have mercy on us."[150] Or the Canaanite woman who cried out, "Lord, Son of David, have mercy on me."[151]

Many other such examples could be cited. Even now I think back to Jesus' encounter with blind Bartimaeus. As he was leaving Jericho, Bartimaeus shouted, "Jesus, Son of David, have mercy on me."[152] Likewise, the despised tax collector in Luke's Gospel beat his breast continuously, crying out, "God, have mercy on me, a sinner."[153] All of these and many more serve as illustrations of sinful humanity crying out for mercy as they sink ever deeper into the cauldrons of their own sin. Sin that not only disconnects them from their Maker, but sin that multiplies suffering and sadness around the globe.

This, I believe, is why repeating the prayer, "Lord Jesus Christ, Son of the living God, have mercy on me, a sinner," is so significant. It provides a way back from the edge of the abyss. It is a way of building a lighthouse in the midst of the gathering storm. Unless we continuously ask for God's mercy, we are in danger of forgetting how desperately we need it. Perhaps this is the very reason that the Jesus Prayer has been so significant throughout the history of the Christian church. It is a "ladder of divine ascent."[154] A way out of the abyss, into the presence of God. In *The Way of a Pilgrim*, an anonymous nineteenth-century Christian practiced the Jesus Prayer until it became as natural as breathing. In the end, it became his gateway into the worship and enjoyment of God.[155]

All of this is but prologue to my own experience. For me the Jesus Prayer has become a game changer. When my wandering and all-too-often anxious mind spins out of control, the Jesus Prayer re-centers me on all that really matters. Often in the middle of the night I repeat the Jesus Prayer again and again. And as I do, my anxious mind becomes quiet and serene. It is as though each time the words flutter from my lips the *dunamis* of God is reawakened within me.

In the beginning I worried that I may be participating in what Jesus described as vain repetitions. The very thing that Jesus charged pagans with doing. "They think they will be heard because of their many words. Do not be like them."[156] Yet after I memorized this warning many years ago, I became aware that as prologue to the Prayer of Jesus, it is not intended to keep us from repeating such a transformative prayer, but rather a warning against the repetition of words that are vain. Empty words, meaningless phrases, insincere contrivances.[157]

The Jesus Prayer, like the Prayer of Jesus, commends itself at once to the most superficial glance. It is short and can be repeated myriad times in the space of minutes. Yet the words are transcendently powerful. *Lord*—the One in whom all things live and move and have their being; *Jesus*—from the Hebrew Yeshua, meaning Yahweh is salvation; *Christ*—the anointed of God; *Son of God*—One who shares the very nature of God; *have mercy on me*—the plea of needy creatures to the One who knit them together in their mothers' wombs; *a sinner*—one who continually misses the mark.

As was communicated with respect to the Prayer of Jesus, the words of the Jesus Prayer are beautiful and balanced, "yet none can say that he is familiar with the heights and depths the prayer reveals, and with the treasures it contains."[158] With every passing day it has become ever dearer to me. I insert it between the words of my adorations and confessions. I repeat it as I drift off to sleep. During the daytime, it has become a principal means by which I discipline my wandering and anxious mind. "Lord Jesus Christ, Son of God, have mercy on me, a sinner . . ."

In sum, it plugs me into "all his energy, which so powerfully works in me."[159] This in essence is *theosis*—being transformed into God.[160] In the words of Paul, "He is before all things, and in him all things hold together."[161] And this is not an isolated or off-handed remark. Again and again, Paul spoke of God's energy, which may so powerfully work not only within creation but within you and me. In her paraphrase of Philippians 2:13, Frederica Mathewes-Green (who has enlightened me greatly respecting the Jesus Prayer) underscores the reality that "God is *energizing* in you, both to will and to *energize* for his good pleasure."[162] When God's energy works within us, life works. When it does not, union with him becomes unimaginable.

"Lord Jesus Christ, Son of the living God, have mercy on me, a sinner."[163]

READING

A second spiritual discipline modeled by our Lord is reading. Reading is not intended to add more stuff to an over-cluttered mind but rather to provide new heights of perspective—new depths of understanding. Some of the greatest breakthroughs I have experienced during the course of my life have come as a direct result of reading.

A great example is the Jesus Prayer. I did not discover this manner of continuous prayer by osmosis. I discovered it through reading. Reading and reflection allowed me to break out of a petrified prayer paradigm into new vistas of prayer I could not have imagined previously. For me it may well have been as transformational as Sir Isaac Newton's design of the first reflecting telescope. Telescopes unveiled vistas of unimagined splendor. The Jesus Prayer allowed me to catch glimpses of what Isaiah must have experienced when he "saw the Lord sitting on a throne, lofty and exalted, with the train of His robe filling the temple."[164]

Newton could never have designed the magnifying power of the telescope on his own. He read and reflected on the accumulated knowledge of those who had come before him. The source of his genius was immersion in a sea of revelation. Revelation is the key that unlocks the mysteries of both created and uncreated energies. And the greatest of all such revelations is the Bible. Newton read it.[165] And so must we.

Bible—Ultimate Power Source of Uncreated Energy

What is the Bible but the study of God (theology)? The very thing that led medieval thinkers to crown reading and reflection on Almighty God "Queen of the Sciences." In the seventeenth century—the century during which Newton developed calculus, discovered the law of gravity, and designed the first reflecting telescope—Peter Paul Rubens memorialized the transformational power inherent in the study of God in a majestic painting titled *The Triumph of the Eucharist*. As noted earlier, the point of the painting was that theology is never absent philosophy and science, but philosophy and science absent reflection on the uncaused First Cause leads inexorably to the blind ditch of ignorance.[166]

Augustine was right to hold God's self-revelation in the Scriptures to be the necessary precondition for all knowledge.[167] No matter how keen a man's eyesight, he can see nothing if confined to pitch-black darkness. Light is axiomatic to seeing; the Bible is indispensable to an experience with the uncreated energies of God.[168]

In *Mere Christianity*, C. S. Lewis told the story of a "hard-bitten" Royal Air Force officer who had little patience for reading the Bible. From his perspective, anyone who has experienced God alone in the desert has little need for the rubbish of reading things about him. On one hand, said Lewis, the officer had a point. As the territory is more real than the map that portrays it, so an experience with God in the cool of a desert night is far more viscerally authentic than just reading things about him in the Bible.

Likewise, looking at the Atlantic Ocean from the vantage of a beach is far more real than merely looking at a map of the Atlantic. "Turning from something real to something less real: turning from real waves to a bit of coloured paper."[169]

But here is what needs to be understood. The map is based on the experience of thousands of people who have had a real encounter with the Atlantic. Not isolated experiences—innumerable experiences. Moreover, "if you want to go anywhere, the map is absolutely necessary." After all, wrote Lewis, "The map is going to be more use than walks on the beach if you want to get to America."[170]

The Bible is like that map. Merely reading it is less real (less exciting) than the R. A. F. officer's experience in the desert. But without it one is bound to get lost. While the territory may be more significant than the map, the map nonetheless matters.

As the map is not the territory, so the Bible is not God. What it entails, however, is *the experience of hundreds of people who really were in touch with God—experiences compared with which any thrills or pious feelings you and I are likely to get on our own are very elementary and very confused.*[171] You won't get anywhere by just looking at a map. But you will likely not get to where you're going without one. Thus, again, while it is true that life matters more than truth, the life that matters more is ultimately dependent on truth.

In his high priestly prayer, Jesus prayed, "sanctify them by the truth; your word is truth."[172] Did you get that? The Bible is truth. It is not just about truth. It *is* truth. It begins with God. The uncaused First Cause—Creator of all that is. It continues with a memorable history of God's creative prowess in a way that may be remembered and recalled through an association with the continuous seven-day cycle of life. The first six days outline a hierarchy of creation that culminates in you and me as the crowning jewels of God's creation. Jewels created with volition. Made so we could choose to love him or not. With volition came the *potential* for sin. A potential actualized when Adam and Eve fell into lives of perpetual sin terminated by death. The fall marring the imago Dei—the image of God within.

The revelation that references the fall, however, also records the divine plan for deification. The means by which we may do what the first man and woman were designed to experience. To ascend the Edenic mountain toward the Shekinah glory and there partake of the deifying fruit by which we will be transformed from one glory to another. To achieve our intended union with God.

Our lives are not only *changed* through reconciliation—peace with God. We have been saved unto *exchanged* lives. The life of Christ *engrafted* into ours.[173] Jesus said, "I have come that they may have life, and have it to the full."[174] The apostle John testified, "God has given us eternal life, and this life is in his Son. Whoever has the Son has life; whoever does not have the Son of God does not have life."[175] Through the life of Christ we are organically united with the divine. And as that life is nurtured and grows we begin to enjoy life to the full.

Such life is not just *Bio*. It is *Zoe*. Not merely biological, but spiritual. Such a glorious truth elevates our prayer life from a forced biological exercise whereby we get down on our knees, mumble a few words, and then rush back into our frenetic existence. The *Zoe* life—the spiritual life, the engrafted life of Christ—works from within. It makes union with God an organic actuality.

This is likewise the case with our reading of the Bible. Said Watchman Nee, "Should we not read the Bible? Of course we should, or our spiritual life will suffer. But that should not mean forcing ourselves to read. There is a new law in us which gives us a hunger for God's Word. *Then* half an hour can be more profitable than five hours of forced reading."[176] Hunger for the Word of God must be as natural as hunger for food. We do not force ourselves to become hungry for physical sustenance. Neither should we force ourselves to become hungry for spiritual sustenance. In the authentic Christian life it is as natural as breathing or blinking our eyes.

I love how Nee illustrated this wonderful truth in *The Normal Christian Life*! His illustrations are so keen, so practical. "I used to suffer from sleeplessness," said Nee. "Once after several sleepless nights, when I had prayed much about it and exhausted all my resources, I confessed at length to God that the fault must lie with me and asked to be shown where." The answer that God provided was as simple as it was profound. "Believe in nature's laws." Sleep like hunger is the law of nature! "I realized that, though I had never thought of worrying whether I would get hungry or not, I had been worrying about sleeping. I had been trying to help nature, and that is the chief trouble with most sufferers from sleeplessness. But now I trusted not only God but God's law of nature, and very soon slept well."[177]

This, of course, is not to suggest that you cannot thwart natural sleep patterns through bad habits. If you overeat (or eat the wrong things at the wrong time) natural sleep is affected. Drinking a glass of wine (or two) may make you sleepy, but because wine has a relatively short half-life, you may find yourself waking up in the middle of the night and not being able to get back to sleep. The point is, we must live lives of discipline. That's why *life practices* are often referred to as living or spiritual *disciplines*.

The tragedy is that many suppose the overcoming life can be achieved apart from the embrace of life practices such as reading the Bible. It can't. Reading the Bible must become as routine as eating breakfast. Not forced, but regular. Then what starts out as a discipline *will* become a delight.

The question now is how. How should the Bible be read? The Bible can be used in various ways. It can be used as a basis for prayer. (As noted previously, I employ Psalm 139 as an expression of faith; Psalm 145 to articulate adoration; Psalm 51 in confession; and Psalm 118 for thanksgiving.) It can also be used devotionally. The book of Proverbs is particularly suited to this purpose. But the Bible must also be *read!* In fact, if you—like the vast majority of all Christians—have never read through the Bible, you should purpose to do so.

Reading through the Bible—particularly in a year's time—is a daunting proposition. Realizing this, I have developed the "Legacy Reading Plan" designed to empower you to "eat the elephant" one book at a time.[178] The format is specifically formulated to make your time in the Bible the best it can be. You'd be hard-pressed to come up with a better legacy than that of reading through the Bible once a year, every year, for the rest of your life. (To put it in perspective, for me that's likely to be less than twenty more times.)

The "Legacy Reading Plan" is unique in that it requires you to process books of the Bible rather than piecing together bits of books. The goal is to comprehend the essence God is communicating by reading each biblical book as a whole. The reading calendar is naturally segmented into seasons and the seasons into months.

At the beginning of each year, you know that during the winter your focus will be on the Pentateuch and Poetry (249 chapters); in spring, the Historical books (249 chapters); in summer the Prophets (250 chapters); and during the fall, the New Testament (260 chapters). Each season is further broken down into months.

Thus, every January your goal is to read through Genesis and Exodus and every December the Synoptic Gospels and Acts. There are times when you will naturally read ten chapters at a time and others when you will read one or two. More importantly you will read the Bible just as you read other literature.

The exceptions are Psalms and Proverbs. As Psalms constituted a hymn-book or devotional guide for ancient Israel, it can do so for you in the present. And because Proverbs is replete with principles for successful daily living, you may find it helpful to read a chapter of Proverbs each day, progressing through the entire book once a month.

Nothing should take precedence over getting into the Word and getting the Word into us. If we fail to eat well-balanced meals on a regular basis, we will eventually suffer the physical consequences. Likewise, if we do not regularly feed on the Word of God, we will suffer the spiritual consequences. You cannot do next week's eating today. D. L. Moody was right: "A man can no more take in a supply of grace for the future than he can eat enough for the next six months, or take sufficient air into his lungs at one time to sustain life for a week. We must draw upon God's boundless store of grace from day to day as we need it."[179]

Books

From *the* Book we progress to books—the reading of which must become an ever-more-disciplined life practice for us all. I am sorely tempted to cite the statistics. But here's the bottom line. The numbers of people not reading the Bible (or books in general) is staggering. A full quarter of the population did not read so much as a single book in the past year![180]

The good news is that, as with technology, all of us can get hooked on reading all over again. There are so many benefits it's hard to know where to begin. Reading improves discipline, vocabulary, memory, creativity, reasoning, and relaxation; plus, it can even stave off diseases such as Alzheimer's.[181] Most importantly, reading engages you with *another* mind.

When it comes to reading Scripture, the implications are simply staggering. By its words we are brought into direct communion with the mind of God. And not only so. We have access to the minds of writers directly inspired by the divine. Thus, in the pages of the inspired text we have a mind-to-mind connection with minds that were awash in uncreated energy.

Think about it. Some of the most engaging conversations imaginable may occur in mute communion with absent authors. The vistas are virtually limitless. A few hours ago I boarded a plane to California. In my hand was a copy of *Mere Christianity*. For the next five hours I reconnected with one of the great minds of the twentieth century. To say the experience was exhilarating is an understatement. Though Lewis is dead, I was brought back to a time in which he was very much alive. He was thinking as he wrote; and I had the privilege of engaging his ideas.

Allow me an illustration that comes from the preface of *Mere Christianity*. Here Lewis engaged objectors who might cringe at his use of the word *Christian*. He imagined the objectors asking who he thinks he is to define *Christian* as someone holding to the main and the plain doctrines of the Christian faith. He could almost hear them saying, "May not many a man who cannot believe these doctrines be far more truly a Christian, far closer to the spirit of Christ, than some who do?" As spiritual as this sounds, said Lewis, "we simply cannot, without disaster, use language as these objectors want us to use it."[182] The sentiment might be noble, but the consequences are disastrous.

Lewis employed the word *gentleman* as an example. In its original form *gentleman* meant someone who had a coat of arms and a landed estate (formerly a British symbol of status). Thus, in calling someone a gentleman you are neither paying him a compliment nor insulting him. You are simply stating a fact. However, the word *gentleman*, once "spiritualised and refined out of its old coarse, objective sense, means hardly more than a man whom the speaker likes. As a result, *gentleman* is now a useless word." Why? "We had lots of terms of approval already, so it was not needed for that use; on the other hand if anyone (say, in a historical work) wants to use it in its old sense, he cannot do so without explanations. It has been spoiled for that purpose."[183]

And so it is with the word *Christian*. The moment we begin spiritualizing or "deepening" the word *Christian*, we rob the word of its usefulness. "Christians themselves will never be able to apply it to anyone. It is not for us to say who, in the deepest sense, is or is not close to the spirit of Christ.... It would be wicked arrogance for us to say that any man is, or is not, a Christian in this refined sense. And obviously a word which we can never apply is not going to be a very useful word."[184]

Whether you agree with Lewis or not, my point is that in reading a book like *Mere Christianity*, we, in the present, connect with a mind from the past, and can make application to the future. Today I did a broadcast on an issue Lewis himself may never have imagined—the redefinition of *marriage*. Yet his writings so many years ago were eerily relevant as I interviewed the coauthor of a book titled *Same-Sex Marriage*.[185]

In the book, the authors forward the notion that "marriage has at all times and in all societies been a relationship between men and women." That "marriage *exists* because of the dual, gender-distinct nature of humanity."[186] As such, "the connection between marriage and procreation is more than just incidental."[187] They note that in a contrary opinion, Supreme Court justice Anthony Kennedy holds that marriage, as historically defined, fosters little more than ill will and animosity. In his considered opinion anyone who embraces the historical definition of marriage—thus excluding same-sex couples—"does so out of hate and animus."[188] Curiously, Justice Kennedy's opinion was the very thing I had read Lewis on—the danger of redefining words. What must surely have been self-evident to this supremely erudite arbiter of justice is that virtually every redefinition of marriage, including his own, *excludes* someone (siblings, the polygamous, those underage, etc.). But is this due to hate or to common sense? If marriage means everything, in the end it may well mean nothing at all.

As Maggie Gallagher, founder of the National Organization for Marriage, noted, "Social institutions like marriage are created, sustained, and transmitted by words, and the images, symbols, and feelings that surround words. Change the meaning of the word, and you change the thing itself." If you redefine the word "cat" to mean "furry, domestic animal with four legs and a tail," it becomes quite difficult to know whether you are talking about a cat, a dog, or something else. "If we want to speak to each other about cats, we will either have to invent a new term, and hope it will still communicate the full valence of the old word (rich with historic associations and symbolic overtones), or we will have to do without a word for 'cat' at all. One might reasonably foresee, without charting all the particular specific mechanisms, that it might become harder to communicate an idea for which we no longer have any word."[189]

My point is that by reading classics such as *Mere Christianity*, I am engaging minds from the past, just as in reading *Same-Sex Marriage* I am engaging minds in the present. The net result is a synergy by which I am equipped in matters of life and truth. During the past decade, Kathy and I have been gaining great insights by reading early church fathers. Reading their thoughts and learning from their actions continues to give perspective to our present-day living.

A while back I read an article in the *Washington Post* written by Barronelle Stutzman. As I read, my mind flashed back to words I encountered as I read a history on the life of Polycarp. Like Polycarp, Barronelle was faced with a matter of conscience. Her article was titled "I'm a florist, but I refused to do flowers for my gay friend's wedding."[190] She noted that Rob Ingersoll was one of her favorite clients. "I knew he was gay but it didn't matter—I enjoyed his company and his creativity." When Rob asked her to create the floral arrangements for his wedding, she talked it over with her husband. After carefully considering what was at stake, she was struck by the conviction that "marriage is a sacred religious ceremony between a man, a woman and Christ. It's a covenant with the church. To participate in a wedding that violates those principles violates the core of my faith." Feeling badly that she could not share this day with Rob as she had so many others before, she "took his hands and said, 'I'm sorry I can't do your wedding because of my relationship with Jesus Christ.'" After providing Rob with the names of three floral artists who would make his same-sex wedding special, they hugged.

Barronelle could hardly have imagined what would happen next. First, she was sued by Washington State Attorney General Bob Ferguson; shortly thereafter Rob and his partner Curt filed suit as well. Barronelle noted that she had employed gays and lesbians, that Rob had been a long-time customer, and that he had other wonderful vendors to choose from. Nonetheless, the state and the same-sex couple were determined to impose their will. "However they want to punish me, they can't change my faith," wrote Barronelle. "What happens in my business or my life is in God's hands. Having a clear conscience means much more to me than any amount of money or my business."

Polycarp was of the same persuasion. He cared more for eternal verities than earthly vanities. Whether Barronelle's faith was bolstered by stories of saints and martyrs I do not know. What I do know is that reading stories such as Barronelle's inspires us to continue on as cultural change agents rather than cultural conformists. Whether one agrees with Barronelle's present persuasions or those of Polycarp in the past, their testimonies cause us to think deeply about our life and living.

In the middle of the second century, when persecution broke out against the church in Smyrna (Turkey), Christians were fed to wild animals or sacrificed to the flames. Polycarp was their leader and as such a primary target of their pagan hatred. Yet when the governor threatened to engulf him in earthly fire, Polycarp simply educated him on the terrors of eternal fire. Rather than curse God and live, Polycarp confessed Christ and died. Reading his story not only transports us back in time but fuels a future faith.[191] Who knows when we, like Barronelle, will be called upon to stand for deeply held convictions no matter the cost?

I could not help but wonder if Polycarp himself had been emboldened by the story of Ignatius. If you haven't read this one, you should. Ignatius was one of the last church leaders personally acquainted with the New Testament apostles themselves. At the turn of the century, he was forcibly removed from service to the saints in Antioch and thrown to the beasts in a Roman amphitheater. His testimony of faith in the face of a horrifying death has inspired multitudes to stand for Christ no matter the cost. "Allow me to become food for the wild beasts, through whose means it will be granted me to reach God," he said. "I am the wheat of God and am ground by the teeth of the wild beasts, that I may be found the pure bread of Christ."[192]

Along with biographies of martyrs in early church history, I have been greatly inspired by reading stories of modern-day saints. Last night I read the account of a man who survived the horrendous social experiment that Mao Zedong imposed on the Chinese populace.[193] Some thirty million died in what was imagined to be the Great Leap Forward into the heaven of communism. Reading in the comforts of my home, I was transported back to a time in which millions considered a tiny piece of bread and a small cup of water a luxury. As I read, I imagined myself in the circumstances that were being depicted. It felt as though I had been lifted out of myself and into the life of another. Their suffering became my suffering. Their story became my own.

As I read, I could not help but contemplate the immense growth of Christianity in the face of modern persecutions. Even as thousands are daily turning away from Christ in the West, tens of thousands are turning toward him in the East. On the one hand are genuine encounters with uncreated energy in the epicenter of religious persecution. On the other, an epidemic of complacency and spiritual malnourishment, "having a form of godliness but denying its power."[194] As faith without works is form devoid of substance, so religion devoid of God's uncreated energy is little more than baptized secular humanism. Acquiescence to logical truth propositions devoid of living realities.

All these thoughts and many more coursed through my mind as I read. But that is precisely what reading does. It provides an enhanced perspective on reality. As we see the divine actively participating in the lives of people past and present, East and West, we begin to realize how God works redemptively in and through our lives as well.

If there was a secret to John Wesley's otherworldly ministry, I am convinced it was reading. Depth of understanding gained through reading allowed him to tap into wellsprings of uncreated energies. In exhorting other preachers to read, Wesley pulled no punches. "What has exceedingly hurt you in time past, nay, and I fear, to this day, is, want of reading." Wesley urged his hearers to begin at once. To make the discipline of reading a daily routine. "Fix some part of every day for private exercises. You may acquire the taste which you have not: what is tedious at first, will afterward be pleas-ant. Whether you like it or no, read and pray daily. It is for your life; there is no other way; else you will be a trifler all your days, and a petty, superficial preacher. Do justice to your own soul; give it time and means to grow. Do not starve yourself any longer."[195]

Lewis is another great example. He may well have been the most influ-ential British writer in history. Perhaps reading made it so. Like his parents, Lewis read voraciously. As a young child he was already immersed in the classics. As with my wife, Lewis loved reading George MacDonald. Upon reading a copy of *Phantastes*, which he happened upon at a train station book-stall, Lewis said he felt as though he had "crossed a great frontier." Like G. K. Chesterton, who famously said that the writings of MacDonald "made a difference to my whole existence,"[196] Lewis was forever hooked. He claimed to have never written a book in which he did not quote MacDonald.[197] "I know hardly any other writer who seems to be closer, or more continually close, to the Spirit of Christ Himself. Hence his Christ-like union of tenderness and severity. Nowhere else outside the New Testament have I found terror and comfort so intertwined."[198]

Lewis loved a wide variety of genres, not the least of which was fantasy and fiction. Though he was a prodigious intellect, such genres continually stoked his imagination. He knew that by prodding readers through the ward-robe into Narnia they might well emerge with renewed sensitivities to all that is real. Likewise, to reside for a time within the minds of fiction writers and their characters is a means by which to ponder existent realities. Far from escapism, such writings can propel us into the mystery of an unseen world as real as flesh on bone.

While Lewis loved contemporary writings, he most treasured the clas-sics. Thus, he counsels you and me to augment the reading of every new book with one that has withstood the test of time. Not only so. He counsels us to read the classics until we own their contents. Said Lewis, "an unliterary man may be defined as one who reads books once only."[199]

One of the books that I myself have read more than once is *Mere Christianity*. (Unfortunately, I just left my dog-eared, highlighted, underlined, prized personal copy on an airplane seat!) One of the chapters is titled "The Obstinate Toy Soldiers." In it Lewis concerns himself with the business of becoming a son of God—transitioning from a temporary biological existence to a timeless spiritual existence. "Humanity is already 'saved' in principle. We individuals have to appropriate that salvation. But the really tough work— the bit we could not have done for ourselves—has been done for us. We have not got to try to climb up into spiritual life by our own efforts; it has already come down into the human race. If we will only lay ourselves open to the one Man in whom it was fully present, and who, in spite of being God, is also a real man, He will do it in us and for us." Lewis's point is that "one of our own race has this new life: if we get close to Him [like an infection] we shall catch it from Him."[200]

I own many more books that, like *Mere Christianity*, are dog-eared and worn from use. Watchman Nee's *The Normal Christian Life* is one of them. As is my custom, I first read it with a yellow highlighter. I then went back and underlined portions with a pen. Some of the passages I memorized. Others I refer back to time and time again. Whenever I feel myself gravitating toward living life and serving the Lord in my own gifting and energies, I am reminded of Nee's admonition. "In us who have received Christ, there is a new life. We all have that precious possession, the treasure in the vessel. Praise the Lord for the reality of life within!"[201] This life is not merely a "changed life." "What God offers us is an 'exchanged life'—a 'substituted life,' and Christ is our Substitute within." The exchanged life "is not something which we ourselves have to produce. It is Christ's own life reproduced in us."[202] As Paul put it, "I no longer live, but Christ lives in me."[203]

Yet another book I refer back to frequently is Dallas Willard's *The Spirit of the Disciplines*. By it I am reminded that the purpose of life practices or living disciplines is transformation. We are not just waiting to experience life after death; we are afforded life straightaway. If we limit salvation to forgiveness of sins, we will fail to understand what our present lives have to do with our redemption. What I consider again and again as I return to highlighted and underlined portions of Willard's book is that "the idea of redemption as the *impartation of a life* provides a totally different framework of understanding."

Through "the spirit of the disciplines" my "life will be poised to become a life of the same quality as Christ's, because it indeed *is* Christ's. He really does live on in us. The incarnation continues."[204]

The point in all this is to emphasize that reading is a life practice by which our minds may be renewed and transformed.[205] It is a principal tool through which God changes us. Turn off the television! Get in the habit of reading! Engage the mind of God and the marvelous minds of those who have learned to think his thoughts after him!

Johannes Kepler was one of them. He studied the universe, for in creation he experienced the image and energies of God. It was Kepler who said of his planetary breakthroughs, "I was merely thinking God's thoughts after him. Since we astronomers are priests of the highest God in regard to the book of nature, it benefits us to be thoughtful, not of the glory of our minds, but rather, above all else, of the glory of God."[206] Kepler faithfully read the Bible, voraciously consumed a wide variety of books, and resolutely fixed his substantial talents on the book of nature, for through it God spoke to him as a Father to a child.

Book of Nature

The book of nature is not for sale. Nor can it be found in any bookstore. It's as free as the air we breathe and as vast as the universe. By reading it you and I can experience God's invisible qualities—"His eternal power and divine nature."[207] Johannes Kepler read the book of nature,[208] as did Albert Einstein. Though he was neither a Christian theist nor an atheist, he read with "an attitude of humility corresponding to the weakness of our intellectual understanding of nature and of our own being."[209]

He saw himself as "a little child entering a huge library filled with books in many different languages. The child knows someone must have written those books. It does not know how. It does not understand the languages in which they are written. The child dimly suspects a mysterious order in the arrangement of the books but doesn't know what it is. That, it seems to me, is the attitude of even the most intelligent human being toward God."[210]

Though Einstein rejected the personal God of the Bible, he revered the

God who gives glimpses of himself in the library of nature. The One "who reveals himself in the harmony of all that exists."[211] For Einstein, such library books were as wonderful as they were mysterious. And this he found intoxicating. "The most beautiful emotion we can experience is the mysterious. It is the fundamental emotion that stands at the cradle of all true art and science. He to whom this emotion is a stranger, who can no longer wonder and stand rapt in awe, is as good as dead, a snuffed-out candle."[212]

A child may as yet view a chrysalis with wonder. Or thrill at the emergence of a butterfly. Too many simply yawn—blind to the wonders of the universe. We glance at the moon and fail to grasp its significance for our survival. We order yet another glass of water and forget its uniqueness among the liquids. Were it like virtually any other fluid, it would freeze from the bottom up rather than from the top down, killing aquatic life, destroying the oxygen supply, making earth uninhabitable.[213] We fail to grasp the gravity of gravity. Were it infinitesimally weaker or stronger, the universe would not—could not—support intelligent life. We swat at an ant without thinking to trace its path into the domain of the learned. Far better, said Solomon, to "observe her ways and be wise."[214]

We must ever remember that God has revealed himself in two books: the Bible and the book of nature. The parallel between them so complete, said Origen, that "the person who is asking questions of nature and the person who is asking questions of Scripture are bound to arrive at the same conclusion."[215] Luther was similarly persuaded. "God writes His Gospel, not in the Bible alone, but in trees, and flowers, and clouds, and stars."[216]

The great American reformer George Cheever may have said it best. "The man who can really, in living union of the mind and heart, converse with God through nature, finds in the material forms around him, a source of power and happiness inexhaustible." Cheever went on to say that "the highest life and glory of man is to be alive unto God; and when this grandeur of sensibility to Him, and this power of communion with Him is carried, as the habit of the soul, into the forms of nature, then the walls of our world are as the gates of heaven."[217]

The American poet Henry Wadsworth Longfellow was similarly

persuaded. He described the book of nature as an old nurse who takes us upon her knee, "Saying: 'Here is a story-book / Thy Father has written for thee.' / 'Come, wander with me,' she said, / 'Into regions yet untrod; And read what is still unread / in the manuscripts of God.'"[218]

Intimacy with the book of nature is directly linked to spiritual renaissance. When we give in to the power and presence of the Spirit, we encounter the hand of omnipotence in all of creation. It is resplendent in the stars, reveals itself in the diversity of plants and trees, roils in the rhythm of the waves, and resides in the mystery of the wind. Those who ignore the book of nature do so at their own peril. Spurgeon, the prince of preachers, found it exceedingly strange for one to claim to love God and yet be "afraid to study the God-declaring book of nature." He bemoaned "the mock-spirituality of some believers, who are too heavenly to consider the heavens."[219]

What we need is a cleansing of the toxins. An escape from light pollution so as to see that "the heavens declare the glory of God; the skies proclaim the work of his hands. Day after day they pour forth speech; night after night they display knowledge. There is no speech or language where their voice is not heard. Their voice goes out into all the earth, their words to the ends of the world."[220] Watch the eagle soar. Listen to the babbling brook. Consider the myriad flowers and leaves. Allow the differentiated snowflakes to fall softly upon your eyelids. Open your eyes and know that God is near. Said Einstein, "To know what is impenetrable to us really exists, manifesting itself as the highest wisdom and the most radiant beauty which our dull faculties can comprehend only in their most primitive forms—this knowledge, this feeling, is at the center of true religiousness."[221]

Einstein was half right. On one hand the Mind who spoke and trillions of galaxies leapt into existence is impenetrable. Inaccessible. On the other he is immanent. Scripture affirms both his ineffability and his immanence. He is "a God nearby" *and* "a God far away."[222] Impenetrable in his essence, present in his energies. As such, reading the book of nature is tantamount to a para-eucharistic practice. Para-eucharistic, in that it stands alongside the Eucharist, as a means by which we may experience the mystery of union with God. All that he has created is a sacred sacrament through which we may be mysteriously interpenetrated and indwelt. God's creative handiwork is replete with *logoi* (little words) that speak to us as through a mighty rushing wind.[223] The tragedy is this. Creation surrounds us with its presence, but we are far too much like the proverbial fish swimming in water yet complaining of thirst.

Perhaps some wilderness therapy is in order. Wilderness therapy deepens our appreciation of the book of nature. Reacquaints us with its rhythms. Permits us to perceive our place in the purposes of God. Allows us to struggle with uncreated energy rather than struggling with our own. Disconnects us from the spirit of this age and reconnects us with the Spirit of the ages.

Our greatest example is Jesus. He often withdrew to lonely places to experience union with the Father. John, too, withdrew to unpopulated places so as to remove the impediments and better bear witness to the Light. Elijah, after whom the ministry of John was patterned, likewise cried out from the wilderness: "Prepare the way of the Lord; make straight the paths of our God."[224] With the noise of the city no longer pounding in their brains, they sensed God's speaking in the sounds of silence. They encountered the ineffable in the mountain crags and in the desert sands. In the flight of the fearsome falcon, in the glassy eye of the owl. In the darting of the hummingbird, in the beauty of a butterfly. They communed with God and like the bush that burned they were consecrated but not consumed.

It is in the wilderness that our anxious hearts may be quiet and know that he is God (see Psalm 46:10). In our apartness there is an intuitive knowing that he who is above and beyond is also within. Saint Gregory Palamas, archbishop of Thessalonica, accentuated the paradox: "He is both existent and nonexistent; he is everywhere and nowhere; he has many names and he cannot be named; he is ever-moving and he is unmoved and, in short, he is everything and nothing [no-thing]." The Western mind tends to shun such paradox, but not Palamas. God, he said, "remains wholly within himself and yet he dwells wholly within us, causing us to participate not in his nature but in his glory and radiance."[225] This does not mean that we are "united to God with respect to his essence," since "with respect to his essence God undergoes no participation." What this means is that "those privileged to attain union with God are united to him with respect to his energy."[226]

And as the contemporary Orthodox theologian Metropolitan Kallistos Ware aptly reminds us, "the divine energies are not an intermediary between God and humankind, not a 'thing' that exists apart from God. They are, on the contrary, *God himself*, God in action, God in his self-revelation, God indwelling his creation through his direct and unmediated presence."[227]

The point of wilderness therapy is precisely that—to experience God's unmediated presence. Though he is ineffable in his essence; he is nonetheless immanent in his energies. As such, we who are joined to the Lord are one spirit with him.[228] In the shimmering between light and darkness, we may well experience the beatific vision—Adam and Eve walking with God in the cool of the day. Said Lewis, "If I find in myself a desire which no experience in this world can satisfy, the most probable explanation is that I was made for another world."[229] As Christian apologist Dan Story has so beautifully expressed it, "Wild nature is a privileged peek through earthly shutters to a Garden of Eden reborn; a future Paradise with all the joy and peace and unspoiled beauty of Eden—and more! In God's timing, the wilderness—indeed, all of creation—will be transformed.[230] The dim memory of Eden hovering in the recesses of our minds will someday become a living reality."[231]

In the meantime we are to read. Read the Bible and experience the mind of God; read books and engage minds he created in his image and likeness; read the book of nature with its myriad logoi, which in unison express the Logos. Purge the toxins. Cleanse the lens. Let the shining begin.

ABSTINENCE

For four consecutive years (2015–18), the Cleveland Cavaliers played the Golden State Warriors in the NBA finals. LeBron James versus Steph Curry. Had LeBron not left for the Los Angeles Lakers, that trend may well have continued in perpetuity. LeBron is by all accounts the best basketball player on the planet. Steph is the heir apparent to bump out LeBron as the face of the NBA.

LeBron, a four-time MVP, says he could see immediately that Stephen

Curry was destined for stardom. He saw in Curry a wonderful blend of finesse, skill, drive, as well as the discipline and dedication necessary for greatness.[232] I have personally witnessed all of that and more. Having played a fair amount of golf with Steph, I have seen his progress in that arena as well—today he is not only an NBA superstar but arguably the best golfer in the NBA. In sum, Steph is a fierce competitor. What seems automatic in the spotlight is the result of a lifetime of discipline. Years of regimen, exercise, study, diet, practice, practice, and more practice.

And not only so, but abstinence. Put another way, self-enforced restraint. What that means is that Steph has had to abstain from all sorts of appetites in order to master the game he loves. What Curry has accomplished in the physical realm Christians are called to accomplish in the spiritual realm. Abstinence is a living discipline by which we master our appetites for food, sex—even for our favorite pastime—so that we may partake of heavenly manna. Abstinence vitalizes our vigor, amplifies our affections, and compounds our contentment. While such things as food and sex are glorious gifts from God, little compares with mastery over the appetites that seek to master us.

Wishing does not win a race. Nor does it produce an NBA superstar. To compete in the games takes strict training. It takes disciplining the appetites—making them your slave. It's wonderful to win an NBA championship, yet all such glory pales in comparison to experiencing communion with God. One is temporary. It will not last. The other is forever. Thus, like a coach, the apostle Paul urged his young protégé Timothy to forgo endless myths and legends and train hard in the gymnasium of life. "For physical training is of some value, but godliness has value for all things, holding promise for both the present life and the life to come."[233]

Writing on abstinence in a culture screaming indulgence is no small task. Prejudice against the spiritual gymnasium is breathtaking. To abstain from food, sex, a favorite sport, an evening cocktail, or even television is foreign to our sensibilities. We live in a self-indulgent culture in which feeling good is deemed to be the highest value.

The apostles had a decidedly different perspective. Paul practiced abstinence because emulating Christ was the highest virtue. Thus, as Christ fasted, Paul fasted too. He lived and practiced the things his Lord had taught and practiced so that he might be empowered by God's energies, not just his own. Many talk a good game. But what about the walk? If we are brutally honest with ourselves, more often than not we walk in the way of the world. How many of us can truly say that we "have crucified the flesh with its passions and desires"?[234] Who among us can truthfully say that we are engaged in mastering those passions that for far too long have mastered us?

Yet this is precisely what Christ calls his disciples to do. "If anyone would come after me, he *must* deny himself and take up his cross and follow me."[235] Paul knew precisely what that meant. And so he wisely enrolled in the school of self-restraint. The world, said Paul, has given itself "over to sensuality so as to indulge in every kind of impurity with a continual lust for more. You, however, did not come to know Christ that way." Instead, "you were taught, with regard to your former way of life, to put off your old self, which is being corrupted by its deceitful desires; to be made new in the attitude of your minds; and to put on the new self, created to be like God in true righteousness and holiness."[236]

Giving assent to the truth propositions of the historic Christian faith is important. As I have been saying all along—truth matters. But mental assent and good intentions do not in and of themselves produce transformation. It is not just our beliefs that need changing. It's our behaviors. If our habits remain the same, our lives will as well.[237] I can't tell you how many people have told me that they would dearly love to memorize Scripture. Few, however, are willing to embrace the disciplines necessary to carve the Scriptures into the canvas of their consciousness. Good intentions are many. Disciplines few. Steph Curry did not become the NBA's "Baby-Faced Assassin" by accident. He yielded his members wholeheartedly to the rigors of the gym. We must do so as well.

We all have weaknesses that are essential to master. NBA great Dwight Howard is a case in point. He can dunk a basketball with the best of them. Free throws are another matter. One of the reasons the Rockets lost to Curry and the Golden State Warriors during the 2015 NBA Western Conference finals was Howard's inefficiency at the free throw line. The point is (and he should have made a whole lot more of them) that Howard would be well served to discipline his weakness, even more than practicing his strengths.

Moreover, we must practice abstinence for the right reasons. *We must not seek abstention from food and water in order to curry God's favor. We abstain from food and water in order to experience union with God.* I fear that a primary reason there is so little emphasis on fasting in the modern church is that it is perceived to be a warped monastic practice by which medieval Christians sought to attain righteousness apart from faith.[238] One need only think back to Luther who, prior to the Reformation, quite nearly killed himself in order to gain right standing before God. Afterward he ruefully noted that extreme abstinence had quite likely done permanent damage to his digestive system.[239]

The fact that "the just shall live by faith,"[240] however, is hardly an excuse to give up on abstinence. No need to throw out the baby with the bathwater. Nor pour dirty water on the baby! Defect is no reason to disdain discipline. Neither should orthopraxy be sacrificed on the altar of orthodoxy. Doctrinal correctness is not a replacement for correct discipline—as though what we do and what we think have no bearing upon one another.

While abstinence for the sake of abstinence is most surely sin, abstinence for the sake of spiritual attainment is a divine imperative. To abstain from physical pleasures for a season serves to intensify the greatest pleasure of all—that of communing with the living God. And, while I am most interested in focusing this chapter on the oft-neglected discipline of fasting, allow me to first say a few words about abstinence in other areas as well.

Abstinence from a Favorite Pastime

I have played the game of golf now for over fifty years. To say it has become a consuming passion would be an understatement. Like Steph Curry, I have sought to master the game I love. Over time, however, I fear it has begun to master me. I could scarcely imagine a week without it. Despite advancing age, I was always trying to get better. I lifted weights, worked on stretching exercises, and pounded thousands of golf balls. Like Paul, I beat my body to make it my slave—but for entirely different reasons. I wanted to continue hitting a golf ball as far as the flat bellies—Hank Jr., Steph, and so on.

I discovered just how strong my addiction to golf was when my car was front-ended by a young lady momentarily blinded by the sun. The result was significant damage to my left wrist. Twelve days later, I was rear-ended as Kathy and I were driving to a function for one of our boys. As I began to regain my senses, I felt an acute pain in my left shoulder and subsequently my left hamstring.

Twelve days, two accidents. And nothing I could have done about either. The result was damage to the three major levers of my golf swing. I could no longer set my wrists properly, make a complete shoulder turn, or pivot efficiently onto my left side. Coincidence? I cannot say for sure. What I do know is that I was unable to play golf efficiently for several years following the accidents.

While my abstinence was involuntary, it was abstinence nonetheless. And it revealed just how addicted I had become to the game of golf. This is not to imply that it has not been a great outlet, nor that there is anything intrinsically wrong with it. Rather, what my time away from golf revealed was the matter of imbalance. As the quotable British theologian William Inge put it, "If we feel that any habit or pursuit, harmless in itself, is keeping us from God and sinking us deeper in the things of earth; if we find that things which others can do with impunity are for us the occasion of falling, then abstinence is our only course." Why? Because "we should steadily resolve to give up anything that comes between ourselves and God."[241]

Sexual Abstinence

Resolving to give up anything that comes between ourselves and God stretches as far as the hallowed mystery of sexual intimacy—one of the greatest gifts God has given humankind. Sexual intimacy is as profound as it is mysterious. Intercourse consummates marriage as a multifaceted mystery in which two people are forged together as one flesh. In mysterious union, a man and a woman procreate children fashioned in the image and likeness of their Creator. Sexual union, however, is even more profound than procreation and paradisiacal pleasure—it is a mysterious parable of Christ and his church. The union of two people a poignant portrait of the unity of Christ and his bride.

The parable has its roots in Genesis and bears ultimate fruit in Revelation. Human history rooted in the union of Adam and Eve and yielding its fruit in the wedding supper of the Lamb. The full complement of God's people "prepared as a bride beautifully dressed for her husband."[242] This mystery we are to ponder and preserve. It is a divine meta-narrative transcending our individual marriage narratives.

In the mystery of marriage, the husband is the image of Christ; the wife the image of the church. Thus, as Christ is sufficient to our every need, a husband is commanded to fulfill the needs of his wife. The biblical language is arresting. "Husbands, love your wives, just as Christ loved the church and gave himself up for her to make her holy, cleansing her by the washing with water through the word, and to present her to himself as a radiant church, without stain or wrinkle or any other blemish, but holy and blameless."[243]

A husband is thus called to fulfill his wife. To understand her needs and to fill them. To esteem her satisfaction as greater than his own. To love his wife as his own body. "After all, no one ever hated his own body, but he feeds and cares for it, just as Christ does the church."[244]

A wife, likewise, is to fulfill the needs of her husband—and this in every way including physical union. Thus, according to Scripture, "the husband should fulfill his marital duty to his wife, and likewise the wife to her husband. The wife's body does not belong to her alone but also to her husband. In the same way, the husband's body does not belong to him alone but also to his wife."[245]

As Thomas Aquinas explained, "the man should give to his wife her conjugal rights, namely, with his own body through carnal union, and likewise the wife to her husband, because in this matter they are judged equal. Hence the woman was not formed from the feet of the man as a servant, nor from the head as lording it over her husband, but from the side as a companion." To fail to do so is called fraud, "because one is taking away what belongs to another."[246]

Yet in full view of the mystery of marriage—replete with its parabolic profundity in Christ and the church, its potential for procreating children in the image and likeness of God, and its promise of psychophysical pleasure— there is an exception. "Do not deprive each other *except* by mutual consent and for a time, so that you may devote yourselves to prayer. Then come together again so that Satan will not tempt you because of your lack of self-control."[247]

First, as Paul emphasized, sexual abstinence must be by "mutual consent." Neither husband nor wife may make a unilateral decision. Both must agree. For there is no more beautiful expression of Christ and the church than that of husbands and wives dwelling together in harmony, peace, and mutual fulfillment.

Furthermore, sexual abstinence is to be practiced only "for a time." That is, only for an agreed-upon specific season. In the words of King Solomon, "there is a time for everything, and a season for every activity under the heavens." That includes "a time to embrace and a time to refrain from embracing."[248]

Finally, sexual abstinence is to be done for a suitable purpose. Most specifically, to "devote yourselves to prayer." Aquinas, in concert with the early church fathers, quite naturally expanded the meaning of prayer to "spiritual acts, for which continence renders one more suitable."[249] This self-evidently includes all the spiritual disciplines by which we are fashioned in the image and likeness of God through his grace or divine energies. Not the least of which is abstinence through fasting from food.

Abstinence Through Fasting from Food

Perhaps I should begin this section with another confession. For the vast majority of my Christian life, I have neglected the spiritual discipline of fasting. As with anyone who has read through or studied the Scriptures, I was well aware of the numerous references to this discipline but never seriously considered putting it into practice. Thus, today as I write, I do so as a novice. A novice committed to fasting as a normal part of my spiritual journey.

In considering the subject of fasting from food, I cannot help but think of one of the most wicked cities of antiquity. Its wickedness so pronounced it had become a stench in the nostrils of the Almighty. Thus, God commissioned the prophet Jonah to go to Nineveh, diamond of Assyria, embedded in the golden arc of the Fertile Crescent midway between the Mediterranean and Caspian seas. There he proclaimed that the great city would be overthrown.[250] Read *utterly destroyed*.

In sober response, the Ninevites "declared a fast, and all of them, from the greatest to the least, put on sackcloth."[251] Imagine. A prostituted pagan city fasting in sackcloth and ashes. "When God saw what they did and how they turned from their evil ways, he had compassion and did not bring upon them the destruction he had threatened."[252]

And the great Assyrian city is not alone. Many nations throughout history have fasted and prayed for the mercy of God. America is one of them. In the midst of civil war, Lincoln called on all Americans to participate in a national day of humiliation, fasting, and prayer. "We have grown in numbers, wealth and power, as no other nation has ever grown. But we have forgotten God. We have forgotten the gracious hand which preserved us in peace, and multiplied and enriched and strengthened us; and we have vainly imagined, in the deceitfulness of our hearts, that all these blessings were produced by some superior wisdom and virtue of our own. Intoxicated with unbroken success, we have become too self-sufficient to feel that necessity of redeeming and preserving grace, too proud to pray to the God that made us!"

Thus, said Lincoln, "It behooves us, then, to humble ourselves before the offended Power, to confess our national sins, and to pray for clemency and forgiveness."[253] And that is what happened. On April 30, 1863, the American people in compliance with the request of the Senate and the proclamation of President Lincoln abstained from their ordinary secular pursuits, humbled themselves, and devoted themselves to fasting and prayer for the restoration of a divided country.

Such days of national fasting find precedent in sacred Scripture. Twelve centuries before Christ, Samuel, the last judge of Israel, assembled the Israelites at Mizpah for a national day of fasting. There they poured out water upon the earth and begged the Lord to forgive their idolatry and wash away their sins.[254] In the days of Nehemiah, the seed of Israel separated themselves in the sanctuary and renounced their heathenism, "fasting and wearing sackcloth and putting dust on their heads."[255] Joel, who likened the invasion of foreign hordes that plundered Jerusalem and left her desolate to an apocalyptic army of locusts, likewise consecrated a sacred fast in Jerusalem. There the people of the promise begged the Lord to forgive their iniquities, "with fasting and weeping and mourning."[256]

The most exceptional fasting account in the whole of the Old Testament took place at the time of the exodus. Not an ordinary fast. An extraordinary one. A fast from food *and* water for forty days and forty nights. And not just once, but on three separate occasions and over a relatively short period of time. A total of 120 days and nights without food and water! Even more amazing is that the one fasting was already in his eightieth year of life.

The story, of course, is that of Moses, who climbed up to the top of Mount Sinai and was absorbed into the cloud of God's glory. There he experienced God as the archetypal source of life and living. On the mountaintop, Moses was permitted to experientially *know* that "man does not live on bread alone but on every word that comes from the mouth of the LORD."[257] He was not kept alive by bread and water, but by being interpenetrated by uncreated energy. A life-source not physical but manifestly divine in origin.

Had Moses not participated in the divine nature, he would most certainly have died. Humans can abstain from food for forty days but not from water. Within a weeks' time death becomes unavoidable. Yet Moses did not die. Nor did he grow weary. After forty days and forty nights without food and water, he traversed Mount Sinai from its top all the way to its bottom and watched in horror as the children of Israel, engorged on food and drink, worshiped the golden calf. With supernatural energy he ground the detestable idol into dust and then fell prostrate before the Lord for yet another forty days and forty nights during which he "ate no bread and drank no water."[258] On top of all of that, Moses ascended Mount Sinai, fasting yet again for forty days and forty nights.[259] When he came down from Mount Sinai his face quite literally glowed with the glory of the Lord.[260]

This account of fasting is of course miraculous. Not in the sense of a momentary disruption of natural law but rather in the sense of the divine disclosure of another reality. Moses, as it were, had stepped through the wardrobe into Narnia and encountered a world in which the ingestion of food and water was superfluous.

And Moses was not alone. Elijah, the prototypical prophet, likewise fasted forty days and forty nights. Thereafter he, too, experienced the graces of God. Not in a cloud of glory, nor in a fiery vision, but in the "sound of a gentle breeze."[261] Jesus likewise abstained from food. As the new Moses leading us into a better covenant, he fasted forty days and forty nights in the wilderness. Israel murmured against God in the midst of wilderness manna. Immanuel did not. He cherished the manna from heaven more than life itself. His rebuke of Satan says it all: "Man shall not live on bread alone, but on every word that comes from the mouth of God."[262]

The normal human mode of existence depends on the ingestion, digestion, and metabolism of food and water. As Jesus makes plain, however, there is an alternate energy supply. This he referred to when he spoke to the Samaritan woman at Jacob's well: "Whoever drinks of this water will thirst again, but whoever drinks of the water that I shall give him will never thirst."[263] Shortly thereafter, "His disciples urged him saying, 'Rabbi, eat.' But He said to them, 'I have food to eat of which you do not know.'"[264]

This was the way of the Master. Communicating spiritual realities by means of earthly, empirically perceptible realities—what might best be described as living metaphors. The disciples understood food and water. Jesus desired for them to understand nourishment on a higher plane. They were acquainted with the energy that is derived from food; Jesus acquainted them with the energy that comes from the Father.

The disciples gained a glimpse of this otherworldly reality on the Mount of Transfiguration. There Peter, James, and John were witness to a dazzling display of uncreated energy. The face of Christ "shone like the sun, and His clothes became as white as the light."[265] Moreover, Moses and Elijah—who themselves had experienced divine energy during their times of fasting—appeared as the disciples were enveloped in a bright cloud.[266] They experienced the ultimate lawgiver and archetypal prophet in "glorious splendor."[267] They were eyewitness to the majesty of the One who fulfilled the law and the prophets. And they themselves were immersed in the bright cloud of God's presence.

Peter, James, and John were well aware of the fact that Moses and Elijah, after fasting forty days and forty nights, had encountered a partial disclosure of the *dunamis* underlying the created order. But what they experienced on the Mount of Transfiguration was even more profound. They were eyewitnesses to the transfigured majesty of the One who like Moses and Elijah had fasted from food and feasted on a far more substantial reality. Jesus had previously explained the dynamics of energy on a higher plane. On Mount Sinai they experienced it.

This, then, is the primary purpose of fasting. To experience God as the source and substance of life that is truly life.[268] To taste the heavenly manna. To drink divine water so as to never thirst again. To recognize union with Christ as the apex of human existence. In the words of one who himself had been blinded by the light: "We all, with unveiled face, beholding as in a mirror the glory of the Lord, are being transformed into the same image from glory to glory, just as by the Spirit of the Lord."[269] As we behold him, we become what we were designed to be—*Christ*-ians growing in his image and being transformed into his likeness.

As glorious as this high peak truth is, there are myriad other reasons to fast. The Ninevites fasted in sackcloth and ashes, and God stayed his hand of judgment. Ezra "ate no food and drank no water"[270] as he mourned the unfaithfulness of exiles who had returned to the land but had not returned to the Lord. Esther fasted from food and water for three days and nights and begged Jews in the province of Susa to do likewise—thus they averted the genocidal plot of Haman, personal advisor to the Persian king Xerxes.[271] Saul was "three days without sight, and neither ate nor drank." Thereafter "there fell from his eyes something like scales, and he received his sight at once; and he arose and was baptized."[272] The church at Antioch fasted and prayed as Saul, turned Paul, was being set apart for his glorious commission as Apostle to the Gentiles.[273]

Fasting has all this and much more to commend it. In the Sermon on the Mount Jesus placed fasting on par with prayer and almsgiving as "an act of righteousness."[274] Not to be seen by men, but by our Father "who sees what is done in secret."[275] Indeed, prayer, almsgiving, and fasting are inextricably woven as one. As the living discipline of fasting fortifies our supplications, so also it opens our hearts to the needs of the poor and downtrodden.

In a series of sermons, the revered Cappadocian Father Saint Basil exhorts us to walk through history and investigate the ancient origins of fasting. "All the saints have protected it, like an inheritance passed down from the fathers. They in turn passed it down, like a father passing something down to a child. So we are the successors of this long line, and this possession has been entrusted to us." For Basil, fasting was no trifling matter. He chided those who appeared to be more eager to pleasure the stomach than provide for the soul. "While getting filled up does a favor for the stomach, fasting returns benefits to the soul. Be encouraged, because the doctor has given you a powerful remedy for sin. Strong, powerful medicines can get rid of annoying worms that are living in the bowels of children. Fasting is like that, as it cuts down to the depths, venturing into the soul to kill sin. It is truly fitting to call it by this honorable name of medicine."[276]

As Moses, Elijah, and Jesus fasted forty days, so the church from its earliest days onward has fasted forty days in spiritual preparation for the festival of the Lord's resurrection.[277] During those forty days our Lord's words concerning fasting remain foremost in our thoughts. Fasting is not for outward appearances. Hypocrisy is repugnant to him. But when your fasting is attended by purity of heart, you will be fully rewarded by the Father. As such, Jesus weaves fasting together with prayer and almsgiving as a three-braided cord connecting us to our Father who is in heaven and to our own flesh and blood who are on the earth.[278] And says Isaiah, "Is not this the kind of fasting I have chosen: to loose the chains of injustice and untie the cords of the yoke, to set the oppressed free and break every yoke? Is it not to share your food with the hungry and to provide the poor wanderer with shelter—when you see the naked, to clothe them, and not to turn away from your own flesh and blood?"[279]

When you fast in such a way, your prayers will rise up as a sweet-smelling savor. "Then your light will break forth like the dawn, and your healing will quickly appear; then your righteousness will go before you, and the glory of the LORD will be your rear guard. Then you will call, and the LORD will answer; you will cry for help, and he will say: Here am I."[280] The genuine love of God will inevitably stimulate a reciprocal love for needy human beings who bear his image and likeness upon the earth. And when this is so, God will infuse you with his uncreated energy. Though your stomach may be empty, your spirit will be fully satisfied. You will experience the life of God springing up within you like a river of living water. Says Isaiah, "The Lord will guide you always; he will satisfy your needs in a sun-scorched land and will strengthen your frame. You will be like a well-watered garden, like a spring whose waters never fail."[281]

If we are satiated with food and drink, we are prone to a false sense of self-sufficiency and easily blinded to the needs of those lacking bread and water. But in fasting we are refashioned as "the poor in spirit,"[282] illumined to our dependence on God and to the needs of those fashioned in his image and likeness. As we fast, we are reminded that he is the bread of heaven. And that his body was broken so that we may even now experience the life that is truly life and in the consummation of all things an eternal banquet table.

Fasting is a many-splendored discipline. It not only satisfies the spirit but is strong medicine for the body. In his sermon series, Saint Basil enumerates the benefits. "What's easier to the stomach," he asks, "a plain diet that carries you through the night, or rich foods that weigh you down like a rock when you lie down?"[283]

The wise Cappadocian father used a merchant ship as an apt illustration. Such a ship is far safer and more maneuverable when light than when excessively weighed down. "The ship completely loaded down is sunk by a minor swell in the waters. But the boat that has a captain smart enough to toss overboard the extra weight will ride high above even surging waves." And so it is with over-indulged bodies. "A person gets absorbed with filling up, getting weighed down until finally falling into ill health. But those who are well-equipped, light, and truly nourished, avoid the prospect of serious disease. They are like the boat in stormy weather that goes right over a dangerous rock."[284] Moreover, "to those who are traveling, fasting is a favorable traveling partner. While luxury forces them to bear burdens by carrying their enjoyments around, fasting prepares them to be light and unencumbered."[285]

Basil continues with ironic humor. "The stomach should give a vacation to the mouth!" It "never stops demanding, and what it takes in today is forgotten tomorrow. Whenever it is filled, it philosophizes about abstinence; whenever it is emptied, it forgets those opinions."[286] How foolish to dig a grave with your own knife and fork. "A full belly not only makes running a race difficult, it even makes sleep tough. When you are weighted down completely and can't find a way to rest, you are forced instead to continually turn from side to side."[287]

The stomach is very much like an undisciplined child, forever demanding its fill of empty calories. The discipline of fasting restores balance and self-control. "One fasting has a gentle eye, a calm gait, and a thoughtful face. There is no intemperate, arrogant laughter, but rather fitting speech, and purity of heart. Remember the saints of old, 'Of whom the world was not worthy, who went around in sheepskins, in goatskins, destitute, persecuted, mistreated.'[288] Remember their mode of life, if indeed you are seeking after the same inheritance as them."[289]

With all that fasting has to commend it, the question that remains to be answered is, How can we celebrate this discipline for the remainder of our lives? As with the memorization of Scripture, I have found it exceedingly helpful to set small, attainable goals. Thus, I began my initial fasts following the Orthodox manner of fasting on Wednesday and Friday. During both days I fortified myself with prayer, considered the needs of others, and drank ample amounts of water. During these fasts, I maintained an acute awareness that my fasting was not about outward appearances (although I did lose a substantial amount of weight) but inner transformation.

In time I felt adequately prepared to follow the Orthodox fasting calendar, which in essence is "a mostly vegan diet for more than half the days of the year."[290] When I begin to feel hungry during some of the more challenging fasts (e.g., the Lenten fast before Pascha), I pray not only for perseverance but for multitudes worldwide experiencing involuntary deprivation—and for millions more who could not assuage their hunger by drinking bottles of fresh water as I have the luxury of doing.

As I write, I am in spiritual preparation for a three-day fast and eventually one that will be seven days in duration. During a seven-day fast the first three days are the most difficult. During this time the body is in process of eliminating toxins that have accumulated over years of undisciplined eating. Day four is typically transitional. From that time forward your mind will become increasingly clear and you may even feel physically invigorated. Most of the toxins will have been eliminated and you will experience what Basil described as a "calm gait" and "purity of heart." After seven days a feeling of well-being will likely motivate continuance of the fast.

Wherever fasting takes you—perhaps even toward a forty-day mountain-top experience—it is crucial to remain mindful of the purposes for practicing abstinence. Four immediately spring to mind: forgiveness, almsgiving, supplication, transformation.

- **Forgiveness:** As we fast we are to continually seek forgiveness from sin. "If we confess our sins, he is faithful and just and will forgive us our sins and purify us from all unrighteousness."[291]
- **Almsgiving:** In fasting we intuitively consider the needs of others—and our responsibility to give alms to the poor. "I tell you the truth," said Jesus, "whatever you did for one of the least of these brothers of mine, you did for me."[292]
- **Supplication:** As almsgiving is inextricably woven together with fasting, so too are our prayers and supplications. "This is the confidence we have in approaching God: that if we ask anything according to his will, he hears us. And if we know that he hears us—whatever we ask—we know that we have what we have asked of him."[293]
- **Transformation:** We fast so that we might be transfigured in the manner of Peter, James, and John. As Saint Basil so wonderfully exhorted: "Anoint your head with a holy oil, so that you may be a partaker of Christ, and then go forth to fast."[294] Appetites pleasure the body; abstinence gives wings to the spirit so that we may ascend to the mount of transfiguration and there discover communion with God as the apex of life.

Living disciplines such as prayer, reading, and fasting characterized the life of Jesus. So, too, they must characterize ours. Every year millions make confessions of faith. But there's a problem. Their habits of life are appreciably the same after conversion as they were before. Why? Because of the accumulated deposits of life experiences that remain entrenched in their embodied selves.[295] They "have the desire to do what is good" but "cannot carry it out."[296]

Peter vowed never to forsake his Lord.[297] Yet when a young woman wondered whether he followed Caesar or was a follower of Christ, he renounced the Master with vile oaths.[298] He swore he had no personal knowledge of the very One he had previously announced as "the Christ, the Son of the living God."[299] Preservation of life and limb overwhelmed his better intentions.

This is the self-same problem we face in the cauldron of adversity. We may have correct inner beliefs, yet lacking a full measure of the authentic Christian life we stumble in the moment of truth. How different our Lord. When the Pharisees and teachers of the law threatened to undo him, he exhibited an otherworldly calm—a peace in the midst of the storm.

Such peace is accessible to you and me as well. "My peace I give you," said Jesus.[300] The words of our Lord highlight a glorious truth. The peace manifested by Jesus may be actualized in our lives. Not by asking what Jesus would do in this or that circumstance. But by doing what Jesus did throughout the entirety of our lives. Such is the role of living disciplines.

Force of will is entirely insufficient—indeed impotent—in dealing with the deeply ingrained tendencies embedded in the embodied self.[301] Jesus said to his disciples in the Garden of Gethsemane, "The spirit is willing, but the flesh is weak."[302] Supposing we can transform ourselves from carnality to Christlikeness through force of will is delusional.

Imagine trying to hit a six-iron out of a bunker to a green ominously guarded by sand and water in the manner of Tiger Woods. I can promise you force of will is wholly insufficient. Or imagine leading a fourth-quarter game-winning drive in the manner of Tom Brady. It will not happen by asking what Tiger or Tom would do. The only way to do what Tiger or Tom do in the heat of battle is to prepare for the moment of truth in the manner they do.

In sum, willpower is insufficient to eradicate the layers of sin embedded in our embodied selves. Living disciplines can do what force of will cannot. They are the means through which we may sow to the Spirit instead of sowing to the sinful nature. As Paul took pains to explain, sowing to the sinful nature reaps ever-escalating corruption. Sowing to the Spirit produces life.[303] As Richard Foster has well said, "A farmer is helpless to grow grain; all he can do is provide the right conditions for the growing of grain. He cultivates the ground, he plants the seed, he waters the plants, and then the natural forces of the earth take over and up comes the grain. This is the way it is with the Spiritual Disciplines—they are a way of sowing to the Spirit. The Disciplines are God's way of getting us into the ground; they put us where he can work within us and transform us. By themselves the Spiritual Disciplines can do nothing; they can only get us to the place where something can be done. *They are God's means of grace.*"[304]

FUSION

The Secret to Global Transformation

There is a direct link between the oneness of Christians, after the image of the Trinity, and the missionary dimension of the Church. The Church looks not inward but outward. It exists not for the sake of itself but for the sake of the world's salvation. The Church, as a mystery of mutual Trinitarian love, is true to itself only if the circle of love is being constantly enlarged, only if new persons are continually being brought within it. Faith in the Triune God signifies that we are each of us missionaries, dedicated to the preaching of the Gospel.

—ECUMENICAL PATRIARCH BARTHOLOMEW I[1]

"Unlimited energy. For everyone. Forever."[2] Such is the promise of fusion. As an energy source, nuclear fusion is perfect. It produces approximately four times as much power as fission and runs on hydrogen, the most plentiful element in the universe. If something goes wrong, fusion reactors don't melt down; they stop. No toxicity; no radioactive waste; no pollution.

The opposite is true of fission. While fusion is union, fission is division.

It is the splitting of atoms as opposed to their unification. Splitting larger atoms such as uranium 235 releases a tremendous amount of energy. *But with fission comes radioactive toxic waste.* Think Chernobyl—the most disastrous nuclear fission accident in the world. Due to the division inherent in fission, Chernobyl will continue to be unsafe for human habitation for at least another three thousand years.[3]

As with fission, division within the body of Christ—"The church of God which He purchased with His own blood"[4]—produces tremendous toxicity. In contrast, a global church fused together around the essentials of the historic Christian faith is a transformational repository of *unlimited energy. For everyone. Forever.*

Fusion is the answer to the High Priestly Prayer of Jesus. "I do not pray for these alone, but also for those who will believe in Me through their word; that they all may be one, as You, Father, are in Me, and I in You; that they also may be one in Us, that the world may believe that You sent Me."[5] Union with God and unity with one another is thus the goal of our salvation and the means of global transformation. Not divided as in fission. But united as in fusion.

God became incarnate in the form of humanity so that humanity might rise up to union with God. United to God and to one another, the church is empowered by an unlimited flow of divine energy by which to provide life and light to the world. Divided, the church's energy remains limited and toxic. And therein lies the billion-dollar question. Will we continue to fissure? Or will we fuse with God and with one another in answer to the Lord's High Priestly Prayer, that we all may be one so that "the world may believe"? Believe and receive the life that matters more!

As with fusion in the natural realm, fusion in the body of Christ may seem an impossible dream. Though the world needs clean energy and plenty of it, atomic nuclei quite naturally resist fusion. They are fundamentally opposed to it. The nuclei of hydrogen atoms contain the same positive charge and, as such, are predisposed to repel one another. And yet "fusion may just turn out to belong to that category of human achievement, like powered flight and moon landings, that appeared categorically impossible right up until the moment somebody did it."[6] "We need an energy miracle," said Bill Gates.[7]

And he is betting billions that the fusion that happens routinely within the sun will one day soon be birthed in miniature suns on earth.[8]

Our response to the notion of fusion in the spiritual realm may well be one of denial. Too good to be true. How realistic is it to believe that the church would move toward unification as opposed to continuing the slide of divide? But we must immediately catch ourselves. Do we really have the temerity to ask the Lord God Most High, the One in whose presence we could not so much as stand, whether his prayer to the Father might actually be realistic?

How can an infinitesimally tiny speck of dust question the One who created that dust? We can pose questions only because the breath of heaven has blown upon us. The question, therefore, is not one of realism but one of obedience. Jesus in his High Priestly Prayer is not inviting us to comprehend the infinite or to grasp the eternal. The Lord, the Savior, the Redeemer, the Logos by whom all things were made and by whom all things will be liberated from bondage to decay, is simply asking us to obey.

Fusion as an energy source would be "so cheap and clean and plentiful that it would create an inflection point in human history, an energy singularity that would leave no industry untouched." Were fusion science to become reality, it "would mean the end of fossil fuels. It would be the greatest antidote to climate change [hysteria] that the human race could reasonably ask for. Saving the world."[9]

Whatever the reality respecting fusion science, spiritual fusion *is* the greatest antidote to the cultural captivity of the contemporary church. Were the authentic church to embrace fusion in place of fission, she may well experience a second iteration of Pentecost. The sound from heaven. The mighty rushing wind. The baptism of the Holy Spirit and fire. The manifestation of the uncreated, inexhaustible energy supply that alone is sufficient to save the world.

During the first iteration of Pentecost, the growth of the Christian church was quite simply beyond the pale. Within an astonishingly short time frame eucharistic assemblies appeared as if by magic throughout the Roman Empire. The magic rooted not in sleight of hand nor sleight of mind, but in an organic miracle of unity within diversity. As with the Trinity, the church, a miraculous assembly of subjects (human hypostases), was united in a single essence. "Just as each of us has one body with many members, and these members do not all have the same function, so in Christ we who are many form one body, and each member belongs to all the others."[10] At Baptism, we are birthed into the body of Christ. And in the Eucharist, we are united to Christ and to one another. "For we, though many, are one bread and one body; for we all partake of that one bread."[11] Thus, the one body of Christ creates the unity of the one body of *Christ*-ians.

DISUNITY—FISSURING THE BODY OF CHRIST

"Disunity," proffered Patriarch Bartholomew, the Ecumenical Patriarch of the three hundred million Orthodox worldwide, "is not simply an inconvenience, not simply a hindrance and a scandal, but it is a contradiction of the basic essence of the Church as an icon of God's mutual Trinitarian love."[12]

Nevertheless, disunity invaded the church. On a "summer afternoon in the year 1054, as a service was about to begin in the Church of the Holy Wisdom at Constantinople, Cardinal Humbert and two other legates of the Pope entered the building and made their way up to the sanctuary. They had not come to pray. They placed a Bull of Excommunication upon the altar and marched out."[13] One millennium after Pentecost, disunity had become an evident reality.

In that fateful eleventh-century moment, the rumblings of a schismatic volcano erupted, leaving behind a blackened lava trail stretching from East to West. Eruption was inevitable. East and West had become progressively alien to one another. "Latin thought was influenced by juridical ideas, by the concepts of Roman law, while the Greeks understood theology in the context of worship and in the light of the Holy Liturgy. When thinking about the Trinity, Latins started with the unity of the Godhead, Greeks with the threeness of the persons; when reflecting on the Crucifixion, Latins thought primarily of Christ the Victim, Greeks of Christ the Victor; Latins talked more of redemption, Greeks of deification."[14]

There were other divergences as well. The West insisted on priestly celibacy, while the East allowed for marriage in the priesthood; the West used unleavened bread in the Eucharist, the East leavened bread; and both assigned different parameters to fasting. Yet despite such divergences, unity may as yet have prevailed were it not for the egregious sin of fratricide.

During its first millennium, the church had effectively functioned as a sisterhood of five patriarchates. Antioch, where the disciples were first called Christians; Alexandria, the patriarchate founded by the Gospel writer Mark; Jerusalem, home to the first Ecumenical Council; Constantinople, capital of the Christian Greek Roman Empire; and Rome, the patriarchate designated by the others with a primacy of honor—but not supremacy.

And therein lay the fissure of fratricide. In the era of the Ecumenical Councils, the church functioned as a collegial and conciliar move of the Spirit. The bishop of Rome was afforded a primacy of honor, but not the state of supremacy he arrogated unto himself.[15] As Nicetas, Archbishop of Nicomedia, once the eastern capital of the Roman Empire, put it in a twelfth-century letter addressed to the Roman pontiff, "We do not deny to the Roman Church the primacy amongst the five sister Patriarchates; and we recognize her right to the most honourable seat at an Ecumenical Council. But she has separated herself from us by her own deeds, when through pride she assumed a monarchy which does not belong to her office."[16]

The church must never function in supreme and autonomous fashion. Were she to do so, said Nicetas, "the Roman see would not be the pious mother of sons but a hard and imperious mistress of slaves."[17] The sin of fratricide was thus a sin against the common mind of the church.

This was no small matter. To sin against the mind of the church is to sin against "the pillar and ground of the truth."[18] From the beginning, the church revered the Bible as "the supreme expression of God's revelation to the human race."[19] As with the Bible, the ancient church afforded a sacred primacy to the creeds—the most important of which was the Niceno-Constantinopolitan Creed. From ancient times it was recited or sung at every eucharistic celebration. And that without addition or subtraction. The very thought of altering it was anathema. Thus, when the *Filioque* (Latin for *"and the Son"*) was added to the Creed, disunity between East and West became inevitable.

From the Eastern perspective, altering the creed such that the Holy Spirit proceeds from the Father *and the Son* has significant theological ramifications. To begin with, it altered the sacred text of Scripture. For as the Gospel of John would have it, the Spirit of truth "proceeds from the Father" rather than in double procession from the Father *and the Son*.[20] Furthermore, in concert with the creed, *unbegottenness* belongs to the Father; *begottenness* to the Son, and *procession* to the Spirit. Tampering with the creedal formulation was thus tantamount to the subordination of the Spirit.[21] Moreover, the subordination of the Spirit such that he does not possess an attribute common to the Father and the Son was believed to spell disastrous consequences for the doctrine of deification.[22]

While there may be valid counterarguments to such Eastern contentions, one thing can be stated with absolute certainty. The unilateral addition of the *Filioque* to the Niceno-Constantinopolitan Creed struck a mortal blow to the unity of the church and fractured relations between the Western papacy and the Eastern patriarchates.

Half a millennium after the scandal of fratricide had fissured the church from East to West, another schism shattered Western Christianity. This time the fissure separated Rome from the Reformers. This time the catalyst was indulgences.

It was the summer of 1517 and a crass and carnal Dominican friar named Johann Tetzel was conning commoners into buying special releases from sin. Tetzel proved to be a master at his trade. He took a complex Catholic creed on purgatory and reduced it to a catchy couplet. "As soon as the coin in the coffer rings; the soul from purgatory springs."[23]

His pitch was intoxicatingly simple. People could purchase a pardon from God that would purge them from a place called Purgatory. Thousands fell for the ruse. The masses—from monks to magistrates—hailed Tetzel as a messenger from heaven. Capitalizing on spiritual insecurity and scriptural illiteracy, he fleeced the flock for the funding of papal projects.

Although Tetzel's merchandizing of the faith was outrageous, no one seemed willing to expose him. His popularity, backed by the power of Rome, seemed too formidable a foe. That is, until a monk named Martin Luther came along. "As a preacher, a pastor, and a professor, he felt it to be his duty to protest."[24] And so, in 1517, Luther mailed the famed *Disputation on the Power and Efficacy of Indulgences* (95 theses) to his archbishop Albrecht of Brandenburg.[25]

Luther's concern was not so much indulgences as it was the pillaging of the poor by the pope. In theses 50 and 51, he stated that the real reason Rome was selling indulgences was not the spiritual well-being of the saints but the financial well-being of the pope and his pet project—the building of the Basilica of Saint Peter's. He wrote with great passion that the mother church in Rome would be better "burnt to ashes, than that it should be built up with the skin, flesh, and bones" of the pope's sheep.[26]

Rome's reaction was swift and severe. Luther was labeled a "child of the devil" and a "drunken German who when sober will change his mind." But Luther did not change his mind.[27] Under the ban of the empire and a bull of excommunication, Luther remained resolute in his contention that the "Romanist Church" was a pawn of the Devil and that the pope was the Devil's antichrist. Were it not for his stranglehold on Scripture, the populace would no longer be duped by his devious deceptions. Thus, the battle cry of the Reformation: *sola Scriptura!*

When Catholic priest and humanist Desiderius Erasmus of Rotterdam warned that translation of the Bible into the vernacular of the masses would "unloose a floodgate of iniquity," Luther responded in cryptic fashion, "if a floodgate of iniquity be opened, so be it."[28]

Erasmus proved prophetic. On one side of the floodgate stood Pope Leo X and a Roman Catholic Church in desperate need of reform. On the other the Protestant Luther and a Reformation that was rapidly turning the Bible into a pathetic caricature of itself. "Reformers inspired directly by Luther, began taking his doctrinal principles—*sola scriptura*, the priesthood of all believers, and justification by faith alone—to places Luther himself thought were heretical."[29] The doctrinal fissures that erupted were deep and devastating.

The year following Luther's publication of the 95 theses, Andreas Rudolph Bodenstein von Karlstadt, who as chancellor of the University of Wittenberg had conferred on Luther a doctorate in theology, and who Luther considered to be his academic superior, published a list of 151 theses.[30] As noted by Dr. Benjamin Wiker in *The Reformation 500 Years Later,* Luther's dictum of justification by faith alone became the basis by which Karlstadt and his followers "rejected all the sacraments—and claimed that there was no support in Scripture for infant baptism, and perhaps not even for adult baptism. Furthermore, some of their followers rejected the doctrine of original sin, the notion that marriage was permanent (it was not, after all, a sacrament), and argued in favor of polygamy (such as existed in the Old Testament)."[31]

And this was but the beginning of sorrows. Wiker goes on to note that "even more infuriating for Luther, who still believed in the necessity of Baptism and the reality of the Eucharist, was that these reformers were attacking the Mass as an idolatrous act and were smashing up church statues, crucifixes, and paintings (even of Christ himself) as idolatrous. And some transformed the religious idea of the equality of all believers into a political cry for equality and political rebellion."[32]

As the Reformation continued, so did the fissuring. Loosed from the restraining fetters of the Apostolic Tradition, the Creeds, and the Councils, Huldreich Zwingli, the Swiss Reformer, reimagined both the Eucharist and Baptism. Dr. Diarmaid MacCulloch, in *The Reformation: A History*, noted that in Zwingli's opinion, Luther "was being crudely literal-minded to take Christ's statement at the Last Supper, 'This is my body . . . this is my blood,' as being true as it stood, and meaning that bread and wine in some sense became the body and blood of Christ."[33] For Zwingli the Eucharist was merely memorial—a remembrance. In like fashion Zwingli altered Baptism from a sacramental burial to sin and resurrection to newness of life, to a mere welcoming ceremony. Said MacCulloch, "For Zwingli, therefore, the meaning of the sacraments shifted from something God did for humanity, to something humanity did for God."[34]

As with the other reformers, there were "serpents in Zwingli's garden: not angry supporters of the pope or troublesome Lutherans, but his own most fervent admirers."[35] Among them were Anabaptists—the so-called radicals or left wing of the Reformation. "Because there were so many different Anabaptist groups with slightly different variations in belief—variations that grew out of the insistence on the believer's right to interpret the Bible as a literal and final authority—it is difficult to give an organized statement of the Anabaptist beliefs."[36] All, however, believed that the Zwinglian commitment to infant baptism was emblematic of the corruption of the church. In retaliation, Zwinglian zealots at Zurich and elsewhere saw to it that the Anabaptists were exiled, drowned, or worse. In one instance of unimaginable brutality, Michael Sattler, an early Anabaptist leader, had his tongue cut out before being burned alive. Days later his wife, Margaretha, was drowned.[37] Even so, the fissuring had just begun.

Though the Swiss Reformer John Calvin married Idelette, widow of an Anabaptist, he had determined to distinguish himself from Anabaptist "fantasists" who, said Calvin, "only wished to govern themselves in accordance with their foolish brains, under the pretence of wishing to obey God."[38] Yet as demonstrated by many a Calvinist, the Reformed "could be as destructive and politically revolutionary as any Anabaptist."[39]

With the burning of the anti-trinitarian Michael Servetus on October 27, 1553, Calvin began to be widely perceived "as not one reformer among many, but the major voice in Reformation Protestantism."[40] He not only opposed "Luther's insistence on finding the body and blood of Christ physically present in the Eucharistic elements,"[41] but, in contrast to Luther, championed the notion of double predestination.[42] He varied his conjecture on the ratios of those preordained to eternal life and those preordained to eternal damnation, from one salvation in every hundred damnations to a more palatable estimate of one in every five.[43] Growing up in the Dutch Calvinist context, I can personally testify that such ratios are far from academic.

Though a great deal more attention could be assigned to the disunity that took place within the Reformation, suffice it to say the fissuring did not end there. Anglicanism was birthed in England when Pope Clement refused to annul the marriage of Henry VIII and Catherine of Aragon. Divergent groups from Baptists (John Smythe), to Quakers (George Fox), to Methodists (John and Charles Wesley) likewise trace their divisional origins to England. As does the nineteenth-century dogma of dispensationalism—which itself is an interesting case study.

In 1831, the same year that Charles Darwin left England and sailed into evolutionary infamy, John Nelson Darby, a disillusioned priest, left the Church of England and joined a separatist millenarian group called the Plymouth Brethren in the English city of Plymouth. Like Darwin, Darby was a trendsetter. In much the same way that Darwin imposed a speculative spin on the scientific data he encountered along the South American coasts of Patagonia, Darby imposed a subjective spin on the scriptural data he encountered in the city of Plymouth.

Darby's contention was that God had two distinct people with two distinct plans and two distinct destinies. Only one of those peoples, the Jews, would suffer tribulation. The other, the church, would be removed from the world in a secret coming seven years prior to the second coming of Christ. While dispensationalism evolved into the poster child for biblical literalism, the Plymouth Brethren initially exposed to Darby's unique twist on the text considered it exegetically indefensible. Thus, Darby's system of dividing the Bible divided the Brethren.

Among the various divisions of the twentieth century, Pentecostalism is particularly noteworthy. In the early morning hours of the first day of the twentieth century, a twenty-seven-year-old preacher from Topeka, Kansas, named Charles Parham placed his hands on the head of a young student named Agnes Ozman. Suddenly, a "halo seemed to surround her head and face" and Agnes began to speak Chinese.[44] For three days she was utterly incapable of speaking a single word in English. And when she tried to write, only Chinese characters would emerge.[45]

Ozman's experience became the catalyst for other students to seek the gift of tongues.[46] It wasn't long before many of them began to speak in languages they had never studied. According to Parham, his students, "Americans all, spoke in twenty-one known languages."[47] Parham therefore proclaimed that while missionaries throughout church history necessarily studied foreign languages, this would no longer be the case. As a result of this twentieth-century Pentecost, "one need only receive the baptism with the Holy Spirit and he could go to the farthest corners of the world and preach to the natives in languages unknown to the speaker."[48]

Pentecostal historian Vincent Synan has noted candidly that when

Parham's theory was put to the test "it ended in failure."[49] Nevertheless, Parham moved to Houston, Texas, and opened a school to propagate his newfound theology. It was at this school that Parham taught a man "given to dreams and visions" who was to become "the Apostle of Azusa Street."[50] His name was William Seymour. While Seymour roundly rejected Parham's teaching that Anglo-Saxons were God's chosen race,[51] he wholeheartedly embraced Parham's theology on tongues. Seymour was so convinced that even before personally speaking in tongues, he told parishioners of a Los Angeles Holiness church that tongues, not sanctification, was evidence of the baptism in the Holy Ghost.[52] Several days later, Seymour experienced the breakthrough he was looking for. He and seven devotees "fell to the floor in a religious ecstasy, speaking with other tongues."[53]

News spread like wildfire, and before long curious onlookers beheld such sights as Jennie Moore (Seymour's future wife) singing in what was believed to be the Hebrew language. Curiosity swelled the size of the crowds so much that Seymour rented an abandoned African Methodist Episcopal Church at 312 Azusa Street and began conducting revival meetings. In time things got so out of hand that "Seymour wrote Parham for advice on how to handle 'the spirits' and begged him to come to Los Angeles to take over supervision of the revival."[54]

When Parham arrived, he denounced the "hypnotists and spiritualists who seemed to have taken over the services."[55] While Seymour was sympathetic to Parham's concerns, he refused correction. Thus, the two pillars of Pentecostalism suffered an irreparable falling out.[56] While the rift between Parham and Seymour was never repaired, the twin pillars of Pentecostalism succeeded in setting the stage for one of the fastest-growing segments of global Christianity[57]—a movement that since has itself fissured into myriad denominations.

The fissuring of the twentieth century continued in the twenty-first. Almost daily new and novel permutations of Christianity have emerged. Sometimes the disputations are minor. At other times major. One of the newest innovations catching the fancy of churches from Singapore to America is the contention that the sacrament of confession—a staple in the church from its very inception—is tantamount to "cheapening God's unmerited favor"[58] or, worse, "mocking God."[59] Private interpretations in this regard are stunning.

One deems confession to be a "Gnostic" heresy[60]; another demeans it as "counterproductive to a healthy Christian life."[61] This in face of the apostle John who urged his "dear children" in the faith[62]—those who have been forgiven on account of Christ—to continually confess their sins.[63] Or, the apostle James, who explicitly exhorts believers to confess their sins to one another and to God.[64]

While accounts of division can be multiplied indefinitely, it is sufficient here to note as did Andrew Stephen Damick in *Orthodoxy and Heterodoxy* that "estimates of the number of Protestant Christian denominations are as high as thirty thousand, though that number includes many single, independent congregations. Among them, you can find a bewildering array of different beliefs. And most of them claim to be 'just going by the Bible.'"[65]

And with each and every division of the atom, the radioactive toxic waste continues to multiply. Yet, as noted at the outset, there is another way. It is the way of fusion.

DOCTRINE OF UNITY—FUSING THE BODY OF CHRIST

If the church is to be one, as Christ and the Father are one, fusion must of necessity overwhelm fission and division. This was the apostolic plea from the beginning. "I appeal to you, brothers, in the name of our Lord Jesus Christ, that all of you agree with one another so that there may be no *divisions* among you and that you may be perfectly *united* in mind and thought."[66]

To the factious who say, "I follow Paul" or "I follow Apollos" or "I follow Cephas" or "I follow Christ," Paul rhetorically retorts, *"Is Christ divided?"*[67] The problem with factionalism in the ancient church, as in its modern-day counterpart, is not one of *tribes*—the tribe of Paul, or Apollos, or Cephas— but one of *tribalism*. Competitors as opposed to coworkers in the fellowship of the undivided Trinity. As Metropolitan Kallistos Ware has rightly said,

"Orthodoxy desires unity-in-diversity, not uniformity; harmony-in-freedom, not absorption. There is room in the Orthodox Church for many different cultural patterns, for many different ways of worship, and even for many different systems of outward organization."[68] Yet with one vital exception.

Authentic Christianity "insists upon unity in matters of faith. *Before there can be reunion among Christians, there must first be full agreement in faith.*"[69] As I have consistently communicated during the entirety of my ministry, there can be liberty in nonessentials and charity in all else, but there must be unity in the faith once for all delivered to the saints. To seek unity at the cost of essential matters of the faith is tantamount to "throwing away the kernel of a nut and keeping the shell."[70] While we are to direct our energies toward the endgame of fusion, we are never to do so at the expense of essential Christian faith and practice.

As with fusion in the physical realm, fusion in the spiritual realm is difficult. Far easier to fissure than fuse. Yet there can be no doubt that you and I have been called for fusion. To be one so that the world may believe. Perhaps you are reading these words as Orthodox or Roman Catholic. Perhaps as Lutheran or Calvinist. Anabaptist or Anglican. Baptist or Pentecostal. Whatever your tribe, our common Lord has specifically called you and me to the doctrine of unity.

As I look back over the course of my life, of one thing I am certain: God has his people everywhere. I grew up in a Calvinist context. At fourteen I walked away from the faith of my parents because I struggled with the notion of hard determinism. Yet as I look back from the perspective of time, I can tell you with absolute certainty that my parents, indeed all my siblings and their spouses who yet remain Calvinist, are friends of God—and deeply committed to essential Christian orthodoxy and orthopraxy. My mom and dad, even now in the presence of the Lord, are heroes of the faith deeply in love with each other and deeply in love with the Lord. Their model of faithfulness to the very end is one I deeply desire to emulate.

Permit me to ramble on a bit. When I came back to the faith at age twenty-nine, Reformed theologian Dr. R. C. Sproul became a hero and mentor. I adored his books and tapes. Particularly those reflecting the holiness of God.

I loved listening to him parse words. I enjoyed the time we spent feeding our mutual addiction to golf. I was perpetually moved by the love and commitment he openly displayed toward his precious bride Vesta. Of this I am confident. He was the real deal!

After moving to Atlanta in the early eighties I met the extraordinary Pentecostal pastor and preacher Dr. Paul Walker. As with R. C. we forged a relationship around the game of golf. It wasn't long before Kathy and I joined Mount Paran Church of God and began teaching memory and personal witness training classes. The relationships we forged in doing so continue to the present. Seldom have I seen people more committed to God, and to the family of God.

In the late eighties I moved to Southern California and became president of the Christian Research Institute. In doing so, I met Christians from a wide variety of spiritual backgrounds. One of my early mentors in countering counterfeit religions was a committed Lutheran named Gretchen Passantino. Gretchen and her husband, Bob, were titans in the field of apologetics. Ferociously committed Christians with fertile minds and fervent hearts. And there were many others. Elliot Miller, editor-in-chief of the *Christian Research Journal*, a giant of the faith. An original of the Jesus Movement and an early Calvary Chapel adherent. In working with Elliot for over thirty years I learned from his commitment to prayer. To truth and to life.

When we began research on the Lord's Recovery, I was privileged to meet believers from all over the world who demonstrated what it means to know the Lord not as a mere logical truth proposition but as a life. Elijah Widjaja, to whom I dedicate this book, opened my eyes to the glories of genuine sonship. To what it is to ascend the paradisiacal mountain and partake of the Tree of Life.

I could go on. At St. Nektarios, I met Father Steve and his wife, Maria, both humble yet brilliant servant leaders. Their commitment to Orthodoxy whet my appetite for the writings of the early church fathers. Within weeks of meeting these precious saints, Kathy had accumulated a library of over a hundred books—all of them now replete with her typical underlining and notes.

One thing Kathy and I have learned together, as we immersed ourselves in the writings of the Fathers, is that just as each of us as individuals are icons of the Triune God, so the body of Christ collectively is a mystery of unity in diversity. In the vernacular of Metropolitan Kallistos, the church "is a new life according to the image of the Holy Trinity, a life in Christ and in the Holy Spirit, a life realized by participation in the sacraments. The Church is a single reality, earthly and heavenly, visible and invisible, human and divine."[71] "The saints," said Symeon the New Theologian, "in each generation, joined to those who have gone before, and filled like them with light, become a golden chain, in which each saint is a separate link, united to the next by faith, works, and love. So in the One God they form a single chain which cannot quickly be broken."[72]

Wherever there is a break in that golden chain—whenever there is a schism—it cries out to be healed. It begs an answer to the Lord's High Priestly Prayer that "all may be one, as you Father, are in Me, and I in You." Even now I am reminded of the Chalcedonian schism that took place more than fifteen hundred years ago. A schism between the Eastern and Oriental Orthodox churches. A division of the atom that has radiated toxic waste for more than fifteen hundred years. A fissure just begging to be healed.

The Chalcedonian schism illustrates how very difficult fusion is. As hydrogen atoms that scientists seek to unify in the interest of fusion naturally repel one another, so also do the factions on either side of a spiritual schism. As Dr. John H. Erickson, Orthodox professor of church history, reminded us, "whatever may have been the issues initially leading to division, a division once established very quickly takes on a life of its own, as each side tries to justify its own role in the division. Differences that would not in themselves have been church-dividing are invested with new meaning, to the point of becoming symbols of division rather than examples of legitimate diversity." As competing factions continue to repel one another, "competing ecclesial structures are erected. Anathemas are hurled. And even if the issues that led to the division are eventually resolved, the division itself—buttressed in these many ways—remains."[73]

Such was the case with Chalcedon. "The Christological issues that initially prompted the division of these churches have been resolved, so that continued division can no longer be justified on dogmatic grounds."[74] The only reason for continued division in the present is division for the sake of division as opposed to division for the sake of essential Christian doctrine.

Thankfully, ongoing dialogue between the Eastern and Oriental Orthodox churches has served to break down old barriers. The breach that began with significant controversy regarding the relationship between the human and divine natures of Christ has gradually been moving toward resolution. Dialogue has ever so slowly moved the divided churches toward unity and full communion. Friendships have been forged and suspicions mitigated. "As two families of Orthodox Churches long out of communion with each other, we now pray and trust in God to *restore that communion* on the basis of the apostolic faith of the undivided Church of the first centuries which we confess in our common creed."[75]

As a reality, this reunification would represent a single chain of some three hundred million believers previously broken. A recognition as succinctly summarized by the Joint Commission for Dialogue between Eastern Orthodox and Oriental Orthodox churches that "we have inherited from our fathers in Christ the one apostolic faith and tradition."[76] The tribes may continue with their own historical and ecclesiological distinctives; the tribalism, however, would be history.

In the introduction to this book, I recapitulated the more modern division between the Christian Research Institute and the Lord's Recovery. Though the division emitted a significant cloud of radioactive toxic waste, we believed it to be more than justified by the ultimacy of truth. Yet when dialogue prevailed over division, we discovered that as with Chalcedon we were united in "the faith once for all delivered to the saints."[77] That our differences were not essential but secondary. That there was much that we could learn from one another.

Indeed, were it not for the divide that was bridged by dialogue, this book would never have been written. I would likely never have understood that truth matters, but life matters more. I may never have discovered the authentic Christian life. The life of fellowship in the Trinity.

Whether fusion takes place within the body of Christ on a global basis may be as speculative as fusion within the natural realm. But were it to happen—were the global church to fuse together around the essentials of historic Christianity—it would be a transformational repository of *unlimited energy. For everyone. Forever.*

Epilogue

DISCOVERING THE
AUTHENTIC CHRISTIAN LIFE

All creation is a gigantic Burning Bush, permeated but not
consumed by the ineffable and wondrous fire of God's energies.

—METROPOLITAN KALLISTOS WARE OF DIOKLEIA[1]

We live in perilous times. Islam is now the fastest-growing religion in the
world—poised to replace not only Christianity but secularism as the cultural
foundation of civilization. Not just by jihad but by the virulent demographic
reality I wrote about in *MUSLIM: What You Need to Know About the World's
Fastest-Growing Religion*.[2] A civilization that is becoming Islamic demograph-
ically will inevitably succumb to Islam politically as well. While polygamous
Muslims boast a robust birthrate, native Westerners are moving rapidly
toward self-extinction. Filling the void are multiplied millions of Muslims
who have little or no intention of assimilating into Western culture. Equally
grave is the specter of global Islamic jihadism now exacting mass genocide on
Christians in the East and ever-multiplying atrocities throughout the West.

Think back to when Muslims renamed Constantinople, Istanbul, and
replaced the cross adorning Hagia Sophia with a crescent. From the fall of

Constantinople, the Ottoman Empire advanced steadily into Europe—their sights set on the wealth of Austria and Germany. Had it not been for the leadership of Poland's King Jan Sobieski, who on September 11, 1683, halted the Muslim menace at the gates of Vienna, Europe might have already been renamed Eurabia.[3]

On September 11, 2001, the Western world faced yet another such moment of truth. This time no Jan Sobieski arrived on the scene fully understanding that the destiny of the West hung in the balance. Instead, obsessively self-loathing Western elites such as Angela Merkel pontificated that "Islam belongs to Germany"[4] and vicariously to the best of the West.

As astutely noted by Dr. Benjamin Wiker, the contemporary Islamic takeover of Western civilization can be linked in no small manner to the ascendency of illiberal liberalism, which "simultaneously declares Christianity to be the worst of all religions, and welcomes Muslims as the best of all neighbors, *even though everything about Islam is diametrically opposed to secular liberalism.*"[5] This is no doubt the reason that the genocide of Christians in the East remains squarely in the blind spot of the West.

"This strange attitude of the secular Left isn't new, but has been part and parcel of modern European atheism from the late Middle Ages on; it wasn't just the ancient pagans who were considered superior to the Christian culture of Europe, so was just about every other culture, including most particularly Islamic culture, which was simple and manly and permitted polygamy and had supposedly enjoyed its own period of glorious learning in the past." Therein lies the irascible idiosyncratic illiberal ideology that "*anything* is better than Judeo-Christianity, especially Islam." Which is precisely why the radical left "seems to love Islam and despise Christianity, even at the cost of its own self-destruction."[6]

The denigration of Christian civilization is hardly symptomatic of a fevered imagination. It is astonishingly real, as evidenced by the three quintessential building blocks of civil society—marriage, government, and church—all of which rest atop the foundation of human life.

The building block of marriage was once correctly believed to be the unique, permanent, and "comprehensive union of body, mind, emotion, and soul, a proper end of which is children."[7] Today, life has become expendable. Even as I write, the news cycle is awash with tributes to the progressive thinking of Governor Andrew Cuomo as he signs New York's "Reproductive Health Act," effectively permitting abortion up until the very moment of delivery.[8] Moreover, the US Supreme Court's redefinition of marriage has not only undermined the foundation of human civilization but has opened Pandora's grizzly box. If there is no special virtue in gender-differentiated parenting, is there any magic in the number two? And why arbitrarily assign eighteen as the magical age of consent? Once we abandon the biblical definition of marriage, there is virtually no limit on where unsanctified passions will lead us.

Western governments mandated by God to ennoble life, promote justice, and restrain sin[9] are instead leading the charge toward social chaos. Toward militant egalitarianism, radical individualism, multiculturalism, political correctness, and religious pluralism.[10] Even toward the eradication of the gender distinctions ordained by God from the inception of human civilization. Government agencies now create, manipulate, and disseminate ideological constructs that are driving the whole of civilization in a very dangerous direction.

Of the three building blocks of civil society resting upon the foundation of life, perhaps the most colossal failures belong to the church itself. "Evangelicals," wrote the award-winning journalist John S. Dickerson in *The Great Evangelical Recession*, "are dividing and not conquering over a number of issues: politics, theology, church models and methods, views of Scripture, new approaches to the atonement. The list goes on."[11] The composite picture is a prescription for disaster. We are not only "losing most of our kids" but "our evangelism efforts are not keeping pace with population growth." Moreover, "in the midst of all this, or actually as a result of all this, the unified evangelicalism of the 20th century is splintering and fraying, turning against itself."[12] And what is true of the evangelical church is true of the global church as well.

For all intents and purposes, the church has succumbed to the crushing onslaught of illicit Islam and illiberal liberalism. Jacob Neusner, one of the most published authors in history, hauntingly reminds us that "civilization hangs suspended, from generation to generation, by the gossamer strand of memory. If only one cohort of mothers and fathers fails to convey to its children what *it* has learned from its parents, then the great chain of learning and wisdom snaps. If the guardians of human knowledge stumble only one time, in their fall collapses the whole edifice of knowledge and understanding."[13]

In concert with Neusner, philosopher and award-winning author Rabbi Jonathan Henry Sacks underscored the criticality of constant conversations between the generations. "You achieve immortality not by building pyramids or statues—but by engraving your values on the hearts of your children, and they on theirs, so that our ancestors live on in us, and we in our children, and so on until the end of time."[14]

His admonition is reminiscent of Moses, who exhorted the people of the promise to impress the words of the Almighty upon the hearts of their children and their children's children. "Talk about them when you sit at home and when you walk along the road, when you lie down and when you get up. Tie them as symbols on your hands and bind them on your foreheads. Write them on the doorframes of your houses and on your gates." Above all, exhorted Moses, "do not forget."[15]

If truth matters, and it most surely does, the church must take the task of Christian education seriously. Not "edutain" but educate. Equip our children and theirs to always be ready to give an *answer* to everyone who asks you to give a reason for the hope that you have. But do this with gentleness and respect.[16] Or as the apostle Paul would have it, "Let your conversation be always full of grace, seasoned with salt, so that you may know how to *answer* everyone."[17]

As noted in chapter 1, I, like many in the current generation, walked away from the faith during my teenage years. I was hungry for answers but found little or no relief within the context of my church or Christian school. Though I would slip in and out of spirituality over the next fifteen years, it wasn't until I discovered satisfactory answers to the pressing questions that churned through my teenage mind that I came to realize my need for Ecclesia.

Permit me to state the obvious. There are myriad professors and cultural pundits ready to steal away the faith of your progeny. Ready to tell them, as does Dr. Alex Rosenberg, professor of philosophy at the prestigious Duke

Center for Philosophy of Biology, that "physical and biological science makes the existence of God less probable than the existence of Santa Claus."[18]

Because truth matters, it is likewise critical to continue to educate ourselves and our children in the art and science of *biblical interpretation*. As discussed in chapter 2, multitudes distrust the message of the Bible because they mistake its meaning. Thus, when the Bible is so much as mentioned in polite company, it is not uncommon to see expressions of polite exasperation etched on modern faces. After all, the Bible is not only hopelessly contradictory, but also suggests that slavery is perfectly acceptable. "Which passages of Scripture should guide our public policy?" intoned former President Barack Obama. "Should we go with Leviticus, which suggests slavery is okay and that eating shellfish is abomination? Or we could go with Deuteronomy, which suggests stoning your child if he strays from the faith? Or should we just stick to the Sermon on the Mount—a passage that is so radical that it's doubtful that our own Defense Department would survive its application."[19]

What Obama is saying is hard to mistake: the Bible cannot possibly be divine. No God worthy of worship would teach that slavery is okay. What parent in his right mind would stone a child who strays away from the faith? Calling consumption of shellfish an abomination is just plain silly. And the Sermon on the Mount? Way too radical!

Obama is hardly original. His sentiments echo daily through the halls of academia and are radically reinforced by public personalities—and now most notably through the Internet. Thus, the need to equip our generation to read and interpret the Bible for all its substantial worth.

Because truth matters, the church must also prepare herself to counter such counterfeit religions as Islam. Yet, as Robert Spencer rightly pointed out in the foreword to *MUSLIM*, the church as a whole has "been notably slow, not only to meet this challenge but even to recognize it as such. While Muslim groups are making concerted efforts to convert young Christians to Islam . . . Christian leaders of all denominations have been notably remiss. . . .

"The seriousness of this omission is compounded by the fact that Islam shares a feature common to many spiritual counterfeits: a simplicity and directness that seem to contrast favorably with what can appear to be

Christianity's complexity and difficulty (indeed, one of the favorite tactics of Muslim proselytizers is to attack the doctrine of the Trinity as illogical and therefore false and evidence of the falsity of Christianity as a whole)."[20]

The antidote is to demonstrate "that Islam's simplicity and superficial clarity dissolve, upon closer inspection, into a chaos of self-contradiction, illogic, and absurdity, featuring doctrines borrowed from Christianity, severely misunderstood, and twisted beyond recognition to form part of the incoherence that is Islamic theology."[21]

When compared with the straight stick of Scripture, such crookedness is readily apparent. Thus, whether countering Islam or the deviations of some other counterfeit, we are well-served to be so familiar with the truth that when a forgery looms on the horizon, we spot it straightaway.

It is hardly sufficient, however, to be *intellectually* equipped to communicate truth via answers, the art and science of biblical interpretation, or by countering counterfeit religions. Thus, in part two, our focus was on life—the life that matters more. The absolute necessity of being *internally* equipped for this anything-but-Christian moment. What that means is that the church must be energized for its mission—by a power that is *in* it but not *of* it.

As underscored in chapter 4, the goal is not for saved humanity to remain in the "port of salvation." It is to continue on a "journey whose sole goal is union with God."[22] It is the experience of life. All attempts to understand the Christian ethic from a solely rational perspective remain partial and inadequate. While the life that matters more is not a prohibition upon knowledge, it *is* the transcending of knowledge. The transcending of all philosophical speculation.

When the disciples saw the face of Jesus shining like the sun, they came face-to-face with the poverty of their own petrified paradigms. The notion that they might be transfigured like unto their Teacher was as remote to Peter, James, and John as $E = mc^2$ would have been to a consensus scientist prior to the genius of Albert Einstein. As previously noted, "we are not merely saved *from* sin; we are saved *for* sonship, to be divinely adopted sons and daughters of God." The Fathers of the embryonic church "were so bold as to call this process 'divinization' and 'deification,' because it is the means by which we enter the life of the Trinity."[23]

God became incarnate in the form of humanity that humanity might rise up to union with God. This, said Maximus the Confessor, is the very purpose for which God created us, "that we may become partakers of the divine nature, in order that we may enter into eternity, and that we may appear like unto Him, being deified by that grace out of which all things that exist have come, and which brings into existence everything that before had no existence."[24]

God became man that man might become god! The echo of the Fathers pound at our psyches seeking to extricate us from our pyscho-epistomological cocoons. Christ invaded time and space. He took on our humanity. That we might experience "the *perichoretic* movement" inherent to the "divinization of Christ's flesh." A movement "undeniably commenced by the divine nature of the Logos who 'united our nature to himself in a single hypostasis, without division and without confusion.'" In "reciprocal movement, 'the image returns to the archetype,' who, in turn, imparts to it the divine life."[25]

As highlighted in chapter 5, Ecclesia is the primary "sphere within which union with God takes place in this present life, the union which will be consummated in the age to come, after the resurrection of the dead."[26] It is the reincarnation of Eden. A place in which you and I may access the Tree of Life replete with its eucharistic bounty. A bounty by which our nature is unified with Christ and with other *Christ*-ians.

The Eucharist is thus the central mystery of Ecclesia. The chief sacrament of the church. By it we are changed from human multiplicity to one body in Christ, the temple of the Holy Spirit. Within the eucharistic assembly, "divine life flows into us and penetrates the fabric of our humanity. The future life is infused into the present one and is blended with it, so that our fallen humanity may be transformed into the glorified humanity of the new Adam, Christ."[27] As such, Ignatius christened the Eucharist our "medicine of immortality and the antidote against death, enabling us to live forever in Jesus Christ."[28]

The church is simultaneously a spiritual gymnasium wherein we exercise living disciplines. Disciplines that become the basis for life and living. Fasting is but one of them. It not only satisfies the spirit but is strong medicine for the body. The stomach is very much like an undisciplined child, forever demanding its fill of empty calories. The discipline of fasting restores balance and self-control. Living disciplines such as prayer, reading, and fasting characterized the life of Jesus. So, too, they must characterize ours. Churches have majored on teaching right things about Christ, but often have neglected to become his imitators. Millions profess faith in the death of Christ but have little concept of the power inherent in his life.

Last—but most certainly not least—"is a direct link between the oneness of Christians, after the image of the Trinity, and the missionary dimension of the Church."[29] Plainly put, division produces tremendous toxicity. Conversely, a global church fused together around the essentials of the historic Christian faith is a transformational repository of unlimited, unpolluted energy. Thus, in chapter 6 we explored the answer to the High Priestly Prayer of Jesus. "I do not pray for these alone but also for those who will believe in me through their word; that they all may be one, as You, Father, are in Me, and I in you; that they may also be one in us *that the world may believe that you sent Me*."[30] Union with God and unity with one another is thus the goal of our salvation and the means of global transformation. Not divided as in fission. But united as in fusion.

Whatever the reality respecting fusion science, spiritual fusion *is* the greatest antidote to the cultural captivity of the contemporary church. Were the authentic church to embrace fusion in place of fission, you and I may as yet experience the authentic Christian life. The manifestation of the uncreated, inexhaustible energy supply, which alone is sufficient to save the world. Allow me to close with an illustration that involves life in the natural realm. A life force by which the world has been irrevocably changed. On September 27, 1905, Albert Einstein published a paper titled "Does the Inertia of a Body Depend Upon Its Energy Content?" The answer to his poignant question is encapsulated in the elegant yet visibly simple equation $E = mc^2$.[31] An answer replete with the capacity for unleashing a transformational energy supply previously unimagined.

What Einstein discovered was the power inherent in mass. The stunning reality that microscopic atomic molecules contain an enormous amount of energy that when released can vaporize the world—or conversely, transform it. With $E = mc^2$ Einstein confirmed the previously unrealized reality "that mass (m) and kinetic energy (E) are equal since the speed of light (c^2) is constant. *In other words, mass can be changed into energy.*"[32]

What Einstein revealed to be true in the physical realm must likewise be revealed in the spiritual realm—mass can be changed into energy. And the energy inherent in mass (mission), Eucharist (thanksgiving meal), Communion (union with Christ) or the Lord's Table (1 Corinthians 10:21), has the power to transform the world.

Such is the energy manifested by Jesus on the Mount of Transfiguration, when "his face shone like the sun, and his clothes became as white as the light." When "a bright cloud enveloped" Peter, James, and John.[33] This is the energy that Paul invoked when he spoke of being energized by all his energy, which so powerfully energizes me.[34]

This is the energy that alone can unite the church and transform the world. This is what it means to discover the unexpected beauty of an authentic Christian life.

Acknowledgments

It is with profound gratitude that I first wish to acknowledge my dear brother and friend Elijah Widjaja. Apart from the exercise of his prophetic gift—not in the sense of *foretelling* but *forthtelling*—the notion that "life matters more" may never have occurred to me. As noted in the introduction to part two, without Elijah I would have had little concept of what the life that mattered more might entail. Why? Because the notion that it might involve what the early church designated deification or union with God existed outside my conceptual framework.

Furthermore, I am deeply grateful to my dear friend and brother Jack Countryman, without whom this volume (like the last) would not be a Harper Collins publication. To be back with Daisy Blackwell Hutton and her team has been truly delightful. Daisy is not only a marvelously talented publisher but has been a great encouragement to me in my battle with cancer, which coincided with the writing of this book. Daisy afforded me the privilege of working with talented team members including Sam O'Neal and Dawn Hollomon.

Finally, I am deeply grateful for my colleagues at the Christian Research Institute—many have been with me going on three decades. I am particularly grateful for Stephen Ross and Paul Young, who have worked closely with me during the past thirty years! I truly could not imagine life without them. I am also profoundly thankful for my family, the apex of which is my beloved wife

Kathy. We have walked together in solidarity throughout every step of our exhilarating spiritual journey. There are of course many others who deserve acknowledgment, not the least of which include Father Alex Karloutsos, Father Steve Dalber, my oldest son David, and the many authors whose books and articles are reflected in the endnotes.

Notes

Foreword

1. See Paul L. Maier, "The Fate of Pontius Pilate," *Hermes* 99, no. 3 (1971): 362–71, JSTOR, www.jstor.org/stable/4475698.
2. Timothy J. Keller, *The Reason for God* (New York, NY: Penguin, 2008), 229–230.
3. The first two sentences in this quote paraphrase C. S. Lewis (see page 158).

Before You Begin

1. John 14:6.
2. Story from Watchman Nee, *The Normal Christian Life* (Peabody, MA: Hendrickson, 1961), 59–61.
3. Witness Lee, *Watchman Nee: A Seer of the Divine Revelation in the Present Age* (Anaheim: Living Stream Ministry, 1991), 280.
4. The "Local Churches" of Watchman Nee and Witness Lee painstakingly "define *mingling* in a way that does not suggest a change in the essential nature of God or man." Elliot Miller, "Part 1: The 'Local Church' as Movement and Source of Controversy," *Christian Research Journal* 32, no. 6 (2009): 10–13, www.equip.org /PDF/EnglishOpt.pdf. See the sidebar, "'Mingling'—Was There Ever a Better Word?" in Kerry S. Robichaux, ". . . That We Might Be Made God," *Affirmation and Critique* 1, no. 3 (July 1996): 31, 62, www.affcrit.com/pdfs/1996/03/96_03_a3.pdf.
5. Jennifer Lin, *Shanghai Faithful: Betrayal and Forgiveness in a Chinese Christian Family* (Lanham, MD: Rowman & Littlefield, 2017), 132. I draw from Lin in what follows concerning the life and ministry of Watchman Nee.
6. Lin, *Shanghai Faithful*, 149.
7. Lin, 178–79.
8. Lin, 168.

9. Lin, 169.

10. Lin, 169.

11. Lin, 179.

12. Lin, 181–82.

13. Lin, 185.

14. Lin, 241.

15. Andrew Yu and Chris Wilde, interview by *Bible Answer Man*, Christian Research Institute, September 8, 2008, www.oneplace.com/ministries/bible-answer-man. Speaking from the floor of the US House of Representatives, Congressman Chris Smith aptly summed up Nee's worldwide impact. "Madam Speaker, I rise today to acknowledge the immense spiritual achievement of Watchman Nee, a great pioneer of Christianity in China."

Smith went on to communicate that *Christianity Today* memorialized Nee "as one of the 100 most influential Christians of the twentieth century" (see "Survey Results: What Do You Think?" *CT*, www.christianitytoday.com/history/issues/issue-65/survey-results-what-do-you-think.html) and that "his life and work continue to influence millions of Protestant Christians in China." Also that "today more than three thousand churches outside of China, including several hundred in the United States, look to him as one of their religious and theological leaders."

Though "Nee was never released," said Smith, "several of his books continued to grow in influence and popularity, particularly in the United States, and his best-known book, *The Normal Christian Life*, sold over one million copies world-wide and became a twentieth-century Christian classic.

"Madam Speaker, it is estimated that China has more than one hundred million Christians, and millions of them consider themselves the spiritual heirs of Watchman Nee. Millions more are rightly proud of the contribution Watchman Nee made to global Christianity—he was the first Chinese Christian to exercise an influence on Western Christians—and indeed of his contribution to world spiritual culture." Christopher H. Smith, "In Recognition of Watchman Nee," 155 Cong. Rec. 118 (2009), www.gpo.gov/fdsys/pkg/CREC-2009–07–31/html/CREC-2009–07–31-pt1-PgE2110–2.htm.

16. Cf. Walter Martin, ed., *The New Cults* (Ventura, CA: Regal Books, 1980), 381.

17. Quote (reflecting Martin's published views) paraphrased from Cal Beisner, Bob Passantino, and Gretchen Passantino, "The Teachings of Witness Lee and the Local Church," Christian Research Institute, statement DL–075, 1978, 1996, withdrawn 2003. Cf. Martin, *New Cults*, 379–408.

18. See Beisner, Passantino, and Passantino, "Teachings of Witness Lee."

19. Martin, *New Cults*, 406.

20. Martin, 382.

21. See, e.g., Beisner, Passantino, and Passantino, "Teachings of Witness Lee"; Martin, *New Cults*.

22. Neil T. Duddy and Spiritual Counterfeits Project, *The God-Men: An Inquiry into Witness Lee and the Local Church* (Downers Grove, IL: InterVarsity Press, 1981).

23. Jack Sparks, *The Mindbenders* (Nashville: Thomas Nelson, 1977).

24. Defense and Confirmation Project, "The Facts That Belie Charges of 'Litigiousness by the Local Churches to Silence and Control What Is Written about Them,'" unpublished manuscript, 2008, in Elliot Miller, "Part 5: Addressing the Open Letter's Concerns: On Lawsuits with Evangelical Christians," *Christian Research Journal* 32, no. 6 (2009): 45, available at www.equip.org/PDF/EnglishOpt.pdf.

25. Defense and Confirmation Project, "Facts That Belie Charges of 'Litigiousness.'"

26. Modalism is an anti-trinitarian heresy in which a radically unitarian deity is revealed in three modes, manifestations, or masks.

27. See *Christian Research Journal* 32, no. 6 (2009); cover.

28. Li Li-hong, testimony, *History and Testimony: An Account of the Lord's Recovery in Mainland China*, trans. and ed. Zhao Shihe (unpublished manuscript), 248.

29. Li Li-hong, *History and Testimony*, 248–49.

30. Cf. Li Li-hong *History and Testimony*.

31. See *Christian Research Journal* 32, no. 6 (2009); cover.

32. Elliot Miller, "Cultic, Aberrant, or (Unconventionally) Orthodox? A Reassessment of the 'Local Church' Movement," *Christian Research Journal* 32, no. 6 (2009): 7.

33. Hank Hanegraaff, *Christianity in Crisis* (Eugene, OR: Harvest House, 1993), back cover.

34. Norm Geisler and Ron Rhodes, "A Response to the *Christian Research Journal's* Recent Defense of the 'Local Church' Movement," n.d., 2, www.open-letter.org /pdf/Geisler_Rhodes_Response_to_CRI.pdf, emphasis added by Geisler and Rhodes to quotation from Elliot Miller, "The Conclusion of the Matter: We Were Wrong," *Christian Research Journal* 32, no. 6 (2009): 47.

35. "Press Release: 'Leading Evangelical Scholars Call On "Local Churches" to Renounce Doctrines, Legal Attacks,'" January 9, 2007, www.open-letter.org/pdf /OL_PressRelease.pdf. See also "An Open Letter to the Leadership of Living Stream Ministry and the 'Local Churches,'" January 9, 2007, www.open-letter .org/.

36. Geisler and Rhodes, "Response to the *Christian Research Journal's* Recent Defense," 15.

37. "Open Letter." Quote from Witness Lee, *A Deeper Study of the Divine Dispensing* (Anaheim: Living Stream Ministry, 1990), 53.

38. Lee, *Deeper Study*, 53, emphasis added. In fact, in the paragraph immediately preceding the passage quoted in the open letter, Lee wrote, "The ultimate purpose of God is to work Himself into us that He may be our life and everything to us so that one day we may become Him. But this does not mean that we can become part of the Godhead and be the same as the unique God. We have to know that although we are born of God and have God's life to become God's children, His house, and His household, we do not have a share in His sovereignty or His Person and cannot be worshiped as God." See the clear and helpful discussion in Elliot Miller, "Part 3: Addressing the Open Letter's Concerns: On the Nature of Humanity," *Christian Research Journal* 32, no. 6 (2009): 24–31.

39. Witness Lee, *The Christian Life* (Anaheim: Living Stream Ministry, 1994), 134, see all of chap. 12, sect. 5. See also Witness Lee, *Life-Study of 1 & 2 Samuel* (Anaheim: Living Stream Ministry, 1996), chap. 25, sects. 1 and 2; Witness Lee, *The Move of God in Man* (Anaheim: Living Stream Ministry, 1993), chap. 2, sect. 6; Witness Lee, *God's New Testament Economy* (Anaheim: Living Stream Ministry, 1986), chap. 42, sect. 1; Ron Kangas et al., *The Truth Concerning the Ultimate Goal of God's Economy: A Refutation of J. S.'s Slanderous Accusations* (Anaheim: Living Stream Ministry, 1994), 11–12. Most references accessible at www.ministrybooks.org or available through www.livingstream.com.

    See also the careful discussion in Kerry S. Robichaux, "Can Human Beings Become God?" *Affirmation & Critique* 7, no. 2 (2002): 42, www.affcrit.com/pdfs /2002/02/02_02_a2.pdf.

40. Dario Fernández-Morera, *The Myth of the Andalusian Paradise: Muslims, Christians, and Jews under Islamic Rule in Medieval Spain* (Wilmington, DE: ISI Books, 2016), 4.

41. Athanasius (c. 296–373), "On the Incarnation of the Word" 54.3, in *Nicene and Post-Nicene Fathers*, 2nd ser., vol. 4, *St. Athanasius: Select Works and Letters*, ed. Philip Schaff (repr., Grand Rapids: Eerdmans, 1980), 65; accessible at Christian Classics Ethereal Library (CCEL hereafter), www.ccel.org/ccel/schaff/npnf204 .vii.ii.liv.html.

42. Pss. 90:2; 93:2; 102:12; Eph. 3:21; Heb. 9:14.

43. Gen. 1:26–31; see also Job 38:4, 21.

44. Job 14; 34:20; Pss. 90:10; 102:11–12; 103:15; Isa. 40:6–8; James 1:10–11; 4:14; 1 Peter 1:24.

45. John 5:26; see also Isa. 43:10; 41:4; 44:6; 48:12; Rev. 1:8, 17; 2:8; 3:14; 21:6; 22:13; and Exod. 3:14 with John 8:58.

46. Acts 17:28; see Gen. 2:7 with Ps. 104:24, 29.

47. Job 42:2; see also Jer. 32:17; Matt. 19:26; Mark 10:27; Luke 1:37; 18:27.

48. 1 Cor. 1:25; see also Job 23; 2 Cor. 12:9; Heb. 4:15.

49. Job 37:16; Ps. 147:5; Isa. 40:13–14; 41:22–23; 42:9; 44:7; 46:10; Jer. 17:10; Rom. 11:33.

50. Isa. 55:8–9; 1 Cor. 1:25; 2:14; 13:12; see also Job 11:7–12; 21:22; 36:22–33; 38:4.

51. Jer. 23:23–24; see also Ps. 139:7–12; Matt. 28:20; Eph. 1:23; 4:10; Col. 3:11. Also, *God is immutable with respect to his nature* (Ps. 102:26–27; Mal. 3:6; Heb. 1:11–12; 13:8; James 1:17), *and God is absolutely sovereign over all creation* (Jer. 32:17; Ps. 103:19; Col. 1:16; Heb. 1:3; see also Rom. 8:28). *God is holy* (Lev. 19:2; Ps. 99:5; Isa. 6:3; 8:13; 1 Peter 1:14–19), *good* (Ps. 118:1; Nahum 1:7; Luke 18:19), *and perfectly righteous* (Isa. 45:21; Zeph. 3:5; Rom. 3:26) *and loving* (Deut. 7:7–8; Jer. 31:3; Joel 2:13; John 3:16; Eph. 2:4; Heb. 12:6; 1 John 4:7–8).

As St. Anselm of Canterbury (eleventh century) realized, God is a being a greater than which cannot be conceived (*Prosologian*). Thus, *God, and God alone, is worthy of worship* (Deut. 5:7–8; 6:13–14; 2 Kings 17:35–36; 1 Chron. 16:25; Ps. 96:4–5; Matt. 4:10).

52. Ps. 139:1–12. See also Job 23; 37:23; 38–41. Paragraph and sentence preceding adapted from Hank Hanegraaff, *MUSLIM: What You Need to Know About the World's Fastest-Growing Religion* (Nashville: W Publishing Group, 2017), 165.

53. 2 Cor. 5:17 NKJV, emphasis added.

54. See Nee, *Normal Christian Life*, 59–61, 119, 170–71.

55. Vladimir Lossky, *Orthodox Theology: An Introduction*, trans. Ian Kesarcodi-Watson and Ihita Kesarcodi-Watson (Crestwood, NY: St. Vladimir's Seminary Press, 1978), 84.

56. See Donald Fairbairn, *Life in the Trinity: An Introduction to Theology with the Help of the Church Fathers* (Downers Grove, IL: IVP Academic, 2009).

57. Martin Luther, *Weimarer Ausgabe* (WA) 1, 28, 25–32, quoted in Mannermaa, "Theosis," 43, quoted in Veli-Matti Kärkkäinen, *One with God: Salvation as Deification and Justification* (Collegeville, MN: Liturgical Press, 2004), 47, emphasis added; cf. discussion and a slightly different translation of the same quote in Kurt E. Marquart, "Luther and Theosis," *Concordia Theological Quarterly* 64, no. 3 (2000): 186–87, www.ctsfw.net/media/pdfs/marquartlutherandtheosis .pdf. Marquart dates the sermon to 1515.

58. Martin Luther, *Weimarer Ausgabe* (WA) 2, 247–48; *Luther's Works* (LW) 51, 58, quoted in Kärkkäinen, *One with God*, 47. Cf. John Climacus (died early seventh century), *The Ladder of Divine Ascent*.

59. Quoted in G. Mantzaridis, *The Deification of Man* (Crestwood, NY: St Vladimir's Seminary, 1984), 29; cf. Daniel B. Clendenin, "Partakers of Divinity: The Orthodox Doctrine of Theosis," *Journal of the Evangelical Theological Society* 37, no. 3 (September 1994); 374.

60. 2 Peter 1:4.

61. Vladimir Lossky wrote, "In the tradition of the Eastern Church there is no place for a theology, and even less for a mysticism, of the divine essence. The goal of Orthodox spirituality, the blessedness of the Kingdom of Heaven, is not the vision of the essence, but, above all, a participation in the divine life of the Holy Trinity; the deified state of the co-heirs of the divine nature, gods created after the uncreated God, possessing by grace all that the Holy Trinity possesses by nature." Lossky, *The Mystical Theology of the Eastern Church*, trans. Fellowship of St. Alban and St. Sergius (1976; repr., Crestwood, NY: St. Vladimir's Seminary Press, 2002), 65. See, e.g., Maximus the Confessor, *Ambiguum*, 7.

   In the Western church, Augustine wrote, "If we have been made sons of God, we have also been made gods: but this is the effect of Grace adopting, not of nature generating. For the only Son of God, God, and one God with the Father, Our Lord and Saviour Jesus Christ, was in the beginning the Word, and the Word with God, the Word God. The rest that are made gods, are made by His own Grace, are not born of His Substance, that they should be the same as He, but that by favour they should come to Him, and be fellow-heirs with Christ." Augustine, *Exposition on the Book of Psalms* 50.2, in *Nicene and Post-Nicene Fathers*, 1st ser., vol. 8, ed. Philip Schaff (repr., Grand Rapids: Eerdmans, 1983), 178; , www.ccel .org/ccel/schaff/npnf108.ii.L.html.

62. John 1:12; cf. Gal. 4:5–7; 1 John 3:2.

63. I discuss the distinction between God's *essence*, which is and always will be incomprehensible to created beings, and God's *energies*, by which we can know God, in chapter 4.

64. C. S. Lewis, *Mere Christianity*, rev. ed. (New York: HarperOne, 2001), 189.

65. See "Statement of Decision—Lee v. Duddy re: The God-Men by Neil Duddy and the SCP," June 27, 1985, Alameda, CA, Leon Seyranian, Judge of the Superior Court, 28, 31, web.archive.org/web/20060212144127/http://www.contendingforthefaith .com/libel-litigations/god-men/decision/completeText.html.

66. See Acts 23:12ff.

67. See Num. 14.

68. See Hank Hanegraaff, *The Covering: God's Plan to Protect You from Evil* (Nashville: W Publishing Group, 2002), 41.

69. Os Guinness, *Time for Truth* (Grand Rapids: Baker, 2000), 39.

70. Jack Crowe, "Kamala Harris Ignores Questions on Smollett Hoax after Dining with Sharpton," *National Review*, February 21, 2019, www.nationalreview.com /news/jussie-smollett-case-kamala-harris-ignores-questions-on-hoax-after-dining -with-al-sharpton/.

71. Guinness, *Time for Truth*, 39–40. Previous three paragraphs adapted in part from Hanegraaff, *Covering*, 41–42.

72. Hank Hanegraaff, *The Millennium Bug Debugged* (Minneapolis, MN: Bethany House, 1999).

73. Tom Junod, "365 Days to the Apocalypse and We Still Don't Know Where to Hide the Jews . . . and Other Notes from Pat Robertson's Y2K Conference," *Esquire*, January 1999, 96.

74. Eph. 6:14.

75. John 14:6.

76. Guinness, *Time for Truth*, 79–80. Previous three paragraphs adapted from Hanegraaff, *Covering*, 42–44.

77. "St. Thomas Aquinas: 'All I Have Written Seems Like Straw!'" Holy Trinity Lutheran Church, www.holytrinity.net/st-thomas-aquinas-all-i-have-written-seems-like-straw/.

78. "St. Thomas Aquinas," Holy Trinity Lutheran Church. See also Eleonore Stump, *Aquinas* (New York: Routledge, 2003), 12.

79. Lee, *Watchman Nee*, 280.

80. Lossky, *Orthodox Theology*, 84.

Part 1: Truth Matters

1. Blaise Pascal, *Pensees*, XIV, 864.

2. *1964* (WGBH Educational Foundation, 2014), *American Experience*, PBS, transcript, web.archive.org/web/20160531000408/http://www.pbs.org:80/wgbh/americanexperience/features/transcript/1964-transcript/.

3. Bob Dylan, "The Times They Are A-Changin'," *The Times They Are A-Changin'* (Warner Bros., 1963, 1964), www.bobdylan.com/songs/times-they-are-changin/.

4. John Lennon [and Yoko Ono], "Imagine," *Imagine* (Ascot Sound Studios, 1971), genius.com/John-lennon-imagine-lyrics.

5. The Reformer John Calvin wrote, "Since the arrangement of all things is in the hand of God, since to him belongs the disposal of life and death, he arranges all things by his sovereign counsel, in such a way that individuals are born, who are doomed from the womb to certain death, and are to glorify him by their destruction." *Institutes of the Christian Religion*, 3.23.6, trans. Henry Beveridge, accessible at CCEL, www.ccel.org/ccel/calvin/institutes.v.xxiv.html.

6. Calvin, *Institutes*, 3.21.5, www.ccel.org/ccel/calvin/institutes.v.xxii.html.

7. Lossky, *Orthodox Theology*, 84.

8. 1 Peter 3:15.

9. Sentence adapted from Hank Hanegraaff, *The Complete Bible Answer Book—Collector's Edition*, rev. ed. (Nashville: Thomas Nelson, 2016), 66–67.

10. Christopher Hitchens, *God Is Not Great: How Religion Poisons Everything* (New York: Twelve, 2007), 102.

11. See 1 Tim. 1:10. Paragraph adapted from Hank Hanegraaff, *Has God Spoken? Memorable Proofs of the Bible's Divine Inspiration* (Nashville: Thomas Nelson, 2011), 241.

12. The late atheist Christopher Hitchens accused the Bible of warranting such evils (see Hitchens, *God Is Not Great*, 102). For discussion, see Hanegraaff, *Has God Spoken?*, pt. 4.

13. This sentence adapts two often-quoted lines. The first is frequently attributed to Mark Twain but appears to trace to Jonathan Swift and others including C. H. Spurgeon (see Niraj Chokshi, "That Wasn't Mark Twain: How a Quotation is Born," *New York Times*, April 26, 2017, www.nytimes.com/2017/04/26/books/famous -misquotations.html). The second comes from Gordon D. Fee and Douglas Stuart, *How to Read the Bible for All Its Worth* (Grand Rapids: Zondervan, 1981, 2014).

14. Joseph Smith, *History of the Church*, 4:461, emphasis added.

15. See Hank Hanegraaff, *The Mormon Mirage: Seeing Through the Illusion of Mainstream Mormonism* (Charlotte, NC: Christian Research Institute, 2008).

16. See Hanegraaff, *MUSLIM*.

Chapter 1: Answers

1. 1 Peter 3:15.

2. Sir Julian Huxley, *Essays of a Humanist* (New York: Harper & Row, 1964), 78, 79.

3. Huxley, *Essays of a Humanist*, 125.

4. See Charles Darwin, *The Life and Letters of Charles Darwin*, vol. 1, ed. F. Darwin (London: John Murray, 1888), 45, darwin-online.org.uk.

5. Michael Denton, *Evolution: A Theory in Crisis* (Bethesda, MD: Adler & Adler, 1985), 25. Previous four paragraphs adapted from Hank Hanegraaff, *The FACE That Demonstrates the Farce of Evolution* (Nashville: Word Publishing, 1998), 9, 17, 20.

6. Charles Darwin, *On the Origin of Species: Or the Preservation of Favoured Races in the Struggle for Life* (London: John Murray, 1859), chap. 6, www.gutenberg.org /files/1228/1228-h/1228-h.htm.

7. Charles Darwin, *The Descent of Man*, chap. 6 in *Great Books of the Western World*, vol. 49, *Darwin*, ed. Robert Maynard Hutchins (Chicago: Encyclopædia Britannica, 1952), 336.

8. Benjamin Wiker, *10 Books That Screwed Up the World* (Washington DC: Regnery Publishing, 2008), 96.

9. Richard Dawkins, *The Greatest Show on Earth: The Evidence for Evolution* (New York: Free Press, 2009), 62n.

10. Richard Dawkins, "Ignorance Is No Crime," Free Inquiry 21, no. 3 (2001), www .secularhumanism.org/2001/07/ignorance-is-no-crime/; see also Lawrence M. Krauss and Richard Dawkins, "Should Science Speak to Faith? (Extended Version)," *Scientific American*, June 19, 2007, www.scientificamerican.com/article /should-science-speak-to-faith-extended/. Previous two paragraphs adapted from Hanegraaff, *Has God Spoken?*, 257–58.

11. For cutting-edge analysis of molecular evidence against the Darwinian view of life, see Michael J. Behe, *Darwin Devolves: The New Science about DNA That Challenges Evolution* (New York: HarperOne, 2019).

12. "Sir Francis Galton F.R.S. 1822–1911," www.galton.org/main.html.

13. Francis Galton, "Hereditary Character and Talent," *Macmillan's*, 1865, www .galton.org/essays/1860–1869/galton-1865-macmillan-hereditary-talent.html.

14. Charles Darwin, *The Descent of Man and Selection in Relation to Sex*, 2nd ed. (1874), chap. 5, emphasis added, www.gutenberg.org/files/2300/2300-h/2300-h.htm.

15. George William Hunter, *A Civic Biology, Presented in Problems* (New York: American Book Company, 1914), www.digitalhistory.uh.edu/disp_textbook .cfm?smtID=3&psid=1134.

16. Hunter, *Civic Biology*. See Wiker, *10 Books*, 89–91.

17. Henry M. Morris and Gary E. Parker, *What Is Creation Science?* rev. ed. (El Cajon, CA: Master Books, 1987), 67.

18. Henry M. Morris, *Creation and the Modern Christian* (El Cajon, CA: Master Books, 1985), 72. See Stephen Jay Gould, "Dr. Down's Syndrome," *Natural History* 87 (April 1980): 142–48, reprinted in *The Panda's Thumb: More Reflections in Natural History*, ed. Stephen Jay Gould (New York: W. W. Norton, 1980), 160–68.

19. "History of Down's Syndrome," Down's Syndrome Association, www.downs -syndrome.org.uk/about/history-of-downs-syndrome-2/.

20. Julian Quinones and Arijeta Lajka, "'What Kind of Society Do You Want to Live In?': Inside the Country Where Down Syndrome Is Disappearing," CBS News, August 15, 2017, www.cbsnews.com/news/down-syndrome-iceland/.

21. See Marvin L. Lubenow, *Bones of Contention: A Creationist Assessment of the Human Fossils* (Grand Rapids, MI: Baker Book House, 1992), 47. This and following four paragraphs adapted from Hanegraaff, *Has God Spoken?*, 258–59.

22. Michael Crichton, *State of Fear* (New York: HarperCollins Publishers, 2004), 576. 575–80 is a concise overview of the history of eugenics. I follow Crichton in the subsequent discussion.

23. Alex Rosenberg, *The Atheist's Guide to Reality: Enjoying Life Without Illusions* (New York: W. W. Norton, 2011), 71.

24. Rosenberg, *Atheist's Guide to Reality*, viii.

25. Rosenberg, 17.

26. Rosenberg, 17.

27. Rosenberg, 43, emphasis original.

28. Rosenberg, 94–95.

29. Rosenberg, 109.

30. Rosenberg, 98.

31. Rosenberg, 2–3, emphasis original.

32. Rosenberg, 312.

33. Rosenberg, 313.

34. Cf. Rosenberg, 312.

35. Rosenberg, 299.

36. Rosenberg, 315.

37. Rosenberg, 275.

38. Rosenberg, 276.

39. Bruce L. Shelley, *Church History in Plain Language* (Nashville: Thomas Nelson, 1995), 61. Remainder of this paragraph adapted from Hanegraaff, *Has God Spoken?*, 281 (see 268n167 in the present book).

40. Jacques Monod, *Chance and Necessity* (New York: Vintage Books, 1972), 112, emphasis original.

41. See publisher's blurb on cover of Rosenberg, *Atheist's Guide to Reality.*

42. Rosenberg, 111.

43. Charles Darwin, *The Descent of Man*, chap. 29 in *Great Books of the Western World*, vol. 49, 566.

44. J. P. Moreland, "A Philosophical Examination of Hugh Ross's Natural Theology," *Philosophia Christi*, 21, no. 1 (1998): 33, web.archive.org/web/20130625163402 /www.reasons.org/articles/philosophia-christi#heading4.

45. Sociologist Rodney Stark has noted, "Augustine was heir to the entire legacy of Greek philosophy, and Aquinas and his peers acknowledge their deep debts to Hellenic scholarship. But the antiscientific elements of Greek thought were withstood by Augustine and by the Scholastics, and long before Greco-Roman learning was confined to classics departments, it was *not* the philosophy of scientists. While it is true (and constantly cited by the classicists) that Newton remarked in a letter to Robert Hook in 1675 that 'if I have seen further (than you and Descartes) it is by standing on the shoulders of giants,' such high regard for the ancients is not expressed or reflected in his work or in his usual presentations of self. Instead, Newton and his peers achieved their breakthroughs in obvious opposition to the Greek 'giants.' What the great figures involved in the sixteenth- and seventeenth-century blossoming of science—including Descartes, Galileo,

Newton, and Kepler—did confess was their absolute faith in a creator God, whose work incorporated rational rules awaiting discovery.

"The rise of science was not an extension of classical learning. It was the natural outgrowth of Christian doctrine: nature exists because it was created by God. In order to love and honor God, it is necessary to fully appreciate the wonders of his handiwork. Because God is perfect, his handiwork functions in accord with *immutable principles*. By the full use of our God-given powers of reason and observation, it ought to be possible to discover these principles." Rodney Stark, *The Victory of Reason: How Christianity Led to Freedom, Capitalism, and Western Success* (New York: Random House, 2006), 22–23, emphasis original. See also Vishal Mangalwadi, *The Book That Made Your World: How the Bible Created the Soul of Western Civilization* (Nashville: Thomas Nelson, 2011), 220–45. I am indebted to the work of Stark and Mangalwadi concerning the historical relationship between revelation and reason in the development of Western civilization.

46. Rom. 1:20 NIV 1984.

47. Rom. 1:21–22; see context of vv. 18–32.

48. Scott M. Huse, *The Collapse of Evolution*, 2nd ed. (Grand Rapids, MI: Baker Books, 1993), 71. Paragraph adapted from Hanegraaff, *FACE*, 68–69, 188.

49. Gen. 1:1.

50. Rosenberg, *Atheist's Guide to Reality*, 313.

51. Discussion drawn from Henry M. Morris, *Men of Science, Men of God: Great Scientists Who Believed the Bible* (El Cajon, CA: Master Books, 1990).

52. List of Christian men and women of science drawn from Morris, *Men of Science*; cf. Fred Heeren, *Show Me God*, rev. ed. (Wheeling, IL: Day Star, 1997), 334–63. Previous twelve paragraphs adapted from Hanegraaff, *Has God Spoken?*, 281–86.

53. Jonathan Wells, *Zombie Science: More Icons of Evolution* (Seattle: Discovery Institute Press, 2017), 17–18.

54. Darwin, *On the Origin of Species*, chap. 14, www.gutenberg.org/files/1228/1228 -h/1228-h.htm.

55. Darwin, emphasis added.

56. Richard Dawkins, *The Blind Watchmaker: Why Evidence of Evolution Reveals a Universe Without Design* (New York: W. W. Norton, 1996), 229. Three previous paragraphs adapted from Hank Hanegraaff, *The Creation Answer Book* (Nashville: Thomas Nelson, 2012), 158–59.

57. Duane T. Gish, *Evolution: The Fossils Still Say No!* (El Cajon, CA: Institute for Creation Research, 1995), 133.

58. Pierre Lecomte du Noüy, *Human Destiny* (New York: Longmans, Green, and Co., 1947), 72.

59. Gould and Eldredge continue with the explicit clarification, "curious mosaics like *Archaeopteryx* do not count." Stephen Jay Gould and Niles Eldredge, "Punctuated Equilibria: The Tempo and Mode of Evolution Reconsidered," *Paleobiology*, 3 (1977): 147. Previous four paragraphs adapted from Hanegraaff, *FACE*, 34–38. For an incisive analysis of the fossil record, see Günter Bechly and Stephen C. Meyer, "The Fossil Record and Universal Common Ancestry," in *Theistic Evolution: A Scientific, Philosophical, and Theological Critique*, ed. J. P Moreland, Stephen C. Meyer, et al. (Wheaton, IL: Crossway, 2017), 331–62.

60. I have adapted this humorous way of describing *Pithecanthropus erectus* from Phil Saint, *Fossils That Speak Out* (Greensboro, NC: Saint Ministries International, 1985), 42.

61. Paragraph adapted from Hanegraaff, *FACE*, 3.

62. Factual information adapted from Gish, *Evolution*, 280–81.

63. Lubenow, *Bones of Contention*, 115; see 113–19 for a good overview of the Selenka Expedition.

64. Michael D. Lemonick, "How Man Began," *Time*, March 14, 1994, www.content .time.com/time/magazine/article/0,9171,980307,00.html.

65. Henry M. Morris and Gary E. Parker, *What Is Creation Science?*, 154. Section adapted from Hanegraaff, *FACE*, 50, 52.

66. Lubenow, *Bones of Contention*, 40–43; William R. Fix, *The Bone Peddlers: Selling Evolution* (New York: Macmillan, 1984), 12, 13.

67. Lubenow, *Bones of Contention*, 43.

68. Fix, *The Bone Peddlers*, 12.

69. *The Cambridge Encyclopedia of Human Evolution*, ed. Steve Jones, Robert Martin, and David Pilbeam (Cambridge: Cambridge University Press, 1992), 448.

70. *Cambridge Encyclopedia*, 448; Lubenow, *Bones of Contention*, 42–43. Section adapted from Hanegraaff, *FACE*, 52–54.

71. Ian T. Taylor, *In the Minds of Men*, 3rd edition (Toronto: TFE Publishing, 1991), 235.

72. Taylor, *In the Minds of Men*, 236.

73. Taylor, 237.

74. Taylor, 240; some of the most interesting facts for reconstructing the Peking man story are found on pages 234–41.

75. See Gish, *Evolution*, 292–93; Taylor, *In the Minds of Men*, 238–40.

76. Taylor, *In the Minds of Men*, 240.

77. This quip is not original to me. I heard it many years ago.

78. *Illustrated London News*, June 24, 1922, cited in Gish, *Evolution*, 327–28; Taylor, *In the Minds of Men*, 231–32.

79. See Gish, *Evolution*, 326–28; Taylor, *In the Minds of Men*, 233.

80. See Robert Bazell, "The Missing Link: Worth the Hype?" Daily Nightly, May 19, 2009, MSNBC, web.archive.org/web/20090522170215/http://dailynightly.msnbc.msn.com/archive/2009/05/19/1937065.aspx.

81. "Fossil Frenzy: Is This the Mother of All Monkeys?" NBC Nightly News, video recording, May 19, 2009, web.archive.org/web/20090523163129/http://www.msnbc.msn.com/id/21134540/vp/30833464.

82. James Randerson and Ed Pilkington, "Deal in Hamburg Bar Led Scientist to Ida Fossil, the 'Eighth Wonder of the World,'" Guardian, May 19, 2009, web.archive.org/web/20180112194912/www.theguardian.com/science/2009/may/19/fossil-ida-missing-link-discovery.

83. Samantha Strong and Rich Schapiro, "Missing Link Found? Scientists Unveil Fossil of 47 Million-Year-Old Primate, Darwinius Masillae," New York Daily News, May 19, 2009, www.nydailynews.com/news/us_world/2009/05/19/2009–05–19_missing_link_found_fossil_of_47_millionyearold_primate_sheds_light_on_.html.

84. Rex Dalton, "Fossil Primate Challenges Ida's Place," Nature, October 21, 2009, www.nature.com/news/2009/091021/full/4611040a.html; "Darwinius Masillae," American Museum of Natural History, www.amnh.org/exhibitions/extreme-mammals/meet-your-relatives/darwinius-masillae; Siw Ellen Jakobsen, "The Fossil Ida—Five Years On," Science Nordic, May 19, 2014, www.sciencenordic.com/fossil-ida-%E2%80%93-five-years.

85. For further study, see the articles in sec. 1, part 2 in Moreland, Theistic Evolution. Section adapted from Hanegraaff, FACE, 49, 54–55, 56; Hanegraaff, Creation Answer Book, 168, 187.

86. Paragraph adapted from Hanegraaff, FACE, 93.

87. Stephen Jay Gould, Ontogeny and Phylogeny (Cambridge, MA: Bellknap Press, 1977), n.430.

88. Gould, Ontogeny and Phylogeny, back cover.

89. Gould, 1.

90. See Gavin de Beer, "Darwin and Embryology," in A Century of Darwin, ed. S. A. Barnett (Cambridge, MA: Harvard University Press, 1958), 159; see also Taylor, In the Minds of Men, 274.

91. Taylor, In the Minds of Men, 276. Ian Taylor wrote, "Haeckel stated that the ova and embryos of different vertebrate animals and man are, at certain periods of their development, all perfectly alike, indicating their supposed common origin. Haeckel produced the well-known illustration showing embryos at several stages of development. In this he had to play fast and loose with the facts by altering several drawings in order to make them appear more alike and conform to the theory.... In a catalog of errors, His (1874) showed that Haeckel had used two

drawings of embryos, one taken from Bischoff (1845) and the other from Ecker (1851–59), and he had added 3–5 mm to the head of Bischoff's dog embryo, taken 2 mm off the head of Ecker's human embryo, reduced the size of the eye 5 mm, and doubled the length of the posterior."

92. Walt Brown, *In the Beginning: Compelling Evidence for Creation and the Flood*, 6th ed. (Phoenix: Center for Scientific Creation, 1995), 45.

93. J. Assmusth and Ernest R. Hull, *Haeckel's Frauds and Forgeries* (India: Bombay Press, 1911), cited in Luther D. Sunderland, *Darwin's Enigma*, 4th ed. rev. (Santee, CA: Master Books, 1988), 120; see also Wilbert H. Rusch Sr., "Ontogeny Recapitulates Phylogeny," *Creation Research Society Annual* (June 1969): 30, creationresearch.org/wp-content/uploads/crsq-1969-volume-6-number-1.pdf.

94. Henry M. Morris, *Scientific Creationism*, public school edition (San Diego: C.L.P., 1981), 77.

95. Morris, *Scientific Creationism*, 77; see pp. 75–78 on alleged evolutionary vestiges and recapitulations.

96. Carl Sagan, *The Dragons of Eden* (New York: Random House, 1977), 57–58.

97. "The throat (or pharyngeal) grooves and pouches, falsely called 'gill slits,' are *not* mistakes in human development. They develop into absolutely essential parts of human anatomy. The middle ear canals come from the second pouches, and the parathyroid and thymus glands come from the third and fourth. Without a thymus, we would lose half our immune systems. Without the parathyroids, we would be unable to regulate calcium balance and could not even survive. Another pouch, thought to be vestigial by evolutionists until just recently, becomes a gland that assists in calcium balance." (Morris, Parker, *What Is Creation Science?*, 64.) Section adapted from Hanegraaff, *FACE*, 93–96.

98. Sagan, *The Dragons of Eden*, 197.

99. Jerome LeJeune, "The Human Life Bill: Hearings on S-158 before the Subcommittee on Separation of Powers of the Senate Judiciary Committee," 97th Congress, 1st Session (1981), in Norman L. Geisler, *Christian Ethics: Options and Issues* (Grand Rapids, MI: Baker Books, 1989), 149. Punctuation as in "Watch: Why Jerome Lejeune's Work Advances the Pro-Life Cause," Jerome Lejeune Foundation, August 10, 2018, www.lejeunefoundation.org/jerome-lejeune-advances-pro-life-cause/.

100. The Human Life Bill—S. 158, Report 9, Hathi Trust Digital Library, www.babel.hathitrust.org/cgi/pt?id=mdp.39015018597867;view=1up;seq=11. Section adapted from Hanegraaff, *FACE*, 96–97, 99.

101. See Stephen Jay Gould, "Dr. Down's Syndrome," *Natural History* 87 (April 1980): 142–48; also reprinted in Gould, *The Panda's Thumb*, 160–168.

102. Morris and Parker, *What Is Creation Science?*, 67. According to "many recapitulationists," says Gould, "throwbacks, or atavisms, represent the spontaneous reappearance in adults of ancestral features that had disappeared in advanced lineages," Gould, "Dr. Down's Syndrome," in *The Panda's Thumb*, 164.

103. Gould, "Dr. Down's Syndrome," in *The Panda's Thumb*, 163.

104. Stephen Jay Gould, "The Episodic Nature of Evolutionary Change," in *The Panda's Thumb*, 182.

105. David Berlinski with William F. Buckley Jr., *Firing Line*, season 32, episode 36, "A Firing Line Debate," directed by Warren Steibel, aired December 5, 1997, on PBS. Section adapted from Hanegraaff, *FACE*, 100, 102, 103–104.

106. Monod, *Chance and Necessity*, 112, emphasis original.

107. Monod, 180.

108. James F. Coppedge, *Evolution: Possible or Impossible?* (Northridge, CA: Probability Research in Molecular Biology, 1993), 218.

109. Darwin, *On the Origin of Species*, chap. 6, www.gutenberg.org/files/1228/1228-h /1228-h.htm. Of course, Darwin's life work was intended to show that all biological organisms, with their "organs of extreme perfection and complication," were formed through natural selection.

110. Michael J. Behe, *Darwin's Black Box: The Biochemical Challenge to Evolution* (New York: Free Press, 1996), 22; see also 15–22.

111. Eye description adapted from Gordon Rattray Taylor, *The Great Evolution Mystery* (New York: Harper & Row, 1983), 101–2; see 98–103.

112. See Coppedge, *Evolution: Possible or Impossible?*, 218–20; and Denton, *Evolution: A Theory in Crisis*, 332–33. Section adapted from Hanegraaff, *FACE*, 62, 63, 64–65.

113. *The Wonders of God's Creation: Human Life*, vol. 3 (Chicago: Moody Institute of Science, 1993), VHS.

114. A. E. Wilder-Smith, *The Natural Sciences Know Nothing of Evolution* (Costa Mesa, CA: T. W. F. T. Publishers, 1981), 82.

115. A. E. Wilder-Smith, *The Origin of Life*, episode 3, videotape (Gilbert, AZ: Eden, 1983).

116. See Behe, *Darwin's Black Box*, 24; see 3–25.

117. Coppedge, *Evolution: Possible or Impossible?*, 52. "Section adapted from Hanegraaff, *FACE*, 64–67.

118. *The Wonders of God's Creation: Planet Earth*, vol. 1, videotape (Chicago: Moody Institute of Science, 1993).

119. *Wonders of God's Creation.*

120. *Wonders of God's Creation*; Huse, *Collapse of Evolution*, 71.

121. Huse, *Collapse of Evolution*, 71–72.

122. Ps. 14:1 NIV 1984. Section adapted from Hanegraaff, *FACE*, 67, 68, 69, 73.

123. Albert Einstein, *Ideas and Opinions—The World as I See It* (1954; repr., New York: Three Rivers Press, 1982), 40.

124. Heeren, *Show Me God*, 88.

125. Morris, *Scientific Creationism*, 19–20.

126. See Kenneth Boa and Larry Moody, *I'm Glad You Asked* (Wheaton, IL: Victor Books, 1982), 38–39.

127. For a sketch of this argument, see Hanegraaff, *FACE*, 193–94n12. Section adapted from Hanegraaff, *FACE*, 78, 80, 81.

128. *New Encyclopædia Britannica*, Macropædia, 15th ed., vol. 10 (Chicago: Encyclopædia Britannica, 1981), 415.

129. Isaac Asimov, "In the Game of Energy and Thermodynamics You Can't Even Break Even," *Journal of the Smithsonian Institute* (June 1970): 6; as quoted in Heeren, *Show Me God*, 128–29; also in Morris, *Scientific Creationism*, 21.

130. See Behe, *Darwin's Black Box*, 23–24.

131. Section adapted from Hanegraaff, *FACE*, 81–85.

132. Heeren, *Show Me God*, 129.

133. See Phillip E. Johnson, *Reason in the Balance* (Downers Grove, IL: InterVarsity Press, 1995).

134. Arthur S. Eddington, *The Nature of the Physical World* (New York: Macmillan, 1928), 74.

135. Myron Tribus and Edward C. McIrvine, "Energy and Information," *Scientific American* 224 (September 1971): 188, www.scientificamerican.com/magazine /sa/1971/09–01/.

136. See Morris, *Scientific Creationism*, 43–46; Willem J. J. Glashouwer and Paul S. Taylor, *The Origin of the Universe*, videotape (Mesa, AZ: Eden, 1983). See also Granville Sewell, *In the Beginning: And Other Essays on Intelligent Design*, 2nd ed. (Seattle: Discovery Institute Press, 2015).

137. See Hanegraaff, *FACE*, 198–99n28; see also R. C. Sproul, *Not a Chance: The Myth of Chance in Modern Science and Cosmology* (Grand Rapids, MI: Baker Books, 1994).

138. See Hanegraaff, *FACE*, 199–200n29.

139. Gen. 1:1.

140. Gen. 1:1. Section adapted from Hanegraaff, *FACE*, 85–89, 103–104.

141. The Nicene Creed.

142. Col. 1:15–17, 18 NIV 1984, emphasis added.

143. 1 Cor. 15:32 NIV 1984.

144. 1 Cor. 15:17–19 NIV 1984.

145. See Hugh J. Schonfield, *The Passover Plot: A New Interpretation of the Life and Death of Jesus* (New York: Bernard Geis Associates, 1965), back cover publisher's blurbs.

146. See Gary R. Habermas, *The Historical Jesus: Ancient Evidence for the Life of Christ* (Joplin, MO: College Press, 1996), 90–91. Donovan Joyce, *The Jesus Scroll* (New York: New American Library, 1972).

147. See Edwin M. Yamauchi, "Jesus Outside the New Testament: What Is the Evidence?" in *Jesus Under Fire: Modern Scholarship Reinvents the Historical Jesus*, ed. Michael J. Wilkins and J. P. Moreland (Grand Rapids: Zondervan, 1995), 210. Barbara Thiering, *Jesus and the Riddle of the Dead Sea Scrolls: Unlocking the Secrets of His Life Story* (San Francisco: HarperSanFrancisco, 1992).

148. See Qur'an 4:157–9, quoted in Abdullah Yusuf Ali, *The Meaning of the Holy Qur'an*, 10th ed. (Beltsville, MD: Amana, 1999).

149. See Ali, *Meaning of the Holy Qur'an*, 236 (4:157n663).

150. See Norman L. Geisler and Abdul Saleeb, *Answering Islam: The Crescent in Light of the Cross*, 2nd ed. (Grand Rapids, MI: Baker Books, 2002), app. 3.

151. See Hanegraaff, *MUSLIM*, 171ff; Geisler and Saleeb, *Answering Islam*, 65–66.

152. See, e.g., *Let God Be True*, rev. ed. (Brooklyn: Watchtower Bible and Tract Society, 1952), 41.

153. See, e.g., *Things in Which It Is Impossible for God to Lie* (Brooklyn: Watchtower Bible and Tract Society, 1965), 354–55.

154. See *The Kingdom Is at Hand* (Brooklyn: Watchtower Bible and Tract Society, 1944), 259; *Reasoning from the Scriptures* (Brooklyn: Watchtower Bible and Tract Society, 1985), 334; *From Paradise Lost to Paradise Regained* (Brooklyn: Watchtower Bible and Tract Society, 1958), 144.

155. Section adapted from Hank Hanegraaff, *Resurrection* (Nashville: Word Publishing, 2000), chap. 1.

156. 1 Cor. 15:3.

157. See Josephus, *Antiquities* 18.63. While *Antiquities* 18.63 may contain Christian interpolations, a majority of scholars view it as containing historically reliable and authentic core material—particularly in view of the text discovered by Melkite historian Agapius, which bears no indication of tampering. See *Josephus: The Essential Works: A Condensation of* Jewish Antiquities *and* The Jewish War, trans. and ed. Paul L. Maier (Grand Rapids: Kregel, 1994), 269–70, 282–84; Hanegraaff, *Has God Spoken?*, 40–42.

158. See, e.g., Josephus, *Antiquities* 20.200.

159. Tacitus, *Annals* 15.44, trans. Alfred John Church and William Jackson Brodribb, www.classics.mit.edu/Tacitus/annals.11.xv.html.

160. See Tacitus, *Annals* 15.44. See Hanegraaff, *Has God Spoken?*, 42. Primary source information on Christ and Christianity in ancient Jewish and pagan writings can be found in C. K. Barrett, *The New Testament Background: Selected Documents*

(New York: Macmillan, 1957); Darrell L. Bock and Gregory Herrick, *Jesus in Context: Background Readings* (Grand Rapids: Baker Academic, 2005); H. Wayne House, *Chronological and Background Charts of the New Testament* (Grand Rapids: Zondervan, 1981); Maier, *Josephus: The Essential Works*; Robert E. Van Voorst, *Jesus Outside the New Testament: An Introduction to the Ancient Evidence* (Grand Rapids: Eerdmans, 2000).

Based on the available extrabiblical early material, it is possible to piece together highlights of the life and death of Christ. See Habermas, *Historical Jesus*, 187–228 (esp. 224–28).

161. See Hanegraaff, *Resurrection*, 18–26; Habermas, *Historical Jesus*, 143–70 (esp. 158); *Will the Real Jesus Please Stand Up? A Debate Between William Lane Craig and John Dominic Crossan*, ed. Paul Copan (Grand Rapids: Baker Book House, 1998), 26–27; William Lane Craig, "Did Jesus Rise from the Dead?" in *Jesus Under Fire*, 147–48.

162. See Luke 22:44. For medical descriptions concerning Christ's suffering and death, I draw from C. Truman Davis, "The Crucifixion of Jesus: The Passion of Christ from a Medical Point of View," *Arizona Medicine* 22 (March 1965): 183–87; and William D. Edwards, Wesley J. Gabel, and Floyd E. Hosmer, "On the Physical Death of Jesus Christ," *Journal of the American Medical Association* 255, no. 11 (March 21, 1986): 1455–63. See also Dr. Alexander Metherell, interview in Lee Strobel, *The Case for Christ* (Grand Rapids: Zondervan, 1998), 191–204; Hanegraaff, *Resurrection*, 18–20.

163. Matt. 27:33.

164. Strobel, *Case for Christ*, 197–98.

165. Or wrists, which in Jewish understanding were part of the hands.

166. For further discussion see Hanegraaff, *Resurrection*, chap. 2.

167. 1 Cor. 15:4. For the tomb of Joseph of Arimathea, see Matt. 27:57–60; Mark 15:42–46; Luke 23:50–53; John 19:38–42.

168. John A. T. Robinson, *The Human Face of God* (Philadelphia: Westminster, 1973), 131, quoted in Copan, *Will the Real Jesus Please Stand Up?*, 27.

169. See n161.

170. See Raymond E. Brown, *The Death of the Messiah: From Gethsemane to the Grave*, 2 vols. (New York: Doubleday, 1994), 2:1240 (see 1239–41); Craig, *Reasonable Faith*, 364.

171. Craig, "Did Jesus Rise from the Dead?," 149.

172. Craig, 148, 152.

173. Craig, 147–48; For arguments establishing early dates for the writing of Mark, see John Wenham, *Redating Matthew, Mark & Luke* (Downers Grove, IL: InterVarsity Press, 1992), chaps. 6–8; Gregory A. Boyd, *Cynic Sage or Son of God?* (Wheaton, IL: Bridge Point, 1995), chap. 11.

174. See William Lane Craig, interview in Strobel, *Case for Christ*, 217–18.

175. See Ronald F. Youngblood, ed., *Nelson's New Illustrated Bible Dictionary* (Nashville: Thomas Nelson, 1995), 1318.

176. For discussion, see Craig, *Reasonable Faith*, 367–69.

177. See Matt. 28:13.

178. See Craig, "Did Jesus Rise from the Dead?," 146–47, 152; Habermas, *Historical Jesus*, 205–6.

179. For an excellent defense of the empty tomb, see Craig, *Reasonable Faith*, 361–77. See also Hanegraaff, *Resurrection*, chap. 3.

180. Craig, "Did Jesus Rise from the Dead?," 147.

181. 1 Cor. 15:3–7 NIV 1984.

182. Habermas, *Historical Jesus*, 154; Craig L. Blomberg, "Where Do We Start Studying Jesus?" in *Jesus Under Fire*, 42–43; cf. Craig, *Reasonable Faith*, 362.

183. Cf. Craig, *Reasonable Faith*, 366, esp. n48.

184. In this sentence I am closely paraphrasing—virtually quoting—Gary Habermas in Strobel, *The Case for Christ*, 233.

185. See 1 Cor. 15:6. Paul received this creed from the believing community (v. 3), perhaps from Peter and James in Jerusalem (see Gal. 1:18–19) if not sooner (see Habermas, *Historical Jesus*, 155).

186. See C. H. Dodd, "The Appearances of the Risen Christ: A Study in the Form Criticism of the Gospels," in *More New Testament Studies* (Manchester: University of Manchester, 1968), 128; Craig, *Reasonable Faith*, 378–79.

187. See Acts 9:1–9; 1 Cor. 15:7.

188. See Acts 22:3; Rom. 11:1; Phil. 3:3–8.

189. Acts 7:58–8:1; 8:3; 9:14; 26:10–11; 1 Cor. 15:9; Gal. 1:13, 23; 1 Tim. 1:13.

190. Sean McDowell explains, "The traditional view is that Paul was beheaded in Rome during the reign of Nero in AD 64 to 67. Scripture does not directly state his martyrdom, but there are hints in both Acts and 2 Timothy 4:6–8 that Paul knew his death was pending. The first extrabiblical evidence is found in *1 Clement* 5:5–7 (c. AD 95–96) in which Paul is described as suffering greatly for his faith and then being 'set free from this world and transported up to the holy place, having become the greatest example of endurance.' While details regarding the manner of his fate are lacking, the immediate context strongly implies that Clement was referring to the martyrdom of Paul. Other early evidences for the martyrdom of Paul can be found in Ignatius (*Letter to the Ephesians* 12:2), Polycarp (*Letter to the Philippians* 9:1–2), Dionysius of Corinth (Eusebius, *Ecclesiastical History* 2.25.4), Irenaeus (*Against Heresies* 3.1.1), The Acts of Paul, and Tertullian (*Scorpiace* 15:5–6). The early, consistent, and unanimous testimony is that Paul died as a martyr." Sean

McDowell, "Did the Apostles Really Die as Martyrs for Their Faith?" *Christian Research Journal* 39, no. 2 (2016), www.equip.org/PDF/JAF1392.pdf. See also Sean McDowell, *The Fate of the Apostles: Examining the Martyrdom Accounts of the Closest Followers of Jesus* (Surrey, England: Ashgate, 2015).

191. See 1 Cor. 15:7.

192. See Mark 3:21, 31–35; John 7:5.

193. Craig, *Reasonable Faith*, 379–80; Strobel, *Case for Christ*, 248; See Josephus, *Antiquities of the Jews*, 20.200. That James became an apostle and leader in the Jerusalem church is evident from such passages as Acts 12:17; 15:13–21; 21:18ff; 1 Cor. 15:3–8; Gal. 2:9–12.

194. Norman Perrin, *The Resurrection According to Matthew, Mark, and Luke* (Philadelphia: Fortress, 1974), 80, quoted in Copan, *Will the Real Jesus Please Stand Up?*, 28. For further discussion, see Hanegraaff, *Resurrection*, chap. 4.

195. See 1 Cor. 15:5, in which the original apostles, minus Judas, are referred to as the Twelve (cf. John 20:24).

196. Peter, like Paul, suffered a martyr's death. See Clement of Rome (c. A.D. 30–100), *First Epistle to the Corinthians*, chap. 5 Tertullian (c. 160–225), *On Prescription Against Heretics*, chap. 36; Eusebius (c. 260–340), *History of the Church*, bk 2: 25. See also McDowell, "Did the Apostles Really Die?"

197. J. P. Moreland, *Scaling the Secular City: A Defense of Christianity* (Grand Rapids: Baker Book House, 1987), 179–180; see also Moreland, interview in Strobel, *Case for Christ*, 250–54.

198. See Gen. 2:2–3.

199. See Deut. 5:15; cf. Exod. 20:11.

200. See Col. 2:16–17; Heb. 4:1–11.

201. Norman Geisler and Thomas Howe, *When Critics Ask* (Wheaton, IL: Victor Books, 1992), 78. See Matt. 28:1–10; John 20:26ff; Acts 2:1; 20:7; 1 Cor. 16:2.

202. Adapted from Moreland, interview in Strobel, *Case for Christ*, 251.

203. See Heb. 8–10.

204. John 1:29.

205. Cf. Strobel, *Case for Christ*, 252–53.

206. Merrill C. Tenney, "Baptism and the Lord's Supper," in *Basic Christian Doctrines*, ed. Carl F. H. Henry (Grand Rapids: Baker Book House, 1971), 256.

207. Acts 2:36–41; see also Matt. 28:19; Acts 8:16; 10:48; 19:5; Rom. 6:3–5; 1 Cor. 6:11.

208. Strobel, *Case for Christ*, 253. See also chap. 3, 60–62. Preceding paragraphs adapted from Hanegraaff, *Resurrection*, 59–62.

209. 1 Cor. 15:42–43.

210. John 11:25 NIV 1984.

211. See Hank Hanegraaff, *AfterLife: What You Need to Know about Heaven, the Hereafter, and Near-Death Experiences* (Brentwood, TN: Worthy Publishing, 2013). Previous two paragraphs adapted from Hanegraaff, *Has God Spoken?*, 184–85.

212. I. A. Ibrahim, *A Brief Illustrated Guide to Understanding Islam*, 2nd ed. (Houston: Darussalam, 1997), 5; see also Sayyid Abul A'La Maududi, *Towards Understanding Islam*, 2nd ed. (n.p.: International Islamic Federation of Student Organizations, 1989), 60.

213. Joseph Smith in *The Teachings of the Prophet Joseph Smith*, ed. Joseph Fielding Smith (Salt Lake City: Deseret Book Company, 1976), 194.

214. Journal of Oliver B. Huntington, page 168 of typed copy at Utah State Historical Society, in Jerald Tanner and Sandra Tanner, "Introduction," in *3,913 Changes in the Book of Mormon* (Salt Lake City: Utah Lighthouse Ministries, 1996), www.utlm.org/onlinebooks/3913intro.htm.

215. See Hanegraaff, *MUSLIM*, chap. 2.

216. See note 161, page 236.

217. The claim that the Book of Mormon was written in "reformed Egyptian" is found in Mormon 9:32.

218. See Ether 7 in the Book of Mormon.

219. Two DVDs I highly recommend for personal and group study are *The Bible vs. The Book of Mormon* (Brigham City, UT: Living Hope Ministries, 2003), and *DNA vs. The Book of Mormon* (Brigham City, UT: Living Hope Ministries, 2003).

220. Bart D. Ehrman, *Forged: Writing in the Name of God—Why the Bible's Authors Are Not Who We Think They Are* (New York: HarperOne, 2011), 250.

221. Quoted in Cathleen Falsani, "The God Factor," *Chicago Sun-Times*, October 24, 2004, News 16.

222. See Hanegraaff, *Has God Spoken?*

223. See F. F. Bruce, *The Books and the Parchments: How We Got Our English Bible* (Grand Rapids: Revell, 1950), 178; for a more recent discussion, see Clay Jones, "The Bibliographical Test Updated," *Christian Research Journal* 35, no. 3 (2012), www.equip.org/article/the-bibliographical-test-updated/.

224. James R. White, *The King James Only Controversy: Can You Trust the Modern Translations?* (Minneapolis, MN: Bethany House Publishers, 1995), 47–48.

225. See Hanegraaff, *Has God Spoken?*, chap. 3. Two previous paragraphs adapted from Hanegraaff, *Complete Bible Answer Book*, 142–43.

226. 2 Peter 1:16, emphasis added.

227. See Luke 1:1–4.

228. Darrel L. Bock, *Studying the Historical Jesus: A Guide to Sources and Methods* (Grand Rapids: Baker Academic, 2002), 47–49.

229. See Habermas, *Historical Jesus*, 187–228 (esp. 224–28). See also 235–36n160.

230. See 235n157–58. See also Hanegraaff, *Has God Spoken?*, pt. 1, from which the previous two paragraphs are adapted.

231. See Thomas H. Maugh II, "Biblical Pool Uncovered in Jerusalem," *Los Angeles Times*, August 9, 2005, A8.

232. John 9:7 NKJV, emphasis added. See Hershel Shanks, "The Siloam Pool: Where Jesus Cured the Blind Man," *Biblical Archeology Review* 31, no. 5, (Sept./Oct. 2005): 16–23.

233. See John 5:1–15; Timothy McGrew and Lydia McGrew, "The Argument from Miracles: A Cumulative Case for the Resurrection of Jesus of Nazareth," in *The Blackwell Companion to Natural Theology*, ed. William Lane Craig and J. P. Moreland (West Sussex, United Kingdom: Wiley-Blackwell, 2009), 600; Shimon Gibson, *The Final Days of Jesus: The Archaeological Evidence* (New York: HarperCollins, 2009), 74–75.

234. See Hanegraaff, *Has God Spoken?*, chap. 8.

235. See Hanegraaff, chap. 9.

236. See Hanegraaff, chap. 10. Section adapted from Hanegraaff, pt. 2.

237. Isa. 48:5.

238. John 14:29.

239. See Hanegraaff, *Has God Spoken?*, chap. 12.

240. Josephus, *Antiquities* 10:186.

241. Josephus, 10.11.7. See also F. F. Bruce, *The Canon of Scripture* (Downers Grove, IL: InterVarsity Press, 1988), 32–36; James Patrick Holding, "The Authenticity of Daniel: A Defense," Tekton Apologetics, www.tektonics.org/af/danieldefense.html.

242. Matt. 24:15; see Dan. 9:27; 11:31; 12:11. For further defense of the sixth-century authorship of the book of Daniel, see Hanegraaff, *Has God Spoken?*, 153–54.

243. See Hanegraaff, chap. 16. Section adapted from pt. 3.

244. Paragraph adopted from Hanegraaff, chap. 22.

245. Hanegraaff, *Complete Bible Answer Book*; Hanegraaff, *Creation Answer Book*.

Chapter 2: Biblical Interpretation

1. Clement of Alexandria (d. 215), quoted in R. P. C. Hanson, *Origen's Doctrine of Tradition* (London: SPCK, 1954), 48, accessed via Google Books, http://books.google.com; see Clement of Alexandria, *Stromata*, 7.16 in *The Ante-Nicene Fathers*, vol. 2, eds. Alexander Roberts and James Donaldson, , www.ccel.org/ccel/schaff/anf02.vi.iv.vii.xvi.html.

2. See especially discussions below under subheadings "Holy Fathers" and "Seven Ecumenical Councils" in chap. 4 and "Disunity—Fissuring the Body of Christ" in chap. 6. Paragraph above adapted from Hanegraaff, *Has God Spoken?*, 211.

3. Jean-Claude Larchet aptly notes that paleontology refers only to history outside of Paradise. And that "the original condition of man as it is presented in Scripture and the Fathers is situated in another temporal order than that of historical knowledge: itD. L.does not belong to the time of sensible realities (*chronos*), but to the duration of spiritual realities (*aiōn*), which eludes historical science because it belongs to the sphere of spiritual history. Without being 'non-temporal' . . . the existence of Adam in his primitive state is 'ante-historical,' just as human existence following the parousia will be post-historical. Spiritual history, then, cannot be replaced by historical science. The teaching of Tradition about human origins is neither more nor less incompatible with our present knowledge of human paleontology than is the faith of the Church in the eucharistic transformation of bread and wine into Body and Blood of Christ with the findings of the science of chemistry, or faith in the Ascension of Christ with the findings of physics and astronomy. . . . Faith and spiritual knowledge correspond to a domain in which the laws of nature are transcended and to a mode of existence that is, in the proper sense of the term, 'super-natural.'" Jean-Claude Larchet, *The Theology of Illness* (Crestwood, NY: St. Vladimir's Seminary Press, 2002), 23n.

4. John 6:35.

5. William Gurnall, *The Christian in Complete Armour*, vol. 2, rev. ed., ed., Ruthanne Garlock, Kay King, Karen Sloan, and Candy Coan (1658; repr., Edinburgh, Great Britain: Banner of Truth Trust, 1988), 150, emphasis added.

6. Section adapted from Hanegraaff, *Has God Spoken?*, chap. 17.

7. 1 Cor. 2:12 NIV 1984.

8. 1 Sam. 3:9 (see also v. 10).

9. John 10:27.

10. Widely used saying without attribution.

11. 1 John 4:1.

12. Section adapted from Hanegraaff, *Has God Spoken?*, chap. 18.

13. Matt. 16:15.

14. Mark 4:41.

15. John 10:32–33 NIV 1984.

16. See John 1:1 (and Col. 1:15–17) in the New World Translation published by the Jehovah's Witnesses.

17. Section adapted from Hanegraaff, *Has God Spoken?*, chap. 19.

18. See Ezek. 1; 10–11; 43; Ezra 3; 8; Neh. 1–8; Hag. 1–2; Mal. 3; also Dan. 9–11. Section adapted from Hanegraaff, *Has God Spoken?*, chap. 20.

19. See, e.g., Heb. 9:24; Rom. 5:14; 1 Cor. 10:11; Col. 2: 17. Section adapted from Hanegraaff, *Has God Spoken?*, chaps. 13, 21.

20. Matt. 26:64 NIV 1984.

21. See Bart D. Ehrman, *Jesus: Apocalyptic Prophet of the New Millennium* (Oxford University Press, 1999), 130–31; and Bart D. Ehrman, *The New Testament: A Historical Introduction to the Early Christian Writings*, 3rd ed. (New York: Oxford University Press, 2004), 128–29.

22. Cf. George B. Caird, *Jesus and the Jewish Nation* (London: Athlone, 1965), 20–22. For discussion, see Hank Hanegraaff, *The Apocalypse Code: Find Out What the Bible Really Says About the End Times . . . and Why It Matters Today* (Nashville: Thomas Nelson, 2007), 105–8.

23. Section adapted from Hanegraaff, *Has God Spoken?*, chaps. 2, 22.

Chapter 3: Countering Counterfeit Religions

1. 2 Cor. 11:3–4 NKJV.

2. "How to Detect Counterfeit Money," *Los Angeles Times*, August 9, 1999, www.articles .latimes.com/1999/aug/09/local/me-64066; see also "How to Protect Yourself from Counterfeiting," University of Florida Police Department, www.police.ufl.edu /resources/brochures-safety-tips/property-crimes/#how-to-detect-counterfeit-money.

3. Popularly attributed to D. L. Moody. Introductory paragraphs adapted from Hanegraaff, *MUSLIM*, 129, 131; Hanegraaff, *Complete Bible Answer Book*, 6, 7.

4. See "Who Is Michael the Archangel?" Jehovah's Witnesses, www.jw.org/en /publications/books/bible-teach/who-is-michael-the-archangel-jesus/.

5. Jess L. Christensen, "How Can Jesus and Lucifer be Spirit Brothers When Their Characters and Purposes Are So Utterly Opposed?" Church of Jesus Christ of Latter-Day Saints, June 1986, www.lds.org/ensign/1986/06/i-have-a-question /how-can-jesus-and-lucifer-be-spirit-brothers-when-their-characters-and -purposes-are-so-utterly-opposed?; Hank Hanegraaff, "Is Jesus the Spirit Brother of Satan?" *Christian Research Journal* 31, no. 2 (2008), www.equip.org/article /is-jesus-christ-the-spirit-brother-of-satan/.

6. Cf. Elliot Miller, "From 'New Age Christ' to Born-Again Christian," *Christian Research Journal* 11, no. 1 (1988), www.equip.org/article/from-new-age-christ-to -born-again-christian/.

7. John 5:18.

8. See John 8:58–59; cf. Exod. 3:14.

9. John 10:30–33 NIV 1984.

10. Mark 14:61–62.

11. Dan. 7:13–14.

12. Mark 14:64. See Gary. R. Habermas, *The Risen Jesus & Future Hope* (Lanham, MD: Rowman & Littlefield, 2003), 104–6.

13. John 8:46. The apostle Paul wrote, "We do not have a high priest who is unable to empathize with our weaknesses, but we have one who has been tempted in every way, just as we are—yet he did not sin" (Heb. 4:15). See also Isa. 53:9; Matt. 12:18; 17:5; Luke 2:40; 3:22; 4:1–13; 23:41, 47; John 8:29; 10:36–38; Heb. 7:26; 9:14; 1 Peter 1:19; 2 Peter 1:17.

14. See Matt. 27:45ff; Mark 15:33ff; Luke 23:44ff; John 19:28ff; see also 1 Cor. 15:1–11. See also chap. 1, "Answers on Resurrection."

15. Additionally, in Rom. 10:13, Paul equates calling on Christ with calling on Yahweh (Joel 2:32); and in Phil. 2:9–11, he equates bowing to and confessing the name of Jesus with bowing to and confessing the name of Yahweh (Isa. 45:22–25), further demonstrating that Jesus is himself Almighty God.

16. Particularly compelling is the way John presents in Revelation a set of two corresponding divine declarations of God and Christ:

God: "I am the Alpha and the Omega" (1:8; cf. Isa. 44:6).

Christ: "I am the First and the Last" (1:17).

God: "I am the Alpha and the Omega, the Beginning and the End" (21:6).

Christ: "I am the Alpha and the Omega, the First and the Last, the Beginning and the End" (22:13).

See Richard Bauckham, *The Theology of the Book of Revelation* (Cambridge, United Kingdom: Cambridge University Press, 1993), 26 (see chaps. 2–3).

17. In his comprehensive study of the New Testament use of the term θεός (*theos*, "God"), New Testament scholar Murray J. Harris concluded, "While the [New Testament] customarily reserves the term θεός for the Father, occasionally it is applied to Jesus in his preincarnate, incarnate, or postresurrection state. As used of the Father, θεός is virtually a proper name. As used of Jesus, θεός is a generic title, being an appellation descriptive of his *genus* as one who inherently belongs to the category of Deity. In this usage θεός points not to Christ's function or office but to his nature." See John 1:1, 18; 20:28; Rom. 9:5; Titus 2:13; Heb. 1:8; 2 Peter 1:1. Murray J. Harris, *Jesus as God: The New Testament Use of the Term Theos in Reference to Jesus* (Grand Rapids: Baker Book House, 1992), 298.

Furthermore, Christ receives worship due to God alone: Matt. 2:11; 14:33; 28:9, 17; John 9:37–38; Phil. 2:9–11 (cf. Isa. 45:23–24); Heb. 1:6; Rev. 5:6, 8, 13–14; 22:1–3 (cf. Exod. 20:3–6; Deut. 4:35; 6:4; 13–16; 32:39; Matt. 4:10; John 4:24; Acts 10:25–26; 14:11–15; Rev. 19:9–10; 22:8–9).

Section adapted from Hanegraaff, *Complete Bible Answer Book*, 244–45, 246–50, 275–76; Hanegraaff, *MUSLIM*, 131–34, 258–59.

18. Gen. 2:16–17 NIV 1984.

19. Frederica Mathewes-Green, *First Fruits of Prayer: A Forty-Day Journey Through the Canon of St. Andrew* (Brewster, MA: Paraclete Press, 2006), xiv–xv.

20. Rom. 5:12. See also Rom. 5:14–21; 1 Cor. 15:21–22, 45–49; Eph. 2:3; Ps. 51:5; also Rom. 3:9ff.

21. Athanasius (c. 296–373), *Discourse 1 Against the Arians*, 1.51, trans. John Henry Newman and Archibald Robertson, in *Nicene and Post-Nicene Fathers*, vol. 4, eds. Philip Schaff and Henry Wace (Buffalo, NY: Literature Publishing Co., 1892), www.newadvent.org/fathers/28161.htm.

22. Gen. 3.

23. Gen. 12:3.

24. Heb. 11:16.

25. Gen. 17:5.

26. Rom. 4:13.

27. The apostle Paul wrote, "Now the promises were spoken to Abraham and to his seed. He does not say, 'And to seeds,' as referring to many, but rather to one, 'And to your seed,' that is, Christ" (Gal. 3:16 NASB). See Gen. 12:7; 22:17–18 in which the Hebrew for "seed" is singular.

28. Four previous paragraphs adapted from Hanegraaff, *Apocalypse Code*, 51–52, 53.

29. Jane Idleman Smith and Yvonne Yazbeck Haddad, *The Islamic Understanding of Death and Resurrection* (Oxford: Oxford University Press, 2002), 14.

30. See Smith and Haddad, *Islamic Understanding*, 12; Salaam Corniche, "Fitrah and Fig Leaves: Islamic and Christian Teachings on Sin," *St. Francis Magazine* 9, no. 5 (2013).

31. *Sahih Muslim*, bk. 033, no. 6426, bracketed insertion in original, trans. Abdul Hamid Siddiqui, Center for Muslim-Jewish Engagement, University of Southern California, web.archive.org/web/20160511165648/http://www.usc.edu/org /cmje/religious-texts/hadith/muslim/033-smt.php.

32. Abdullah Yusuf Ali, *The Meaning of the Holy Qur'an*, 10th ed. (Beltsville, MD: Amana Publications, 1999, 2001), 1016 (n3541 at Sura 30:30), emphasis added. Although humankind has been created weak (Sura 4:28) and inclines toward forgetfulness, there is "nothing inherently debased about man; he has been given every natural opportunity to live a life of well-being and honor." Smith and Haddad, *Islamic Understanding*, 14, 15.

33. Ps. 51:5. Four previous paragraphs adapted from Hanegraaff, *MUSLIM*, 138, 139.

34. Dennis Prager, "Are People Born Good?" PragerU, www.prageru.com/sites/ default/files/courses/transcripts/prager-are_people_born_good-transcript.pdf.

35. Tree of Life content adapted from Hanegraaff, *Creation Answer Book*, 57–58.

36. For further study see Hanegraaff, *MUSLIM*.

37. *The Book of Mormon*, Introduction, Church of Jesus Christ of Latter-Day Saints, www.lds.org/scriptures/bofm/introduction.

38. 2 Nephi 5:21; *The Book of Mormon* (Salt Lake City: Church of Jesus Christ of Latter-Day Saints, 1987), introduction, emphasis added.

39. *Book of Mormon*, introduction. The claim that the Book of Mormon was written in "reformed Egyptian" is found in Mormon 9:32.

40. *Book of Mormon*, introduction.

41. *Book of Mormon*, introduction.

42. Paul L. Maier, "Archaeology: Biblical Ally or Adversary?" *Christian Research Journal* 27, no. 2 (2004), www.equip.org/PDF/DA111.pdf.

43. See William M. Ramsay, *The Bearing of Recent Discovery on the Trustworthiness of the New Testament* (repr., Grand Rapids: Baker Book House, 1953); *St. Paul the Traveler and the Roman Citizen* (Grand Rapids: Baker Book House, 1962).

44. See Jeffrey L. Sheler, "Is the Bible True?" *U.S. News and World Report*, October 25, 1999, 58, reprinted from Jeffrey L. Sheler, *Is the Bible True?* (San Francisco: HarperSanFrancisco, 1999).

45. Sheler, *Is the Bible True?*, 111. Previous paragraphs adapted from Hanegraaff, *Has God Spoken?*, 58–60.

46. For further resources see the flipchart, "Memorable Keys to the M-O-R-M-O-N Mirage," www.equip.org; and Hanegraaff, *The Mormon Mirage*.

47. "Oneness Pentecostalism," Stanley M. Burgess, Gary B. McGee, Patrick H. Alexander, eds., *Dictionary of Pentecostal and Charismatic Movements* (Grand Rapids: Zondervan Publishing House, 1988), 644.

48. See "Should You Believe in the Trinity?" (Brooklyn: Watchtower Bible and Tract Society of New York, 1989); Hanegraaff, *MUSLIM*, 37–39, 156–59.

49. See Alexander Vilenkin, "The Beginning of the Universe," *Inference* 1, no. 4 (2015), www.inference-review.com/article/the-beginning-of-the-universe.

50. See Gen. 1, esp. v. 1; Ps. 33:6–9; 148:1–6; Prov. 8:22–29; John 1:3; Rom. 4:17; Col. 1:16–17; Heb. 1:2–3; 11:3.

51. See John 3:35; 5:20; 14:31; Rom. 5:5; 1 John 4:8, 16. For a helpful discussion, see Fairbairn, *Life in the Trinity*, chaps. 2–4.

52. C. S. Lewis, *Mere Christianity*, 174.

53. Fairbairn, *Life in the Trinity*, 54. Three previous paragraphs adapted from Hanegraaff, *MUSLIM*, 156–57.

54. Leonardo Boff, *Trinity and Society* (New York: Orbis Books, 1988), 89; see also Millard J. Erickson, *God in Three Persons* (Grand Rapids: Baker Books, 1995), 233.

55. Norman L. Geisler, *Baker Encyclopedia of Christian Apologetics* (Grand Rapids:

Baker Books, 1999), 732. This and following three paragraphs adapted from Hanegraaff, *Complete Bible Answer Book*, 50–51.

56. Deut. 4:35, emphasis added.

57. Matt. 28:19. See also Luke 1:35; 3:22; John 8:16–18; 14:26; 15:26; 16:13–15; Rom. 8:9–11.

58. See John 1:12; 14:16–17, 19–20; 16:13–15; 20:31; Rom. 8:15–16; 2 Peter 1:4. Our sharing in the loving relationship the Son has with his Father (*theosis*) is the subject of chap. 4.

59. 1 Thess. 4:13–14.

60. See the illustrative presentation of this miraculous process in *Metamorphosis: The Beauty and Design of Butterflies*, directed by Lad Allen (La Mirada, CA: Illustra Media, 2011), DVD.

61. 2 Cor. 5:8.

62. 1 Cor. 15:42–44.

63. Rev. 21:1.

64. Dan. 12:2–3.

65. Isa. 26:19 NIV 1984.

66. John 5:28–29.

67. Scientism is the view that science (especially the hard sciences such as physics and chemistry) provides the only (or at least the most reliable) means of gaining knowledge. Recall Alex Rosenberg's claim that "physics fixes all the facts." Rosenberg, *Atheist's Guide to Reality*, 94–95.

68. "Americans Describe Their Views about Life After Death," Barna Group, October 21, 2003, www.barna.com/research/americans-describe-their-views-about-life-after-death/. The Barna Group also reports that one in five Americans believes in reincarnation.

69. John Leo, "I Was Beheaded in the 1700s," *Time*, September 10, 1984, 68.

70. Section adapted from Hanegraaff, *AfterLife*, 1–3, 117–19, 155–56; Hanegraaff, *Has God Spoken?*, 173.

71. John 1:14 NKJV.

72. Dan Brown, *The Da Vinci Code* (New York: Doubleday, 2003).

73. Jeff Ayers, *Library Journal* (February 1, 2003): 114.

74. *Publisher's Weekly*, March 18, 2003, 76.

75. Brown, *Da Vinci Code*, back cover.

76. Brown, 232, emphasis added.

77. Brown, 232.

78. Hank Hanegraaff and Paul L. Maier, *The Da Vinci Code: Fact or Fiction?—A Critique of the Novel by Dan Brown* (Wheaton, IL: Tyndale House Publishers, 2004).

79. Maier, in Hanegraaff and Maier, *Da Vinci Code,* 2–3.

80. Maier in Hanegraaff and Maier, *Da Vinci Code,* 3.

81. J. Ed Komoszewski, M. James Sawyer, and Daniel B. Wallace, *Reinventing Jesus: How Contemporary Skeptics Miss the Real Jesus and Mislead Popular Culture* (Grand Rapids: Kregel Publications, 2006), 221–22.

82. See W. B. Yeats, "Leda and the Swan" (1924), Academy of American Poets, www.poets.org/poetsorg/poem/leda-and-swan.

83. John Burt, "Mary and Leda," message delivered at First Universalist Church of Orange, Massachusetts, December 1996, www.people.brandeis.edu/~burt/ledasermon.pdf.

84. John 1:14.

85. Five previous paragraphs adapted from Hanegraaff, *Complete Bible Answer Book,* 257–58, 260, 269, 270.

86. John 1:12.

87. 2 Cor. 5:17, emphasis added.

88. Hanegraaff, *MUSLIM,* 166.

89. See Nee, *Normal Christian Life,* 59–61, 119, 170–71.

90. Lossky, *Orthodox Theology,* 84.

91. See Fairbairn, *Life in the Trinity.*

92. C. H. Spurgeon, "The Believer a New Creature," sermon no. 881, delivered July 18, 1869, www.spurgeongems.org/vols13–15/chs881.pdf. This version has been lightly edited to conform to modern-day language; compare original at Christian Classics Ethereal Library, www.ccel.org/ccel/spurgeon/sermons15.i_1.html.

93. Hanegraaff, *MUSLIM,* 169.

94. Hanegraaff, *Apocalypse Code.*

95. Ehrman, *Jesus,* x.

96. Ehrman, *Jesus,* 159–60. Ehrman is quoting Mark 13:24–25.

97. Isa. 13:9–10 NIV 1984.

98. Other instances of a prophet predicting judgment within his generation include Ezek. 32:7 (judgment on Egypt); Joel 2:10, 31; Amos 5:18–20 (judgment on Israel); Zeph. 1:14–18 (judgment on Judah).

99. Bertrand Russell, "Why I Am Not a Christian," in *Why I Am Not a Christian: And Other Essays on Religion and Related Subjects,* ed. Paul Edwards (New York: Simon and Schuster, 1957), 16.

100. Matt. 24:30 NIV 1984.

101. Ezek. 30:3 NIV 1984, emphasis added.

102. Joel 2:1–2 NIV 1984, emphasis added.

103. Isa. 19:1 NIV 1984, emphasis added.

104. Caird, *Jesus and the Jewish Nation*, 22; quoted in N. T. Wright, *Jesus and the Victory of God*, vol. 2, *Christian Origins and the Question of God* (Minneapolis: Fortress, 1996), 341.

105. Matt. 24:34 NIV 1984.

106. Section adapted from Hanegraaff, *Apocalypse Code*, 1–2, 136, 237; Hanegraaff, *Has God Spoken?*, 147–48, 150–51.

107. 1 Peter 3:15.

108. This quote is a widely disseminated, abridged paraphrase of several lines from Daniel Webster, *An Address Delivered Before the New York Historical Society, February 23, 1852* (New York: Press of the Historical Society, 1852), 47, www .catalog.hathitrust.org/Record/100765773.

109. 2 Peter 1:4.

110. Dallas Willard, *The Divine Conspiracy: Rediscovering Our Hidden Life in God* (New York: HarperSanFrancisco, 1997), 30–31.

111. Willard, *Divine Conspiracy*, 58.

Part 2: Life Matters More

1. Lossky, *Orthodox Theology*, 84.

2. Prov. 20:15.

3. John 10:10, in Holy Bible: Recovery Version (Anaheim: Living Stream Ministry, 2003), https://online.recoveryversion.bible.

4. Thanks to Larry Johnston for these insights.

5. Rosenberg, *Atheist's Guide to Reality*, 21.

6. See *Information and the Nature of Reality: From Physics to Metaphysics*, ed. Paul Davies and Niels Henrik Gregersen (Cambridge, UK: Cambridge University Press, 2010).

7. John 17:22 ESV. For Christ's transfiguration, see Matt. 17:1–9; Mark 9:2–9; Luke 9:28–36.

8. 2 Cor. 3:18 NIV 1984.

9. John 14:6, emphasis added.

10. Lossky, *Mystical Theology*, 9.

11. Lossky, *Mystical Theology*, 9.

Chapter 4: Deification

1. Martin Luther, *Weimarer Ausgabe* (WA) 1, 28, 25–32, quoted in Mannermaa, "Theosis," 43, quoted in Veli-Matti Kärkkäinen, *One with God: Salvation as Deification and Justification* (Collegeville, MN: Liturgical Press, 2004), 47; cf. discussion and a slightly different translation of the same quote in Kurt E.

Marquart, "Luther and Theosis," *Concordia Theological Quarterly* 64, no. 3 (2000): 186–87, www.ctsfw.net /media/pdfs/marquartlutherandtheosis.pdf.

2. Gen. 3:5.

3. Hanegraaff, *Christianity in Crisis*, 107–120; see also Hank Hanegraaff, *Christianity in Crisis: 21ˢᵗ Century* (Nashville: Thomas Nelson, 2009) 131–42.

4. M. Scott Peck, *The Road Less Traveled* (New York: Simon & Schuster, 1978), 270.

5. Margot Adler, *Drawing Down the Moon*, rev. ed. (Boston: Beacon Press, 1986), 25.

6. Bhagwan Shree Rajneesh, quoted in *Fear Is the Master* (Hemet, CA: Jeremiah Films, 1987).

7. Maharishi Mahesh Yogi, *Meditations of Maharishi Mahesh Yogi* (New York: Bantam, 1968), 178; quoted in James W. Sire, *Scripture Twisting* (Downers Grove, IL: InterVarsity Press, 1980), 34. Cf. Ps. 46:10 (45:10 LXX).

8. Jim Jones, quoted in James Reston Jr. and Noah Adams, "Father Cares: The Last of Jonestown," program on National Public Radio (April 23, 1981).

9. Kenneth E. Hagin, *Zoe: The God-Kind of Life* (Tulsa, OK: Kenneth Hagin Ministries, 1989), 35–36, 41.

10. Kenneth Copeland, "Spirit, Soul and Body I" (Fort Worth, TX: Kenneth Copeland Ministries, 1985), audiotape 01–0601, side 1.

11. Joseph Smith Jr., "Classics in Mormon Thought: The King Follett Sermon," April 7, 1844, www.lds.org/ensign/1971/04/the-king-follett-sermon.

12. Stephen E. Robinson, "The Doctrinal Exclusion," in *Are Mormons Christians?* (Salt Lake City: Bookcraft, 1991), chap. 6, www.lightplanet.com/mormons /response/general/christians/ser6.htm.

13. Hanegraaff, *Christianity in Crisis*, 110–11.

14. Robichaux, "Can Human Beings Become God?" 41.

15. Robichaux, 45–46.

16. Andrew Louth, "The Place of *Theosis* in Orthodox Theology," in *Partakers of the Divine Nature: The History and Development of Deification in the Christian Traditions*, ed. Michael J. Christensen and Jeffrey A. Wittung (Grand Rapids: Baker Academic, 2007), 33.

17. Robichaux, "Can Human Beings Become God?" 31.

18. Robichaux, 45.

19. Lossky, *Orthodox Theology*, 84, emphasis added.

20. Louth, "The Place of *Theosis* in Orthodox Theology," 34.

21. Louth, 35.

22. Louth, 36.

23. Matt. 13:44–46 NIV 1984.

24. Scott Hahn, "Foreword," in *Called to Be the Children of God: The Catholic*

Theology of Human Deification, ed. David Vincent Meconi and Carl E. Olson (San Francisco: Ignatius Press, 2016), 7, emphasis in original.

25. Hahn, "Foreword," 8.

26. Hahn, 8.

27. Meconi and Olson, "Introduction," in *Called to Be the Children of* God, 12, emphasis added. See also Norman Russell, *The Doctrine of Deification in the Greek Patristic Tradition* (New York: Oxford University Press, 2004), 262, 267, 294. "Kenosis" (from Greek) refers to Christ's act of self-emptying in the incarnation (see Phil. 2:6–7), though Christ never divested himself of any divine attribute.

28. Donald Fairbairn, *Life in the Trinity: An Introduction to Theology with the Help of the Church Fathers* (Downers Grove, IL: IVP Academic, 2009), 6.

29. Gregory Palamas (c. 1296–c. 1359), *In Dormitionem*, 472B, in Lossky, *Mystical Theology*, 194. The title "Panagia" (from Greek) means "All-holy."

30. Lossky, *Mystical Theology*, 194.

31. From a Hymn to Mary, chanted in Eastern Orthodox and Eastern Catholic Divine Services.

32. Luke 1:47.

33. Luke 1:42–43 KJV.

34. Matt. 13:55–56.

35. See Gen. 29:15. The Septuagint reads, "Laban said to Jacob ... thou art my brother [ἀδελφός]." *The Septuagint with Apocrypha: Greek and English*, trans. Lancelot C. L. Brenton (Peabody, MA: Hendrickson Publishers, 1851), 1999.

36. See Gen. 13:8. Note that the KJV translators rendered the Hebrew word אָחִי ['a-hi] in Gen. 29:15 as "brother" and in Gen. 13:8 (אֲנָשִׁים ['a-him]) as "brethren."

37. Matt. 1:25.

38. *The Septuagint Version of the Old Testament*, vol. 1, trans. Lancelot Charles Lee Brenton (London: Samuel Bagster and Sons, 1844), 335, accessed via Google Books, http://books.google.com.

39. See *The Protoevangelium of James* (mid-second century A.D.), accessible at CCEL, www.ccel.org/ccel/schaff/anf08.vii.iv.html.

40. Or possibly in virtue of simply being Joseph's brother, Cleopas's "children were our Lord's 'brothers' (using the terminology of Israel, which ... made no distinction between brothers and cousins but referred to all as 'brothers')." Fr. John Hainsworth, "The Ever-Virginity of the Mother of God," Greek Orthodox Archdiocese of America, www.goarch.org/-/the-ever-virginity-of-the-mother-of-god. Cf. St. Jerome (c. 340–420), *The Perpetual Virginity of Blessed Mary*, accessible at CCEL, www.ccel.org/ccel/schaff/npnf206.vi.v.html.

41. John 19:27 NKJV. The reference to Mosaic Law is Exod. 20:12; cf. Mark 7:8–13.

42. Martin Luther, "That Jesus Christ Was Born a Jew," in *Luther's Works*, vol. 45, ed. Walther I. Brand (Muhlenberg Press, 1962), 199, emphasis added. Also available online at University of Duisburg-Essen, www.uni-due.de/collcart/es/sem/s6/txt09_1.htm.

43. "Who Are the Theotokos and St. John?" Theotokos & Saint John Orthodox Mission, www.fountainhills.arizonaorthodox.com/who-are-the-theotokos-and-st-john/.

44. Quoted in Lossky, *Mystical Theology*, 140.

45. 1 Tim. 2:14.

46. Lossky, *Mystical Theology*, 140, 193, 194.

47. Palamas, *In Dormitionem*, 468AB.

48. Lossky, 195. Lossky cites Palamas, *In Dormitionem*. For this helpful and freeing insight concerning rhetorical flourish, I thank Frederica Mathewes-Green.

49. Hanegraaff, *Resurrection*, chap. 5. I allude to the hymn by Reginald Heber, "The Son of God Goes Forth to War."

50. Jude v. 3 ESV.

51. *Martyrdom of Polycarp*, 9, paraphrase from trans. J. B. Lightfoot, Early Christian Writings, www.earlychristianwritings.com/text/martyrdompolycarp-lightfoot.html; see similar trans. Cyril C. Richardson, accessible at CCEL, www.ccel.org/ccel/richardson/fathers.vii.i.iii.html.

52. Paraphrase of 1 John 1:1.

53. Ignatius (c. 35–c. 107), *Epistle to the Romans* 4, in *Ante-Nicene Fathers*, vol. 1, eds. Alexander Roberts and James Donaldson (repr., Grand Rapids: Eerdmans, 1985), 75, , www.ccel.org/ccel/schaff/anf01.v.v.iv.html.

54. Ignatius, *Epistle to the Ephesians* 20, in *Ante-Nicene Fathers*, vol. 1, 57, 58, www.ccel.org/ccel/schaff/anf01.v.ii.xxi.html.

55. 2 Peter 1:4 NASB.

56. "St. Irenaeus," New Advent, www.newadvent.org/cathen/08130b.htm.

57. Philip Kariatlis, "St Irenaeus of Lyons," www.orthodoxchristian.info/pages/St_Irenaeus.htm; I've altered Dr. Kariatlis's sentence slightly from the original, "Just like a surgeon, when performing a major operation, Irenaeus too, through his writings lays bare the nerves and sinews so as to take his reader to the very heart of a heresy with the sole purpose of healing the Church from such disease."

58. Vincent of Lérins (d. 456), *Commonitorium* 2, quoted in Fr. John Behr, "Orthodoxy," St. Vladimir's Seminary, March 23, 1998, www.svots.edu/content/orthodoxy, emphasis added; slightly different translation at www.newadvent.org/fathers/3506.htm.

59. George Florovsky, "The Function of Tradition in the Ancient Church," *Greek Orthodox Theological Review* 9, no. 2 (1963), reprinted in Daniel B. Clendenin ed.,

Eastern Orthodox Theology: A Contemporary Reader, 2nd edition (Grand Rapids: Baker Academic, 2003), 99.

60. Irenaeus (c. 130–c. 200), *Against Heresies* 1.8.1. in *Ante-Nicene Fathers,* vol. 1, 326.

61. Cf. M. David Litwa, "The Wondrous Exchange: Irenaeus and Eastern Valentinians on the Soteriology of Interchange," *Journal of Early Christian Studies,* 22, no. 3 (Fall 2014): 311–41, www.muse.jhu.edu/article/553684.

62. Irenaeus, *Against Heresies* 5, Preface, in *Ante-Nicene Fathers,* vol. 1, 526.

63. Irenaeus, *Against Heresies,* 2.19.1, in *Ante-Nicene Fathers,* vol. 1, 448. Irenaeus cited Ps. 82:6–7 (81:6–7 LXX).

64. Origen (c. 185–c. 254), *Commentary on the Epistle to the Romans* 4.9.12, trans. Thomas P. Scheck, *Commentary on the Epistle to the Romans: Books 1–5,* in *The Fathers of the Church,* vol. 103 (Washington, DC: Catholic University of America Press, 2001), 292–93.

65. See Daniel A. Keating, "Deification in the Greek Fathers," in *Called to Be the Children of God,* 46. The Fifth Ecumenical Council in Constantinople (553) condemned Origen and his errors.

66. Athanasius, *On the Incarnation* 54, in *Nicene and Post-Nicene Fathers,* 2nd ser., vol. 4, 65.

67. Keating, "Deification," 46, emphasis in original.

68. Keating, 47.

69. See Athanasius, Festal Letter 39.5, in *Nicene and Post-Nicene Fathers,* 2nd ser., vol.4, 552.

70. Robichaux, "Can Human Beings Become God?" 32.

71. Jules Gross, *The Divinization of the Christian According to the Greek Fathers,* trans. Paul A. Onica (Anaheim: A & C Press, 2002), 176.

72. Gregory of Nyssa (c. 335–c. 394), *Great Catechism,* 25, in Gross, *Divinization of the Christian,* 182.

73. This sentence paraphrases Gross, *Divinization of the Christian,* 180; text in quotation marks from Gregory of Nyssa, *On the Soul and the Resurrection.*

74. Gross, *Divinization of the Christian,* 180; text in single quotation marks from Gregory of Nyssa, *On the Creation of Man,* 16, and *Great Catechism,* 21.

75. Gross explains that Gregory of Nyssa "subordinates individual divinization, not only to the moral effort of the subject, notably to his free 'acceptance of the [evangelical] message and his renunciation of sin, but also to the receiving of Baptism and the Eucharist. . . . In order to permit us to partake of His body 'raised to the divine dignity,' Christ instituted the Eucharist, by means of which He, like a seed, is put into the body of the believers. By this union He makes them partakers of incorruptibility; in other words, He deifies them." *Divinization of the Christian,* 185–86; see Gregory of Nyssa, *Great Catechism,* 31, 33, 36, 37, accessible at CCEL, www.ccel.org/ccel/schaff/npnf205.toc.html.

76. Gregory of Nyssa, *Homilies on the Song of Songs*, 15, in Gross, *Divinization of the Christian*, 187. See Song of Songs 6:3; cf. 2:16; 7:10.

77. See John 10:10; cf. 1 Tim. 6:19.

78. Robichaux, "Can Human Beings Become God?," 33.

79. See St. Basil (c. 329–c. 379), *On the Spirit*, 9.23, in John Behr, *The Nicene Faith*, part 2 (Crestwood, NY: St. Vladimir's Seminary Press, 2004), 316; quoted in Keating, "Deification in the Greek Fathers," 47; cf. Basil, *On the Spirit*, 9.23, trans. Blomfield Jackson, in *Nicene and Post-Nicene Fathers*, 2nd ser., vol. 8 (Grand Rapids: Eerdmans, 1983), 16.

80. Gross, *Divinization of the Christian*, 192; text in single quotation marks from Basil, *Against Eunomius*, 3.2.

81. Gross, 197; Gross cites Gregory of Nazianzus, *Orations*, 23.11.

82. Augustine (c. 354–c. 430), *Trinity* 11.5.8, trans. Edmond Hill, (Hyde Park, NY: New City Press, 1991), 310, emphasis in original; quoted in David Vincent Meconi, "No Longer a Christian but Christ: Saint Augustine on Becoming Divine," in *Called to Be the Children of God*, Meconi, Olson, 88.

83. Meconi, "No Longer a Christian," 88.

84. Meconi, 86; Meconi cites Augustine, *Trinity* 1.6.11.

85. Augustine, *Sermon* 23B.1, quoted in Meconi, "No Longer a Christian," 89.

86. John 1:12.

87. Augustine, *Expositions of the Psalms* 49.2, trans. Maria Boulding, *Expositions*, vol. 3/16 (Hyde Park, NY: New City Press, 2000), 381; quoted in Meconi, "No Longer a Christian," 90.

88. Maximus the Confessor (c. 580–c. 662), *Epistle 2*, trans. Andrew Louth, *Maximus the Confessor* (London and New York: Routledge, 1996), 85, quoted in Keating, "Deification in the Greek Fathers," 53. Cf. Meconi, "No Longer a Christian," 91–94.

89. Maximus the Confessor, *Ambigua* 41, trans. Elena Vishnevskaya, "Divinization as Perichoretic Embrace in Maximus the Confessor," in *Partakers of the Divine Nature*, 141.

90. Russell, *Doctrine*, 8.

91. Russell, 262. Cf. Keating, "Deification in the Greek Fathers," 53n55.

92. Maximus the Confessor, trans. K. Juessen, "Maximus Confessor," *Lexikon für Theologie und Kirche* 7:22, in Gross, *Divinization of the Christian*, 249.

93. Maximus the Confessor, *Epistle 43 Ad Joannem cubicularium*, in Lossky, *Mystical Theology*, 90.

94. Gregory Palamas, *Theophanes*, in Lossky, *Mystical Theology*, 69.

95. Lossky, 67.

96. Lossky, 69–70. Lossky inserts the Greek word *murinpóstatos* just before "of

myriads of hypostases." In this context, the term "hypostasis" refers to a particular subject or individual that is the bearer of a certain nature. A person, we can say, is a hypostasis bearing a rational nature.

97. Maximus the Confessor, in the *Panoplia Dogmatics* of Euthymius Zigabenus, III, in Lossky, *Mystical Theology*, 73.

98. See Lossky, 69, 87–88.

99. Lossky, 74.

100. Lossky, 75.

101. Lossky, 76.

102. Hab. 3:3–4 NASB.

103. Gal. 2:20 NKJV.

104. Kirsten H. Anderson, "Gregory Palamas: On Divine and Deifying Participation," in *Analogia* 4, no. 3 (2017), 7.

105. John 1:12.

106. Cf. Augustine, *Confessions*, VII.5.

107. See Exod. 33:20.

108. Basil, *Epistle* 234, trans. Blomfield Jackson, in *Nicene and Post-Nicene Fathers*, 2nd ser., vol. 8, 274, modified; see David Bradshaw, "The Concept of the Divine Energies," in *Divine Essence and Divine Energies: Ecumenical Reflections on the Presence of God in Eastern Orthodoxy*, ed. Constantinos Athanasopoulos and Christoph Schneider (Cambridge, United Kingdom: James Clark & Co., 2013), 39. The word "energies" is used in place of "operations" in the original translation.

109. For further study concerning the distinction between the essence and energies of God, see Lossky, *Mystical Theology*, 67–90; Kallistos Ware (Metropolitan of Diokleia), "God Immanent yet Transcendent: The Divine Energies According to Saint Gregory Palamas," in *In Whom We Live and Move and Have Our Being*, ed. Philip Clayton and Arthur Peacocke (Grand Rapids: Eerdmans., 2004), 157–68; Bradshaw, "The Concept of the Divine Energies," 27–49.

110. Previous two paragraphs adapted from Hanegraaff, *Creation Answer Book*, 36–37.

111. Thomas Buchan, "Paradise as the Landscape of Salvation in Ephrem the Syrian," in *Partakers of the Divine Nature*, 148.

112. Buchan, "Paradise," 148.

113. Buchan, 149.

114. Ephrem the Syrian (c. 306–c. 373), *Commentary on Genesis*, 2.23.1, K. E. McVey, ed. *St. Ephrem the Syrian: Selected Prose Works; Commentary on Genesis, Commentary on Exodus, Homily on Our Lord, Letter to Publius*, trans. E. G. Matthews Jr. and J. P. Amar, FC 91 (Washington, DC: Catholic University of America Press, 1994), in Buchan, "Paradise," 150.

115. Buchan, "Paradise," 152.

116. I should say that Solomon was the wisest of mere mortal men (see 1 Kings 3:7–12; 4:29–31; 10:27), second to Theanthropos—the God/Man—the Lord Jesus Christ (Matt. 12:42; John 1:1–5, 14, 18; 1 Cor. 1:24–25, 30).

117. Prov. 3:18; 11:30; 13:12.

118. Rev. 2:7 NKJV.

119. Text in this paragraph thus far adapted from Hanegraaff, AfterLife, 16.

120. Ephrem the Syrian, Hymns on Paradise 6.8, S. P. Brock, St. Ephrem the Syrian: Hymns on Paradise (Crestwood, NY: St. Vladimir's Seminary Press, 1990), in Buchan, "Paradise," 154.

121. Exod. 33:11 ESV.

122. Dionysius (fifth or sixth century), On Mystical Theology, 1.3, 1001A, trans. Andrew Louth, in Andrew Louth, The Origins of the Christian Mystical Tradition (Oxford: Clarendon Press, 1981), 173, in Russell, Doctrine, 260.

123. Russell, Doctrine, 260.

124. See Exod. 33:11; Deut. 34:10.

125. See Exod. 20:18–21; 32:10–14; Deut. 5:22–33; Ps. 106:23.

126. See Exod. 7:1.

127. See Exod. 34:29–35; cf. 2 Cor. 3:13.

128. See Matt. 17:1–8; Mark 9:2–8; Luke 9:28–36.

129. See 2 Cor. 3:18.

130. See Rev. 21:2.

131. See Matt. 6:9; Luke 11:2; see also Rom. 8:14–17; Gal. 4:4–7.

132. John 1:12.

133. John 12:36 NKJV.

134. John 1:13 NKJV.

135. See Becoming Truly Human directed by Nathan Jacobs (Ancient Faith Films, 2017), DVD.

136. See Phil. 2:5–8.

137. 2 Cor. 8:9 NKJV.

138. See Russell, Doctrine, 262, 294.

139. 2 Peter 1:4; 1 Peter 5:1 NKJV.

140. Rev. 22:14.

141. Rev. 22:2–4.

142. Lossky, Mystical Theology, 10.

143. Lossky, Mystical Theology, 10.

144. In addition to Lossky's pithy overview of the dogmatic battles of the early church in the introductory chapter of Mystical Theology, see the following helpful,

concise summaries of the seven ancient ecumenical councils: "Short Summaries of the Ecumenical Councils," OrthodoxPhotos.com, www.orthodoxphotos.com /readings/LGFLS/summaries.shtml; "The Church of Seven Councils," Saint George Greek Orthodox Cathedral, www.stgeorgegreenville.org/our-faith /catechism/church-history/church-of-councils. For "all the doctrinal definitions of the Seven Ecumenical Councils . . . and all the canons, disciplinary and doctrinal, which were enacted by them," see *Nicene and Post-Nicene Fathers*, 2nd ser., vol. 14, *The Seven Ecumenical Councils of the Undivided Church*, ed. Henry R. Percival (for quote by Percival, see General Introduction, xi), www.ccel.org/ccel /schaff/npnf214.

145. Vincent of Lérins, *Commonitorium* 2.

146. Witness Lee, *Life-Study of Job, Psalms Part 1* (Anaheim: Living Stream Ministry, 1996), 122. See the careful discussion in Robichaux, "Can Human Beings Become God?" 42. See also 222n38–39.

147. See Nicholas Needham, "Truly God, Truly Man: The Council of Chalcedon," Ligonier Ministries, www.ligonier.org/learn/articles/truly-god-truly-man-council -chalcedon/. Donald Fairbairn clarifies, "Neither the early church as a whole nor the Chalcedonian Definition in particular is affirming merely that Christ has two natures united into one person. Both the church and Chalcedon affirm that the person who possesses both divine and human natures is the eternal second person of the Trinity, the Son of God. . . . This is what the church needed to say about Christ, since only if Christ was God the Son as a person could he give us a share in his eternal, personal relationship to God the Father" (*theosis*). Fairbairn, *Life in the Trinity*, 145.

148. Lossky, *Mystical Theology*, 10.

149. See 2 Peter 1:4.

150. Gregory the Great (c. 540–c. 604), Epistle to John, Bishop of Constantinople, and the other Patriarchs, quoted in Archbishop Peter L'Huillier, *The Church of the Ancient Councils: The Disciplinary Work of the First Four Ecumenical Councils* (Creswood, NY: St. Vladimir's Seminary Press, 2000), ix. Epistle is accessible in slightly different translation at CCEL, www.ccel.org/ccel/schaff/npnf212 .iii.v.i.xviii.html.

151. Lossky, *Mystical Theology*, 10.

152. Lossky, *Mystical Theology*, 10.

153. Jude 3, my paraphrase.

154. 1 Tim. 3:15. It is worth noting here the words of the nineteenth-century Protestant Episcopalian divine Henry R. Percival that in "the Seven Ecumenical Councils, the question the Fathers considered was not what they supposed Holy Scripture might mean, nor what they, from *à priori* arguments, thought would

be consistent with the mind of God, but something entirely different, to wit, what they had received. They understood their position to be that of witnesses, not that of exegetes. They recognized but one duty resting upon them in this respect—to hand down to other faithful men that good thing the Church had received according to the command of God. The first requirement was not learning, but honesty. The question they were called to answer was not, What do I think probable, or even certain, from Holy Scripture? but What have I been taught, what has been instrusted to me to hand down to others? When the time came, in the Fourth Council, to examine the Tome of Pope St. Leo, the question was not whether it could be proved to the satisfaction of the assembled fathers from Holy Scripture, but whether it was the traditional faith of the Church. It was not the doctrine of Leo in the fifth century, but the doctrine of Peter in the first, and of the Church since then, that they desired to believe and to teach, and so, when they had studied the Tome, they cried out: 'This is the faith of the Fathers! This is the faith of the Apostles! . . . Peter hath thus spoken by Leo! The Apostles thus taught! Cyril thus taught!', etc." *Nicene and Post-Nicene Fathers*, 2nd ser., vol. 14, 2, www.ccel.org/ccel/schaff/npnf214.

155. Lossky, *Mystical Theology*, 154–55. Lossky cites Gregory Nazianzen (c. 329–c. 389), who said, "What has not been assumed [taken up into God] has not been healed; it is what is united to his divinity that is saved." Nazianzen, *Critique of Apollinarius*, Epistle 101.

156. Athanasius, *On the Incarnation* 54, in Nicene and Post-Nicene Fathers, 2nd ser., vol. 4, 65, emphasis added.

157. The mystery of the Holy that causes us to tremble and yet attracts us. Kallistos Ware (Metropolitan of Diokleia), "Light and Darkness in the Mystical Theology of the Greek Fathers," in *Light from Light: Scientists and Theologians in Dialogue*, ed. Gerald O'Collins and Mary Ann Meyers (Grand Rapids: Eerdmans, 2012), 140; see Rudolf Otto, *The Idea of the Holy*, trans. John W. Harvey (1917; repr., New York: Oxford University Press, 1964), 12–40.

158. Cf. Robichaux, "Can Human Beings Become God?" 40.

159. John 1:14 NASB.

160. Qur'an 112:3, quoted in Ali, *Meaning of the Holy Qur'an*.

161. Nicholas D. Kristof, "Believe It, or Not," *New York Times*, August 15, 2003, www.nytimes.com/2003/08/15/opinion/believe-it-or-not.html, last accessed September 12, 2014.

162. Previous paragraph and previous sentences of this paragraph adapted from Hanegraaff, *Has God Spoken?*, 287–88.

163. Carl Sagan, *Cosmos: A Personal Voyage*, episode 7, "The Backbone of the Night"

directed by Adrian Malone, aired November 9, 1980, on PBS; clip available at "Carl Sagan—Where Are We? Who Are We? [Cosmos]," September 16, 2011, YouTube, www.youtube.com/watch?v=kMJ9H3uBqZM; cf. Carl Sagan, *Cosmos* (New York: Ballantine Books, 1985), 159.

164. Bill Nye, "The Best Idea We've Had So Far," The Humanist, December 10, 2010, www.thehumanist.com/magazine/november-december-2010/features/best-idea-weve-far; see also "Bill Nye Speaks at the 2010 AHA Conference: Part 3/3," June 6, 2010, video clip, YouTube, https://www.youtube.com/watch?v=S4dZ WbFs8T0.

165. Carl Sagan, *Pale Blue Dot: A Vision of the Human Future in Space* (New York: Ballantine Books, 1994), 7.

166. Ps. 19:1–4 NIV 1984.

167. Col. 1:19–20 NIV 1984.

168. Col. 1:15–16 NIV 1984.

169. Partially adapted from Hanegraaff, *AfterLife*, 30.

170. 2 Cor. 3:18.

171. John Lennon and Yoko Ono, "Imagine" (New York: Apple, 1971).

172. Rom. 8:21 NIV 1984.

173. N. T. Wright, *Surprised by Hope: Rethinking Heaven, the Resurrection, and the Mission of the Church* (New York: HarperOne, 2008), 115.

174. Carl Sagan, *Cosmos* (New York: Ballantine Books, 1980, 1985), 1.

175. Vishnevskaya, "Divinization as Perichoretic Embrace in Maximus the Confessor," in *Partakers of the Divine Nature*, 132, emphasis in original, quoting Maximus the Confessor, *Ambiguorum liber* 7.

176. Vishnevskaya, "Divinization"136, quoting Maximus the Confessor, *Ambiguorum liber* 7.

177. Maximus the Confessor, *Ambigua* 41, quoted in Keating, "Deification in the Greek Fathers," in *Called to Be the Children of God*, 53.

178. Maximus the Confessor, Epistle 24, in Hieromonk Artemije Radosavljević, "Deification as the End and Fulfillment of Salvation According to St. Maximos the Confessor," in *The Mystery of Salvation According to St. Maximos the Confessor* (Athens: n.p., 1975), www.scribd.com/document/114284087/Maximus-and-Deification.

179. Luke 19:10 NIV 1984.

180. 1 Tim. 1:15 NIV 1984.

181. Hahn, "Foreword," in *Called to Be the Children of God*, 7, emphasis in original.

182. Lossky, *Orthodox Theology*, 84. These two sentences paraphrase Lossky.

183. Matt. 1:23. See also Isa. 7:14.

184. Lossky, *Mystical Theology*, 136.

185. Lossky, 135.

186. Nicholas Cabasilas (1322–c. 1391), *Life in Christ* III, quoted in Lossky, *Mystical Theology*, 136, emphasis added.

187. Isa. 7:14 NIV 1984.

188. Matt. 1:21 NIV 1984.

189. Isa. 7:2 NIV 1984.

190. Isa. 7:4 NIV 1984.

191. Isa. 7:14–16 NIV 1984.

192. See Isa. 8:3–4 NIV 1984.

193. I am especially indebted to two excellent articles concerning typological prophecy in general and the nature of the relationship between Isa. 7:14 and Matt. 1:22–23 in particular: James M. Hamilton Jr., "The Virgin Will Conceive: Typology in Isaiah and Fulfillment in Matthew, the Use of Isaiah 7:14 in Matthew 1:18–23," Tyndale Fellowship Biblical Theology Study Group, July 6–8, 2005, online at web. archive.org/web/20120111141750/http://www.swbts.edu/resources/SWBTS /Resources/FacultyDocuments/Hamilton/TheVirginWillConceive.7_19_05 .pdf; Duane A. Garrett, "Type, Typology," in *Evangelical Dictionary of Biblical Theology*, ed. Walter A. Elwell (Grand Rapids: Baker, 1996), 785–87.

     Previous four paragraphs adapted from Hanegraaff, *Has God Spoken?* 134–35.

194. Gen. 3:24.

195. Isa. 53:5 NIV 1984.

196. Quotations in this paragraph from Isa. 53: 2, 3, 4, 9, 6, 5, 7, 12, respectively (NIV 1984).

197. 1 Peter 2:24–25 NIV 1984.

198. Zech. 12:10 NIV 1984.

199. 1 Cor. 15:22 NIV 1984.

200. See 1 Cor. 15:54–57.

201. Isa. 53:3 NIV 1984.

202. Isa. 53:11 NIV 1984.

203. 1 Cor. 15:54; see also Dan. 12:2; John 5:28–29.

204. Isa. 26:19 NIV 1984.

205. See Gen. 2:7.

206. Cf. Ecc. 12:7.

207. Ezek. 37:7–8 NIV 1984.

208. Ezek. 37:10 NIV 1984.

209. Ezek. 37:14 NIV 1984.

210. John 5:28–29 NIV 1984.

211. Previous five paragraphs adapted from Hanegraaff, *AfterLife*, 156–57.

212. Lossky, *Mystical Theology*, 135–36, emphasis original.

Chapter 5: Ecclesia

1. Cyprian, *On the Unity of the Church*, 6.

2. Brent Kelly, "Lee Trevino Quotes: 30 Great Quips About Golf and Life," ThoughtCo, March 17, 2017, www.thoughtco.com/lee-trevino-quotes-1561257; see also Josh Morris, "1975: Lee Trevino Is Struck by Lightning at the Western Open During a Weather Delay," Golf History Today, www.golfhistorytoday.com/1975-lee-trevino-western-open/.

3. Gilbert King, "Hit by a Bus, How Ben Hogan Hit Back," Smithsonian, January 25, 2012, www.smithsonianmag.com/history/hit-by-a-bus-how-ben-hogan-hit-back-24870580. Story details from King.

4. Ben Hogan with Herbert Warren Wind, *Ben Hogan's Five Lessons: The Modern Fundamentals of Golf* (New York: Simon and Schuster, 1957), xiv, emphasis added.

5. 1 Cor. 9:25–27 NIV 1984.

6. See *The Martyrdom of Saint Polycarp*, 2 and 3, in Early Christian Fathers, vol. 1, ed. and trans. Cyril C. Richardson (Grand Rapids: Christian Classics Ethereal Library, 1953.), www.ccel.org/ccel/richardson/fathers.vii.i.iii.html.

7. *Martyrdom*, 9.

8. *The Martyrdom of Saint Polycarp*, 11, in *Eusebius: The Church History*, 4.15, trans. Paul L. Maier (Grand Rapids: Kregel, 1999), 150; cf. trans. Richardson.

9. Polycarp (c. 69–c. 156); Ignatius (c. 35–c. 107).

10. Timothy Ware (Metropolitan Kallistos of Diokleia), *The Orthodox Church: An Introduction to Eastern Christianity*, 3rd ed. (1963; repr., London: Penguin Books, 2015), 13.

11. Ware, *Orthodox Church*, 13, emphasis original.

12. Matt. 16:18 ESV.

13. Skye Jethani, *The Divine Commodity: Discovering a Faith Beyond Consumer Christianity* (Grand Rapids: Zondervan, 2009), 9–10, emphasis original.

14. Lossky, *Mystical Theology*, 177.

15. Cyprian (d. 258), *On the Unity of the Church*, 6, quoted in "Cyprian on Church Unity," ed. Dan Graves, Christian History Institute, www. christianhistory institute.org/study/module/Cyprian. *On the Unity of the Church* is accessible in a slightly different translation at New Advent, www.newadvent.org/fathers/050701.htm.

16. Georges Florovsky, "The Catholicity of the Church" (1934), in *Bible, Church, Tradition: An Eastern Orthodox View* (Belmont, MA: Nordland Publishing, 1972), 37–38, emphasis in original; see also discussion in Ware, *Orthodox Church*, 240. See also Irenaeus, *Against Heresies*, Book III; Cyprian, *Epistle* 73; *On the Unity of the Church*, 6; Augustine, *Sermo ad Caesariensis Ecclesia plebem*.

17. Lossky, *Mystical Theology*, 178, 179.

18. John of Damascus (c. 676–c. 749), *Exposition of the Orthodox Faith*, 4.13, trans. S. D. F. Salmond in *Nicene and Post-Nicene Fathers*, 2nd ser., vol. 9, ed. Philip Schaff (repr., Grand Rapids: Eerdmans, 1983), 84; www.ccel.org/ccel/schaff/npnf209 .iii.iv.iv.xiii.html.

19. Rev. Protopresbyter Panagiotis Papanikolaou, "Living A Eucharistic Life Is Living with Gratitude," Dormition of the Virgin Mary Greek Orthodox Church, Oct. 29, 2017, Weekly Bulletin, www.bulletinbuilder.org/dormitionva/current/20171029.

20. Ignatius, *Epistle to the Ephesians*, 20, quoted in Papanikolaou, "Living a Eucharistic Life Is Living with Gratitude"; accessible at CCEL, www.ccel.org/ccel/schaff /anf01.v.ii.xx.html.

21. Fr. Alkiviades Calivas, "An Introduction to the Divine Liturgy," in *The Divine Liturgy of Saint John Chrysostom*, 3rd ed., trans. Members of the Faculty of Hellenic College/Holy Cross Greek Orthodox School of Theology (Brookline, MA: Holy Cross Orthodox Press, 1985), xxiii–xxiv.

22. Calivas, "An Introduction to the Divine Liturgy," xxv. Cf. Alciviadis C. Calivas, "The Sacramental Life of the Orthodox Church," Greek Orthodox Archdiocese of America, September 3, 1998, www.goarch.org/-/the-sacramental-life-of-the-orthodox-church.

23. Gregory Palamas, *On the Holy and Dread Mysteries of Christ*, 9, quoted in Calivas, "An Introduction to the Divine Liturgy," xxvi.

24. For further reading on the Orthodox Eucharist, see Fr. Emmanuel Hatzidakis, *The Heavenly Banquet: Understanding the Divine Liturgy* (Chicago: Orthodox Witness, 2010); Anthony M. Coniaris, *These Are the Sacraments: The Life-Giving Mysteries of the Orthodox Church* (Edina, MN: Light & Life Publishing Co., 1981); Alexander Schmemann, *The Eucharist: Sacrament of the Kingdom* (Crestwood, NY: St. Vladimir's Seminary Press, 2003).

25. Matt. 26:26–28 NKJV.

26. Martin Luther, *Tischreden*, 6.6775, in the Weimar edition, quoted in *What Luther Says: A Practical In-Home Anthology for the Active Christian*, comp. Ewald M. Plass (St. Louis: Concordia Publishing House, 1959), 795 selection 2472. For the Lutheran view of the Lord's Supper, see Martin Chemnitz, *The Lord's Supper* (1590), trans. J. A. O. Preus (St. Louis: Concordia Publishing House, 1979); John R. Stephenson, *The Lord's Supper* (St. Louis: Luther Academy, 2003).

27. See Martin Luther, "Confession Concerning Christ's Supper, 1528," in *Luther's Works*, vol. 37, *Word and Sacrament III*, ed. and trans. Robert H. Fischer (Philadelphia: Fortress Press, 1961), 151–372.

28. Cyril of Jerusalem (c. 315–386), *Catechetical Lecture*, 22.3, quoted in J. N. D. Kelly, *Early Christian Doctrines*, rev. ed. (New York: HarperSanFrancisco, 1978),

450; see also similar translation and full context accessible at New Advent, www
.newadvent.org/fathers/310122.htm.

29. Kelly, *Early Christian Doctrines*, 450.

30. See, e.g., Huldreich Zwingli, "The Presence of Christ's Body in the Supper" (1531).

31. Martin Luther, *The Babylonian Captivity of the Church* (1520), 2.29, emphasis added, www.lutherdansk.dk/web-babylonian%20captivitate/martin%20luther.htm.

32. Martin Luther, *Large Catechism*, art. 5.12–13, in *The Book of Concord: The Confessions of the Evangelical Lutheran Church*, ed. Robert Kolb and Timothy J. Wengert (Minneapolis: Fortress Press, 2000), 468, emphasis added. Two instances of "etc." omitted.

33. See John R. Stephenson, "Reflections on the Appropriate Vessels for Consecrating and Distributing the Precious Blood of Christ," *Logia* 4, no. 1 (1995): 12; cf. David P. Scaer, "Did Luther and Melanchthon Agree on the Real Presence?" *Concordia Theological Quarterly* 44, nos. 2–3 (1980): 141–47, www.ctsfw.net/media/pdfs /scaerresponsetohagglund.pdf.

34. John 15:5 NKJV (see vv. 1–11).

35. John 6:56–58 NIV 1984, emphasis added.

36. John 6:53 NKJV, emphasis added.

37. Luther, *Large Catechism*, art. 5.23–25, in Kolb and Wengert, *Book of Concord*, 469. Words "as I have said" omitted from "However, our human flesh and blood, as I have said, have not lost their old skin."

38. 1 Tim. 4:7–8 NIV 1984, except I'm using the term "gymnasize" for the Greek verb γύμναζε (*gymnaze*), meaning "to discipline, train, or exercise."

39. Willard, *Divine Conspiracy*, 9–11.

40. See Rom. 12:1.

41. Quoted in Donald S. Whitney, *Spiritual Disciplines for the Christian Life* (Colorado Springs: NavPress, 1991), 20.

42. Whitney, *Spiritual Disciplines*, 20.

43. C. H. Spurgeon, quoted in *Spurgeon at His Best*, comp. Tom Carter (Grand Rapids: Baker, 1988), 99–100.

44. C. S. Lewis, *The Screwtape Letters* (New York: Collier, 1961), 11, emphasis original.

45. Previous four paragraphs adapted from Hanegraaff, *Covering*, 51–53.

46. Dallas Willard, *The Spirit of the Disciplines: Understanding How God Changes Lives* (New York: HarperSanFrancisco, 1988), 152.

47. Says Dallas Willard, "By modest estimate, more than a quarter of the entire population of the United States have professed an evangelical conversion experience. William Iverson wryly observes that 'a pound of meat would surely be affected by a quarter pound of salt, if this is real Christianity, the 'salt of the earth,' where is the effect of which Jesus spoke?'" Willard, *Spirit of the Disciplines*, 23.

48. Rom. 5:10.

49. Matt. 23:5.

50. Lewis, *Mere Christianity*, 189.

51. Lewis, 191–92.

52. 1 Cor. 6:17 NRSV.

53. Eph. 5:32.

54. Col. 4:2 ESV.

55. Luke 11:1 paraphrase. The Greek word translated "teach" is an aorist imperative, which may imply a slight sense of urgency: "teach us now to pray." See Darrell L. Bock, *Luke, vol. 2, Baker Exegetical Commentary on the New Testament* (Grand Rapids: Baker Books, 1996), 1050.

56. Matt. 6:9–10 NIV 1984.

57. Tertullian (c. 160–c. 225), "On Prayer," chap. 6, trans. S. Thelwall, in *Ante-Nicene Fathers*, vol. 3, *Latin Christianity: Its Founder, Tertullian*, eds. Alexander Roberts and James Donaldson (repr., Grand Rapids: Eerdmans, 1986), 683, emphasis added, www.ccel.org/ccel/schaff/anf03.vi.iv.vi.html.

58. Matt. 6:11–13 NIV 1984.

59. 1 Peter 5:8.

60. "Deep is where the noisy, trashy surface of the ocean gets quiet and serene." The tragedy, says Calvin Miller, is that most believers "spend their lives being whipped tumultuously through the surface circumstances of their days. Their frothy lifestyles mark the surface nature of their lives. Yet those who plumb the deep things of God discover true peace for the first time." Miller, *Into the Depths of God: Where Eyes See the Invisible, Ears Hear the Inaudible, and Minds Conceive the Inconceivable* (Minneapolis: Bethany House, 2000), 15.

61. See John 1:12.

62. Rom. 8:15 NKJV.

63. Rom. 8:16–17.

64. Matt. 6:9.

65. 1 Peter 2:5.

66. Matt. 6:9 NKJV.

67. Augustine, *Our Lord's Sermon on the Mount, According to Matthew*, 2.5.19, trans. William Findlay, in *Nicene and Post-Nicene Fathers*, 1st ser., vol. 6, ed. Philip Schaff (repr., Grand Rapids: Eerdmans, 1980), 40, www.ccel.org/ccel/schaff /npnf106.v.iii.v.html.

68. Matt. 6:10 NKJV.

69. Lewis, *Mere Christianity*, 46.

70. Anthony A. Hoekema, *The Bible and the Future* (Grand Rapids: Eerdmans, 1979), 21.

71. Matt. 6:10 NKJV.
72. See Rom. 8:28.
73. C. H. Spurgeon, "God's People Melted and Tried," sermon no. 2274, Feb. 19, 1891, at Spurgeon Gems, www.spurgeongems.org/vols37–39/chs2274.pdf.
74. Matt. 6:10.
75. Hab. 2:14.
76. Gen. 28:16–17. See Gen. 12:7–8; 13:3; 28:11–22; 31:13; 35:7.
77. Exod. 24:17.
78. Josh. 5:15.
79. See Exod. 3.
80. Isa. 6:1, 5.
81. Heb. 12:22–23.
82. Matt. 6:11, emphasis added.
83. Luke 12:19, 20.
84. John 6:35.
85. Matt. 6:12.
86. Matt. 18:35.
87. Matt. 6:14–15.
88. Matt. 6:13 ESV.
89. Eph. 6:11.
90. Said Tertullian: "Let us take note of the devices of the devil, who is wont to ape some of God's things with no other design than, by the faithfulness of his servants, to put us to shame, and to condemn us." *De Corona*, 15, in *The Ante-Nicene Fathers*, vol. 3, ed. Alexander Roberts and James Donaldson (repr., Grand Rapids: Eerdmans, 1986), 103. Cf. *de Baptismo*, 5, in Ante-Nicene Fathers, vol. 3, 671, www.ccel.org/ccel/schaff/anf03.iv.vi.xv.html.

    Said Luther: "[The devil] is always aping God and trying to imitate and improve everything God does." Weimar edition of Luther's Works, 50, 645, quoted in Plass, *What Luther Says*, 465, selection 1371.
91. Said Luther, "God uses the devil and the evil angels. They, of course, desire to ruin everything; but God blocks them, unless a well-earned scourging is in order. God allows pestilence, war, or some other plague to come, that we may humble ourselves before Him, fear Him, hold to Him, and call upon Him. When God has accomplished these purposes through the scourge, then the good angels come again to perform their office. They bid the devil stop the pestilence, war, and famine. So the devil must serve us with the very thing with which he plans to injure us; for God is such a great Master that He is able to turn even the wickedness of the devil into good." Weimar edition of Luther's Works, 34.2.240, quoted in Plass, *What Luther Says*, 401–2, selection 1184.

Cf. Timothy George, "Where Are the Nail Prints?: The Devil and Dr. Luther," *Journal of the Evangelical Theological Society* 61, no. 2 (2018): 253 (see 245–57), www.etsjets .org/files/JETS-PDFs/61/61-2/JETS_61.2_245-257_George.pdf.

92. Matt. 4:1, emphasis added.

93. See Rev. 20:10.

94. Rev. 21:27.

95. Adolph Saphir, quoted in Philip Graham Ryken, *When You Pray* (Wheaton, IL: Crossway Books, 2000), 9. Section adapted from Hank Hanegraaff, *The Prayer of Jesus: Secrets to Real Intimacy with God* (Nashville: Thomas Nelson, 2001); Hanegraaff, *AfterLife.*

96. I am paraphrasing Calvin Miller in this sentence and drawing from him in this paragraph. Miller, *Into the Depths of God*, 15.

97. Luke 5:16.

98. Job 13:15.

99. Matt. 10:30–31.

100. Ps. 139:1–10 NIV 1984 (Ps. 138 in the Orthodox Old Testament).

101. Ps. 139:15–16 NIV 1984.

102. Ps. 139:24 NIV 1984.

103. Ps. 145:1–2 NIV 1984, emphasis added.

104. 2 Peter 1:4 NIV 1984.

105. William C. Placher, *The Domestication of Transcendence: How Modern Thinking about God Went Wrong* (Louisville, KY: Westminster John Knox Press, 1996).

106. Ps. 145:13.

107. Ps. 145:3–5 NIV 1984.

108. See 2 Sam. 12. Quotation from 2 Kingdoms 12:7, 9–10, *The Orthodox Study Bible* (Nashville: Thomas Nelson, 2008).

109. Ps. 51:1 (Ps. 50 Orthodox Old Testament).

110. 1 John 1:9–10.

111. Matt. 15:22 NKJV.

112. Luke 17:13 NKJV.

113. Mark 10:47 NKJV.

114. Frederica Mathewes-Green, *The Jesus Prayer: The Ancient Desert Prayer That Tunes the Heart to God* (Brewster, MA: Paraclete Press, 2009), xii, emphasis added.

115. Scripture quotations from Ps. 51:1–3.

116. Luke 15:18–19, 22–23, 24.

117. Ps. 118:19–21 (Ps. 117 Orthodox Old Testament).

118. William Hendriksen, *New Testament Commentary: Exposition of Philippians* (1962; repr., Grand Rapids: Baker Books, 1995), 196.

119. Ps. 100:4 (Ps. 99 Orthodox Old Testament).

120. Rom. 1:21.

121. Luke 17:12–13, 16, 17, emphasis added.

122. Col. 2:7; 4:2.

123. See Matt. 6:8; 7:7–12.

124. 1 Thess. 5:16–18; see also Eph. 5:20.

125. Col. 1:29 NIV 1984. Ps. 118 is 117 in the Orthodox Old Testament.

126. Phil. 4:6–7 ESV.

127. Benny Hinn, "*Rise and Be Healed!" God's Promises for Healing* (Orlando, FL: Celebration Publishers, 1991), 47–48.

128. For a critique of the Word of Faith movement and its theology, see Hanegraaff, *Christianity in Crisis: 21st Century*.

129. Matt. 6:10 KJV.

130. Matt. 26:39 .

131. James 4:15.

132. Rom. 1:10.

133. Rom. 15:32.

134. See, e.g., Deut. 10:14; 1 Sam. 2:6; 2 Chron. 20:6; Ps. 115:3; 135:6; 147:5; 148; Prov. 16:1–4; Isa. 40:13–14; 46:10; 55:8–9; Jer. 10:23; Dan. 4:34–37; Rom. 8:28; 11:36; 1 Cor. 15:27–28; Eph. 1:9–12; Col. 1:15–18; 1 Tim. 6:15–16; Heb. 1:3; Rev. 4:11.

135. Paraphrase of such passages as Matt. 26:39; Mark 14:36; Luke 22:42.

136. Rom. 8:28.

137. "The F-A-C-T-S Prayer Guide" section adapted from Hanegraaff, *Christianity in Crisis: 21st Century*; Hanegraaff, *Prayer of Jesus*.

138. Hanegraaff, *Prayer of Jesus*.

139. 1 Thess. 5:17 NASB.

140. Eph. 6:18 NASB.

141. Col. 4:2 ESV.

142. Rom. 12:12 NASB.

143. Deut. 4:7. In its context this passage is part of a rhetorical question.

144. Lam. 3:57.

145. Zeph. 3:9, emphasis added.

146. See, e.g., Witness Lee, *Calling on the Name of the Lord* (Anaheim: Living Stream Ministry, n.d.), www.ministrybooks.org/books.cfm?xid=1DG326Q3I6GY9.

147. 2 Peter 1:4.

148. See Gal. 2:20; Eph. 2:19–22; 3:16–21; Phil. 1:21; 3:7–11; Col. 1:27; see also John 14:20; 15:4.

149. Ps. 51:1.

150. Luke 17:13 ESV.

151. Matt. 15:22.

152. Mark 10:47.

153. Luke 18:13.

154. See John Climacus (died early seventh century), *The Ladder of Divine Ascent*. It is interesting that John Climacus, who offers instructions for raising one's soul and body to God by acquiring virtues through ascetic practices, does not actually address the Jesus Prayer. Nonetheless, the prayer is rightly characterized as a "ladder of divine ascent." Thanks to Frederica Mathewes-Green for this insight.

155. See *The Way of a Pilgrim and The Pilgrim Continues His Way*, trans. Olga Savin (Boston: Shambhala Publications, 2001).

156. Matt. 6:7–8.

157. See Mathewes-Green, *Jesus Prayer*, 93–94.

158. Quoting with slight paraphrase from Dr. Adolph Saphir, who wrote these words specifically concerning the Prayer of Jesus (Matt. 6:9–13), in Ryken, *When You Pray*, 9.

159. Col. 1:29.

160. In Christ we become "more and more like God, without identifying with Him. Man will continue to become like God forever, in an even fuller union with Him, but never will he reach full identification with Him; he will be able to reflect God more and more, but he will not become what God is. This distinguishes likeness from identity, or the quality of god by grace, from God by nature." Dumitru Staniloae, *Orthodox Spirituality: A Practical Guide for the Faithful and a Definitive Manual for the Scholar*, trans. Archimandrite Jerome and Otilia Kloos (South Canaan, PA: St. Tikhon's Seminary Press, 2003), 365.

161. Col. 1:17.

162. Says Mathewes-Green, "The word energy occurs frequently in St. Paul's letters; he says, for example, 'God is *energon* [energizing] in you, both to will and to *energein* [energize] for his good pleasure' (Phil. 2:13)." She explains that "*energy* is a word we imported into English directly from the Greek. But there was no equivalent for this word in Latin, so in his masterful translation of the Bible, St. Jerome (AD 347–420) used *operare*, that is, 'operate' or 'work.' When the Bible began to be published in English, its translators stood at the end of a thousand years of devout reading, preaching, and studying the Bible in Latin translation. Our English Bibles refer to God 'working,' not 'energizing,' but isn't there a difference? If we hear that God's energy is within us, then union with him becomes more imaginable." Mathewes-Green, *Jesus Prayer*, 23.

163. For further study on the Jesus Prayer, see *The Mysteries of the Jesus Prayer* (Passion

River, 2011), directed by Norris Chumley, DVD, mysteriesofthejesusprayer.com /wp1/.

164. Isa. 6:1 NASB.

165. Yet the orthodoxy of Newton's Christian confession has been called into question in modern times. See Avery Cardinal Dulles, "The Deist Minimum," *First Things*, January 2005, www.firstthings.com/article/2005/01/the-deist-minimum; Robert Lliffe, "Newton's Religious Life and Work" (2013), The Newton Project, www. newtonproject.ox.ac.uk/view/contexts/CNTX00001; Stephen D. Snobelen, "Isaac Newton, Heretic: The Strategies of a Nicodemite," *British Journal for the History of Science*, 32, no. 115 (Dec. 1999), 381–419, archived online at web.archive.org /web/20160423224541/http://www.toriah.org/articles/snobelen-1999-1.pdf.

166. For the Rubens illustration, I am indebted to J. P. Moreland, "A Philosophical Examination of Hugh Ross's Natural Theology," in *Journal of the Evangelical Philosophical Society* 21, no. 1 (1998): 33, web.archive.org/web/20130625163402 /www.reasons.org/articles/philosophia-christi#heading4. For further study on this point, see Stark, *Victory of Reason*; Mangalwadi, *Book That Made Your World*.

167. See Augustine, *Trinity*, 1.2 and bks. 8–15; *Confessions*, bks. 10–11. See also Robert Crouse, "Knowledge," in *Augustine Through the Ages: An Encyclopedia*, ed. Allan D. Fitzgerald (Grand Rapids: Eerdmans Publishing, 1999), 486–88; R. C. Sproul, *The Consequences of Ideas: Understanding the Concepts That Shaped Our World* (Wheaton, IL: Crossway, 2000), 58–59.

168. Previous two paragraphs adapted from Hanegraaff, *Has God Spoken?*, 281.

169. Lewis, *Mere Christianity*, 154.

170. Lewis, 154.

171. Lewis, 154 (see 153–155), emphasis added.

172. John 17:17.

173. See Nee, *Normal Christian Life*, 59–61, 119, 170–71.

174. John 10:10.

175. 1 John 5:11–12.

176. Nee, *Normal Christian Life*, 126, emphasis in original.

177. Nee, 126, emphasis added.

178. Hank Hanegraaff, "Legacy Reading Plan," Christian Research Institute, www .equip.org/article/legacy-reading-plan.

179. As quoted in Whitney, *Spiritual Disciplines*, 28, emphasis added. Legacy Reading Plan discussion adapted from Hanegraaff, *Has God Spoken?*, 223, 291–93.

180. See Andrew Perrin, "Who Doesn't Read Books in America?" Pew Research Center, March 23, 2018, www.pewresearch.org/fact-tank/2018/03/23/who-doesnt-read -books-in-america/; cf. John Maher, "Wondering Where Publishing Is Headed? Ask

Its Future Leaders," Publishers Weekly, January 4, 2019, www.publishersweekly.com /pw/by-topic/industry-news/publisher-news/article/78932-wondering-where -publishing-is-headed-ask-its-future-leaders.html.

181. See Alan Castel, "Can Reading Help My Brain Grow and Prevent Dementia?" *Psychology Today*, April 11, 2018, www.psychologytoday.com/us/blog /metacognition-and-the-mind/201804/can-reading-help-my-brain-grow -and-prevent-dementia; Robert S. Wilson, et al., "Life-Span Cognitive Activity, Neuropathologic Burden, and Cognitive Aging," Neurology, American Academy of Neurology, July 23, 2013, neurology.org/content/81/4/314.

182. Lewis, *Mere Christianity*, xiii.

183. Lewis, xiv.

184. Lewis, xiv.

185. Sean McDowell and John Stonestreet, *Same-Sex Marriage: A Thoughtful Approach to God's Design for Marriage* (Grand Rapids: Baker Books, 2014).

186. McDowell and Stonestreet, Same-Sex Marriage, 32, emphasis added.

187. McDowell and Stonestreet, 57.

188. McDowell and Stonestreet, 43. See Justice Anthony Kennedy, *United States v. Windsor* (2013), www.supremecourt.gov/opinions/12pdf/12–307_6j37.pdf.

189. Maggie Gallagher, "(How) Will Gay Marriage Weaken Marriage as a Social Institution: A Reply to Andrew Koppelman," *University of St. Thomas Law Journal* 2, no. 1 (2004): 53, www.ir.stthomas.edu/cgi/viewcontent.cgi?article=1047 &context=ustlj. See also McDowell and Stonestreet, *Same-Sex Marriage*, 57–58.

190. Baronelle Stutzman, "I'm a Florist, but I Refused to Do Flowers for My Gay Friend's Wedding," *Washington Post*, May 12, 2015, www.washingtonpost.com /posteverything/wp/2015/05/12/im-a-florist-but-i-refused-to-do-flowers-for -my-gay-friends-wedding/.

191. *Martydom of Polycarp* is accessible at Christian Classics Ethereal Library, www .ccel.org/ccel/richardson/fathers.vii.i.iii.html.

192. See Ignatius, *Epistle to the Romans* 4, in *The Ante-Nicene Fathers*, vol. 1, ed. Alexander Roberts and James Donaldson (repr., Grand Rapids: Eerdmans, 1985), 75, www .ccel.org/ccel/schaff/anf01.v.v.iv.html.

193. See Frank Dikötter, *The Cultural Revolution: A People's History, 1962–1976* (New York: Bloomsbury Press, 2016).

194. 2 Tim. 3:5.

195. John Wesley to Mr. John Trembath, August 17, 1760, in *The Works of the Rev. John Wesley*, vol. 6 (New York: Carlton and Porter, 1856), 750, accessed via Google Books, http://books.google.com.

196. G. K. Chesterton, foreword to Greville MacDonald, *George MacDonald and*

His Wife (London: George Allen & Unwin, 1924), 9, quoted in Tanya Ingham, "George MacDonald: An Original Thinker," *Knowing and Doing*, Fall 2009, C. S. Lewis Institute, www.cslewisinstitute.org/webfm_send/509.

197. C. S. Lewis, preface to *George MacDonald: An Anthology*, quoted in Marianne Wright, ed., *The Gospel in George MacDonald: Selections from His Novels, Fairy Tales, and Spiritual Writings* (Walden, NY: Plough Publishing, 2016), 316.

198. Lewis, preface to *George MacDonald: An Anthology*, quoted in Wright, *Gospel in George MacDonald*, viii.

199. C. S. Lewis, "On Stories," in *Of Other Worlds: Essays and Stories* (1966; repr., New York: HarperCollins Publishers, 1994), 25. See also Lewis's introduction (1944) in Saint Athanasius, *On the Incarnation*, trans. John Behr (Yonkers, NY: St. Vladimir's Seminry Press, 2012).

200. Lewis, *Mere Christianity*, 181.

201. Nee, *Normal Christian Life*, 171.

202. Nee, *Normal Christian Life*, 119.

203. Gal. 2:20.

204. Willard, *Spirit of the Disciplines*, 38, emphasis in original.

205. See Rom. 12:2.

206. Quoted in "Johannes Kepler," *New World Encyclopedia*, www.newworldencyclopedia .org/entry/Johannes_Kepler. Cf. Johannes Kepler, *Werke* VII (1953), 25; Letter to Herwath von Hohenburg, March 26, 1598, *Werke* XIII (1945), 193, in *Gesammelte Werke*, 20 vols. (Munich: C. H. Beck, 1937–45), as cited in Peter Harrison, *The Bible, Protestantism, and the Rise of Natural Science* (Cambridge, UK: Cambridge University Press, 1998), 198.

207. Rom. 1:20.

208. See Harrison, *Bible*, 193–204.

209. Michael R. Gilmore, "Einstein's God: Just What Did Einstein Believe About God?" *Skeptic* 5, no. 2 (1997): 64, web.archive.org/web/20020126112239 /http://www.skeptic.com/archives50.html; quote in Albert Einstein to Guy Raner Jr., September 28, 1949, web.archive.org/web/20150612112530 /https://i.dailymail.co.uk/i/pix/2015/06/11/11/6ZCNTH5HT-HSK1– 3119437-For_sale_This_undated_image_provided_by_Profiles_in_History _show-m-1_1434020122921.jpg.

210. Albert Einstein, interview by George Sylvester Viereck, quoted in Denis Brian, *Einstein: A Life* (New York: John Wiley & Sons, 1996), 186.

211. Albert Einstein to Herbert S. Goldstein, April 25, 1929, quoted in Walter Isaacson, *Einstein: His Life and Universe* (New York: Simon and Schuster Paperbacks, 2007), 551.

212. Albert Einstein, "What I Believe," quoted in Isaacson, *Einstein*, 387.

213. See *The Wonders of God's Creation: Planet Earth*, vol. 1 (Chicago: Moody Institute of Science, 1993),VHS.

214. Prov. 6:6 NASB. For further discussion, see Hanegraaff, *Creation Answer Book*, 13–15; Guillermo Gonzalez and Jay W. Richards, *The Privileged Planet: How Our Place in the Cosmos Is Designed for Discovery* (Washington, DC: Regnery Publishing, 2004).

215. Origen, *Commentary on Psalm 1*, 3.

216. Attributed to Martin Luther, "Hearth and Home: The Schoenberg-Cotta Family, by Mrs. Andrew Charles, Part XX.—Else's Story, Wittenberg, June, 1530," prepared by Martin J. Heinicke, *The Lutheran Witness*, vol. 36 (1917): 106, St. Louis, Concordia Publishing House, accessed via Google Books, http://books.google.com.

217. Widely attributed to the nineteenth-century clergyman George Barrell Cheever.

218. Henry Wadsworth Longfellow, "The Fiftieth Birthday of Agassiz," May 28, 1857, Bartleby Great Books Online, www.bartleby.com/42/787.html. Although Longfellow was a member of the Unitarian Church, he was "Christ-haunted" by the Christian claim that Jesus of Nazareth was God in human flesh (see Charles A. Coulome, "Longfellow and the Faith," Catholicism, March 23, 2015, catholicism.org/longfellow-and-the-faith.html).

219. C. H. Spurgeon, *The Treasury of David*, vol. 1 (London: Passmore and Alabaster, 1870), 305, accessed via Google Books, http://books.google.com.

220. Ps. 19:1–4 NIV 1984.

221. Albert Einstein, "What I Believe," *Form and Century*, 84, no. 4 (October 1930): 193–94 as quoted in Alice Calaprice, Daniel J. Kennefick, and Robert Schulmann, *An Einstein Encyclopedia* (Princeton, NJ: Princeton University Press, 2015), xiii, accessed via Google Books, http://books.google.com.

222. Jer. 23:23. Paul tells us there is "one God and Father of all, who is over all and through all and in all" (Eph. 4:6). Concerning the immanence of God, see also Deut. 4:7; Ps. 139:7; Acts 17:27; Col. 1:17; Heb. 1:3; and concerning the transcendence of God, see also 1 Kings 8:27; Ps. 8:1; 113:5–6; Isa. 40:22, 25–26; John 8:23; Acts 17:24; Heb. 7:26.

223. See Lossky, *Mystical Theology*, 96–100; Ware, "God Immanent yet Transcendent," 160–61.

224. Isa. 40:3, St. Athanasius Academy of Orthodox Theology, Elk Grove, California, Septuagint translation.

225. Gregory Palamas, *On the Divine Energies and Participation in Them* 2, ed. P. K. Christou, *Syngrammata*, vol. 2 (Thessaloniki, 1966), 97, as quoted in Ware, "God Immanent yet Transcendent," 162.

226. Gregory Palamas, *One Hundred and Fifty Chapters* 75, ed. Robert E. Sinkewicz,

Studies and Texts 83 (Toronto: Pontifical Institute of Medieval Studies, 1988), 170, as quoted in Ware, "God Immanent yet Transcendent," 163.

227. Ware, "God Immanent yet Transcendent," 165, emphasis in original.

228. See 1 Cor. 6:17.

229. Lewis, *Mere Christianity*, 136–37.

230. See Rom. 8:19–23.

231. Dan Story, "Homesick for Heaven: A Story to Share with Non-Christians," *Christian Research Journal* 38, no. 2 (2015): 36.

232. See, e.g., Associated Press, "Ohio Homeboys: Superstars LeBron, Curry Both Born in Akron," USA Today, June 1, 2015, www.usatoday.com/story/sports /nba/2015/06/01/ohio-homeboys-superstars-lebron-curry-both-born-in-akron /28291563/.

233. 1 Tim. 4:8.

234. Gal. 5:24.

235. Matt. 16:24 NIV 1984.

236. Eph. 4:19–24 NIV 1984.

237. See Willard, *Spirit of the Disciplines*, 3–6, 20, 31, 53, 67–68, 72, 151–53.

238. Cf. Willard, *Spirit of the Disciplines*, 19, 25.

239. Roland H. Bainton, *Here I Stand: A Life of Martin Luther* (1950; repr., Nashville: Abingdon Press, 1978), 30.

240. Rom. 1:17 NKJV.

241. W. R. Inge, *Goodness and Truth* (London: Mowbray, 1958), 76–77; quoted in Willard, *Spirit of the Disciplines*, 159.

242. Rev. 21:2 NIV 1984.

243. Eph. 5:25–27.

244. Eph. 5:29 NIV 1984 (see vv. 21–33).

245. 1 Cor. 7:3–4 NIV 1984.

246. Saint Thomas Aquinas (c. 1225–c. 1274), *Commentary on the First Epistle to the Corinthians*, 321, 323, trans. Fabian Larcher, Priory of the Immaculate Conception at the Dominican House of Studies, www.dhspriory.org/thomas/SS1Cor.htm#71. Previous four paragraphs adapted from Hanegraaff, *MUSLIM*, 68.

247. 1 Cor. 7:5 NIV 1984.

248. Ecc. 3:1, 5.

249. Aquinas, *Commentary*, 324.

250. See Jonah 3:4.

251. Jonah 3:5 NIV 1984.

252. Jonah 3:10 NIV 1984.

253. Abraham Lincoln, "Proclamation Appointing a National Fast Day," March 30,

1863, Abraham Lincoln Online, www.abrahamlincolnonline.org/lincoln/speeches /fast.htm.

254. See 1 Sam. 7:6.

255. Neh. 9:1.

256. Joel 2:12.

257. Deut. 8:3.

258. Deut. 9:18 (see 9:7ff); see also Exod. 24:18 (see 24:1–18).

259. Regarding this reckoning of three forty-day fasts, Kent D. Berghuis explained that "the first explicit reference to a case of total fasting one encounters in the biblical text is found in Exod 34:28. This second occasion of Moses on the mountain follows on the heels, however, of the first forty day period mentioned in Exod 24:18, and both incidents are acts of fasting, as Deut 9:9 and 10:10 make clear. In between the events, Deut 9:18 suggests that there was another intercessory period of forty days' fasting. So the story line as presented by Deuteronomy actually contains three incidents of Moses engaged in forty-day fasts from food and water on Sinai, although the Exodus account only explicitly mentions one fasting episode." Kent D. Berghuis, *Christian Fasting: A Theological Approach* (n.p.: Biblical Studies Press, 2007), 12, web.archive.org/web/20120627195346/https://bible.org/seriespage /chapter-1-fasting-old-testament-and-ancient-judaism-mourning-repentance-and -prayer-hope-g. For this intriguing interpretation, Berghuis cites Jeffrey H. Tigay, *Deuteronomy*, JPS Torah Commentary (Philadelphia: Jewish Publication Society, 1996), 100–101.

260. See Exod. 34:28–35; cf. 2 Cor. 3:1–4:6.

261. See 1 Kings 19:12. Quotation from 3 Kingdoms 19:12, St. Athanasius Academy of Orthodox Theology, Septuagint translation, in *Orthodox Study Bible*.

262. Matt. 4:4.

263. John 4:13–14 NKJV.

264. John 4:31–32 NKJV.

265. Matt. 17:2 NKJV.

266. Matt. 17:5 (see NIV 1984).

267. Luke 9:31 NIV 1984.

268. Alexander Schmemann, *Great Lent: Journey to Pascha* (Crestwood, NY: St. Vladimir's Seminary Press, 1969), 93–99; Willard, *Spirit of the Disciplines*, 166–68.

269. 2 Cor. 3:18 NKJV.

270. Ezra 10:6.

271. See Esther 4:16.

272. Acts 9:9, 18 NKJV.

273. See Acts 13:2–3.

274. Kent D. Berghuis, *Christian Fasting: Theological Approach*, "Chapter 2: Fasting in the New Testament: Remembrance and Anticipation in the Messianic Age," Biblical Studies Foundation, 2007, bible.org/seriespage/chapter-2-fasting-new -testament-remembrance-and-anticipation-messianic-age.

275. Matt. 6:18.

276. Basil, *About Fasting* (Περὶ Νηστείας), sermon 1, trans. Berghuis, *Christian Fasting*, "Appendix 1: Basil's Sermons About Fasting," Biblical Studies Foundation, 2007, www.web.archive.org/web/20170430025311/bible.org/seriespage/appendix -1-basil's-sermons-about-fasting.

277. See Schmemann, *Great Lent*.

278. See Matt. 6:1–18.

279. Isa. 58:6–7.

280. Isa. 58:8–9.

281. Isa. 58:11.

282. Matt. 5:3.

283. Basil, *About Fasting*, sermon 1.

284. Basil, sermon 1.

285. Basil, sermon 2.

286. Basil, sermon 1.

287. Basil, sermon 2.

288. Basil is citing Heb. 11:38.

289. Basil, sermon 1.

290. Frederica Mathewes-Green, *Welcome to the Orthodox Church: An Introduction to Eastern Christianity* (Brewster, MA: Paraclete Press, 2015), 275.

291. 1 John 1:9.

292. Matt. 25:40 NIV 1984.

293. 1 John 5:14–15.

294. Basil, *About Fasting*, sermon 1.

295. Willard, *Spirit of the Disciplines*, 113–14; C. S. Lewis also emphasized this point in *The Screwtape Letters and Screwtape Proposes a Toast*.

296. Rom. 7:18.

297. See Matt. 26:34.

298. See Matt. 26:69–74.

299. Matt. 16:16 NIV 1984.

300. John 14:27.

301. Willard, *Spirit of the Disciplines*, 6.

302. Mark 14:38.

303. See, e.g., Gal. 6:7–10.

304. Richard J. Foster, *Celebration of Discipline: The Path to Spiritual Growth*, 20th Anniversary Edition (New York: HarperSanFrancisco, 1998), 7, emphasis added.

Chapter 6: Fusion

1. Sermon of His All Holiness Ecumenical Patriarch Bartholomew, Uppsala Cathedral, August 22, 1993, quoted in Thomas FitzGerald, *The Ecumenical Patriarchate and Christian Unity*, 3rd rev. ed. (Brookline: MA: Holy Cross Orthodox Press, 2009), 47.

2. Front cover headlines for feature article, Lev Grossman, "Inside the Quest for Fusion, Clean Energy's Holy Grail," *Time*, Nov. 2, 2015, www.time.com/magazine /us/4082927/november-2nd-2015-vol-186-no-18-u-s/.

3. Matthew Schofield, "Ruined Chernobyl Nuclear Plant Will Remain a Threat for 3,000 Years," McClatchy DC Bureau, April 24, 2016, www.mcclatchydc.com /news/nation-world/world/article73405857.html; cf. "Chernobyl Accident 1986," World Nuclear Association, updated April 2018, http://www.world-nuclear.org /information-library/safety-and-security/safety-of-plants/chernobyl-accident .aspx; "Commemoration of the Chernobyl Disaster: The Human Experience Twenty Years Later," Kennan Institute, April 6, 2006, Wilson Center, www.wilson center.org/event/commemoration-the-chernobyl-disaster-the-human-experience -twenty-years-later.

4. Acts 20:28 NKJV.

5. John 17:20–21 NKJV.

6. Grossman, "Inside the Quest for Fusion."

7. James Bennet, "We Need an Energy Miracle," *Atlantic*, November 2015, www.the atlantic.com/magazine/archive/2015/11/we-need-an-energy-miracle/407881/.

8. Jonathan Tirone, "Billionaires Chase 'SpaceX Moment' for the Holy Grail of Energy," *Bloomberg*, October 30, 2018, www.bloomberg.com/news/articles /2018–10–30/nuclear-fusion-financed-by-billionaires-bill-gates-jeff-bezos.

9. Grossman, "Inside the Quest for Fusion." The insertion is my commentary, as with Alexandria Ocasio-Cortez's prediction that "the world is going to end in twelve years" (see William Cummings, "'The World Is Going to End in 12 Years if We Don't Address Climate Change,' Ocasio-Cortez Says," USA Today, January 22, 2019, www.usatoday.com/story/news/politics/onpolitics/2019/01 /22/ocasio-cortez-climate-change-alarm/2642481002/).

10. Rom. 12:4–5 NIV 1984.

11. 1 Cor. 10:17 NKJV.

12. Sermon of His All Holiness Ecumenical Patriarch Bartholomew, Uppsala Cathedral, August 22, 1993, 47.

13. Ware, *Orthodox Church*, 41.

14. Ware, *Orthodox Church*, 46.

15. See Ware, *Orthodox Church*, 47.

16. As quoted in Ware, *Orthodox Church*, 47–48.

17. As quoted in Ware, *Orthodox Church*, 48.

18. 1 Tim. 3:15 NKJV.

19. Metropolitan Kallistos Ware went on to explain that Christians were by definition "People of the Book." And if Christians were "People of the Book," then the Bible must in truth be "the Book of the People." In fact, "it is from the Church that the Bible ultimately derives its authority, for it was the Church which originally decided which books form a part of Holy Scripture; and it is the Church alone which can interpret Holy Scripture with authority. There are many sayings in the Bible which by themselves are far from clear, and individual readers, however sincere, are in danger of error if they trust their own personal interpretation. 'Do you understand what you are reading?' Philip asked the Ethiopian eunuch; and the eunuch replied, 'How can I, unless someone guides me?' (Acts viii, 30–1)." (Ware, *Orthodox Church*, 193–94.)

20. See John 15:26.

21. Robert Letham explains that for Photius (c. 810–c. 895) and the East, "The Western doctrine subordinates the Holy Spirit. . . . The Son is begotten *immediately* by the Father, but for the West the Spirit proceeds from the Father *remotely*, since he also proceeds from the Son, who is himself begotten. Thus, the Spirit's procession is subsequent to the begetting of the Son, since these cannot occur at the same time or else the Spirt would also be begotten by the Son. This argument is reinforced by the Western teaching on the Spirit (following Augustine) as the bond of love between the Father and the Son, which gives him subpersonal status" (Robert Letham, *The Holy Trinity: In Scripture, History, Theology, and Worship* (Phillipsburg, PA: P&R Publishing, 2004), 243; cf. 201–220). Christopher Iacovetti explains that Gregory Palamas "worries that by conceiving of the Holy Spirit as a product of the 'joint causation' of Father and Son, the *filioque* ["and the Son"] renders him indistinguishable from creatures, who are likewise jointly caused by the Father and Son." Christopher Iacovetti, "*Filioque, Theosis,* and *Ecclesia*: Augustine in Dialogue with Modern Orthodox Theology," *Modern Theology* 34, no. 1 (2018): 73–74 (cf. 75ff.), www.doi.org/10.1111/moth.12369).

22. See Vladimir Lossky, *In the Image and Likeness of God* (Crestwood, NY: St. Vladimir's Seminary Press, 1974), 71–110. Christopher Iacovetti explains, "Like Palamas, Lossky worries that the *filioque* effectively subordinates the Spirit to the Father and Son and that this subordination has dire consequences

for the doctrine of *theosis*. . . . As a consequence of this error, charges Lossky, Western theologians from Anselm to Aquinas have found themselves unable to conceive of salvation in properly trinitarian terms, i.e., in terms of *theosis*. For whereas, from the Orthodox perspective, salvation is a process of deification initiated by the Father, made possible by the work of the Son, and brought to 'final realization' by the Spirit, for filioquist theology the Spirit has essentially no place in the soteriological picture. Thus, according to Lossky, what one finds in Western treatises like Anselm's *Cur Deus Homo* is a description not of *theosis* but of a purely juridical form of 'redemption' purchased by Christ's death and offered to the satisfaction of the Father." Iacovetti suggests an "excellent Orthodox defense of Anselm against Lossky on this score" is found in David Bentley Hart, *The Beauty of the Infinite: The Aesthetics of Christian Faith* (Grand Rapids: Eerdmans, 2003), 155–67. (Iacovetti, *"Filioque, Theosis, and Ecclesia,"* 74; cf. 75ff.)

23. According to church historian Philip Schaff, *"'Sobald der Pfennig im Kasten klingt, / Die Seel' aus dem Fegfeuer springt.'* Mathesius and Johann Hess, two contemporary witnesses, ascribe this sentence (with slight verbal modifications) to Tetzel himself. Luther mentions it in Theses 27 and 28, and in his book *Wider Hans Wurst* (Erl. ed. XXVI. 51)." Philip Schaff, *History of the Christian Church*, 8 vols. (1888; repr., n.p.: AP & A, n.d.), 7:345n11 (see 7:68).

24. Schaff, *History of the Christian Church*, 7:69.

25. See Katherine Arcement, "Martin Luther Shook the World 500 Years Ago, But Did He Nail Anything to a Church Door?" *Washington Post*, Oct. 31, 2017, www .washingtonpost.com/news/retropolis/wp/2017/10/31/martin-luther-shook -the-world-500-years-ago-but-did-he-nail-anything-to-a-church-door/; cf. Volker Leppin and Timothy J. Wengert, "Sources for and Against the Posting of the Ninety-Five Theses," *Lutheran Quarterly* 29 (2015): 373–98, www.luther anquarterly.com/uploads/7/4/0/1/7401289/lq-95theses-leppin_wengert.pdf.

26. Schaff, *History of the Christian Church*, 7:73. See also "Theses, Ninety-Five, of Luther," *Christian Cyclopedia*, The Lutheran Church Missouri Synod, www .cyclopedia.lcms.org/display.asp?t1=T&word=THESES.NINETY-FIVE .OFLUTHER.

27. Schaff, *History of the Christian Church*, 7:78. Previous five paragraphs adapted from Hanegraaff, *Christianity in Crisis: 21ˢᵗ Century*, 209–10.

28. Desiderius Erasmus and Martin Luther, *Discourse on Free Will*, trans. Ernst F. Winter (New York: Continuum, 2006), 96; see R. C. Sproul, "The Word of God in the Hands of Man," *Tabletalk*, April 1, 2009, www.ligonier.org/learn/articles /word-god-hands-man.

29. Benjamin Wiker, *The Reformation 500 Years Later: 12 Things You Need to Know* (Washington DC: Regnery History, 2017), 138.

30. Cf. Ronald J. Sider, *Andreas Bodenstein Von Karlstadt: The Development of His Thought, 1517–1525* (Leiden: E. J. Brill, 1974), 9–11.

31. Wiker, *Reformation 500 Years Later*, 138. Cf. Stryder Matthews, "Andreas Bodenstein von Karlstadt and Martin Luther: It's Complicated," *Tenor of Our Times*, vol. 6, article 9 (2017), www.scholarworks.harding.edu/tenor/vol6/iss1/9; Sider, *Andreas Bodenstein Von Karlstadt*.

32. Wiker, *Reformation 500 Years Later*, 138–39.

33. Diarmaid MacCulloch, *Reformation* (New York: Viking, 2004), 143.

34. MacCulloch, 143.

35. MacCulloch, 144.

36. Earle E. Cairns, *Christianity Through the Centuries: A History of the Christian Church* (Grand Rapids: Academie Books, 1981), 307.

37. See Ken Curtis, "Reformation Radicals: The Anabaptists," Christianity, April 28, 2018, www.christianity.com/church/church-history/timeline/1501–1600 /reformation-radicals-the-anabaptists-11629935.html.

38. Calvin preaching on Acts 5:29 in Geneva, quoted in MacCulloch, *Reformation*, 190. MacCulloch cites J. Calvin, Sermons on the Acts of the Apostles, in Supplementa Calviniana, (ital.), vol. 8, ed. J. W. Balke and W. H. T. Moehn (Neukirchen-Vluyn: Neukirchener Verlag, 1994), 160–61.

39. MacCulloch, *The Reformation*, 190.

40. MacCulloch, 238.

41. MacCulloch, 241.

42. Wiker, *Reformation 500 Years Later*, 132.

43. MacCulloch, *Reformation*, 237. See Calvin, *Institutes*, 1.4.1; 1.5.8; 3.20.14; 3.24.12.

44. Vinson Synan, *The Holiness-Pentecostal Movement in the United States* (Grand Rapids: Eerdmans, 1971), 101. Previous two paragraphs adapted from Hanegraaff, *The Apocalypse Code*, 40–41, 45.

45. Synan, *Holiness-Pentecostal Movement*, 101.

46. Sincere Christian believers are divided on this theological issue. Some believe that the "gifts of the Spirit" ceased at the close of the apostolic age or with the closing of the canon of Scripture. Others do not believe that there is clear biblical evidence that they would ever cease. In any case, the "prostitution" of the gift of tongues only serves to bring unnecessary division. This is an issue we may vigorously debate, but over which we should never divide.

47. Synan, *Holiness-Pentecostal Movement*, 102.

48. Synan, 102–3.

49. Synan, 111.

50. Synan, 103.

51. Daniel G. Reid et al., *Dictionary of Christianity in America* (Downers Grove, IL: InterVarsity Press, 1990), 865.

52. George C. Bedell, Leo Sandon Jr., and Charles T. Wellborn, *Religion in America* (New York: Macmillan, 1975), 159–60.

53. Synan, *Holiness-Pentecostal Movement*, 106.

54. Synan, 110.

55. Synan, 112.

56. Discussion of Pentecostalism adapted from Hank Hanegraaff, *Counterfeit Revival* (Nashville: Thomas Nelson, 2001), 141–44.

57. "Spirit and Power—A 10-Country Survey of Pentecostals," Pew Research Center, October 5, 2006, www.pewforum.org/2006/10/05/spirit-and-power/.

58. Joseph Prince, *Unmerited Favor: Your Supernatural Advantage for a Successful Life* (Lake Mary, FL: Charisma House, 2010), 195.

59. Bob George, "What about 1 John 1:9?" Bob George Ministries, March 10, 2013, www.bobgeorge.net/1-john-1-9/.

60. See Prince, *Unmerited Favor*, 188ff.

61. Greg Koukl, "Clarification on Confession," Stand to Reason, March 22, 2013, www.str.org/articles/clarification-on-confession#.XEnyv1VKiUk.

62. 1 John 2:1.

63. 1 John 1:8–10.

64. James 5:16. For further study, see Steven Parks, "Grace Upon Grace: 1 John 1:8–9 and the Forgiveness of Sins," *Christian Research Journal* 38, no. 2 (2015), www.equip.org/article/grace-upon-grace-1-john-18–9-forgiveness-sins/.

65. Andrew Stephen Damick, *Orthodoxy and Heterodoxy: Finding the Way to Christ in a Complicated Religious Landscape*, 2nd ed. (Chesterton, IN: Ancient Faith Publishing,2017), 37–38.

66. 1 Cor. 1:10 NIV 1984, emphasis added.

67. Scripture quotations from 1 Cor. 1:10–13 NIV 1984.

68. Ware, *Orthodox Church*, 303.

69. Ware, 303, emphasis in original.

70. Ware, 303.

71. Ware, 37–38.

72. Symeon the New Theologian, *Centuries*, 111, 4, quoted in Ware, *Orthodox Church*, 248.

73. John H. Erickson, "Beyond Dialogue: The Quest for Eastern and Oriental Orthodox Unity Today," Symposium on 1700th Anniversary of Christian

Armenia, October 27–28, 2000, St. Vladimir's Orthodoxy Theological Seminary, www.svots.edu/content/beyond-dialogue-quest-eastern-and-oriental-orthodox -unity-today.

74. Erickson, "Beyond Dialogue."

75. First Agreed Statement (1989), Anba Bishoy Monastery, Wadi-El-Natroun, Egypt, June 20–24, 1989, Joint Commission of the Theological Dialogue Between the Orthodox Church and the Oriental Orthodox Churches, emphasis added, www .orthodoxjointcommission.wordpress.com/2013/12/14/first-agreed-statement -1989/. See discussion in Ware, *Orthodox Church*, 305–6.

76. "History of Dialogue," in "Various Documents Concerning Eastern Orthodox and Oriental Orthodox Joint Commission and Unity," Orthodox Joint Commission, www.orthodoxjointcommission.wordpress.com/.

77. Jude 1:3, my paraphrase.

Epilogue

1. Ware, *Orthodox Church*, 65.

2. Hanegraaff, *MUSLIM*.

3. A nice account is offered by Baron Bodissey, "The Other September 11th," Gates of Vienna, September 11, 2006, accessed October 1, 2016, www.gatesofvienna .blogspot.com/2006/09/other-september-11th.html.

4. Andreas Rinke, "Merkel says Islam 'belongs to Germany' ahead of Dresden rally," Reuters, January 12, 2015, www.reuters.com/article/us-germany-islam-merkel -idUSKBN0KL1S020150112. Three previous paragraphs adapted from Hanegraaff, *MUSLIM*, xix–xx.

5. Wiker, *Reformation*, 85, emphasis original.

6. Wiker, 85, emphasis original.

7. Jay Richards, "To Defend Marriage We Should Learn a Lesson from Apologetics," *Christian Research Journal* 35, no. 4 (2012), www.equip.org/PDF/JAF6354.pdf; see also Sherif Girgis, Ryan T. Anderson, Robert P. George, *What Is Marriage? Man and Woman: A Defense* (New York: Encounter Books, 2012).

8. Micaiah Bilger, "New York Governor Andrew Cuomo Signs Bill Legalizing Abortions Up to Birth," LifeNews, Jan. 23, 2019, www.lifenews.com/2019 /01/23/new-york-governor-andrew-cuomo-signs-bill-legalizing-abortions-up -to-birth/. This paragraph and previous paragraph adapted from Hanegraaff, *Complete Bible Answer Book*, 430–32.

9. See Rom. 13:1–7; 1 Peter 2:13–17; cf. John 19:11. See Charles Colson, *God and Government* (Grand Rapids: Zondervan, 2007), 101–2.

10. Specifically, *militant* (or totalitarian) *egalitarianism* as economic, social, and

political equality of outcomes as opposed to opportunities, and as equality of subjective desires at the expense of objective ethical facts that would inhibit fulfillment of one's subjective desires; *radical individualism* as unbridled craving for self-gratification; *multiculturalism* as mandating that one set of cultural values must not be deemed inferior to another; *political correctness* as repression of honest dialogue and tolerant disagreement, especially at the expense of religious liberty; *religious pluralism* as all religions being equally true and valid ways to God or whatever definition of ultimate reality one sees fit to use. See Os Guinness, *Last Call for Liberty* (Downers Grove, IL: IVP Books, 2018); Walter E. Williams, "Multiculturalism: A Failed Concept," June 29, 2016, www.creators.com/read/walter-williams/06/16/multiculturalism-a-failed-concept; Walter E. Williams, "Multiculturalism Is a Failure," September 17, 2014, www.creators.com/read/walter-williams/09/14/multiculturalism-is-a-failure. Adapted from Hanegraaff, *MUSLIM*, 182, 272.

11. John S. Dickerson, *The Great Evangelical Recession: 6 Factors That Will Crash the American Church . . . and How to Prepare* (Grand Rapids: Baker Books, 2013), 65.

12. Dickerson, *Great Evangelical Recession*, 76.

13. Jacob Neusner, *Conservative, American and Jewish: I Wouldn't Have It Any Other Way* (Lafayette, LA: Vital Issues Press, 1993).

14. Quoted in Guinness, *Last Call for Liberty*, 39; cf. Jonathan Sacks, *Radical Then, Radical Now* (London: Bloomsbury, 2001), 32–33.

15. Deut. 6:7–9, 12 NIV 1984.

16. 1 Peter 3:15, my paraphrase.

17. Col. 4:6 NIV 1984, emphasis added.

18. Rosenberg, *Atheist's Guide to Reality*, 275.

19. Barack Obama, "News and Speeches: Call to Renewal Key Note Address" June 28, 2006, http://blog.beliefnet.com/stevenwaldman/2008/11/obamas-historic-call-to-renewa.html.

20. Robert Spencer, "Foreword: The Bible Answer Man Becomes the Qur'an Answer Man," in Hanegraaff, *MUSLIM*, xi.

21. Spencer, "Foreword," xi.

22. Lossky, *Mystical Theology*, 84.

23. Hahn, "Foreword," in *Called to Be the Children of God*, 7, 8.

24. Maximus the Confessor, *Epistle 43 Ad Joannem cubicularium*, in Lossky, *Mystical Theology*, 90.

25. Vishnevskaya, "Divinization," 132, 136, emphasis in original, quoting Maximus the Confessor, *Ambiguorum liber 7*.

26. Lossky, *Mystical Theology*, 179.

27. Rev. Protopresbyter Panagiotis Papanikolaou, "Living a Eucharistic Life Is Living with Gratitude," Dormition of the Virgin Mary Greek Orthodox Church, Oct. 29, 2017, Weekly Bulletin, www.bulletinbuilder.org/dormitionva/current/20171029.

28. Ignatius, *Epistle to the Ephesians*, 20, quoted in Papanikolaou, "Living a Eucharistic Life"; see also CCEL, www.ccel.org/ccel/schaff/anf01.v.ii.xx.html.

29. Bartholomew, sermon, 47.

30. John 17:20–21 NKJV.

31. "E = mc²: The Unforgettable Equation of Einstein's Miracle Year," Encyclopædia Britannica, September 27, 2010, www.blogs.britannica.com/2010/09/e-mc2-the-unforgettable-equation-of-einsteins-miracle-year-picture-essay-of-the-day/.

32. "E = mc²," emphasis added.

33. Matt. 17:1, 2, 5 NIV 1984.

34. See Col. 1:29.

ABOUT THE AUTHOR

HANK HANEGRAAFF serves as president of the Christian Research Institute (CRI) and host of the *Bible Answer Man* broadcast and the *Hank Unplugged* podcast. He is the author of over twenty books.

Widely regarded as one of the world's leading Christian authors and theologians, Hanegraaff has dedicated his life to a defense of the historic Christian faith. For the greater part of his life and ministry, Hank's clarion call was to communicate Christian truth—*because truth matters!* The discovery that truth matters but *life matters more* has cultivated in him a deep commitment to communicating *why* life matters more and *how* the life that matters more can be experienced today—now—in intimate union with the Triadic One.

Hank and his wife, Kathy, live in Charlotte, North Carolina, and are parents to twelve children.